AF528766

Electronic Resources Management in Libraries

Electronic Resources Management in Libraries

Felicitation Volume brought out in Honour of
Dr Aragonda Lakshmana Moorthy, Director (Retd),
Defence Scientific Information and Documentation Centre,
Defence Research and Development Organisation, Delhi

Editor
Dr Chennupati K. Ramaiah
Professor and Head, Dept. of Library and Information Science
Pondicherry University, R.V. Nagar, Puducherry–605 014

ALLIED PUBLISHERS PVT. LTD.

New Delhi • Mumbai • Kolkata • Lucknow • Chennai
Nagpur • Bangalore • Hyderabad • Ahmedabad

ALLIED PUBLISHERS PRIVATE LIMITED

1/13-14 Asaf Ali Road, **New Delhi**–110002
Ph.: 011-23239001 • E-mail: delhi.books@alliedpublishers.com

47/9 Prag Narain Road, Near Kalyan Bhawan, **Lucknow**–226001
Ph.: 0522-2209942 • E-mail: lko.books@alliedpublishers.com

17 Chittaranjan Avenue, **Kolkata**–700072
Ph.: 033-22129618 • E-mail: cal.books@alliedpublishers.com

15 J.N. Heredia Marg, Ballard Estate, **Mumbai**–400001
Ph.: 022-42126969 • E-mail: mumbai.books@alliedpublishers.com

60 Shiv Sunder Apartments (Ground Floor), Central Bazar Road,
Bajaj Nagar, **Nagpur**–440010
Ph.: 0712-2234210 • E-mail: ngp.books@alliedpublishers.com

F-1 Sun House (First Floor), C.G. Road, Navrangpura,
Ellisbridge P.O., **Ahmedabad**–380006
Ph.: 079-26465916 • E-mail: ahmbd.books@alliedpublishers.com

751 Anna Salai, **Chennai**–600002
Ph.: 044-28523938 • E-mail: chennai.books@alliedpublishers.com

5th Main Road, Gandhinagar, **Bangalore**–560009
Ph.: 080-22262081 • E-mail: bngl.books@alliedpublishers.com

3-2-844/6 & 7 Kachiguda Station Road, **Hyderabad**–500027
Ph.: 040-24619079 • E-mail: hyd.books@alliedpublishers.com

Website: www.alliedpublishers.com

ISBN: 978-81-8424-813-5

Published by Sunil Sachdev and printed by Ravi Sachdev at Allied Publishers Pvt. Ltd. (Printing Division), A-104 Mayapuri Phase II, New Delhi-110064

Dr APJ Abdul Kalam
Former President of India

Message

I am happy to know that the book '**Electronic Resources Management in Libraries**' is being brought out as a felicitation volume in honour of Dr AL Moorthy, on his superannuation as Director, DESIDOC, DRDO. Dr AL Moorthy has been with the ISRO (1979–1984) and DRDO (1984–2012).

DESIDOC has been one of the premier institutions for providing information and science communication through various publications. It has over 1.5 lakh collection covering books, technical reports, standards and bound volumes; has a good digital library with access to over 550 online journals. It has been providing latest information to the DRDO labs as well as Defence establishments. Dr Moorthy was associated with DESIDOC in various capacities and as its Director for over six years during 2006–2012. He has contributed for the development of DESIDOC and its services and has demonstrated utmost sincerity to his work and in developing DESIDOC as a national R&D information centre in the area of Defence Science and Technology. I take this opportunity to congratulate and commend the Editor for bringing out this beautiful volume on the retirement of Dr AL Moorthy.

It is noteworthy that the volume includes 39 papers under eight sections covering professional contributions of Dr Moorthy; Electronic Resources and Management; Electronic Publishing and Internet; Electronic Resource Management Systems; Access and Use of Electronic Resources; Digital Rights Management and IPRs; Standards and Metrics for E-Resources and Electronic Resources; and Pedagogical Issues authored by eminent professionals in the country and from abroad.

I wish Dr AL Moorthy a happy, healthy and busy life ahead.

16 November 2012

APJ Abdul Kalam

Dr Aragonda Lakshmana Moorthy

Foreword

One of the places I was advised to visit, when I first came to India many years ago, was DESIDOC. It was then already well-known in the UK as an institution at the forefront of Indian information activities. I was warmly received and entertained. Indeed, one of my pleasant memories of the visit came from a discussion of cricket that we had one evening. I said how impressed I had been by the Indian cricketers who had come to England when I was beginning to learn the game. The following evening I was taken to meet Lala Amarnath, the Indian cricketer who had impressed me most on that tour. I returned to the UK with the firm belief that DESIDOC combined efficiency with helpfulness. One of the pleasures of revisiting DESIDOC has been to find that under Dr Moorthy these virtues have been not only retained, but developed.

The tributes to Dr Moorthy which begin this volume are from friends and colleagues who know him much better than I do. They all attest to his continuing contributions to the information profession. However, perhaps I could note that he and I have a common interest—an addiction to reading detective stories. I think it is appropriate therefore for me to include in this *Foreword* a very relevant quotation from that master of all fictional detectives, Sherlock Holmes, who said: "I wanted information, Watson". Dr Moorthy will surely be happy to accept this as a statement of what he, himself, has wanted in his working life.

One of Dr Moorthy's great strengths has been to combine a knowledge of information and library science with a knowledge of publishing. The communication of science has traditionally progressed in a series of steps—starting with the author and moving on through the publisher to the librarian and finally to the reader. It has therefore always seemed odd to me that the teaching of library and information science has concentrated almost entirely on the latter two stages. Nowadays, with the growth of new methods of communication, trying to treat the different phases of communication in isolation is becoming less and less feasible. Dr Moorthy can retire happy in the knowledge that his own broad-based approach to information handling will almost certainly be necessary for both individuals and institutions in the future.

The present volume, which my old friend and colleague, Professor C.K. Ramaiah, has planned and edited, reflects this point very well. A glance through the articles included in this festschrift reveals how much traditional concerns relating to information now have to be resolved on a broader basis. They also show how rapidly exploration of new developments in information handling is occurring in India. I am sure that Dr Moorthy will be pleased with the progress reported here, and delighted with the value of the material that has been assembled in his honour.

Prof A. Jack Meadows
Department of Information Science,
Loughborough University,
Ashby Road, Loughborough, Leicestershire LE11 3TU, UK

Preface

Electronic resources refer to those materials or services that require a computer to access, manipulation, or reproduction including, but not limited to, numerical, graphical and textual files, electronic journals, bibliographic or full-text databases and Internet resources. These are any information resources produced or encoded for manipulation by computers or digital devices. It may be written, stored, preserved and accessed either directly from a tangible device such as a PC, DVD-ROM, or remotely through a website or intranet or Internet from a non-tangible electronic resource such as an electronic journal, or a database.

Electronic resources cover bibliographic databases, e-books, full-text e-journals collections, digital collections of data, and all traditional and non-traditional forms of information sources available in digital form. Digital resources offer both the benefits of freedom from paper forms, and the challenges of dealing with different resources in different formats with wide range of prices, terms and conditions. One result of this is that the user may need to employ a wider variety of search strategies to find the required resources. Management of electronic resources has become a challenging task for libraries as their quantity, complexity and varieties increased during the past two decades. The traditional ways of developing and management of collection techniques are not appropriate for electronic resources. Developing efficient and effective ways to manage the staff functions related to the acquisitions, licensing, cataloging, payment, and maintenance has become essential for academic and research libraries. This includes restructuring positions, units, departments and divisions, and creating new positions devoted to electronic resources. A particular challenge for technical services departments is how to integrate the management and processing of electronic resources into existing organizational structures.

The traditional functions of libraries had undergone various changes in present century and e-resources have great importance in libraries and amongst the library users. The library users' requirements and usage of information gone beyond the time and space barriers and that changed the most of the libraries drastically. The workflows from acquisitions to user services and the lifecycle of electronic resources is quite different from that of print resources since it is characterized by access without holding the physical objects. Also, the functional responsibilities for managing electronic resources are often distributed over departments such as serials, acquisitions, and library systems. As licensing electronic resources has greatly increased in recent years, libraries have struggled to control this information in paper files, integrated library systems, separate databases stored on local computers or network. Under these circumstances, a need arose for having knowledge and expertise to handle these resources in a better fashion.

In order to meet the growing needs for integrating e-resources such as online subscription of online full-text journals and e-books, web-resources, databases, and various information retrieval systems, libraries are adopting integrated Electronic Resources Management Systems (ERMS) which conveniently and efficiently provides interfaces to users and librarians by integrating highly complex tasks such as subscription models, licenses, and subject coverage of electronic resources. The ERM Librarian has primary responsibilities for the management of all aspects of acquired electronic resources; providing support for activities including the identification of potential of new products and coordinating the library's trial programs; providing license support including initial negotiation and technical review to ensure that the licenses conform to present library users' requirements. The responsibilities also cover management of ordering new products, link resolvers and other access tools, coordinating the cataloging activities related to e-resources, works with other departments to ensure software and hardware upgradation to maintain correct links to licensed content, and resolving issues identified by staff or users.

The book Electronic Resources Management in Libraries, is a felicitation volume brought out in honour of Dr Aragonda Lakshamana Moorthy who is an eminent Information Scientist and former Director of DESIDOC, Metcalfe House, Delhi with the active support of his friends and admirers. He has contributed immensely to the profession, helped so many junior and senior LIS professionals in various ways during his career particularly while he was working as Director, DESIDOC. He was instrumental in facilitating various professional activities like conferences, seminars and workshops with liberal funding from DRDO. The proposal for this volume was first mooted by Dr K.P. Singh, Assistant Professor from University of Delhi who worked as JRF while I was with DESIDOC which I and many friends warmly welcomed. All friends and admires of Dr Moorthy felt that honouring him is a pleasure and overdue as he is one of the senior most Information Scientists in the country.

A Felicitation Committee was formed with senior most LIS professionals in the country who have extended all the help in this noble endeavour. I would like to thank the assistance of all the Committee Members in getting the papers and review process for this book, without whom this volume would not have been accomplished. A request letter was sent to selected professionals who were closely associated with Dr Moorthy during his career and the response was overwhelming. A few more were to be received which could not be as the volume is delayed. Keeping the scope and size of the publication, nearly a dozen papers could not be accommodated. The publication contains 39 papers including five write-ups on Dr Moorthy and his contributions to the profession. Most of the papers are based on research and few are review articles on a given topic. I am really grateful to His Excellency Dr APJ Abdul Kalam, former President of India, for his message and to my teacher Prof. A. Jack Meadows, Emeritus Professor, Loughborough University, UK for writing Foreword for this book. The authors are all senior professionals with a long standing in the LIS field covering, IITs, Universities, CSIR, DRDO, IIM, and professional Associations. A few papers are received from UK, Thailand and Singapore. I would like to convey my sincere thanks to all the contributors of papers.

Besides intellectual work, the work of this nature needs lot of time commitment from my family members particularly my wife and daughters who encouraged me to do this work. I am grateful to the Allied Publishers Pvt Ltd, New Delhi particularly Shri Sharad Gupta, Publishing Consultant, Editorial Department for his help in bringing out this publication. Finally, but most importantly, I wish to thank once again to all our insightful and expert authors for their excellent contributions to this book and to the field of Electronic Resource Management.

Prof Chennupati K. Ramaiah

Dr AL Moorthy and Smt Shailaja with His Excellency
Dr APJ Abdul Kalam, Former President of India

Dr AL Moorthy Receiving DRDO Best Popular
Science Communication Award – 2009

At the Release of Special Publication by Defence Minister – 2006

ILA-Kaula Best Librarian Award – 2008

Prof SR Ranganathan – Prof PN Kaula Award – 2009

Dr AL Moorthy Receiving SIS Fellowship in 2009

Contents

Section–III: Electronic Publishing and Internet

Section–IV: Electronics Resource Management Systems

Section–V: Access and Use of Electronic Resources

Section–I

Tributes

Electronic Resources Management in Libraries, pp. 3–7

My Association with Dr A.L. Moorthy

S.S. Murthy

Beginning of My Association

During my tenure as the Director of DESIDOC (1979–1999), I used to attend some of the seminars organised by Documentation Research and Training Centre (DRTC, a specialised training school in Documentation and Information Science founded by Dr SR Ranganathan in 1962 at Bangalore under Indian Statistical Institute, Kolkata). The conducting of those seminars was very systematic and purposeful and the deliberations were very objective and educative. They also provided an opportunity of interaction with eminent and internationally reputed professors like Prof A Neelameghan and Prof G Bhattacharya who were teaching in the Centre. It was during one of the seminars there in 1983, I met Shri AL Moorthy for the first time.

During the lunch break in the seminar, I was sitting with Prof Bhattacharya in his office. Then, I casually mentioned to him, the Government had recently sanctioned some posts of scientists and scientific assistants and they would be advertised soon. I told him I was looking for some competent and hardworking candidates to encourage them to apply. He then suggested that he had a candidate in mind who had very good qualifications in science (particularly in physics which is highly relevant to DRDO) and is also a very dedicated worker. He was AL Moorthy who was at that time employed in SHAR Centre of ISRO at Sriharikota and was doing the Master's degree level course in Documentation and Information Science at DRTC. He was also attending the seminar. Prof Bhattacharya immediately sent someone to call him. A few minutes later Shri Moorthy came in and the professor introduced him to me as a very sincere, hardworking and competent information professional. Since Shri Moorthy had been a student of Prof Bhattacharya earlier and also I have a very high confidence in the professor's unbiased and exact assessment of persons, particularly his students, I felt at that time itself it would be good if Shri Moorthy is selected for a scientist post in DESIDOC and joins. So, I suggested to him to await the UPSC advertisement in newspapers for the posts of information scientists for DRDO and apply.

As expected, a few months later (July 1983), the advertisement was published in newspapers. About eight posts of Scientist B were advertised pooling the requirements of some of the DRDO labs like DESIDOC, DLRL (Hyderabad), DL (Jodhpur), etc. ShriMoorthy also applied against the advertisement. UPSC conducted interviews in October 1983 and I was the departmental member on the selection committee. Shri Moorthy performed well in the interview and was selected. The other candidates selected were Smt A Aruna who joined GTRE, Bangalore; Shri M Prahlada Rao (DLRL, Hyderabad); Shri RS Rathore (DL, Jodhpur); Smt Shashi Tyagi, (DESIDOC), and a few others. I was expecting Shri Moorthy's posting to (DESIDOC) but it was a surprise to me when he was posted to DLRL, Hyderabad, by the DRDO Headquarters.

A few years passed. In 1985, two posts of Scientist C were advertised for DESIDOC by the Recruitment and Assessment Centre (RAC), the central recruitment agency of DRDO for scientists. Shri Moorthy also applied for the posts. This time also he was selected. But, since the posts this time were specifically meant for DESIDOC, he was posted to DESIDOC and joined here in January 1987 as Scientist C.

Shri Moorthy's Growth in Publication Work

When he joined DESIDOC, I posted him to the Publications Division. He then met me and pleaded that he must be posted to the Library or the Information Services Division and not to the Publications Division as all his previous service had been in the library and information services work and he had never worked in publication area. He was reluctant to enter a new area of full time publication after doing some years of good work in the other field. But, somehow I felt he would do well in this field also because of his good standard in English and his aptitude for learning new work. So, I requested him to accept the new assignment. He reluctantly accepted and started working under the guidance of Shri GS Sharma, Head of the Publications Division. I believe, this experience, in addition to library and information management work, highly helped him subsequently in becoming a well-rounded information specialist and a very good manager of these areas.

During the year 1988 Shri PG Krishnamurthi was selected as Scientist D against an open advertisement and joined. I posted him also to the Publication Division as I wanted to strengthen this Division which functions as the publication unit of DRDO. After a few months of his joining, Shri GS Sharma was made Joint Director and was given wider responsibilities. Shri Krishnamurthi being the next senior-most in the Division, became its head. Both the Murthys worked in the Division till Shri Krishnamurthi met with a tragic accident and passed away in March 1989. Then, Shri AL Moorthy worked under Shri UR Sharma, who became Head of Publications. He took over as the Head of the Publications Division and continued as the head even after he was promoted as Scientist E a few years later. By then he gained excellent editorial skills and was managing the Division very well. He introduced automation and started using DTP techniques for editorial work. During the period of his work in this Division he also got registration for his doctoral degree with Karnataka University and got his PhD degree a few years later. Considering his request for working in library-related activities, and his pursuance of PhD, he was given responsibilities of a newly created Information Processing Division (IPD) in August 1995. He was made Joint Director in

1997 and some financial powers were also delegated to him which he operated in a very judicial and responsible manner. His responsibilities also became much wider covering more Divisions—Defence Science Library, IPD and Database Development Division of the Centre. He was transferred to DRDL, Hyderabad in February 2001 on his request on personal grounds.

Professional Competency

Dr Moorthy is a voracious reader and a prolific writer. He had developed the reading habit right from the beginning of his career but it was mostly his subject discipline. But, gradually his reading habit extended to science and technology in general. He was regularly reading some journals received in the Defence Science Library of DESIDOC and was also a regular individual subscriber of *National Geographic Magazine* (USA) and *Current Science*, a high standard scientific journal that covers almost all disciplines of science and carries the contributions of eminent scientists. This habit subsequently helped him considerably in his job as an editor of DRDO publications and also in his doctoral research work. Based on his doctoral work and other research and practical work, he contributed many research papers, review articles, etc.

His contributions to the activities of DESIDOC are praiseworthy. He made several improvements in the publication activities of DESIDOC applying current editorial practices and relevant information technologies. As can be seen in the annual reports of the Centre, he also brought several new information technologies into other Divisions after he became the Director, to further improve the quality and speed of the Centre's services. Some of them are the following:

- Providing online access to about 450 e-journals to DRDO scientists.
- Streamlining library procedures and obtaining ISO 9001:2008 certification.
- Revising and updating the DRDO Library Procedures Manual and getting it included in the DRDO Purchase Manual 2012.
- Developing the knowledge repository of DRDO technical reports and an institutional repository.
- Networking of the information resources of DRDO libraries/TICs.
- Bringing out several special/adhoc publications on technology developments made by DRDO and further improving the quality and frequency of the regular publications of DRDO.
- Planning and implementing an e-journal consortium for providing access about 500 publications from 10 publishers.

As per his managerial competence, his management style is largely informal. While following the usual governmental, hierarchical procedures for administrative purposes, he ignored hierarchy in scientific/professional discussions. And, he always had a positive attitude of men and matters. His officers and staff were given freedom to discuss scientific, technical or other professional matters directly with him. Also, he never disliked if someone differed with his views on a subject matter and expressed such difference even in open forums like meetings. He also encouraged his colleagues to contribute papers for conferences and seminars and for publication in reputed journals.

As a manager, he led his colleagues by example. He worked very hard and in a dedicated manner and maintained very high integrity and expected others to function in a similar way. Since he had developed, over the years, practical knowledge of almost all the activities carried out by DESIDOC, it must have greatly helped him to manage the activities of DESIDOC effectively when he became its Director. The improvements he made in the functions and services of the Centre became quite visible even to the users.

Notable Attributes of Dr Moorthy

As mentioned earlier, a notable attribute of his is his reading and writing habit. Because of this habit, he was able to evaluate the writings of others very well and this largely helped him to become an effective editor. I was also taking advantage of this ability of his. Whenever I prepared a paper or other serious document, I used to show it to him at draft stage for his comments/suggestions. Often he made useful suggestions.

Another attribute of Dr Moorthy is his care for detail. This reflected deeply in his editing also. His editing was thorough. But, sometimes going to such detailed editing would have the risk of changing the style of the author. But he is not satisfied till he does job to his satisfaction.

One important attribute of his that sometimes caused some unhappiness in him is his frankness in expressing his opinions or suggestions. If some work is not done properly, he is usually not subtle in expressing his displeasure and expresses in straight terms which often annoys the staff member (or members) concerned. This forthright expression of opinion could be seen even in the meetings I used to conduct as the Director for reviewing the progress of different activities. But he never allowed this displeasure come in his way in the overall assessment of the work of his officials. He always assessed them dispassionately and objectively and often liberally. But this frankness got him some unpopularity with some of those who do not agree with his assessment of them. But he continued this frankness and objectivity as he is sincere to his duty, to the core.

Dr Moorthy is usually liberal in helping people, particularly his officers and staff. He always tried his best to ensure that deserving officials got their promotions or other official benefits when they became due. In this process, sometimes some staff,who did not fully deserve the help, also got the help. But, some of them start accusing him of bias if they didn't get an expected benefit even once. When Dr Moorthy came to know this, he used to feel sorry for their attitude but continued with his objectivity and unbiased decisions on official matters.

Concluding Remark

Based on my long association with Dr AL Moorthy, I strongly feel, he is highly sincere and hard-working with strong commitment to whatever work he undertakes. He is very honest, always maintained very high integrity in official as well as personal matters and is frank in expressing his opinions. At the same time, he extends very high regard to his seniors in the career and all elders in general. With his retirement, DRDO is missing the services of a highly competent and sincere information scientist. I hope DRDO will find some way to continue to use his services.

Electronic Resources Management in Libraries, pp. 8–10

Tribute to Dr A.L. Moorthy, a Professional Friend

K. Sudhakar Goud

Dr Aragonda Lakshmana Moorthy (AL Moorthy) was born in a small agricultural Reddy family at Puthalapattu village in "Gods Own District" (Chittoor) in Andhra Pradesh. His village is surrounded by dark and lush green Sheshcahla mountain range. As he and his elder brother subscribed to socialist ideas, during his school days his name was changed to Lakshmana Moorthy from Lakshmana Moorthy Reddy without parents' approval. This exhibits his radical thinking in the formative years of his young life.

Though his educational career had some ups and downs, Dr Moorthy's schooling went off with flying colours and stood first through out. He has been an active participant in all competitions—essay writing, quiz, elocution and cultural activities—and won prizes; he was a poor athlete and weak sports person. Perhaps this takes Dr Moorthy to visit schools whenever he gets time to interact with children to motivate young minds.

In 1974, he failed in the final year of BSc at SV University in Physics due to the separate Jai Andhra agitation but later finished the course; he has to cancel the passed Mathematics and Chemistry subjects and appeared for all the three to secure second class to enable to enter post-graduate course. But the separate state demand is yet to be a reality and some of his friends and batch mates have become politicians and MLAs. I think he has taken the right direction and completed his MSc in Physics with first class. He attempted competitive exams to enter in banks or public sector for an year, without any success. After trying hard to enter into some job (including private institutions), he joined BLSc (now BLISc) at SV University, Tirupati not by choice but chance; but it proved to be good for LIS profession. Dr Moorthy obtained his PhD in the LIS from Karnataka University, Darward under the supervision of Prof C.R. Karisiddappa, in the year 2000.

Dr Moorthy's career started with the Indian Space Research Organization (ISRO), SHAR Centre (now Satish Dhavan Space Centre) at Sriharikota in Nellore district, Andhra Pradesh in 1979 as a Scientific Assistant in the library. ISRO was a prestigious, elite and glamorous organisation (hope it is still) which recently put 100 satellites in the space orbits with 36 launch vehicles. He was working under Shri VG Bhat who was a non-library professional heading the library which is advantageous for LIS professionals. Dr Moorthy's academic thirst did not end and he wanted to go further. In 1982, he went on to do his Associateship in Documentation and Information Science course at DRTC,

ISI, Bangalore. Fortunately, I joined as an ad-hoc in his leave vacancy and later I was regularized. Thanks to ISRO, during 80's we had the full access to PDP 11 computer of ECIL on our desks. Dr Moorthy exploited all facilities and technology at ISRO and ready to grow further. Unfortunately, after he came back from DRTC training he could not be promoted to the next grade at SHAR due various reasons and he was determined to leave the Organisation in frustration. Our old Indian saying reminds me: "every thing happens for our good" and this happened to Dr Moorthy and no looking back as far his professional career was concerned.

Dr Moorthy moved to DLRL (Defense Electronics Research Laboratory) at Hyderabad as Scientist through Union Public Service Commission in March 1984 and moved to DESIDOC, Delhi on promotion in January 1987. At DESIDOC he worked under two directors Dr SS Murthy and Dr Mohinder Singh. On recognition of his services he was promoted to Sc E and F at a reasonable young age though his subject area is not classified as core R&D. Dr AL Moorthy became Director of DESIDOC in 2006, a third Telugu man after Dr JVSR Anjaneyulu and DR SS Murthy.

Dr A.L. Moorthy's Significant Achievements in DRDO

- Developed a style manual for all DRDO publications.
- As an editor of the *Defence Science Journal (DSJ)*, revamped the editorial processes and introduced automation.
- *DESIDOC Bulletin (*now *DESIDOC Journal of Library and Information Technology)* was revamped and made as an important resource for LIS professionals with quality content and special issues; it is being abstracted in *SCOPUS* of Elsevier Science, an S&T full text database
- Developed library management manual for all DRDO libraries.
- Introduced open access to all priced (except Monographs) publications and hosted on Internet for access to global community.
- Started two new publications: *Technology Focus* and *DRDO Monographs* series.
- Developed DRDO institutional repository, Digital Library and E-journals consortium.
- Edited several high level DRDO HQrs publication for scientific advisors like Dr VS Arunachalam, Dr APJ Abdul Kalam, Shri M Natarajan etc.
- Dr Moorthy had the pleasure of working with Dr Abdul Kalam very closely who knows Dr Moorthy by name.
- Got ISO certification for DESIDOC in 2011.

He has several research papers to his credit, edited books, delivered keynote addresses, chaired technical sessions, and organized national conferences. This is Dr Moorthy's brief professional history.

Now let me turn into his personal side.

Dr Moorthy is a person of very strong convictions and values, a perfectionist. Works and lives more by his brain than heart some times mixes too. His simple lifestyle and down to earth attitude attracts many friends and new acquaintances. He is a materialist and seldom visited Lord Balaji despite being in the temple town for a long time; whenever he visited he accompanied till the temple entrance.

Dr Moorthy got married to a girl (Smt Shailaja) from Mahabubnagar in Telangana while working at DLRL in Hyderabad. Initially there were some cultural differences and practices but over a period of time both appreciated each other cultural differences. His wife Smt Sailaja works for the Govt. of Andhra Pardesh in Protocol Dept at Hyderabad. Due to Dr Moorthy's transfers from Hyderabad to Delhi (1984) to Hyderabad (2001) and again to Delhi (2006) (thereby bettering Mohmmad Bin Tuglak who went from Delhi to Devagiri to Delhi only), Smt Sailaja had lost many opportunities in her career and certainly made sacrifices for her husband. Dr Moorthy and Sailaja are very hospitable, and helping nature. Their residence in Delhi was always a "guest home" for people who come from Hyderabad (far and near relatives, friends, colleagues and their friends). Thanks for them both for their ever willingness to help people.

Dr Moorthy is a lover of nature and a strong conservationist and very stingy in using water and electricity. He practices what he preaches. Many people who meet for the first time may mistake him for his candid views. As a friend of Moorthy for over twenty five years, I describe him as an "egg"; only shell is hard and inside yolk is so smooth.

The greatest tragedy in the life of Dr Moorthy and Sailaja was their only son's tragic and untimely death in May 2011. The boy Chendu (as we call Nitin) whom I knew him since his birth, a tall, handsome and charming boy was to join a job in a multinational company and who had a beautiful girl friend and were to get married. Nitin was doing his MTech from IIT Madras. But his untimely death was a bolt from the blue. Smt Sailaja is yet to recover from the shock and Dr Moorthy put a brave face but I know he is skirting all his feelings. May the God give them strength and long life to Mr and Mrs Moorthys.

Dr Moorthy is a good lover of food and most of the time he over eats and suffers. He is equally good lover of films. I always compare him with Telugu actor Mr. Rajendra Prasad and Dr Moorthy symbolizes him in character and themes.

All the him and keep good health.

Electronic Resources Management in Libraries, pp. 11–12

Down the Memory Lane…

Pushpa Raina

It is a time honoured academic tradition to commemorate a scientist on the occasion of his sixtieth birthday in recognition of a successful career and what he has presented to others to read and discuss in the course of his academic life. This occasion in recognition of achievements and competencies permits all those who accompanied the scientist in question as friends and colleagues for some part of the way, to pay a tribute to him. It gives me a great pleasure to pen down few lines for a boss, a philosopher, a guide and a friend for all times.

My association with Dr AL Moorthy dates back to January 1987 when he first joined Defence Scientific Information and Documentation Centre (DESIDOC), Delhi as the Editor of *Defence Science Journal (DSJ),* a quarterly (now bi-monthly) premier research periodical of DRDO. We were a small team then and being the 80s, the print world was still following traditional methods and procedures. The time lag between the receipt and publishing of the papers was unacceptable to him. Being a visionary that he is, Dr Moorthy made keen and concerted efforts to revamp and streamline the editorial processes by the introduction of automation technology which was followed through during his leadership making the journal a true premier publication in the scientific circles.

After a hiatus, during which Dr Moorthy worked at Defence Research and Development Laboratory (DRDL), Hyderabad, I again got an opportunity to work with him when he returned to DESIDOC as a Director in 2006. Things had changed with time but once at DESIDOC, Dr Moorthy again found trust and faith in his associates with whom he had worked in his earlier posting and chose them as a part of his core working team. Commitment to job, clarity of thought and expression, persuasion and sticking to deadlines were the hallmarks of his professional acumen. He has been a tough and demanding boss, but it has been a learning and challenging experience to work for and with him, which I will always value and cherish even after retirement.

While at DESIDOC, Dr Moorthy again challenged the existing systems and procedures and sought a lot for the organisation. His efforts led to the introduction of many new services and innovative techniques for optimal utilization of information resources. He established a digital library and enhanced digital content. He initiated and established DRDO E-journal Service Consortium for providing online access of over 450 journals to DRDO Labs. He guided the development of Library Automation Software, Database of Library Holdings and Union Catalogue of Periodical Holdings. He was instrumental in starting new publications such as *Technology Focus* and *DRDO Monographs and Special Publications* also.

Dr Moorthy spearheaded the establishment of Knowledge Repository of DRDO Technical Reports and also the DRDO's Institutional Repository. He was instrumental in standardising the work procedures at DESIDOC leading it to the award of ISO 9001:2008 certificate from STQC, Ministry of Information and Technology, New Delhi in the 2011. Dr Moorthy, in addition to being a knowledge management professional, has always been keenly interested in publications. He has an inherent knack for editing which over the years has become a well-nurtured passion and has become a way of life with him. Apart from the regular DESIDOC publications he has a number of other publications to his credit where he has been the editor-in-chief or a guest editor on request. This gives him great insight into what his colleagues on the technical side are doing and facilitates a wholesome team environment. Being a perfectionist by nature, Dr Moorthy brought PERFECTION to the publications of DESIDOC, strictly adhering to the style and punctuality in bringing out the publications.

Dr Moorthy has always led by examples. He believes in disciplined and planned working and teamwork—something he expects from his team always but equally demonstrates it himself also. Unlike the norms of Indian bureaucracy, Dr Moorthy believes in an open door policy and is approachable and available to his team—there to share his knowledge and wisdom. He treats his team members with great respect and regard and this quality endears him to colleagues not only on a professional but a personal level as well. Though a hard task master he is noble at heart. He always stood by his team to the extent of going out of his way to help friends and colleagues in need. I have indeed been fortunate to have a career in an organisation lead by such a capable and visionary scientist.

Dr Moorthy is a connoisseur of good food and along with his better half, Shailija, they make perfect hosts to friends which we cherish and will look forward to continue for times to come.

I wish him a healthy and happy life.

Electronic Resources Management in Libraries, pp. 13–15

A True *Karamyogi*

Manoj Pant

"The great recipe for success is to work, and always work."
—Leon Gambetta

"Try not to be a man of success, but rather to be a man of value."
—Albert Einstein

Success comes with values, vision and the ability to deliver whatever the circumstances may be. Dr Aragonda Lakshmana Moorthy (fondly called ALM) epitomises all the above virtues. My acquaintance with Dr Moorthy dates back to late 1980s when I joined Defence Scientific Information and Documentation Centre (DESIDOC), one of the premier documentation centres of the country, in 1989. After four months of orientation, I was posted to Publications Division of DESIDOC under him. He was Group Head and Editor of *Defence Science Journal* (*DSJ*), a peer-reviewed, primary research journal in the area of defence science and technology. General perception about government jobs is less work, timely pay with more or less no accountability. But I found Dr Moorthy a role model for any aspiring young man starting his career. *DSJ,* though then was a quarterly journal, its timeliness was erratic. Dr Moorthy was trying to maintain its timeliness often working in a punishing schedule. Printing at that time was still being done by the conventional methods. We used to get typed, sometime even handwritten, manuscripts. His involvement in every process of publishing used to be omnipresent, set by example. He would work without any pretentions. I never experienced his ego and status ever interfere for achieving the targets; whenever he found that a certain process is slow he used to be there to streamline the work.

Dr Moorthy brought visible changes in *DSJ*. I found him both a traditionalist and modernist. His biggest contribution to *DSJ* was the standardisation of in-house style of publications prevailing to then international standards. He completely overhauled the look of the journal, right from the contents and size to overall getup. Early nineties was the time when computerisation was the mantra. He perhaps was the first Editor in India who encouraged manuscripts in soft copies (he called these compuscripts). Later as a Head of the Publications Division, he set-up an in-house desktop publishing infrastructure, which helped in saving a lot of time as many intermediary publishing processes got eradicated. In 1993, he started a new publication, *Technology Focus*, on the advice of Dr APJ Abdul Kalam, the then Scientific Advisor to *Raksha Mantri,* Secretary Defence Research and Development and DG Defence Research and Development Organisation (DRDO). The publication highlights products, processes and technologies developed by DRDO in a proper perspective. He also started DRDO Monographs and Special Publications in the same year to capture the tacit knowledge possessed by the superannuating senior scientists and Directors. Till now about 30 books were published under this series. This was followed by Department of Science and Technology and a few other scientific organisations, there by strengthening the S&T knowledge base of the country.

As Dr Moorthy grew in hierarchy, he was assigned new challenges and was made Head of the Defence Science Library (DSL). At DSL, he introduced many new services and innovative techniques for optimal utilisation of information resources and established a digital library. He created a web-based and project oriented information services for the benefit of all R&D scientists of DRDO through a single-window browse facility for 25 services offered by DESIDOC on the Intranet.

For a brief period during 2001–2006, Dr Moorthy was posted to Defence Research and Development Laboratory (DRDL), Hyderabad. At DRDL, he established a Digital Library and made it accessible to the scientists on their desktops. He also created infrastructure for accessing the Digital Library as well as online journals on a 24 × 7 basis.

In February 2006, Dr Moorthy was appointed Director of DESIDOC. Increase in responsibilities never hampered his creativeness to do something new and establish high standards. His first priority after taking over as Director was to improve the standards of services provided by DESIDOC as per international standards. He set the target for getting ISO certification. His encouragement and efforts fructified in July 2011 when DESIDOC was certified an ISO 9001:2008 establishment by the STQC. He networked various Technical Information Centres of DRDO laboratories located at different regions of India by establishing DRDO E-Journal Consortium for providing online access to over 550 journals. He initiated establishment of Knowledge Repository of DRDO Technical Reports, thereby creating DRDO knowledge base. He also established DRDO Institutional Repository, *Gyanstrot*, to archive the intellectual and knowledge capital of scholarly publications of DRDO and made it available for access through Intranet.

Dr Moorthy basically was an information scientist, but he always espoused his attachment with publications. As Editor-in-Chief during 2006–2012, the impact factor of *DSJ* increased three-fold. His other initiative, immediately after taking over as Editor-in-Chief, was to improve the standard of *DESIDOC Journal of Library and Information Technology* (*DJLIT*), a bimonthly primary journal brought out by DESIDOC. *DJLIT* till April 2006 was brought out as *DESIDOC Bulletin of Information Technology* (*DBIT*). He set the task to change it into a journal. Under his editorial guidance, *DJLIT* attained new heights; besides other abstracting agencies *DJLIT* is now being also covered by Scopus, a primary S&T database of Elsevier Science Publishers.

This transition would not have been possible without the able leadership and vision of Dr AL Moorthy who nurtured and presided over the execution of several development initiatives. At the heart of every success lies a philosophy that drives it. Dr Moorthy's philosophy was simple: work, more work and hard work. His days used to end with clearing all the pending work; files which he was unable to clear at office he used to take home so that official decisions should not suffer because of him. He was always available for guidance, both for official as well as personnel problems. After taking over Director, first thing he made was that time of his colleagues is more important because they are the ones who are driving the DESIDOC. He encouraged us to talk to him over intercoms and mobile (even while away on duty) to save the time otherwise wasted in getting appointment and consent. To his colleagues who were working in Publications Division, he used to state, "I am a library professional, but I learned the intricacies of editing by reading, reading and practice. So you can." Though Dr Moorthy is recipient of many awards, his contributions for popularising science and technology were recognised by DRDO when he was awarded the DRDO Award for Best Popular Science Communication in May 2010 from Dr Manmohan Singh, Hon'ble Prime Minister of India.

Dr Moorthy, as I envisage, is a true *Karamyogi.* He epitomises the words of Benjamin Disraeli, "The secret of success is consistency of purpose." Even the personal tragedy, which the fate imposed on him when he lost his only son who was studying in IIT-Madras, could not defeat and deter him and he was back to his hard working ways after a short time.

Dr AL Moorthy had a reputation for being a hard taskmaster and strict disciplinarian but at the same time he is an embodiment of strength and character, courage, dedication and vision. I sincerely hope that he will keep on guiding his admirers and colleagues the same way he used to do not so long ago.

Electronic Resources Management in Libraries, pp. 16–28

Dr Aragonda Lakshmana Moorthy: A Library Wizard

M. Sankara Reddy

"I don't want my house to be walled in on all sides and my windows to be stuffed. I want the cultures of all lands to be blown about my house as freely as possible, but refuse to be flown off my feet by any of them."

—Mahatma M.K. Gandhi

Dr Aragonda Lakshamana Moorthy is an eminent library science professional and former Director of Defence Scientific Information and Documentation Centre (better known by its acronym DESIDOC), Defence Research and Development Organization (DRDO), Ministry of Defence, Metcalfe House, Delhi. He is a well-known person among the LIS professional circles, computer technology savvy and an excellent organiser of men and materials. He is simple in lifestyle but versatile in thinking and action. Through his talent and hard work he built the digital libraries of DRDL and DESIDOC.

Dr Moorthy was born in a middle class peasant family at Puthalapattu village near Tirupathi, Chittoor District on 1 July 1952. He is the youngest of three children—two brothers and one sister—to his parents Shri A Appaswamy Reddy and Smt Sakunthalamma. At a very tender age of 6 months his father passed away. Due to lack of guidance, he was admitted in primary school in the seventh year (as against the normal sixth year). As a kid, he showed interest in books and education. He was a merited student in primary and secondary education. After passing the SSLC (11th class) in 1969, his further studies became a big question mark; mainly due to economic difficulties faced by his family as also the distance involved in attending college at Chittoor which is about 20 km away. At this juncture, his maternal Aunt who had no children came forward to educate. Their village Punepalli is a remote one but nearer to the college at Chittoor (about 11 km). The constraints were that he travels to college by cycle and manage their provisions stores and agriculture. For the love of education and the urge to help his family, he readily agreed to the conditions. He passed PUC, BSc degree in second class and MSc degree in Physics from Sri Venkateswara University, Tirupati in 1974 and 1976, respectively. All through his educational career he was a first class student except in PUC and BSc where he secured second class. From his childhood till he joined Govt service in 1979, he was involved and trained in the various activities of cultivation and farming. He was a voracious reader of books, novels, magazines, etc. throughout his educational career.

Due to family compulsions, although he wanted to pursue PhD in Physics, he tried to enter into some job through competitive examinations; he could not succeed for over a year. To keep himself abreast with his subject field of physics and know the job opportunities, he joined the Bachelor of Library Science at Tirupati. It is not by choice but by compulsion to stay in Tirupathi rather than in a small remote rural village where it was difficult to be in touch with the current events. To lessen his burden on his family, he started tuitions and earned sufficiently to support himself at Tirupathi leading to his liking for teaching as a profession. He passed his BLibSc degree in first class in 1978. Later, while in employment at ISRO, he did his Associateship in Documentation and Information Science (ADISc) at DRTC, Bangalore during 1982–1984. DRTC is a Mecca to all the library professionals. Dr. Moorthy came into contact at DRTC with stalwarts like Dr MA Gopinath and Dr Ganesh Bhattacharya, and Dr S Seetharama. Their impact on Dr Moorthy was seminal and it was later reflected on his work at all institutions he worked. Dr Moorthy's quest higher education was LIS is ever insatiable. He pursued PhD while in service at DESIDOC on the topic "*Impact of Electronic Media on Library Information Centres with a Specific Reference to India*" at Karanatak University, Dharwad in the year 2000 under the supervision of Prof. CR Karisiddappa, a distinguished teacher and professional.

His decision to join BLibSc became a good one as the library and information science was a fast developing profession in the late 70s and early 80s. Within 6 months of completing BLibSc, Dr Moorthy was selected in libraries at Central (ISRO, SHAR Centre), State (Govt Junior College, Pathikonda), and private (Chennai) institutions. With his love for teaching resulted from his tuitions, he tried to join private junior college as lecturer; but the demand for donation or deposit of ₹ 10,000 loomed large and was impossible to meet. Eventually, he chose to join at SHAR Centre, and started his professional career as Scientific Assistant in SHAR Library on 16 January 1979. When he was offered librarian post in February 1979 in the Govt Junior College, Pathikonda, there was compulsion from family to join there and get transferred to Chittoor, at a later date so that he can continue to be nearer to his family. He resisted and chose to stay in ISRO which became another good decision in his professional career. He worked in SHAR Centre 5 years 2 months till 1984. When he was to join Defence Electronics Research Laboratory (DLRL) again the family compulsion was there to stay back at SHAR Centre, which he resisted. During his education (1969–1978, and through his initial professional career, he received generous support from his cousin and bosom friend P. Chandrasekhara Reddy who kindled Dr Moorthy to become officer. His untimely death in August 1984 was a severe blow to Dr Moorthy who took long time to recover from loss.

After joining the profession, he took a bold decision to shun joining teaching or doing PhD in Physics, and continue and do his best and excel in the library field and his determination to complete MLibSc after the mandatory service period. So he was actively involved in all the areas of special library at SHAR Centre (now Satish Dhavan Space Centre) at Sriharikota Range, Nellore District). He would have continued in ISRO but for a minor issue. While pursuing ADISc at DRTC, he applied for the post of Scientific Assistant C in SHAR Centre against an open advertisement. In the interview, he with three-and-half years' service was not recommended; two persons without any experience were selected. This aroused a combative spirit with self-confidence and provoked him to apply and get a senior post. Eventually this led to his selection as an Officer through the Union Public Service Commission, New Delhi, and joining the Defence Research and Development Organisation (DRDO) at the Defence Electronics Research Laboratory (DLRL) Hyderabad in March 1984 as Scientist B. Thereafter for more than 28 years his services revolved around the libraries of DLRL and Defence Research and Development Laboratory (DRDL), Hyderabad and DESIDOC at Delhi in different capacities.

He was selected as Scientist C and joined DESIDOC, Delhi in January 1987 as Editor of *Defence Science Journal (DSJ),* a quarterly (now bi-monthly) premier research periodical of DRDO. He worked at DESIDOC for 14 years; nearly 10 years as Editor of DRDO publications and later as Joint Director of 3 divisions viz. Defence Science Library (DSL), Database Development and Information Services, in 1996. He was transferred to DRDL, Hyderabad to head its library in February 2001. After working for a little over 5 years at DRDL, as a grand finale of his professional career, he was appointed as Director, DESIDOC in February 2006. He rose to the position of the Director, DESIDOC step by step by sheer talent and hard work. He never aspired for positions but positions came to him on their own. He accepts the saying that luck would knock the door but once and the individuals should grab it. He firmly believes that his non-selection to the post of Scientific Assistant C at SHAR Centre was the turning point to his career which aroused a competitive spirit in him. He bore no ill will against anyone and maintained good relations with each and every one.

Dr Moorthy was instrumental in standardising the work at DESIDOC leading it to the award of ISO 9001:2008 certificate from STQC, Ministry of Information and Technology, New Delhi in the year 2011. He ably served both DRDL and DESIDOC libraries and established digital libraries along with introducing new user-friendly services on 24 × 7 basis with enhanced digital content. At DRDL he was instrumental in obtaining sanction for a new library building and with all IT infrastructure and user amenities, At DESIDOC a Knowledge Repository of 20000 technical reports was established along with guidelines for writing and uniform numbering of technical reports brought out in DRDO. Nearly 3500 research papers published by DRDO labs along with photographs, audio and visual material and more than 400 DRDO publications were digitised (DRDO archives) and DRDO Institutional Repository

Gyanstrot was established by Dr Moorthy for preservation and archiving the knowledge capital of DRDO scientific community on DRDO intranet. A DRDO Photo Gallery was also created covering the DRDO Scientific Heritage in terms of photographs of VVIPs, special events, conferences/seminars; products, systems and technologies developed by all 52 DRDO labs, as well as video and audio tapes (of special lectures, addresses, etc. at various events organised by DRDO) on DRDO intranet. He established DRDO E-Journals Service Consortium covering over 550 journals from 10 publishers for all 52 DRDO labs. He introduced several new web-based services, information technologies and infrastructural facilities for optimum utilization of information resources. A novel idea is the single window browse facility for more than 25 web-based and project oriented services for the benefit of all R&D scientists through DRDO intranet. He equipped the DESIDOC digital library with bibliographic databases, reference works and access to online journals.

As Head, DSL, Dr Moorthy was the first LIS professional in India to start subscription of online journals through Elsevier's Science Direct in 1999 when DESIDOC became the first institution to access over 1700 periodicals from two sites in Delhi. Earlier, as Editor (1987–1995), *Defence Science Journal* became the first periodical in 1991 to accept submission of research papers as compuscripts, irrespective of word processing software used. As Head of Publications (1991–1995), he introduced DTP, automation for editorial processes, and standardised the style for DRDO publications and brought out guidelines for house bulletins (*DRDO Newsletter* and *Technology Focus)* and research publications *DSJ* and *Monographs.* He was instrumental in bring out and revising the *DRDO Manual of Procedures for Management of Libraries and Technical Information Centres* which was widely used by all DRDO libraries and also some special libraries. As Editor-in-Chief of Publications, he guided their standardisation, quality of content and printing, timeliness and currency of information. He was responsible for effective dissemination of the achievements and "success stories" of DRDO to academia, institutions, engineering colleges, Military establishments and the public at large. He started profile based info-watch service for top management of DRDO to keep them abreast of latest in the frontier areas of cutting edge defence technologies. He facilitated supply of articles from DESIDOC holdings within 24 hours of request. He guided the revamping of DRDO website which became the second highest visited website (after the CBSE website) of government websites hosted by the National Informatics Centre on Internet. He is a supporter of Open Access and made all DRDO publications including priced ones (except Monographs) openly accessible on Internet. Being a library professional to the core, he revamped and guided the *DESIDOC Journal of Library and Information Technology—DJLIT* (earlier *DESIDOC Bulletin*) into a high quality bi-monthly journal in LIS; it is covered by many abstracting, indexing and full text databases including SCOPUS of Elsevier. Dr Moorthy has flair for journalistic and editorial work. Besides being Editor-in-Chief 2006–20120 and Editor (1991–1995) of DESIDOC publications *DSJ, DJLIT,*

DRDO Newsletter, DRDO Samachar, Technology Focus (BM), and *DRDO Monographs and Special Publications,* and *Popular Science and Technology Series* (1991–1995), he was also Honorary Editor of *ILA Newsletter,* Monthly during 1996–2002 and *AGLIS Journal,* a quarterly during 1989–1991.

Dr Moorthy owes his professional growth to four seniors who honed his skills, trained in specialised areas, above all they shared their knowledge and expertise in as diverse fields as effective services, editing, library management, technology management and change management. In his early professional life at ISRO, Shri VG Bhat, Head, SHAR Library was instrumental in sharpening his professional skills and his all-round development in documentation and services in special library environment. He gave freedom to do and scope to express new ideas. He encouraged Dr Moorthy to go for ADISc, and gave a recommendation letter. He taught how to take adversity as a way of life, besides highly appreciative of Dr Moorthy's work. Secondly, Dr SS Murthy, Director, DESIDOC during 1979–1999, was a hard task master, perfectionist, quality conscious and a skilful manager. He was mentor, philosopher, guide and real Guru to Dr Moorthy, who made the latter to learn editing etiquettes in the hard way. Due to his grinding Dr Moorthy was able to become a good editor and publisher. Dr SS Murthy was a liberal in providing information, copies of articles, and funding to R&D and LIS community in whatever way it is possible wherever they are. He used to say that if any paper is submitted to any conference or a lecture is delivered, DESIDOC's name and eminence should be kept in mind and minimum quality standards to be followed, and that the image of institution is much much larger than an individual's image. These qualities were not only imbibed and followed by Dr AL Moorthy throughout his professional career, but preached the same to the younger scientists in DRDO. Dr Moorthy still follows the maxim of contributing the best and excellence in performance. He introduced DRDO Cash and Performance Excellence Awards in DESIDOC from 2007. He was liberal in deputing the professionals for training and attending conferences. He liberally recommended releasing DRDO grants and funds for organising Conferences, Seminars and Workshops; 35 to 40 such events were funded (7 of them Rs one lakh max) by DRDO during 2006–2012. As Coordinator, Aerospace Resources Panel of Aerospace R&D Board, besides providing scholarships to BTech and MTech students, he recommended 5 LIS projects for funding as also a few Conferences and a Monograph.

Dr Moorthy, joined DRDL in and came under the influence of Dr Prahlada, Director, DRDL, who waited quite some time for his joining the Lab. Dr Moorthy was under a lot of stress and disappointment due to certain professional matters. Dr Prahlada gave moral and psychological support during that period. He was so simple and busy throughout the week and used to work on Saturdays and Sundays to meet the deadlines of missile programme. His simplicity, meeting reaching everyone from the lowest staff members to the senior most officers left an indelible impression on

Dr Moorthy. Dr Prahlada taught the way to deal with employees associations, staff problems, situational behaviour in difficult times, and above all change and technology management for the benefit of R&D community. When he took over as Director, DESIDOC in February 2006, all this managerial experience became handy to Dr Moorthy in successfully meeting the goals and objectives of the establishment. The last one who left an everlasting impression on Dr Moorthy is Prof CR Karisiddappa, to whom he owes his PhD. When Dr Moorthy registered for PhD, he knew editing and etiquettes of writing and presenting papers. Due to official work exigencies and publication deadlines, Dr Moorthy was not able to concentrate on PhD work. Even he forgot to pay the term fee as well as other modalities like extension of time for PhD. The Professor was highly punctual to ring on every Saturday to know the progress and due to guilt of non-progress he used to fear attending phone on those days. Due to the persistence of the Professor Dr Moorthy tried to raise hands and abandon PhD altogether. But it is the Professor who exuded confidence, gave moral support and paid term fees, renewed/extended the period selflessly. Due to his perseverance, Dr Moorthy completed his PhD in 7 years! But the association resulted in a number of research articles, presentations in conferences. Dr Moorthy was to study copyright as part of his study which in the following years made him an expert in the field.

Dr Moorthy is a Life Member of many professional associations viz. AGLIS (GILA), ALSD, IASLIC, ILA, SIS, Indian Physics Association (IPA), Indian Science Writers Association (ISWA) Science Writers Association in Telugu (SWATI) and Member of National Geographic Society, USA (1992–) and the Ranganathan Research Circle, New Delhi (1993–). He is a member of several editorial boards of journals; most notable are the *Annals of Library and Information Science* (NISCAIR), and *World Digital Libraries* (TERI). He never entered into professional politics of Associations although he was an Executive Member of ILA (1996–1999) and SIS (2010–). His deep commitment for his official work kept him away from such work. Otherwise with his popularity among the LIS professionals and official positions he held would have facilitated easily elected to any positions of the associations at any time.

Dr Moorthy is a professional expert of par excellence. He delivered Keynote Addresses many a time, Chairman of Technical Sessions, Panellist and Invited Speaker besides presenting papers at many National Conferences and Seminars. He Chaired Sessions in a couple of international Conferences held in India. Besides DESIDOC and DRDO, he was Chairman/Expert Member of Recruitment and Assessment Boards for several prestigious institutions such as BrahMos, ICMR, CSIR, IIMs, ISRO and NIPER. He was Chairman of ICMR E-Journals Consortium, and Member of DRDO, DST-CSIR NKRC, CeRA, INDEST, consortia. He is Member of Project review committees at DST, ICMR and NISIET. He was evaluator for PhD dissertations for Nagpur, Pune, and GGSIP universities and NISCAIR. He was Academic Counsellor and evaluator for IGNOU. Dr Moorthy was invited resource person to deliver lectures in the

Departments of Library and Information Science by many universities including AMU, Bangalore, Bombay, Guwahati, Jamia Millia, Kurukshetra, RTM Nagpur, Osmania, Sri Venkateswara and also at DRTC, ARCI, DIAT, IGCAR, IGNCA, NISCAIR and IITs. He is an impressive communicator and efficient teacher.

Dr Moorthy during his illustrious professional career received the following awards and honours for his outstanding work and services. These include DRDO Best Popular Science Communication Award-2009 received from Honourable Prime Minister; Life-time Achievement Award-2011 from Pusthakalaya Parishad, Jodhpur; Dr SR Ranganathan-Kaula Award-2009 Medal and Citation from Prof P. N. Kaula Endowment for Library and Information Science, New Delhi; Society for Information Science Fellowship-2009; ILA-Kaula Best Librarian Award-2008; ILA-CD Sharma Best Paper Award-2008; Commendation Certificate-1989 from Dr VS Arunachalam, Scientific Advisor, Ministry of Defence, New Delhi. The NISCAIR Golden Jubilee Lecture, 2011; the Thirteenth Prof S. Dasgupta Memorial Lecture at Delhi Library Association, 2011; Prof PSG Kumar Oration, RTM Nagpur University, Nagpur, 2011; and Prof MR Kumbar Memorial Oration. Karnataka University, Dharwad, 2007 are some of the important recognitions in his professional career.

Dr Moorthy is a prolific and effective writer. He attended during his thirty-three and half years professional career several conferences/seminars/workshops in India. He has authored 52 research articles as chapters in books, conference proceedings and journals. He also edited conference proceedings of ILA and INFLIBNET and several books of DRDO. A list of his papers and selected list of books and monographs edited is enclosed as Appendix A.

Dr Moorthy is an excellent manager of men and materials. He is accessible to one and all without any arrogance, power and position. He is humane in helping library professionals and in solving technical and administrative problems without causing controversy. The secret of his success is his non-assuming nature and leading the team from front as a team member. He simply provided directions, facilitated smooth functioning and solved problems that occurred during execution. He won approbation of his seniors and higher officials for his sincere and efficient work. He never craved for positions or promotions; in fact the fast growth in career was due to open competition where he always succeeded. All his promotions came in normal way and not on fast track. He never complained for his failures and took them sportively; at the same time he fought for career growth of his colleagues, even going out of the way to help the needy and performing staff and officers. He always encouraged and tried to motivate and inspire younger professionals. He never tolerated indiscipline, inefficiency, bureaucratic behaviour, and procrastination among his colleagues and staff.

Lastly, a word about his family. During 1980–1985, Dr Moorthy resisted and shunned marriage proposals for quite some time due his strong convictions to complete PG in LIS and see the family forward. While working at DLRL, Hyderabad, due to his carefree nature and irregular food habits, he suffered with severe jaundice (hepatitis) in 1985. This influenced his decision to marry and become a family man. On 15 May 1986, he married Ms K Shailaja Reddy, daughter of Shri K Venkat Reddy and Smt Sarojini Devi of Kalwakole, Mahbubnagar. Ms Shailaja Reddy, a graduate from Osmania University, with technical qualifications in in typing and telecommunications. To see the professional growth of her husband, she has to sacrifice her Bank job at Mahbubnagar, resign and move to Delhi when Dr Moorthy joined DESIDOC in 1987. Undeterred, she with her own devotion and efforts, secured a job at the AP Bhavan, New Delhi in 1990. She has to suffer in her second career too due to the transfer of Dr Moorthy to DRDL, Hyderabad in 2001 and again when he was appointed Director, DESIDOC in 2006. At present she is working in the Secretariat, Government of Andhra Pradesh in the Protocol section. Both were helpful in nature and their home was a home for friends and visitors to Delhi. They never had any biases of caste, religion or region and were always ready to help. Dr Moorthy and Mrs Sailaja are a happy couple. They had only one son by name Nitin Kumar. He is brilliant throughout his career like his parents. He was tall, handsome and loveable. While doing his BTech (Mech) degree at the IIT, Chennai, unfortunately he passed away in May 2011. This unexpected and untimely death is shock to his parents which left a void in their lives. May God provide strength to Dr Moorthy and Mrs Sailaja Moorthy to recover from the tragic trauma and provide solace to the couple with His Grace.

I hope and wish Dr Moorthy and Mrs Shailaja Moorthy a peaceful post-retired life and extend their experience and wisdom to the profession and professionals. Finally I wish them Good Health.

ANNEXURE A

List of Publications

A. *Articles*

[1] Ankur Pant and AL Moorthy Organizational knowledge management: DRDO initiatives. Paper submitted to IIPA, New Delhi (to be published).

[2] Ankur Pant and AL Moorthy. Knowledge management and need for safeguarding Indian traditional knowledge. (Paper communicated to *Annals of Library and Information Science*).

[3] AL Moorthy and Ankur Pant. DRDO e-journals consortium and use of e-resources. *Annals of Paper Published Library and Information Science*, September 2012, 59(3).

[4] AL Moorthy and Ankur Pant. Digital Rights, Publishers' Monopoly and Digital Content: Need for a Level Playing Field for Librarians. Paper presented at the International Conference on Trends in Knowledge and Information Dynamics (ICTK-2012), 10–13 July 2012, edited by

Devika P Madalli *et al.,* Bengaluru, Documentation Research and Training Centre/ISI, 2012. Vol., pp. 97–510.

[5] K Nageswara Rao and AL Moorthy. eCataloguer: An Automatic Tool for Developing Bibliographic Database using MARCXML Records. *DESIDOC Journal of Library and Information Technology,* 2012, 32(2), 101–108.

[6] AL Moorthy and Ankur Pant. DRDO E-Journals Consortium: An Analytical Study of E-Resources Usage. In Electronic Publications; Papers International Conference held at Puducherry, 1–2 March 2012, edited by C.K. Ramaiah *et al.* Pondicherry, Puducherry University, 2012, pp. 345–352.

[7] Manoj Kumar and AL Moorthy. Bibliographic Analysis of *DESIDOC Journal of Library and Information Technology* during 2001–2010. *DESIDOC Journal of Library and Information Technology,* 2011, 31(3), 203–208.

[8] AL Moorthy. Intellectual Property Rights in Digital Environment. Thirteenth Prof S. Dasgupta Memorial Lecture delivered on 10 March 2011 at the Ranganathan Bhavan, Delhi Library Association, Delhi.

[9] AL Moorthy. Open Access and Scholarly Communication. Dr PSG Kumar Oration Paper. Oration delivered at the RTM Nagpur University, 21 January 2011.

[10] AL Moorthy. Knowledge Management and Traditional Knowledge. Dr PSG Kumar Oration Paper. Oration delivered at the RTM Nagpur University, 21 January 2011.

[11] AL Moorthy. Digital Library Initiatives and Applications. Paper submitted to the Prof N Laxman Rao Felicitation Volume, DLIS, Osmania University, Hyderabad, 2011 (in press)

[12] AL Moorthy. DRDO E-jpurnals Consortium. *DESIDOC Journal of Library and Information Technology,* 2009, 29(5), 18–23.

[13] AL Moorthy. Intellectual Property Rights and Digital Technologies. Paper presented in ILA-TISS International Conference Papers 2008, held at TISS, Mumbai during 12–15 November 2008.

[14] Rajiv Vij and AL Moorthy. Empowering LIS Professionals: Competency development initiatives and programmes of DESIDOC. Paper accepted for publication in 23rd National Seminar of IASLIC at Kolkata during 10–13 December 2008.

[15] AL Moorthy, S Shashi Nath and CM Joshi. Institutional Repositories and their benefits for Organization. *In* Library and Information Science Profession in the Knowledge Society; Prof CR Karisiddappa Festschrift Volume edited by MM Koganuramath *et al.,* New Delhi, Allied, 2007. pp. 227–231.

[16] AL Moorthy. Re-orientation of Library Services in India: Librachine to Digital Libraries. Keynote address delivered at 'National Conference on Reorientation of Library Services in India',18–20 August 2007, on the occasion of Birth Centenary of Kalapoorna Paturi Nagabhushanam. Vijayawada, AP Library Association, 2007. pp. 1–11.

[17] V. Senthil and AL Moorthy. Online Access to DRDO Periodicals Using Open Source Software. Paper presented in the International Conference on Digital Libraries (ICDL-2006) 5–6 December 2006, TERI, New Delhi.

[18] AL Moorthy. Copyright Issues in Digitization Era. *In* Technology management in libraries. Papers presented in honour Dr E Rama Reddy, Librarian, Hyderabad University, edited by AL Moorthy *et al.,* New Delhi, Allied, 2006.

[19] AL Moorthy and CR Karisiddappa. Copyright Issues in Digital Environment. Paper presented in the One-Day Seminar on 'Delivery of Books and Newspapers (Public Libraries) Act, 1954 on 27th April 2006. Karnatak University, Dharwad, pp. 74–119.

[20] AL Moorthy and CR Karisiddappa. Copyright Issues in Digital Environment. Paper presented in the Two-Day State Level Seminar on Perspectives in Intellectual Property Rights, 13–14 August 2005, SDM Dental College, Dharwar. JSS Sakri Law College, Hubli, pp. 32–52.

[21] AL Moorthy and C.R. Karisiddappa. Relevance of Intellectual Property Rights in the Digital millennium. *In* International Conference on Information Management in Knowledge Society (ICIM-2005) 21–25 February 2005, Mumbai, edited by D Kamalavijayan *et al.,* New Delhi, Allied Publishers, 2005, Vol. 1, pp. 201–210.

[22] AL Moorthy and CR Karisiddappa. Cyber Commerce for Libraries. *In* Library and Information Studies in Cyber Age: Essays in honour of Prof JL Sardana, edited by SM Dhavan. Delhi, Authors Press, 2004, pp. 221–238.

[23] AL Moorthy and CR Karisiddappa. Intellectual property rights and copyright in the context of electronic information. *In* Information Technology Application in Libraries: A Text Book for Beginners, edited by M Mahapatra and DB Ramesh. Bhubaneshwar, Reproprint, 2004, pp. 583–589.

[24] AL Moorthy and CR Karisiddappa. Information infrastructure and use of electronic media in Indian libraries. *In* Knowledge Societies and Libraries: Papers in honour of Prof AAN Raju, edited by N Laxman Rao, S Sudarsan Rao and TV Prafulla Chandra. New Delhi, Ess Ess, 2004, pp. 103–118.

[25] CK Ramaiah and AL Moorthy. The impact of continuing education programmes on library and information science professionals. *Library Review*, 2002, 51(1), 24–31.

[26] AL Moorthy, M Prahalada Rao, and CR Karisiddappa. Intellectual property rights of electronic information in the age of digital convergence. *In* NACLIN 2001: Networking of digital resources for national development: Papers of the Fourth National Annual Convention on Library and Information Networking, 6–9 November 2001, University of Hyderabad, edited by HK Kaul. New Delhi, DELNET, 2001, pp. 82–106.

[27] AL Moorthy and CR Karisiddappa. Information infrastructure and use of electronic media in Indian libraries. *In* Role of university and college libraries in the changing information scenario: Papers presented in the First South Indian Conference, 18–19 October 2001, PS Telugu University, Hyderabad, edited by AL Moorthy and M Sankara Reddy. PS Telugu University Library and ILA South Zone, Hyderabad, 2001, pp. 148–162.

[28] AL Moorthy and CR Karisiddappa. Mass Storage Technologies for Libraries and Information Centres. *DESIDOC Bulletin of Information Technology,* 2000, 20(5), 3–20.

[29] AL Moorthy and CR Karisiddappa. Electronic publications: Issues and concerns. *In* Electronic sources of information: Papers presented in the DRTC Annual Seminar held during 1–3 March 2000 at the DRTC, Bangalore, edited by IK Ravichandra Rao. DRTC, Bangalore, 2000.

[30] AL Moorthy and CR Karisiddappa. Copyright in networked environment. *In* CALIBER-2000: Seventh National Convention on Information Services in a Networked Environment, edited by R Vengan, HR Mohan and KS Raghavan. INFLIBNET Centre, Ahmedabad, 2000, pp. 4.18–4.30

[31] AL Moorthy and CR Karisiddappa. Internet for libraries. *In* Vision of future library and information systems: Dr SS Murthy festschrift, edited by T Ashok Babu, LS Ramaiah, SC Saxena, and DS Bedi. Viva Publications, New Delhi, 2000, pp. 67–81.

[32] AL Moorthy and CR Karisiddappa. Infrastructure for accessing electronic information in Indian Libraries. Paper presented in the Seventh Annual Convention on Universal Accessibility to

Information of the Ranganathan Research Circle held on 22 January 2000 at Institute of Integrated Learning in Management, New Delhi.

[33] AL Moorthy and SS Murthy. Electronic commerce and information infrastructure: Indian perspective. *Productivity—A Quarterly Jl of National Productivity Council*, January–March 1999, 39(4), 556–566.

[34] AL Moorthy and CR Karisiddappa. Electronic commerce and networked libraries. *In* NACLIN 98; Library and Information Networking: Papers of the First National Annual Convention on Library and Information Networking, November 1998, India International Centre, New Delhi, edited by HK Kaul. New Delhi, DELNET, 1998, pp. 210–226.

[35] AL Moorthy and CR Karisiddappa. Intellectual property rights and virtual libraries. *In* Towards the New Information Society of Tomorrow: Innovations, Challenges and Impact. Papers presented at the 49th FID Conference and Congress, New Delhi, 11–17 October 1998. NM Malwad, *et al* (Eds). New Delhi, INSDOC, 1998. pp. IV-51–IV-61. FID Publication No. 719.

[36] AL Moorthy and CR Karisiddappa. Impact of Internet on library and information centres: A review. *In* Information Technology: Issues and Trends: Festschrift in honour of Prof N Guruswamy Naidu, Vol. 2. B Satyanarayana, B Ramesh Babu, V Pulla Reddy, and T Ashok Babu (Eds). New Delhi, Cosmo Publications, 1998, pp. 308–324.

[37] AL Moorthy and CR Karisiddappa. Transformation to virtual libraries: Real or virtual? Paper presented at the Seventeenth SIS Annual Convention and Conference on Virtual Libraries: Internet-based L&I Services and Products, University of Hyderabad, 12–14 March 1998. New Delhi, SIS, 1998, pp. 109–122.

[38] AL Moorthy and CR Karisiddappa. Technical report writing: Methods and procedures. *In* Information and Society: Essays in Memory of Prof P Gangadhara Rao. LS Ramaiah, N Guruswami Naidu, T Ashok Babu, B Ramesh Babu and K Ramanaiah (Eds). New Delhi, Ess Ess Publications, 1997, pp. 246–266.

[39] AL Moorthy and SS Murthy. Information technologies and Indian libraries. *In* 50 Years: Library and Information Services in India, edited by PB Mangla, DR Kalia and Neela Jagannathan. Delhi, Shipra Publications, 1998, pp. 249–260.

[40] AL Moorthy and CR Karisiddappa. On citations, references and intellectual debts. *In* Library Science and its Facets, Vol. 1. HR Chopra, Umesh C Sharma and MK Srivastava (Eds). New Delhi, Ess Ess Publishers, 1997, pp. 264–271.

[41] AL Moorthy and CR Karisiddappa. Copyright and Electronic Information. Paper presented at the Sixteenth SIS Annual Convention and Conference on Access to Electronic Information, Regional Research Laboratory, Bhubaneswar, 28–31 January 1997. M Mahapatra *et al.* (Eds). New Delhi, SIS, 1997, pp. 403–415.

[42] AL Moorthy and CR Karisiddappa. Internet and its impact on library and information centres. Paper presented in the 30th DRTC Workshop on Advances in Information Technology: Impact on Library and Information Field, 28–30 October 1996, Bangalore. IK Ravichandra Rao and ARD Prasad (Eds). Bangalore, DRTC, 1996, Paper BF.

[43] AL Moorthy and CR Karisiddappa. Electronic publishing: Impact and implications for library and information centres. *In* Digital libraries: Dynamic store house of digital information. Papers presented at the 15th SIS Annual Convention and Conference, 18–20 January 1996, Bangalore. NM Malwad, TB Rajashekar, IK Ravichandra Rao and NV Satyanarayana (Eds). New Delhi, New Age International Pubs, 1996, pp. 15–35.

[44] AL Moorthy, Manoj Kumar Pant and V Rajendran. Electronic document delivery systems. *In* New Vistas in Library and Information Science: Papers in honour of Prof GVSL Narasimha Raju. AAN Raju, LS Ramaiah, N Laxman Rao and TV Prafulla Chandra (Eds). New Delhi, Vikas Publishers, 1995. pp. 406–422.

[45] AL Moorthy. The role of DESIDOC in science communication. *In* Souvenir of ISWA First National Convention, 12–13 February 1993, New Delhi. New Delhi, ISWA, 1993, pp. 94–96.

[46] AL Moorthy and Manoj Kumar Pant. Desktop publishing. *DESIDOC Bulletin of Information Technology,* 1992, 12(4), 3–12 (also translated into Marathi).

[47] AL Moorthy. Quality of research in published papers. *Defence Science Journa*l, 1992, 42(1), 3–4. (editorial)

[48] AL Moorthy. Of references and intellectual debts. De*fence Science Journal*, 1991, 41(2), v–viii. (editorial)

[49] AL Moorthy. Towards a change. *Defence Science Journal*, 1991, 41(1), v–viii. (editorial).

[50] AL Moorthy and V Rajendran. Information technologies for libraries and information centres. *AGLIS Journa*l, 1990, 8(1), 5–14.

[51] AL Moorthy and V Rajendran. Computer-based document delivery systems for effective dissemination of information. Paper presented at the AGLIS Annual Convention and Seminar, New Delhi, 20–21 December 1990, New Delhi, AGLIS, 1990.

[52] AL Moorthy. Desktop publishing. *In* Workshop on Information Technology, Delhi, 2–27 July 1990. Delhi, DESIDOC, 1990, pp. 181–191.

[53] AL Moorthy. Towards a standard style of bibliographical references. *DESIDOC Bulletin*, 1988, 8(4), 3–8.

[54] MA Gopinath and AL Moorthy. Phase relations associated with mathematical sciences: a case study. *Library Science with a slant to Documentation*, 1983, 20(1), 18–30. (Revised version of the paper presented in the 20th DRTC Annual Seminar on Classification and Indexing in Science and Technology, 21–25 February 1983, Bangalore. DRTC, Bangalore, 1983, pp. BDI–BD19).

B. *Books/Conference Proceedings/Special Publications*

As Editor, he has directly contributed to many regular and ad hoc publications. The following are some important ones:

[1] AL Moorthy (Co-Editor); Electronic Publications: Papers presented at the International Conference, Pondicherry University, 1–2 March 2012. Puducherry, Pondicherry University, 2012, p. 424.

[2] DRDO as Knowledge Generator. Coffee Table Book. DRDO, New Delhi, 2010.

[3] Silent March. Coffee Table Book brought out on the occasion of DRDO Golden Jubilee Celebrations. DRDO, New Delhi, 2008.

[4] AL Moorthy, (Chief Editor). Information Commons: Impact and Implications for Libraries and Information Centres: Seminar Papers of the 52 All India Library Conference of Indian Library Association, 26–29 December 2006, Srinagar, Garhwal. Delhi, ILA, 2006, p. 575.

[5] AL Moorthy, N. Laxman Rao and K. Sudhakar Goud (Eds.). Technology management in libraries: Papers presented in honour Dr E Rama Reddy, Librarian, Hyderabad University, edited by A.L Moorthy *et al.,* New Delhi, Allied, 2006, p. 380.

[6] AL Moorthy (Co-Editor). Electronic Publications. Proceedings of National Seminar, 23–24 March 2006, Hyderabad, edited by Chennupati K. Ramaiah *et al.,* Centre for Information Studies, MGNIRSA, Hyderabad, 2006, p. 480.

[7] AL Moorthy and M Sankara Reddy (Eds). Role of university and college libraries in the changing information scenario: Papers presented in the First South Indian Conference, 18–19 October 2001, PS Telugu University, Hyderabad. PS Telugu University Library and ILA South Zone, Hyderabad, 2001, p. 210.

[8] AL Moorthy, (Co-Editor). Quest for Quality: Papers presented at the 49th All India Library Conference, Ahmedabad, 3–6 January 2001, edited by SM Dhawan *et al.,* ILA, New Delhi, 2000, p. 620.

[9] AL Moorthy and PB Mangla (Eds). CALIBER 97: Papers presented in the Fourth National Convention for Automation of Libraries in Education and Research, 6–8 March 1997, Patiala. Ahmedabad, INFLIBNET, 1997, p. 210.

[10] AL Moorthy (Ed). International directory of defence-related institutions and industries, compiled by Shashi Tyagi and Vinod Kumari. DESIDOC, Delhi, 1996, p. 950.

[11] AL Moorthy (Co-Editor). SHAPE 95: Papers presented at National Seminar on Hospital Architecture and Engineering, New Delhi, 14–15 March 1995, edited by Sudesh Dhiman *et al.* Institution of Military Engineers, MES, New Delhi, 1995, p. 350.

[12] AL Moorthy (Ed). A Nagaratnam. Radiological protection: A summary handbook of ICRP publications and recommendations. DRDO, New Delhi, 1995, p. 1040.

[13] AL Moorthy and DS Bedi (Eds). KAV Pandalai. The other side of science. DRDO, New Delhi, 1994, p. 64.

[14] AL Moorthy (Sp. Ed); S Kumar and AR Reddy (Eds). Solidstate nuclear track detectors. Proceedings of the 7th National Symposium, October 1991. Defence Laboratory, Jodhpur, 1992, p. 250.

[15] AL Moorthy (Co-Editor). Bibliographic databases and networks: Proceedings of the International Conference (ICBDN), New Delhi, 22–25 February 1989, edited by SS Murthy *et al.,* Tata McGraw-Hill, New Delhi, 1990, p. 420.

[16] AL Moorthy (Co-Editor). Bibliographic databases and networks: Papers presented at the International Conference (ICBDN), New Delhi, 22–25 February 1989, edited by SS Murthy *et al.,* Tata McGraw-Hill, New Delhi, 1989, p. 120.

[17] AL Moorthy. Manual of cataloguing. ISRO-SHAR-SP-06-053-84. Sriharikota, ISRO, 1984, p. 35.

Section–II

Electronic Resources and Management

Electronic Resources Management in Libraries, pp. 31–46

Electronic Resources Management in Academic and Research Libraries: Issues and Challenges

M. Koteswara Rao

ABSTRACT

Rapid developments in information and communication technologies, particularly the Internet had paved the way for the creation of vast amount of scholarly content by all the publishers. Consequently, libraries have gradually increased their number of licensed electronic resources such as online journals, databases and e-books. This migration from print to electronic-only journal publishing has been very smooth for the publishers, but it has been a major challenge for libraries in terms of collection, organizing and providing access to these e-resources. This has resulted in the development of new software tools to manage the digital information; and the basic role of the librarian has also shifted form a custodian to a facilitator. This paper discusses various issues and problems of e-resource management including licensing and copyright.

1. Introduction

In the last two decades, the academic and research libraries have shown visible signs of adaptation to the latest Information and Communication Technologies (ICTs) in content creation, collection development, preservation and delivery of information to their members. Further, there has been an increased availability of information in electronic format with better collection management, storage, distribution, dissemination and publishing methods. During this transformation, the librarians' roles too have undergone a major shift from mere providers of documents to facilitators of information. Today, the academic librarians have assumed additional role of a teacher in imparting *information literacy* skills to their users; a publisher and an archivist of institutional repositories.

From the library's point of view, the transition from print to electronic is an action propelled by the ubiquitous Internet. The developments in ICT had a direct bearing on libraries which quickly adopted it to their advantage and started delivering information to their users over intranet and Internet. For large university libraries, e-resources have proved as a boon in space saving, easy access and less administrative work.

From the users' point of view, the rapid developments in ICT have enabled them to access library resources directly without visiting the library and seeking any help from library staff. Today, the Web OPAC, online journals, e-books, digital library and institutional repositories have become the basic components of every academic library webpage. Management of licensed e-resources and providing access to authorized users over a secured network is the only challenge left for librarians to improve upon.

To realize their objectives fully, the academic libraries in the years to come, have to address all the issues pertaining to managing e-resources, technologies, standards, services, and the legal issues required for repositioning academic libraries in the digital environment which is dominated by the Internet. The fundamental challenge is integration *i.e.* bringing together the different components of the library into a coherent unit of knowledge resource centre.

According to the ARL Report (ARL, 2002), approximately 60 percent of the universe of some 20,000 active peer-reviewed journals is available in electronic form. Further, 70 percent of libraries' subscriptions in 2006 were to e-journals or e-journals plus print. The University of California study found that online journals were used 10 times more than print journals. The study predicts that over the next 5–10 years, printed journals will decline and ultimately 95 percent of journals will be electronic.

With too many titles/databases to manage, libraries have realized the need for a record-keeping system that would help manage the details of acquiring and maintaining these e-resources. Managing and delivery of electronic library services is one of the major challenges today for university libraries. Along with the technical issues brought in by the electronic medium, they also need to address the author's copyright without sacrificing free global accessibility of digital resources. An Electronic Resources Management System (ERMS) is one such tool to address these issues. These issues can be grouped under the following heads:

- Selection and acquisition of e-resources
- Licensing of e-resources
- Pricing/subscription models
- Enabling access to e-journals
- ERM tools for librarians
- Value-added services
- Need for library staff training.

2. Acquisition of E-Resources

In the case of printed materials, the acquisition librarian makes the decision to acquire an item with only limited consultation with other departments following established policies and guidelines. E-resources present a number of hurdles not encountered with traditional library materials. In addition to the criteria that apply to printed materials, electronic publications raise complex issues such as licensing, access, networking, pricing, ownership, and rapidly changing technology and standards. Almost all types of documents in print viz. e-journals, e-books, full-text (aggregated) databases, indexing and abstracting databases, reference databases (biographies, dictionaries, directories, encyclopedias, etc.), numeric and statistical databases, e-images (Ex: ARTstor), e-audio/visual resources, have their electronic counterparts.

Unlike print material, the acquisition librarian cannot make a decision to acquire an e-resource in isolation. He/she should coordinate closely with various departments to evaluate the suitability of a resource prior to the decision to acquire. To ensure consistency of approach, it is good practice to establish clear guidelines and processes for the selection of e-resources. These might include developing a checklist for selection and evaluation; establishing clear roles and lines of responsibility and consultation; and the establishment of an e-resource selection committee consisting of faculty, research scholars, students from various departments and the librarian.

To involve library users in collection development, the librarian may consider ways in which to receive their input. This could include feedback on potential new resources as well as on existing resources. To assess whether an e-resource is appropriate for the library's collection and to help determine the true and hidden cost implications of acquisition, storage, maintenance, preservation and other issues, detailed information regarding the resource is required. This information needs to be reviewed against the library's e-resource collection development policy. In some instances, libraries may find it helpful to develop an e-resource selection and evaluation checklist with a detailed set of questions the selector must answer as part of the selection and evaluation process. Such a checklist might include specific rules regarding prioritization of platforms/providers to provide additional guidance for selectors of e-resources which might be available on multiple platforms via different providers.

E-resources can be acquired in many ways. The most common approach is the annual subscription method, by which the library users can have access to the content of current year plus the previous 10 years. We should remember that unless we renew the subscription every year, we have no right of ownership over the data; which means we do not own the content unlike the printed documents. The copyright pertaining to the electronic data lies with the publisher, and he provides only access to the content on payment of a 'fee' on certain terms and conditions laid down in the License agreement.

In a subscription model, the publisher does not provide the archival data to the subscribing library. Even with regard to the printed books, the library can own the copy for reading and circulating, but the content is still protected by copyright. However, some publishers provide free access to 'older' content after certain period of time (usually one year), which is termed as "embargo". Another approach is outright purchase of the electronic content. This is a very expensive proposal where the publisher provides the content to the subscriber (either in DVDs or Hard disk) to be hosted on their local server. Defense and commercial R&D establishments choose this method of content acquisition to maintain confidentiality of information use.

Another method is perpetual access to the e-resources through a one-time payment. The concept of maintaining enduring access to a resource, even if the library has cancelled its subscription or the producer has ceased to maintain it. This is usually applicable to e-books and the library has to make a one-time payment to the publisher. The publishers justify that the high price collected is for maintaining the large amount of data in a large cluster of high-end servers including electricity, staff salaries, and hardware replacements.

The reluctance of some libraries to subscribe expensive e-resources had prompted publishers to evolve newer models of subscription such as pay-per-view. Under this scheme, the library has to pay only for the total number of journal articles it has downloaded from the publisher's website. This method is suitable for small libraries and R&D organizations with limited budgets.

2.1 *Acquisition of Back Files (Archives)*

As more and more publishers have moved from print to e-journals over a period of time, a large volume of old issues or 'back files' have accumulated with every publisher. Today, almost all the leading publishers are offering back files or 'archives' at high cost to libraries on perpetual access basis. Many of the large university libraries are discarding bound volumes of print journals and acquiring 'back files' to save library space and to satisfy the changing user needs. Librarians must exercise caution while purchasing these back files at high cost because the number of articles users would download from old issues of journals could be very small.

3. Licensing of E-Resources

Unlike print media, electronic documents are not generally held or owned by the subscribing library. The amount paid to the publishers is invariably the fee paid to access the content for a specific period of time; except in such cases where the fee paid is for perpetual access (in the case of e-books). Hence, the librarians must negotiate licenses that address the institution's needs and recognize its obligations to the licensor.

A license agreement is a legal contract or a "promise or set of promises constituting an agreement between the parties that gives each a legal duty to the other and also the right to seek a remedy for the breach of those duties. Its essentials are competent parties, subject matter, a legal consideration, mutuality of agreement, and mutuality of obligations."

In the area of licensing electronic resources, failure to read and understand the terms of the agreement may result in such unintended consequences such as loss of certain rights, restrictions, sudden termination of contract, etc. Hence, the library has to negotiate and comply with the vendor's licensing agreements. In many cases, the library has no right to make any change in the agreement. In other words, the librarian has no choice to negotiate or change the terms and conditions in the agreement. However, the librarian should ensure that the agreement is in compliance with the existing copyright laws and guidelines, and does not jeopardize the users' interests.

3.1 *Fair Terms of Use*

Usually, the terms and conditions for using e-resources are spelt out in each of the license agreements signed by the Librarian on behalf of the organisation. In some cases, the administrative head of the institution signs the agreement. The licenses for electronic resources impose two types of restrictions on its usage, namely (i) people who can use these resources; and (ii) how the resources can be used. The first restriction defines authorized users for e-resources, which in academic environment generally includes students, faculty, staff and onsite visitors of the subscribing institution. The second restriction deals with how these resources can be used. It is the responsibility of individual user (library) to ensure that e-resources are used for educational and research purposes only.

Most of the agreements entered into by the consortia and publishers specify items that users are prohibited to do. It is the responsibility of individual library to ensure that the use of electronic resources does not breach the terms and conditions specified in the license agreements. Breaches of the license agreement with publishers could result in the suspension of access to the resources for the member institutions.

License agreements vary from publisher to publisher. These terms and conditions include, but are not limited to, restrictions on copying, republishing, altering, redistributing and reselling the information contained therein. Fee-for-service providers may not copy and resell texts from licensed sources to non-subscribing individuals, institutions or organizations.

3.2 *What Happens if the License is Violated?*

Publishers track the use of electronic resources in terms of number of simultaneous users and downloads made by the subscribing library. Misuse, if any is notified to the librarian with details of kinds of violations and the library is expected to take action. The publishers also suspend the access to e-resource pending suitable action by the subscribing library. The access is stopped not only for journals where license agreement was violated but for all the journals by the same publisher. Moreover, the access is suspended not only for the individual violator but for the entire institution.

3.3 *What is Allowed?*

- Viewing, downloading, copying, printing and saving a copy of search results.
- Viewing, downloading, copying, printing and saving individual articles.
- Using e-resources for scholarly, educational or scientific research, teaching, private study and clinical purposes.
- Sending a copy of an article to another authorized user (*i.e.* current faculty, students or staff).
- Posting the URL to the publisher's version of the article on a class website (publisher links will allow only authorized users access).

3.4 *What is Not Allowed?*

- Use of robots or intelligent agents to do systematic, bulk or automatic downloading is not permitted.
- Systematic downloading or printing of entire journal issues or volumes, or large portions of other e-resources is not permitted.
- Using e-resources for commercial gain is not permitted (*i.e.* reselling, redistributing or republishing licensed content).
- Transmitting, disseminating or otherwise making online content available to unauthorized users (*i.e.* sending to mailing lists or electronic bulletin boards) is not permitted.
- Posting the publisher's version or PDF of an article to an open class website is not permitted (instead, post the URL to the article which will allow only authorized users access).

Keeping the above in view the librarians must ensure that the users are aware of access restrictions given below:

- Restrict access only to authorized users over the campus network
- Fair use licensing agreement to be signed by the librarian
- Saving/printing is limited to few articles only
- Ensure that Systematic Downloading is not done
- Electronic transfer of articles is not done
- Library shall not charge for e-resources
- Strict adherence to copyright laws by the user (library)
- Deny access if any of the IPR conditions are violated.

4. Pricing Models of E-Resources

In India, the market for e-resources is a new concept and is still emerging where pricing models are not yet established. For example, there is enormous variation in e-journal prices from publisher to publisher. This is applicable individually, to subject collections, to take-or-leave-it packages. E-journal pricing models are often based on print subscriptions plus an additional component of content, storage and access fee.

Generally e-journals cost 7 to 8 percent more over the print subscriptions and very often libraries are expected to maintain the paper copies. Emerging e-book services, such as NetLibrary, are quoting prices far in excess of paper prices. There is also the added problem of VAT which is chargeable for electronic resources whereas printed publications are exempt from it.

Many of the publishers are working towards maintaining their market shares and profits even in this new digital era. It reminds us of the earlier problem of serials crisis created in the print environment which is now being transferred to the electronic resources. However, some publishers have realized the dangers of uniform block pricing and started to offer selective pricing to individual libraries. For example, Academic Press pioneered a site license for consortia that includes all journals published by them and gives the user unlimited access to all articles. In this model, titles that are highly used will have a lower cost per-use and be perceived as a better value.

5. Enabling Access to E-Resources

Authentication and authorization are the two major technical issues faced by libraries which have security implications in providing access to licensed e-resources. At present, the best solution is IP-range authentication method. Although the Athens authorization system is more secure and popular in many countries, it is yet to take off in India for various reasons. Further, the demand for off-campus access is also on the rise, but institutions are adopting a wait and watch policy for want of a better software tool that is more secure. Some institutions have already responded to this demand by setting up proxy servers, but we should remember that this is only a temporary solution.

5.1 *IP-based Network Access*

Accessing e-resources over the Internet is the simplest task; however, access to licensed e-resources needs authentication and it comes in many ways. Almost all educational institutions have IP-based campus networks with unique set of IP numbers for connecting to the Internet through internal gateways and proxies. This method is the most secure way of providing access to e-resources. However, users outside the IP range of the domain cannot have access to the campus network using this method. Institutions with multiple campuses need a different configuration but at an extra cost for maintaining multiple IP ranges.

5.2 *Virtual Private Network*

Virtual Private Network (VPN) is a private communication network over a public network, *i.e.* Internet. The VPN is much more secure method, in which every authorized user is given a personal login and password to gain access to the e-resources on the institute's network. The information pertaining to every authorized user is created and maintained on a special server installed with special software. Most of the universities in the West use VPN to enable access to networked e-resources.

Wherever there are no IP-based networks, access to e-resources is provided through a common login and password provided by the publisher. These logins/passwords are maintained and authenticated at the publishers' website. In this method, there is a danger of misuse by unauthorized users who gain access to login/password. This method is suitable for institutions with multiple campuses using broadband connection.

5.3 *Remote Access*

Remote access is concerned with gaining access to subscribed e-journals and databases from outside the physical library or the campus network via special proxy servers or other kinds of web-based authentication. In addition to these there are other remote access methods available in UK, USA and some other countries, but not in India. They are 'Athens' and 'Shibboleth', etc.

A proxy server is a server (a computer system or an application) that acts as an intermediary for requests from clients seeking resources from other servers. A client connects to the proxy server, requesting some service, such as a file, connection, web page, or other resource available from a different server. The proxy server evaluates the request as a way to simplify and control their complexity. The most common ones are mod-proxy (Apache) Squid, IIS (Microsoft) and EZproxy (OCLC).

Considering the security aspects and legal implications of misuse of e-resources by un-authorized users, only a few organizations in India have implemented remote access systems.

6. Electronic Resource Management System

As libraries increase their collections of electronic resources, finding ways to manage them efficiently becomes a major challenge. Managing these electronic resources involves providing the library's user with convenient ways to find and access them and providing library staff with the tools to keep track of them. There are two fundamental aspects to managing electronic resources: (i) the front-end details of delivering the content to library users, and (ii) managing the business details of back-end staff functions related to acquisition, payment, and licensing.

The Digital Library Federation (2004) defines an ERMS as a system that supports management of the information and workflows necessary to efficiently select, evaluate, acquire, maintain, renew/cancel and provide informed access to e-resources in accordance with their business and license terms.

In general, an ERM should support acquisition and management of licensed e-resources, and provide descriptions of resources at the package (database) level and relate package contents (*e.g.* e-journals) to the package record, and linking license documents to resource records. It should enable the library to track electronic resources from the point of order through licensing and final access. It is expected to provide information about the data providers, consortium arrangements, access platform; and the contact information for all content providers.

An ERMS should be able to maintain logging problems with resources and providers, and provide customizable e-mail alerting systems (*e.g.* notices to managers when actions are expected or required). In addition, it should also support retrieval of SUSHI (Standardized Usage Statistics Harvesting Initiative) usage statistics, which is a protocol. Finally, the ERMS should have a public interface, either separately or integrated into the library's web OPAC.

The core elements of every ERMS should include information specific to each resource:

- Authority-controlled resource names.
- URL's and log-in information for resource administration.
- Contact information for sales and technical support.
- Selection and trial process tracking and documentation.
- Access parameters for each resource: access dates, limits on concurrent users if any, physical limitations on access (*i.e.* on-campus only).

Within the acquisitions functionalities, ERMs functionalities should include:

- Multiple funds and discretionary accounts.
- Shared cost allocations.
- Tracking of purchase orders.
- Renewal tracking including reminder emails or other alerts to staff to begin evaluation at an appropriate date and methods of recording decision process.
- Trial tracking reminder emails or other alerts to staff to begin evaluation at an appropriate date and methods of recording decision process.
- Tracking system for communications with vendors including sales staff, technical support staff and others.
- History of payments on a particular resource to chart price increases at the resource level as well as globally.
- User-friendly report generation capabilities to produce on-the-fly reports about the budget from the local college and global perspective.

6.1 *Features and Functions of an ERMS*

Maria Collins and Jill E. Grogg (2011) have conducted a survey on libraries and commercial and open source ERM system vendors to find what librarians want and expect from an ERM, which are summarized in Table 1.

Table 1: E-resources Management Functions expected from an ERMS

Rank	*Feature/Function*	*Description Summary Compiled from Responses*
1.	Workflow management	Support across e-resource life cycle including resource tracking, reminders, status assignments, routing and redistribution of workflow and communication or notifications to stakeholders or patrons as necessary.
2.	License management	Manage license details, provide storage for agreements and display license terms for internal and external users
3.	Statistics management	Obtain, gather and organize usage statistics. Auto upload statistics utilizing SUSHI standard. Provide historical statistics.
4.	Administrative information	Store and make accessible administrative information such as usernames and passwords.
5.	Acquisitions functionality	Provide acquisitions support for budget management, fund management, financial reporting, repository of cost data and invoicing.
6.	Integration/interoperability with other systems	Interoperate across systems, including the ILS, to support auto feeds, data loads and auto updates.
7.	Subscription management	Manage and maintain library subscriptions to electronic content including life cycle changes (new, dropped, cancelled, transferred), vendor changes, maintenance of subscription history, and verification of continued access.
8.	Public display	Support a variety of public display options to the public including A-Z journal listing, database lists and article-level linking.
9.	Vendor contact information	Store and provide access to vendor information including contact data and account numbers.
10.	Support for collection evaluation	Align and report data as appropriate to support the evaluation of the collection and cost analysis.
11.	Consolidate ERM information	Store and provide access to ERM-related data in one place.
12.	Package management	Track titles within packages appropriate to institution including parent/child relationships, business terms, and association of titles with deals.
13.	Holdings management	Identify and maintain appropriate coverage and URLs per title; support holdings display in the catalog.
14.	Reporting	Provide query-based reporting on desired characteristics.
15.	Usability	Provide clean, easy to use interface with consistent displays.

Some of the ERM systems that are developed over the past decade have addressed many of the above issues very well but have left others unresolved. Although ERM systems have been available for a number of years, librarians continue to struggle with the tremendous volume of information needed to effectively manage their e-resources. The most popular commercial and open source ERMs are listed below:

Commercial ERMs

- Millennium ERM system – Innovative Interfaces
- ERM Solution – SirsiDynix
- Verify – VTLS Inc.
- Meridian – Endeavor
- Verde – Ex Libris
- Goldrush – Colorado Alliance
- Erdb – UCLA
- ERM Essentials – EBSCO
- 360 Resource Manager – Serials Solutions
- ERMSS – Total IT Solutions, India.

Open Source ERMs

- CORAL – University of Notre Dame
- CUFTS – Simon Fraser University
- ERMes – University of Wisconsin
- FreERMS – Digital Library Federation
- HERMES – John Hopkins University
- SMDB – SemperToo.

6.2 *Selective List of ERMS Widely Used in Universities*

Electronic Resource Management

Innovative Interfaces, Inc. introduced electronic resource management in 2002. Innovative Interfaces Inc. ranks as one of the leading library automation vendors, offering the Millennium ILS, with a large customer base from all types of libraries, including academic, public, and special. The company's other offerings include the WebBridge OpenURL link resolver, Research-Pro federated search environment, and Encore, a new discovery services platform.

Serials Solutions is an ERM product marketed as **360 Resource Manager**. Since Serial Solutions' acquisition in July 2004, it has operated as a business unit of Proquest, part of Cambridge Information Group, which also owns R.R. Bowker. Serials Solutions got its start on products that leveraged its core expertise in managing e-journal holdings data. The company's **KnowledgeWorks** repository of e-content data continues to provide the foundation for all its products and services.

(a) Verde of ExLibris is a centralized repository through which all e-resource workflows—acquisitions, trial, usage, cost, access and administrative data are managed. Built-in workflow management capabilities enable the library to define consistent and replicable processes, helping staff keep track of task assignments throughout the e-resource life cycle.

(b) The Verde Knowledge Base presents librarians with the most comprehensive view of e-product availability in the electronic products marketplace. Coupled with extensive usage and cost statistics, this information enables library staff to make data-driven collection development decisions regarding serials and e-books. Verde supports multiple collaboration models that allow authorized staff to search across consortium member collections, to share data, and to create a wide range of cross-institution management reports.

TDOne integrates an organization's local, hosted and remote e-Resources with TDNet's searching and browsing modules. This one-stop solution can be integrated into the Library's homepage or portal, so that users can directly search, browse and retrieve information from the library's resources—catalogs, databases, journal and book collections and more. Based on a unified search interface and easy navigation, end-user tasks can be accomplished without ever leaving the library workspace. The fast and easy integration of customers' resources and TDNet modules, and the implementation within the library portal, allows libraries to provide their users with a discovery-to-delivery platform, involving minimal workload on the library side as well as saving money on integration costs.

ERM Essentials of EBSCONET is a comprehensive electronic resource management tool that automatically populates and maintains approximately 100 data fields for your e-journal and e-package orders. ERM Essentials goes beyond what other systems offer, handling the cumbersome task of data input by auto-populating and maintaining data about e-resources acquired through EBSCO. By leveraging the power of the EBSCO Integrated Knowledge Base, information about your entire e-resource collection can be updated across multiple platforms, including EBSCO A-to-Z® and LinkSource®, EBSCO's OpenURL link resolver. By combining auto-population and seamless integration, ERM Essentials significantly reduces the time spent in managing e-resources, allowing you to focus your valuable time on other tasks.

ERMSS of Total IT Solutions (India) is a customized e-resources management and search solution which can be easily integrated with the existing web portal of the library. This solution provides the linking of all the e resources subscribed by the library. ERMSS is useful for the library member students, researcher and all knowledge seekers. They can easily view, access and search within all the e-resources contents with the same interface.

CUFTS is an Open Source serial management system developed by Simon Fraser University library, Canada. CUFTS ERM provides basic electronic resource management services, allowing libraries to centralize all the details about electronic collections, including licensing terms, renewal dates, contacts, and more. CUFTS ERM also features a renewal notification system, reminding you of approaching deadlines and an A-Z list of electronic resources. It comes along with a URL link resolver and a Federated Search Engine.

Gold Rush ERM is a standalone Web-based subscription service developed in 2001 and hosted by the Colorado Alliance of Research Libraries to help its member libraries manage electronic resources. Gold Rush helps patrons to access journal information over the Web and helps librarians manage electronic content. Gold Rush is a complete electronic resource management system containing Real-time A-Z journal title list; subscriptions management system for monitoring contracts, pricing and the renewal process; collection analyzer enabling the library administrator to compare title lists from aggregators, publishers and indexing/abstracting services whether subscribed to or not. During the last few years, Gold Rush has developed into a mature ERM that libraries outside of the consortium now license.

7. ERMS and Open Access Journals

The Open Access (OA) movement of academic publications has already gathered momentum, driven by various issues, including mandates from research funders and authors' concerns regarding loss of rights. The number of open access journals is increasing steadily and more and more researchers are switching away from publishing in commercial journals.

Academic and research libraries cannot ignore open access journals in their collections. It is the duty of the librarian to provide access to the published knowledge to their users irrespective of the origin—commercial or open source. Hence, it would be wise to incorporate open access resources in the ERM system.

Open access journals are peer-reviewed journals whose articles may be accessed online by anyone without any charge. OA publication charges can be often included within the costs of research funding, so the money for access comes through the research funder, rather than through the library budget. There are a growing number of OA Journals in most disciplines.

Creative Commons (CC) is a non-profit organization that enables the sharing and use of creativity and knowledge through free legal tools. Unlike Digital Rights Management (DRM) technology, which tries to restrict use of digital works, CC is providing ways to encourage permitted sharing and reuse of works. Creative Commons licenses are not an alternative to copyright. They work alongside copyright and enable you to modify your copyright terms to best suit your needs.

SHERPA/RoMEO is a database of publishers' policies regarding self-archiving by authors in open access repositories, and related copyright issues. It is used worldwide by repository administrators and academics to check what publishers do and do not allow to be archived. While there is no substitute for a close reading of policies on a publisher's own website, database provides an efficient method of discovering whether a journal will allow one to share published articles, and under the conditions allowed that sharing.

8. ERMS and Usage Statistics

As more and more electronic resources are made available to library users, the librarians are grappled with determining how patrons are making use of the library resources without physically coming to the library. Information related to the use of electronic resources to which a library subscribes needs to be collected, organized and disseminated across various library units and university departments. Such usage statistics can be maintained either by article, resource (title), publisher, user, date/month/year, and measured as units or a 'counter'. Some of the commercial ERM products have features to normalize statistics and improve protocols for transfer and management of such data.

On the other hand the institution shall ensure that the scholarly information, which is subscribed by paying huge amount of money, is properly utilized by its users. Therefore, authentic usage statistics become necessary to take decisions like, which are the subjects that need further support in future and which are the subject areas where university is doing well. It also shows which are the resources not being used by the University and which are in demand. Usage statistics also enables the library to monitor any misuse by unauthorized users. Considering the high cost of subscribing e-resources, the librarian is obliged to justify the expenditure to the finance department as a measure of economy.

9. Value Added Services

Electronic resources offer a variety of advantages over their print counterparts. Added to this the Internet continues to offers unlimited opportunities to information seekers. Technological advances have enabled traditional libraries to become future 'Digital Libraries' capable of delivering user-centric specialized services to the users directly. New social networking tools such as Blogs, RSS, Collaboration Tools, Ask the Librarian, Chat, Personalised alerts, Citation tracker, Wikis, Mobile applications, etc. have become the order of the day.

Many traditional library services like reference service, document delivery, etc. have disappeared along with its 'human presence' and new forms of value-added services have emerged to satisfy the user needs more efficiently. Some of the value-added library services are listed below:

- e-mail alerts on topics of interest to each user (one-time registration required).
- Tagging of articles of interest to each user and managing them.
- Saving searches in personal folders on the publishers website.
- Re-run of saved searches to get new results as and when required.
- Setting up of search alerts to notify when new articles are published that meet the users' search criteria.
- Setting up of Table of Contents alerts to user's email address.
- Viewing of articles that are downloaded in the last few months.
- Personalized homepage to display newly published papers relevant to each user.
- Announcements of new books released with discounts to authors.
- Information about researchers in other institutions/countries having similar research interests (collaboration).

10. Training of Library Staff to Manage ERMS

Cataloging of serials is a complicated specialty, and many libraries may not have adequate staff with the required skills to handle the work. Lack of training, coordination among library units and leadership in the library can be a major bottleneck and negative impact in managing electronic resources. Hence, library staff training is an essential component of ERM implementation and should be given the highest priority by libraries which are moving 'from print to electronic'.

Similar to LMS implementation, the librarian needs to spend much more time to work with all the library units to analyze the work flow, and identify the tasks and assign each task to specific staff members. Only when the tasks are distributed accordingly can the full capabilities and functionalities of the library automation can be realized.

Identification of library staff and providing training in the management of electronic resources requires substantial time and may take many months. It is always better to have the training imparted by the vendor who supplied the ERM solution. Once the ERM workflow is ready, mapping of licenses of e-resources that are subscribed by the library begins. Once identified, the ERM system administrator will set up the resources to be monitored in the system and make changes to the ERM system during and after implementation.

The most critical data to be configured by the ERM system administrator is to convey any changes in the institute's IP addresses to all the publishers, checking for dead/broken links, checking for intruders, maintaining contact email addresses of publishers, and maintaining admin logins and passwords of publishers to access and create usage statistics for all the resources, etc.

11. Conclusions

Today, libraries have tools more powerful than ever before–massive storage capabilities, rapid processing power coupled with global network–and the Internet. The transition of a library from a 'repository' to a site of access has been a major innovation of this century. Libraries have once again proved that given a mandate, they can adapt to any change, be it in the area of Internet, digital libraries, semantics or management of electronic resources in a 'single window' system. It is very clear that the development of ERMs is a library initiative lead by the demand to manage vast amount of digital information. Librarians have learnt to overcome the problem of 'information explosion' to their advantage through the use of ERMs.

The market for ERM is going to expand with a variety of options and choice of vendors. Libraries can mix and match services between ILS modules and/or a library's own portal. A library will need to think deeply and broadly about what kind of services they want to offer, and consider what resources they have internally to devote to such services, before choosing an ERM solution.

Librarians should think very carefully about what they are trying to accomplish in the new electronic resource management environment. Looking at the developments taking place around the world, we can say with confidence that the library of 2020 will be both very similar to, and yet very different from the library of today.

References

[1] Association of Research Libraries: Collections and Access for the 21st Century Scholar: Changing Roles of Research Libraries. Washington DC, ARL, 2002.

[2] Digital Library Federation: Electronic resource management: Final report of the DLF initiative; Washington DC; 2004. Available at: http://www.library.cornell.edu/elicensestudy/dlfdeliverables/DLF-ERMI-FinalReport.pdf

[3] Maria Collins and Jill E. Grogg. Building a Better ERMS. *Library Journal,* 2011, **136**(4); 22–28.

Electronic Resources Management in Libraries, pp. 47–54

Management of E-resources at IISERs: A Consortium Approach

P. Visakhi and Umeshareddy Kacherki

ABSTRACT

Due to tremendous advancements in digital technologies, the scholarly information is being proliferated in the form of e-publications. These e-publications extend numerous like concurrent, remote and multiple accesses, online searching and retrieval, ease of use and requirement of minimal storage space. However the price of journals, especially scientific journals, has continued to rise beyond affordable limit and thus has prompted the librarians to think of resource sharing and to form library consortia. Fluctuation of foreign currency and dwindling of library budgets lead the libraries to opt library consortium to manage their resources. This paper discuss the formation of IISER Consortium, its achievements and also highlights how IISERs are managing to get the e-resources through different consortia like INDEST-AICTE, UGC-Infonet and also through individual institute subscription.

1. Introduction

The concept of library cooperation is not new in India but probably younger than the cooperation results achieved by United States and United Kingdom. Early cooperation among libraries focused on catalogs, inter-library loan and cooperative acquisitions. However these three issues are continued to be cornerstone issues for many library consortia even today.

As per Adrian Alexander, the history of library cooperation is as long as the history of 'professional' librarianship in America. He dated library cooperation to 1876 and highlighted outstanding developments in those areas. The concept of e-Consortium was founded in February 1999 by Rick Craft and a group of 15 prominent service providers who thought the value of collaboration for the benefits of their clients. It started as Virtual Network allowing end users to utilize the e-consortium website to learn about these companies and how they can fulfill their needs (Shinde, 2011).

In the present context the library cooperation has turned into Library Consortium where the sharing of resources among libraries based common organisation and thrust areas of interest has become predominant. The resources that are shared in today's consortium atmosphere are largely in electronic form such as electronic journals and databases. The aim of consortia is to accomplish the task as a group by sharing resources, manpower and money. A Consortium could be expressed as a group of organizations or institutions which come together to fulfill a combined goal that require co-operation and the sharing of resources. The library consortium formation can be at regional, state, national or international level on a functional or format or subject basis. A consortium is said to be a co-operative arrangement among groups or institutions or an association or society. Consortia are commonly formed to increase the purchasing capacity of the collaborating institutions, to expand the resource availability and to offer automated services.

1.1 *Consortium Benefits*

For the participating libraries, the consortia offer several benefits which include access to otherwise unsubscribed content, scope for electronic archives, availability and monitoring of usage statistics, getting deep discounts through joint pricing negotiations which in turn lower content pricing, reduced storage costs, developing common resources databases, effective document delivery system, a single interface and access point, enhanced search facilities, better scope for developing a union catalogue among participating libraries etc. (Sreekumar, 2005).

1.2 *Models of Consortia*

Consortia models are of different types based on their scope, sources of funding etc. But the goal is same with all consortia, *i.e.*, sharing of resources/price with discount. Based on the scope of a consortium, the models are as follows (Rajeev, 2012):

- ***Open End Model:*** It is a flexible model where library can join in/quit at any point of time from a consortium. In this case publishers define a minimum number of libraries to participate at a specific rate per product (*e.g.* FORSAA, partly INDEST).
- ***Closed Group Model***: Generally the consortium formed in an organization, exclusively for its own institutes or consortium formed in a specific subject area either by coalition, affiliation and collaboration of institutes come under this group where there will be no scope for joining libraries other than the organization (*e.g.* IISER Consortium, CeRA).

Based on sources of funding the Consortia models are as follows:

- ***Centrally-Funded Model:*** In this model, libraries/institutes will be facilitated the access through centrally funded body/agency. The existence of the consortium will solely depend upon centrally-funded agency (*e.g.* UGC-Infonet, CeRA, CSIR-NKRC, DRDO and ICMR consortia).
- ***Shared-Budget Model:*** In this model, the participating libraries will take the lead to form consortium and the negotiated price/discount will be shared by participating libraries (*e.g.* HELNET, IIM Consortium, FORSA and IISER Consortium.
- ***Publisher-Initiated Model***: In this model, the publishers quote the consortia price and will provide the attractive discount for the participating libraries with the

condition to retain their print subscription. Publishers like Elsevier Science, Emerald etc. offer such models.

- ***National Consortium:*** National Library and Information Services Infrastructure for Scholarly Content (N-LIST) is the biggest National Consortium in India. It is being jointly executed by the UGC-Infonet Digital Library Consortium, Inflibnet Centre. The INDEST-AICTE Consortium, IIT Delhi provides for cross-subscription to e-resources subscribed by the two Consortia, *i.e.*, subscription to INDEST-AICTE resources for technical institutions and UGC-Infonet resources for universities and access to selected e-resources to colleges.

2. Indian Institutes of Science Education and Research

The Scientific Advisory Council to the Prime Minister (SAC-PM) under the Chairmanship of Prof. CNR Rao, recommended creation of five new institutions devoted to science education and research to be named Indian Institute of Science Education and Research broadly on the lines of IISc, Bangalore. As a result, five Indian Institute of Science Education and Research (IISER) have been established under the Ministry of Human Resource Development (MHRD), Govt of India with a aim to create world class institutes in frontier areas of science education and research. They have been designed to reach the prestigious position in the global setting. These IISERs viz. IISER Kolkata in 2006 in West Bengal, IISER Pune in 2006 in Maharashtra, IISER Mohali in 2007 in Punjab, IISER Bhopal in 2008 in Madhya Pradesh and IISER Thiruvananthapuram in 2008 in Kerala were established with the financial outlay for each IISER is around ₹ 500 crore (US$90.5 million) for the first five years.

These IISERs are autonomous institutions awarding BS-MS integrated five years degree, M.S-PhD integrated, PhD and Post-doctoral in basic sciences. Selection of students for admissions is purely on merit basis through qualifying any of the following examinations:

- *Kishore Vaigyanik Protsahan Yojana* (KVPY), a scholarship program funded by the Department of Science and Technology, Government of India.
- Thosc who feature in the regular merit list of IITJEE. It is used as the sole admission criterion by the sixteen Indian Institutes of Technology (IITs).
- Persons qualifying IISERs Common Entrance Exam conducted by all IISERs together for the students who passed class XII in central and state boards either with marks above the cut-off percent available at DST website or INSPIRE fellowship certificate obtained from the boards.

All students admitted to the 5-year integrated MS programme will receive a monthly fellowship of ₹ 5000 from either from INSPIRE or KVPY.

2.1 *The IISER Consortium*

The year 2010 was a landmark in the history of IISERs with the formation of the IISERs Consortium. The need for strategic partnership and collaboration among the 5 IISER Libraries was highlighted by the IISER Directors in their meeting at IISER Mohali on 08 May 2010 and gave a mandate to form a IISER Library Consortium to share available permissible resources among IISERs and to make collective efforts to subscribe electronic resources to maximize benefits and also to identify the areas of mutual cooperation. In this context, First IISER Librarian's meet was organized at IISER Bhopal on 17 September 2010 during which the IISER Library Consortium was formed.

Objectives

- To subscribe electronic resources not covered under INDEST-AICTE Consortium for IISERs at highly discounted prices and at the best terms and conditions.
- Enriching collection development in subject areas identified as relatively stronger in each IISER Library.
- Strengthening Inter-Library Loan (ILL), including online, Document Delivery Services (DDS) among all the IISER libraries.
- To have better understanding among IISER libraries and information science professionals.
- To find more avenues of cooperation among libraries and interaction among IISERs' library professionals.

3. The Journey of IISER Consortium

Each IISER will take into account day to day requirement of e-resources of their faculty and students of newly born institution in building up of their base in teaching and research activates. Librarians of all five IISERs meet once in six months at one of the IISERs on rotation basis to discuss their e-resources and also to have negotiation with the publishers for required resources at highly discounted prices and at the best terms and conditions. The first meeting of IISER Consortium was held on 17 September 2010 at IISER Bhopal. This was a preliminary meeting and the following guidelines were prepared for IISER Consortium.

- Resources should be available at highly discounted prices and at the best terms and conditions.
- Before negotiation with the publisher, the required product will be reviewed by faculty and students through trail access and usage will be gauged.
- Based on usage Statistics and recommendations made by the faculty/students of IISERs, the IISER Consortium invite the publisher for negotiation.
- IISER Consortium negotiates only with the publisher or "exclusive distributor".

Consequent upon the successful first meeting at IISER Bhopal, the Consortium members have been meeting regularly every six months in various IISER campuses on rotation basis. The Second meeting of IISER Consortium was held on 02 December 2010 at IISER Pune and negotiations were made successfully with the publishers for their resources (Table 1).

Table 1: E-resources Initially Negotiated for the Consortium

Publisher	*Product*
Oxford University Press	Life sciences, mathematics and physics: e-journals collection
Elsevier	Cell press e-journals collection
Royal Society Publishing	All eight journals collections
World Scientific	Customized package of online journals
Thieme Publishing Group	Two journals + one database with back files

The Third IISER Consortium meet was held at IISER Thiruvanathapuram on 13 June 2011. There has been overwhelming response from the publishers offering their products. Since the IISER Consortium was not satisfied with the prices quoted by the publishers, some of the proposals were deferred till next meeting for further discussion or withdrawn. Journal archives from two publishers viz. Institute of Physics (IoP) and Annual Reviews only could be finalized.

The Fourth IISER Consortium meeting held at IISER Kolkata during 23–24 November 2011 was very fruitful. IISER Consortium negotiated with five publishers successfully for their resources (Table 2).

Table 2: E-resources Added for 2012

Publisher	*Product*
Nature Publishing Group	*Scientific American* (current + archives)
Nature Publishing Group	*Nature* archives
Springer	Journals archives (biomedical and life sciences, chemistry and material sciences, mathematics and statistics and physics and astronomy collections)
Oxford University Press	*Science* digital archive
Faculty of 1000	Faculty of 1000
Cambridge University Press	e-Books

Fifth Meeting of IISER Consortium was held during 20–21 July 2012 at IISER Mohali. Consortium members discussed and negotiated with publishers of *Journal of Visualized Experiments* successfully for its complete package.

The Consortium meetings proved to be very successful and productive. Outline of the concept "to pay minimum and get maximum" and build up strong information resources base among IISERs was thus proved successful. After completing two years of establishing the Consortium, IISERs are rich enough and self-sustained to meet the informational requirements of its faculty and students.

IISER Consortium would like to place on record the immense support rendered by INDEST-AICTE Consortium. Since IISERs also come under MHRD and core members of INDEST, the following resources are made available to IISERs by INDEST-AICTE Consortium:

- American Institute of Physics (16 titles)
- American mathematical Society (MathScinet)
- American Physical Society (13 titles)
- Annual Reviews (49 titles)
- Nature Publishing Group (27 titles)
- Project MUSE
- Taylor and Francis (500+ S&T collection).

IISER Consortium place on record the help received from Inflibnet for making the JSTOR online database available for IISERs on payment basis through associate membership option. The subscription cost for the following packages were negotiated by INDEST for IISERs and IISERs are making payment to the publisher as per negotiated price of INDEST. However content fee for some of the packages are being paid by INDEST:

- ScienceDirect—Four Subject Collections
- SCOPUS
- Springer link—Journals
- IEEE's IEL Online
- OSA Optics Infobase
- SciFinder Scholar
- SIAM Journals.

3.1 *Archives*

Since IISERs are newly established institutes and need back volumes of important journals. Keeping in view the advantages of e-versions of journals and long term preservation of scholarly information for future use, the Consortium decided to procure online archives instead of print back volumes 10 online journal archives (Table 3).

Table 3: Online Archives Procured for the Consortium

Sl. No.	*Publisher*	*Product/Titles*	*Coverage*
1.	American Chemical Society*	ACS legacy archives	1879–2011
2.	Annual Reviews	49 titles	1932–2006
3.	Thieme Publishing Group	2 journals + 1 database	Vol.1+
4.	Institute of Physics	86 titles	1874 to 2008
5.	Royal Society of Chemistry	67 titles	1841 to 2004
6.	Scientific American	*Scientific American*	1845–2011
7.	Nature Publishing Group	*Nature Magazine*	1869–2007
8.	Nature Publishing Group	Depending upon requirement	Depending upon requirement
9.	Springer-Verlag Biomed/life sciences Chem/mater sciences Maths/statistics Phys/astronomy	 217 titles 106 titles 125 titles 87 titles	Vol.1 to 1996
10.	Oxford Science Digital Archive	49 titles	Vol.1 to 1996

*Through individual subscription.

4. Conclusion

Creation of consortium is easier than sustaining it. The activity of library consortium is complex and complicate. Bringing the likeminded people together, whole hearted support of management and right amount of efforts by partners plays important role in running a consortium successfully. Also, success of a library consortium depends very much on how to strategically tackle the issues like shrinking of library budgets, fluctuation in foreign currencies, assessing the user requirement, identifying the right resources, consensus on subscription pricing, complicated and vulnerable license terms and conditions, perpetual rights to back files, copyright issues, uninterrupted and hassle free access, bandwidth issues, usage statistics, assessing return on investment and also transfer of publishers rights to other publishers, ceased journals, merging titles, parking digital contents with third party server etc. No doubt by forming a library consortium, IISER libraries are able to strengthen their library's collection base and coverage with maximum benefits possible that too in a record time to meet informational needs of the IISER user community.

Acknowledgments

Authors are extremely grateful to the Directors of all IISERs for their vision, intellectual foresight and their mandate to for IISER Library Consortium. Authors also would like to place on record their acknowledgements to Mr SK Bose, Librarian- IISER, Bhopal and Coordinator of IISER Consortium, Dr. Sainul Abideen P from IISER, Thiruvanthapuram and Mr. Siladitya Jana from IISER, Kolkata for their whole hearted support and for providing information to prepare this paper.

References

[1] NLIST, http://nlist.inflibnet.ac.in/about.php (accessed on 29 August 2012).

[2] Rajeev, M.K.G. (2012). Consortia and prospects of libraries in academic environment: An outline. *In* K. Veeranjaneyulu *et al.* (Eds). Library Services in the Knowledge Web. New Delhi, New India Publishing Agency.

[3] Shinde, P.A., Mohsin, Syed Fayyaz and Ingale, R.N. (2011). Library consortia: Emerging tools of 21st Century. *In* Proceedings of National Conference of Agricultural Librarians and User Community 2011 on Agricultural Libraries in the Knowledge Web, 24–25 February 2011. New Delhi, IARI, pp. 107–112.

[4] Sreekumar, M.G. and Sunita, T. (2005). E-Journal collection development prospects: The IIM Consortium Experience. Paper presented in NACLIN-2005, New Delhi, DELNET, pp. 192–205.

Electronic Resources Management in Libraries, pp. 55–66

An Overview of Information Resources and Services at IIT Libraries in India

Daulat Jotwani

ABSTRACT

This paper describes the role of and contributions made by the Indian Institutes of Technology (IITs) to the higher education and research in engineering, sciences and technology in the country. Each IIT has a well resourced Central Library to support their academic and research information needs. This paper studies the functioning, the resources and the services of all these libraries. The level of automation, availability of ICT infrastructure, access to electronic resources and the digital library initiatives taken by these libraries are also discussed. These libraries are an integral part of the IIT System and are highly valued by their users for their services, along with highly skilled staff, and latest collections not available in most of the other academic institutions.

1. Introduction

Indian Institutes of Technology (IITs) came into their existence due the vision of our first Prime Minister, late Pandit Jawaharlal Nehru, who pioneered the idea of establishing institutions of excellence to impart teaching and conducting research in engineering, sciences and technology so as to produce scientists, engineers and technologists of world class and engage them in building modern and self-reliant India. The IITs at Bombay (now Mumbai), Delhi, Kanpur, Kharagpur, Madras (now Chennai), Guwahati and Roorkee were established as '*Institutions of National Importance*' under The Institutes of Technology Act, 1961. Their main objectives are to impart world-class training in engineering and technology; to conduct research in the relevant fields, and for advancement of learning and dissemination of knowledge. These Institutes are also contributing significantly to education and research in basic sciences and humanities. The IITs offer undergraduate programmes in various branches of engineering and technology; postgraduate programmes with specialization and Ph.D. programmes in various engineering and science disciplines, interdisciplinary areas and conduct basic, applied and sponsored research by national and international agencies. At present, the IITs offer B.Tech., M.Sc., M. Design, M.Phil., M.Tech. and Ph.D. degrees. IITs maintain quality of teaching and research of international standards. These Institutes are continuously evaluating and modifying curricula as per the emerging trends and needs of the industry. They also contribute in updating the knowledge of faculties of other Engineering Colleges through Quality Improvement Programmes. IITs have been effective in enhancing the country's techno-economic strength and technological self reliance. The IITs have distinguished themselves through excellence of their academic activities and research programmes. Sponsored research for different funding agencies in the public and private sectors, industrial consultancy and continuing education programmes are also areas in which the IITs have made significant contribution. In order to provide quality education in science and technology to a larger number of students, the capacities of existing IITs have been regularly enhanced. To keep pace with the changes taking place in new technologies, new programmes are being started in identified areas such as new materials, non-destructive evaluation technology, high speed networking and wireless technology, biotechnology and bio-informatics, smart materials, environmental energy, medical science and technology, medical instrumentation, electronics, electronics communication and membrane technology, etc.

In addition to the seven old IITs, the Government has established six new IITs in 2008–09 in Andhra Pradesh (Hyderabad), Bihar (Patna), Rajasthan (Jodhpur), Gujarat (Gandhinagar), Orissa (Bhubneswar) and Punjab (Ropar), and two new IITs in 2009–10 in Madhya Pradesh (Indore) and Himachal Pradesh (Mandi). However, the libraries of seven old IITs only have been taken for the purpose of this study.

Table 1: Basic Facts about IIT Libraries

Sl. No.	*Institution*	*Name of the Library*	*Year of Estd*	*No. of Books*	*URL*
1.	IIT Kharagpur	Central Library	1951	380 000	http://www.library.iitkgp.ernet.in/
2.	IIT Bombay	Central Library	1958	434 000	www.library.iitb.ac.in
3.	IIT Kanpur	PK Kelkar Library	1959	300 000	http://library.iitk.ac.in/
4.	IIT Madras	Central Library	1959	400 000	http://www.cenlib.iitm.ac.in
5.	IIT Delhi	Central Library	1962	338 000	http://library.iitd.ac.in/index.html
6.	IIT Guwahati	Central Library	1995	96 000	http://www.iitg.ac.in/rs/lib/public_html/index.html
7.	IIT Roorkee	Mahatma Gandhi Central Library	2001	320 000	http://mgcl.iitr.ac.in/

2. IIT Libraries

Each IIT has a large, well maintained, fully automated Central Library which caters to the needs of their students, research scholars, faculties, and staff. Central Libraries are integral part of the IIT System supporting teaching, learning, scholarship and outreach programmes of the institutes. The main thrust at these libraries is to facilitate in creation of new knowledge through acquisition, organization, dissemination of knowledge and provision of value added services.

2.1 *Central Library, IIT Kharagpur*

The IIT Kharagpur is the oldest of all the IITs. The Central Library serves over 5000 students and research scholars, over 500 faculty members and about 1500 technical, administrative and medical staff spread over 18 departments and 7 centres of the institute. Besides, its services are extended to a number of other organizations also. The Library resources stand at about 3,80,000 volumes including books, back-volumes of periodicals, micro forms, video forms, theses, patents and standards. The journals subscription goes beyond 800 titles. A large number of video courses produced by the Centre for Education Technology, IIT Kharagpur are made available to the users for browsing. The Library collection also includes reference books, textbooks meant for the courses running in the institute and books for SC/ST students.

The library is equipped with modern facilities and resources in the form of CD-ROMs, online databases, microforms, video cassettes, etc. It has created a Digital Library using open source software—DSpace—which preserves institutes' intellectual output for campus-wide access. The library uses LIBSYS package for computerization of its house keeping functions including circulation of books. The library has started implementing RFID on a small scale. It has also installed CCTV to improve surveillance and sensitivity.

Table 2: Membership of the Central Libraries of IITs

Sl. No.	*Institute*	*Students*	*Faculty*
1.	IIT, Kharagpur	6625	519
2.	IIT, Bombay	5420	490
3.	IIT, Madras	5011	392
4.	IIT, Kanpur	3810	311
5.	IIT, Delhi	4995	419
6.	IIT, Guwahati	2126	193
7.	IIT, Roorkee	4402	367

2.2 *Central Library, IIT Bombay*

The Central Library is providing an outstanding contribution to IIT Bombay's "Culture of Excellence" to the world of scholarship. Housed in an independent five-storied building, it holds one of the best collections of knowledge resources both in print and electronic form in engineering, sciences, technology, arts and humanities, and social sciences. The library is valued by its users (over 10,000) not just for the facilities, nor for the strength of deep, relevant collections, but rather for the ways the library understands their needs, and supports their academic and research mission through users-focused services, highly skilled staff, and excellent collections. The library has galvanized itself to successfully engage its users in a multifaceted information environment in order to remain their valuable partners in learning and research.

It offers a range of services including reference and consultation, membership and circulation, document delivery, resource sharing, information alert service, book bank for needy students, user awareness programmes, and ICT-enabled web-based services to over 10,000 members. It maintains a 24 × 7 reading hall where students can study even after the library is closed. It also extends support in establishing a library at the IIT Gandhinagar and IIT Indore.

The greatest asset of the library is its collection of books, journals, theses, reports, standards, pamphlets and other reading material that supports academic and research work of the students, faculties, staff and other users. The library added 7099 items to its collection which stands at 4,34,188 as on 31 March 2012. It also subscribed to 1290 journals. The Central Library has its own homepage (http://www.library.iitb.ac.in), provides 24 × 7 access to its resources, subscribes about 15,000 electronic journals and databases, supports online submission of theses and dissertations, and has set-up of an institutional repository of publications brought out by the IIT Bombay community. The library is a part of the institute-wide network and has adequate computing infrastructure to cater to the needs of the users. The Wi-Fi facility in the reading area continues to attract users to bring in their laptops to have seamless access to print and electronic resources. The OPAC (Online Public Access Catalogue) is one of the most heavily used databases of the library and is also accessible 24 × 7 via library's web page. Besides listing all the documents available in the library, it allows online reservation, circulation, fine collection, and indicates status of a particular book. OPAC is searchable by author, title, accession number, subject and several other fields.

The Central Library supports electronic submission of theses and dissertations by the postgraduate and doctoral students. It maintains a full-text database of over 5000 items submitted since 1999–2000 on intranet. During the last year, 377 M.Tech dissertations and 159 Ph.D. theses were submitted online. The library has also developed a database (providing bibliographic details and abstract) using open source software, GSDL of all the Masters dissertations and Ph.D. theses submitted since 1999 and 1965, respectively. This database containing over 2500 records is accessible through the library's homepage. The Central Library has set up an archive of publications (http://dspace.library.iitb.ac.in/jspui) brought out by the institute. The archive already has over 1650 items and is being updated to cover more publications which are permissible within the copyright regulations. The archive is expected to evolve into a database of all publications produced by the IIT Bombay community and is accessible on the Internet through the library's homepage.

Users' education is an important activity of the library to inform, alert, educate and train users about various resources and services of the library. In addition to orientation programmes organized for new students, the library conducted short duration training programmes on "How to Use" various databases for our faculty and students so that they are able to use these resources more effectively. The library also organized half-a-day interactive sessions on "Enhancing User Awareness" for new faculty and research scholars to familiarize them with various library resources and services.

Table 3: Working Hours of IIT Libraries

Sl. No.	*Library Hours*	*IITKg*	*IITB*	*IITK*	*IITM*	*IITD*	*IITG*	*IITR*
1.	Week days (Mon–Fri)	0800–2400 hr	0900–2300 hr	0800–2400 hr	0900–2300 hr	0900–2100 hr	0800–2300 hr	0830–2200 hr
2.	Holidays (Sat, Sunday and Other holidays	0800–2400 hr	1000–1700 hr	0900–2400 hr (Sat) 0900–1730 hr	0900–1730 hr	1000–1800 hr	0930–1730 hr	0945–1830 hr
3.	During Examinations	As above	0900–0100	Open 24 hr	As above	0900–2400 hr		0830–2200 hr
4.	Circulation facility on week days	0900–2000 hr	0900–2000 hr	0900–2100 hr			0930–1730 hr	1030–1900 hr
5.	Circulation facility on holidays	1000–1200 and 1630–1830 hr	1100–1300 hr	0900–1600 hr on Saturdays (closed on other holidays)			closed	Closed
6.	Closed holidays	Institute holidays (19 days)	26 Jan. 15 Aug. 2 Oct. Holi Deepavali	National holidays	7 days in a year	26 Jan 15 Aug 2 Oct., Holi Dashehra Deepavali		Institute holidays (11 days)

2.3 *PK Kelkar Library, IIT Kanpur*

The PK Kelkar Library of the Indian Institute of Technology, Kanpur, housed in a three-storey building with a carpet area of about 6973 sqm, has a collection of more than 3,00,000 volumes and subscribes to more than 1000 periodicals. The Abstracting and Indexing periodicals, Micro-form and CD-ROM databases, technical reports, standards and thesis are important part of this collection. Each year, on an average 4500 books and journal volumes are added to the collection. The library is fully computerized using LIBSYS software. The entire collection of books is searchable through Web-OPAC. Adequate number of computers is placed in the users' area to facilitate OPAC search. The Kelkar library is a creative partner and essential force in the IITK community. It has been rendering essential support to the institutes' teaching research and development programs. The library plans, develops and implements programs to provide latest information, learning resources and information competencies to students, faculty and staff using appropriate technologies

2.4 *Central Library, IIT Madras*

The Central Library is housed in a separate building and caters to the information needs of the institute's faculty, students, staff, research institutions and industries. In addition, there are smaller libraries in each department, which house books borrowed from the main library for quick reference. The collection covering all disciplines of science, engineering, technology, humanities and social sciences, comprises of printed books, reports, theses, standards, atlases, patents and journal back volumes. The non-book collections include material like micro fiche/film, audio/video cassettes and CD-ROM discs. It has a separate collection of prescribed textbooks under 'Book Bank' for the exclusive use of students.

The Central library currently subscribes to around 1,000 scholarly journals in sciences, engineering and humanities. Under the INDEST consortium, the library provides online access to a large number of full-text journals databases from various publishers. These e-journals are accessible on intranet to campus users only. The library provides various services for its members such as—Lending of books and journal back volumes, reservation of books, inter-library loan, document delivery, photocopying, DTP and offset printing, CD-ROM and Internet services, and video screening. All the library activities are computerized, including bar-coded ID cards and separate Online Public Access Catalogue (OPAC) terminals for searching books in the library.

The mission of the Central Library is to provide information services and access to bibliographic and full text digital and printed resources to support the scholarly and informational needs of the Institute Community. The Central Library is well equipped with modern facilities and resources in the form of CD-ROMs, Online databases, audio video cassettes, e-books, e-journals, patents, e-standards, theses, reports, monographs etc. The library's homepage provides electronic access to various full-text and bibliographical databases and e-journals. The Central Library has 9001:2000 certification by RWTUV of Germany along with other units of the Institute for the establishment and maintenance of quality library system, services, and procedures.

2.5 *Central Library, IIT Delhi*

The IIT Delhi Library System consists of a Central Library and 18 departmental libraries which collectively support the teaching, research and extension programmes of the Institute. All students, faculty members and employees of the Institute are entitled to make use of the Library facilities after taking library membership. The Library, besides having a collection of over 4 lakh books on engineering, science and humanities, offers library services through its various Divisions. Setup in 1961, the Library moved into its new building in May, 1988.

Table 4: Services Offered by IIT Libraries

Sl. No.	*Service*	*IITKg*	*IITB*	*IITK*	*IITM*	*IITD*	*IITG*	*IITR*
1.	Reference service	✓	✓	✓	✓	✓	✓	✓
2.	Circulation	✓	✓	✓	✓	✓	✓	✓
3.	Membership	✓	✓	✓	✓	✓	✓	✓
4.	Photocopying service	✓	✓	✓	✓	✓	✓	✓
5.	Inter-library loan	✓	✓	✓	✓	✓	✓	✓
6.	Book bank	✓	✓	✓	✓	✓	✓	✓
7.	Video information service	✓	✓	✓	✓	✓	✓	✓
8.	Database search/Internet access	✓	✓	✓	✓	✓	✓	✓
9.	OPAC/web OPAC	✓	✓	✓	✓	✓	✓	✓
10.	Electronic theses and dissertations	✓	✓	✓	×	✓	×	×
11.	Institutional repository	✓	✓	×	×	✓	×	×
12.	User education/ awareness	✓	✓	✓	✓	✓	✓	✓
13.	Consultancy service	×	✓	×	×	✓	×	✓
14.	Conferences/workshops	✓	✓	×	✓	✓	×	✓
15.	Membership to industrial and corporate houses	✓	✓	×	×	✓	×	✓
18.	Membership to engineering colleges	✓	✓	×	✓	×	×	×
19.	Membership to alumni, retired faculty/officers	✓	✓	×	×	✓	×	✓
20.	Membership to individuals	✓	×	×	×	✓	×	✓
21.	Departmental libraries	✓	×	×	✓	✓	×	✓

The Library uses LibSys software package which is an integrated multi-user library management system that supports all in-house operations of the Library. Bibliographic records of books available in the library can be accessed through the OPAC. The Library is a part of the fiber optic-based campus-wide local area network (LAN). It has 50 Information Outlets (IOs) that link to a computing node to the Campus LAN and to the Internet. The Library has its own sub-LAN consisting of 20 terminals, two terminal controllers and two servers to support OPAC services and other in-house computerization activities within the Library. The Library has 50 Pentium machines including 20 exclusively earmarked for the users for searching of CD-ROM and Internet databases. All 20 terminals, 50 Pentium machines and four servers available in the Library are connected to the Campus LAN. The terminals in the Library can also be used for Internet access.

2.6 *Central Library, IIT Guwahati*

The Central Library currently has over 96,000 volumes, including textbooks, reference books, conference proceedings, back volumes, standards, and non-book material such as CD-ROMs, audio tapes, video tapes, and slides. The Library also subscribes to about 414 current periodicals. All operations of the Library are automated with the help of an integrated library software package. The database for the entire collection has been created and available through Online Public Access Catalogue to the users via campus network. The Library extended facilities to 1600 regular members.

2.7 *Mahatma Gandhi Central Library, IIT Roorkee*

The Central Library of the Institute is one of the best academic libraries in the country. With its collection of more than 3,20,000 documents it provides the world class information support to its users. Besides printed books and journals, its collection contains all forms of documents such as CD-ROMs, online databases, audio-video material, standards, specifications, theses, reports etc. Besides Central Library, every academic department/centre has its own departmental library which contains the core collection required by the concerned department/centre. The collection is strong in sciences and technology, however substantial quality information sources on humanities and social sciences are also available. Library is open for authorized members however; non-members can also utilize its resources with the permission of the Librarian.

The main emphasis of the central library is providing digital information support which is provided through its five servers and more than 70 user terminals. The library has access to more than 8000 electronic journals which are available throughout the campus over its fiber-optic network in the institute. The Library is currently in the process of digitizing its archival collection of theses and dissertation for which an Imaging Centre has been established with latest equipment. The library is housed in a newly built state-of-the-art building since 2007.

3. E-Resources at IIT Libraries

As stated earlier, IIT Libraries are the most modernized libraries in the country and are pioneers in adopting latest tools and techniques of Information and Communication Technologies (ICT) to provide quality services to their users. They have been using

E-Resources during early 1990s' in the form of CD-ROMs. With the expansion of Internet, and the availability of all important information sources on the Web (www) in electronic form (E-Resource) in mid-1990s, IIT Libraries have been the first few in the country to acquire E-Resources for their users (Ali, 2006). Thanks to the formation of a national consortium—INDEST Consortium with the support of the Ministry of Human Resource Development, Government of India. IIT Libraries now have access to over 10,000 full-text e-journals, and databases from following sources (Chauhan and Mahapatra, 2006):

Table 5: E-Resources available through INDEST-AICTE Consortium

Sl. No.	*E-resource Database*
1.	ABI/Inform Complete
2.	ACM Digital Library
3.	Annual Reviews
4.	American Society of Civil Engineering Journals
5.	American Society of Mechanical Engineering Journals (+ A M R)
6.	Capitaline
7.	CRIS INFAC Industrial Information
8.	EBSCO Database
9.	Elsevier's Science Direct
10.	Emerald Full-text
11.	Euromonitor (GMID)
12.	IEC Standards
13.	IEEE/IEE Electronic Library Online (IEL)
14.	INSPEC on EI Village
15.	J-Gate Custom Content for Consortia (JCCC)
16.	MathSciNet
17.	Nature publications group
18.	Optical Society of America(Optics Infobase)
19.	Project Muse
20.	SciFinder Scholar
21.	SCOPUS Database
22.	Springer Link
23.	Web of Science

In addition to above, IIT Libraries are subscribing to various other sources individually or in cross-sharing mode. Complete listing of all E-Resources subscribed to by individual IIT Libraries can be seen on their respective web pages. It is estimated that an amount of ₹ 30 crores is being spent annually for the subscription of the above E-Resources.

4. Digital Library Initiatives at IIT Libraries

IIT Libraries were among first few to adopt digital library applications from the beginning with the acquisition of databases (both primary and secondary) on CD-ROMs and making them available on institute-wide network in late 1980s'. With the availability of increasingly large number of journals, books and databases on the Web, the IIT libraries were again on the forefront to obtain access to these resources for their users. Thanks for the setting up of INDEST/AICTE Consortium with the support of MHRD, now IIT libraries are able to provide access to over 12000 e-journals, e-books and

Table 6: E-Resources Subscribed by IITs Libraries

Sl. No.	*E-Resources (Database)*	*S. No.*	*E-Resources (Database)*
1.	ASTM Standards and Digital Library	26.	Journal of Visualized Experiments
2.	American Chemical Society Journals	27.	JSTOR Journals Archive
3.	AIAA Journals	28.	Lecture Notes—Springer Book Series
4.	AIP/APS	29.	Multi-Science Publishing Journals
5.	American Economic Association Journals	30.	New Scientist
6.	American Geophysical Union Journals	31.	NISCAIR Research Journals
7.	American Mathematical Society	32.	Oxford university Press
8.	ASBMB—Journal of Biological Chemistry	33.	Palgrave-Macmillan Journals
9.	ASCE Proceedings	34.	Proceedings of the National Academy of Sciences
10.	BioOne Journals	35.	POIESIS: Philosophy Online Journals
11.	Cambridge University Press Journals	36.	Project EUCLID Journals
12.	ChemSpider	37.	PsycARTICLES
13.	CMIE Database	38.	PV-Tech
14.	Crisil Research	39.	RSC Journals
15.	EdITLib	40.	Sage Journals
16.	Geological Society of America Journals	41.	Science
17.	ICE Publishing(Thomas Telford)Journals	42.	Science of Synthesis
18.	ICSD: Inorganic Crystal Structure Database	43.	Seismological Society of America
19.	INFORMS Pub Suite	44.	SIAM—Locus(Archives) Journals
20.	Institute Of Materials (Maney) Journals	45.	SPIE: Optical Engineering
21.	Institute of Mathematical Statistics Journals	46.	Taylor and Francis
22.	Institute of Physics Journals	47.	Thieme—Chemistry
23.	International Philosophical Quarterly	48.	Transportation Research Board
24.	Journal Citation Reports	49.	Wiley/Blackwell Journals
25.	Journal of Geophysical Res (All Parts)	50.	World Scientific Journals

databases to their users on 24 × 7 basis. These libraries were also first to move towards creation of digital libraries of research publications including research article (preprint/post-print), technical reports, administrative documents, course notes, learning objects, theses, dissertations and other education and research material (free from copyright restrictions) either by digitization of items from its collection or using digitally born materials. Out of 7 IITs covered under this study, 5 are (IIT Bombay, IIT Madras, IIT Kharagpur, IIT Kanpur, IIT Roorkee) using DSpace Software for creating institutional repositories and electronic submission of theses and dissertations. IIT Delhi uses EPrint software for both institutional repositories and electronic theses and dissertations. In fact, IIT Bombay has been the first in the country to support online submission of theses and dissertations using software developed in-house since 1998 and has a database of over 5000 e-theses and dissertations. IIT Bombay, IIT Delhi, IIT Kanpur and IIT Roorkee IRs are listed in the Open DOAR. IIT Bombay's IR has one of the largest number of records (over 13,500).

5. Conclusion

IIT Libraries are examples for superior infrastructure, efficient services and customer-responsive organization. In addition to housing excellent print collections of knowledge resources in engineering, sciences and technology, these libraries also have acquired access to a large number of electronic resources for their users. These resources have helped IITs in improving their research output both quantitatively and qualitatively because large number of publications are coming out of these institutes. These libraries are valued by the users for their support in academic and research mission through user-focused services, highly skilled staff and latest collections.

References

[1] Ali, N. (2006). The use of electronic resources at IIT Delhi Library: study of search behaviours. *Electronic Library*, 23(6), 691–700.

[2] Arora, J. (2003). Indian National Digital Library in Engineering, Science and Technology (INDEST): a proposal for strategic cooperation for consortia-based access to electronic resources. *International Information and Library Review*, 35(1), 1–17.

[3] Bhattacharya, P. and Choudhary, P. (2008). Digital Library Initiatives in IITs: an overview. *ILA Bulletin*, 44(3–4), 3–17.

[4] Chakravarty, R. and Singh, S. (2005). E-Resources for Indian universities: new initiatives. *SRELS Journal of Information Management*, 42(1), 57–73.

[5] Chauhan, K. and Mahapatra, P.K. (2006). An evaluation of INDEST e-resources. In Proceedings of the National Conference on Information Management in Digital Libraries, 2–4 August 2006, Kharagpur, India. Kharagpur, WB, India: Indian Institute of Technology Kharagpur, pp. 469–480.

[6] Ghosh, T.K. and Panda, K.C. (2010). Collection development and access to serials in the Central Library of IITs in India. *Library Collections, Acquisitions and Technical Services,* 34(2–3), 45–50.

[7] Heckart, R.J. (1999). Imagining the digital library in a commercialized Internet. *Journal of Academic Librarianship,* 25(4), 274–280.

[8] India, Ministry of Human Resource Development (2012). Annual Report 2011–12, New Delhi, India: MHRD. 337pp. http://mhrd.gov.in/documents/term/82 (accessed on 18.6.2012).

[9] Jayarajan, P. (1998). Revenue from library and information science: a case study. In Seetharama, S., ed. Libraries and information centres as profit making institutions. New Delhi, India: Ess Ess, pp. 82–87.

[10] Jeevan, V.K. and Padhi, P. (2008). Infrastructure, resources and services in IIT Libraries: results of a questionnaire survey. *SRELS Journal of Information Management*, 45(4), 455–472.

[11] Kaur, B., and Verma, R. (2008). Use and impact of electronic journals in the Indian Institute of Technology, Delhi, India. *The Electronic Library*, 27(4), 611–622.

[12] Mulla, K.R. and Chandrashekara, M. (2006). E-Resources and services in engineering college libraries: a case study. *Electronic Journal of Academic and Special Librarianship*, 7(1), 7.

[13] Vasanth, N. and Mudhol, M.V. (2007). Advanced approach in using e-resources of the INDEST-AICTE Consortium. *SRELS Journal of Information Management*, 44(4), 367–374.

Electronic Resources Management in Libraries, pp. 67–74

Managing Digital Resources at IICT Library: A Case Study

S.J.D. Varaprasad, D.B. Ramesh, G. Karunakar and U. Baby Soujanya

ABSTRACT

This paper attempts to examine the nature of IICT library, its collections, management of its digital collections with the help of open source software and how the library is supporting the mission of the parent organization and researchers.

1. Introduction

Library profession has become most challenging in the present day knowledge society. Complex changes made librarians to face a challenging situation. Recent advances in Information and Communication Technology (ICT) have changed the work of both the librarians and scientists. Today digital communication and digital information are playing key role in the society. Librarians have to keep abreast a variety of new information resources and implement support mechanisms for proper dissemination of these resources. There are various new fields evolving apart from the existing ones. Libraries—today have to manage old resources as well as scale up to the upcoming technologies to manage and maintain their new digital domain. Chemical science information is unique and it contains a variety of resources like chemical structures, reactions, databases etc. Developing a digital repository is very much useful to the scientific community both for the users inside as well as outside the organisation.

1.1 *What is a Digital Library?*

We may refresh our memory on the definitions of a digital library given by various experts. A Digital Library (DL) is a library in which collections are stored in digital formats and accessible by computers. The content may be stored locally, or accessed remotely. A DL is the combination of content and services and is a tool at the centre of intellectual activity having no logical, conceptual, physical, temporal, or personal borders or barriers on information. According to Gladney *et al.* (1994) a DL service is an assemblage of digital computing, storage, and communications machinery together with the software needed to reproduce, emulate, and extend the services provided by conventional libraries based on paper and other material means of collecting, storing, cataloguing, finding and disseminating information. According to Hill and others (1999), DL information collection can be distinguished as group of objects represented by various forms of item level metadata ranging from ad hoc collections to formally and institutionally managed collection. The difference between traditional and DLs are well defined. While traditional libraries are stable and slowly evolved bodies with print collection or in some other form like microfiche or microfilm etc. and are with flat structure with minimal contextual metadata, DLs have resources in digital form which are dynamic in nature with richer contextual metadata. Traditional libraries have limited access points with physical and logical organization correlated and centrally operated. Whereas digital libraries will have unlimited access points with physical and virtual organization. Digital libraries break the physical boundaries of data and are important for communication and collaboration for information seeking activities.

1.2 *Why Digital Library?*

Digital collection provides access any time, *i.e.*, 24 × 7, 365 days through WAN/LAN to the users simultaneously to access the resources. It promotes efficient delivery of information economically to all users and encourages co-operative efforts in research resource, computing and communication networks. Further the digital resources strengthen communication and collaboration between and among academic and research institutions besides taking a leadership role in the generation and dissemination of knowledge.

Globalization and technological innovations are processes that have created a new global change. This development has benefited the libraries which enable them to serve the information needs of the global village. This has to be welcomed and libraries and librarians have to transform themselves to best fit in the current scenario lest they may lose their identity. There are many advantages with DLs such as unlimited storage space at a much lower cost, lack of physical boundary, round the clock availability, multiuser access, enhanced information retrieval, preservation for some print material, added value, and universal accessibility. However, there are certain limitations also which are true with every new system and some of them are mentioned below.

- ***Hardware*:** The major risk to digital objects is not physical deterioration, but technological obsolescence of the devices to read them. While the lifetime of optical and magneto-optical cartridges is expected to be in decades, that of the reading devices is only about one decade. Solution? Reasonable refreshing schedule and use of widely marketed devices than special purpose devices.
- ***Software*:** A more serious problem is software obsolescence. It has been pointed out that the variety of software formats far exceeds the number of hardware devices manufactured, and that these programs come and go more quickly than the hardware does. Solution? Libraries should rely on standards like Machine-Readable Cataloging (MARC) and Standard Generalized Markup Language (SGML), which are expected to exist for the foreseeable future.

Apart from the two major limitations, a few others include:

- Lack of screening or validation
- Lack of preservation of a fixed copy (for the record and for duplicating scientific research)
- Difficulty in knowing and locating everything that is available
- Differentiating valuable from useless information
- Job loss for traditional publishers and librarians
- Costs are spread and many become hidden.

There are different types of digital resources ranging from electronic journals, electronic books, data bases in many formats like bibliographic, full text images, audio, video, statistical and numeric data sets etc. Indian Institute of Chemical Technology (IICT), Hyderabad is a premier R&D institute in India. The Institute had its origin as the Central Laboratories for Scientific and Industrial Research (CLSIR), established in 1944 by the then Government of Hyderabad State. It has made significant contributions during the last six decades in the fields of chemistry and chemical engineering. The major areas of research at IICT include natural products chemistry, agrochemicals, drugs and intermediates, specialty and fine chemicals, fluoro-organics, inorganic and physical chemistry (catalysis and material science), lipid sciences and technology, coal, gas and energy, chemical engineering, design and engineering. The Institute has been providing engineering designs for commercial plants with standard commercial guarantees. More than 150 technologies developed by IICT are now in commercial production. Its commitment to industry is reflected by the way of several sponsored and consultancy projects received from the industry, year after year. With over 450 highly professional and dedicated scientists and technical officers/technicians, excellent laboratory and instrument facilities for research in chemical sciences and technology and allied sciences, IICT is known nationally as well as internationally for its contributions both in basic and applied research (IICT, 2012).

2. Managing Digital Resources at IICT Library

The IICT library is a hybrid library with a mix of traditional print material such as books and magazines, as well as electronic resources like e-journals and databases. Access for these e-resources has been obtained through institutional and CSIR e-journal consortium, known as National Knowledge Resource Consortium (NKRC). The IICT Library has a large collection of materials in Chemistry, Biological and Engineering Sciences. It provide regular services like circulation, reference, newspaper clippings, inter-library loan, translation service for foreign language research articles along with photocopying and binding activities to in-house scientific staff, and also provides information on the bibliographical details along with the Impact factors of the research papers of IICT and coordinates with NISCAIR. Users include in-house scientific and technical staff, research students of both the laboratories viz. IICT and CCMB, research scholars' number is about 1100 from various universities in India and users from over 100 corporate industrial establishments.

2.1 *Electronic Collections of IICT*

Digital resources of IICT Library include long runs of many important serials published by scholarly societies and associations and other publishers such as the American Chemical Society, Royal Society of Chemistry, American Institute of Physics, and American Society of Mechanical Engineers, Elsevier's Science Direct, Wiley-Blackwell, Springer, Taylor and Francis, Nature etc. Chemical Abstracts (CA) are available from 1907 in print form and from 1996 onwards in CD form. Specialized databases like standards, which include Indian, British and American Society for Testing and Materials, Web of Science, Integrity, Metacore and Qpat databases from Thomson Reuters, Reaxys database from Elsevier, SciFinder from American Chemical Society, Science of Synthesis database from Thieme and some archives of e-journals from Elsevier, Thieme and Royal Society of Chemistry. Library also provides readers with access to about 4000 scientific, technical and peer-reviewed e-journals. Almost all e-journals are accessed through Institutional IP and only a few through user id and password.

2.2 *Management of Digital Collection of IICT*

The electronic collections and research publications, Ph.D. theses and other publications of IICT constitute the digital library of the Institute. These digital library resources are shown in Figure 1. The various modes of acquiring e-resources are as under:

- ***Acquisition of Digital Media:*** Digital media shall contain enormous amount of knowledge. According to the needs of the Institute these may be procured. CA on CD procured by IICT falls under this category.
- ***Buying Access:*** All e-journals accessed by the Institute, either through consortium approach or through individual subscription, falls under this category.
- ***Content Creation:*** In a special library like IICT all the research scientists and scholars' publish articles regularly. Authors may be requested to upload their articles to the digital collection. These are called 'born digital' objects.
- ***Content Creation by Scanning:*** In this type sources of information like archival research articles and other publications of the Institute may be scanned and converted into digital media.
- ***Portal Site:*** This includes URLs of the websites which are of interest to users of the library. If a user is interested to visit a particular site, he can directly click the

hyperlink and get connected to its resources. Such facility has been given in the home page of the IICT library viz. http:libdoc.

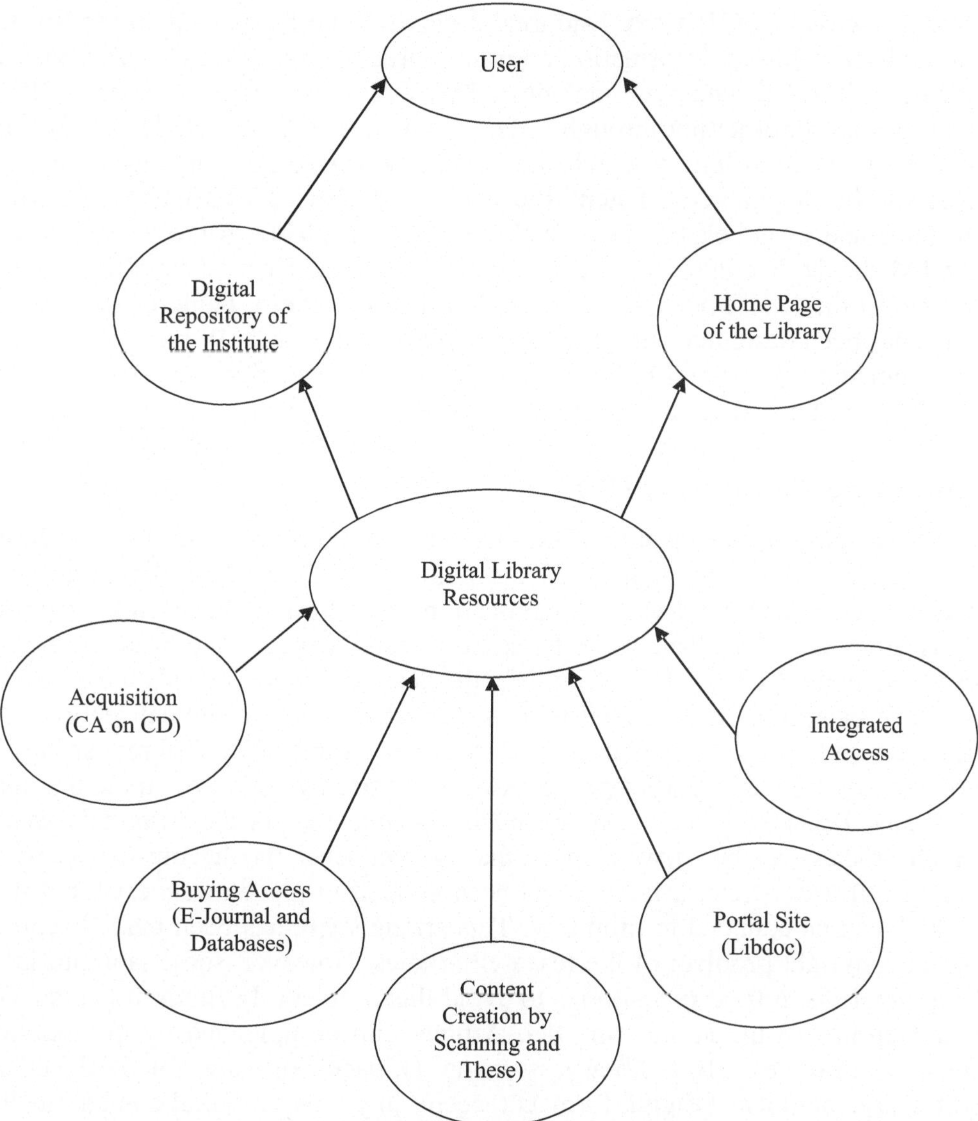

Fig. 1: Digital Resources at IICT Library

- ***Integrated Access:*** Digital collection can also be delivered by combining one or more methods discussed in previous paragraphs.
- ***Library Home Page:*** IICT library home page includes all the activities of the library for the benefit of users. It is a single platform from where one can access

all the e-journals, databases, Open access journals, new arrivals of journals, news papers clippings and included any information that is relevant and freely available in the Web. For all the e-journals hyperlinks have been given for easy and time saving access to IICT users. E-journal archives hyperlinks leads to the full texts of the back volumes. Information on print journal subscription year wise was also included. The CD catalogue includes all the CDs received from other CSIR labs and relevant information through CDs. Downloads section includes all the forms that are relevant to library which can be readily printed and some useful software that can be downloaded. Patent site leads to the subscribed patent sites of the Institute and other related sites which are freely available in the web. Indian and ASTM standards connect to the standards databases. Thus all the digital content related to the IICT library has been included in the library home page. The home page has been designed using the tools Macromedia Dream Weaver MX2004 and Macromedia Fireworks MX2004 using Internet Information Server on Windows 2000 operating system. It is being updated periodically and well managed.

2.3 *Institutional Repository of IICT*

Digital Repository of the Institute (DRI) has been commissioned in the year 2009 at IICT with an intention to include all the publications and Ph.D. theses and other documents of the Institute. Research publications have been included in the repository since its inception. More than seven thousand research papers have been scanned and indexed and included in the DRI. Similarly the details of more than six hundred Ph.D. theses have been included. Annual reports, Newsletters and technical reports of the Institute are on the way to be included. They can be searched by different strings like author, subject, title, date and keyword. Access has been given through the intranet of the Institute. Recently it has been floated in the Internet via the Institute's website. Research articles can be viewed up to the abstract level by the outside users. For obtaining full-text article, a facility has been created to place a request for it in the site which can be attended to promptly. This arrangement has been made keeping in mind the copyright problem of the research articles. However, some laboratories are floating preprints in their repositories to avoid this problem. In future it is planned to upload preprints of the articles in DRI. Articles can be uploaded by the individual scientists themselves. IICT library is using DSpace software for DRI. DSpace supports large number of digital formats (accepts any type of digital content, include: Text Image, Audio and Video). It is an open access soft ware and is to maintain. Hardware component consists of Compaq ML370 server, Intel Xeon3400 CPU, 500GB HDD with 4GB RAM. Software used were Dspace1.5.1, Red hat 9 Linux, JavaJDK1.5, Apache Tomcat 6.0.20, Apache Ant1.7., Apache Maven 2.1 and PostgreSQL8.3fro the DRI.

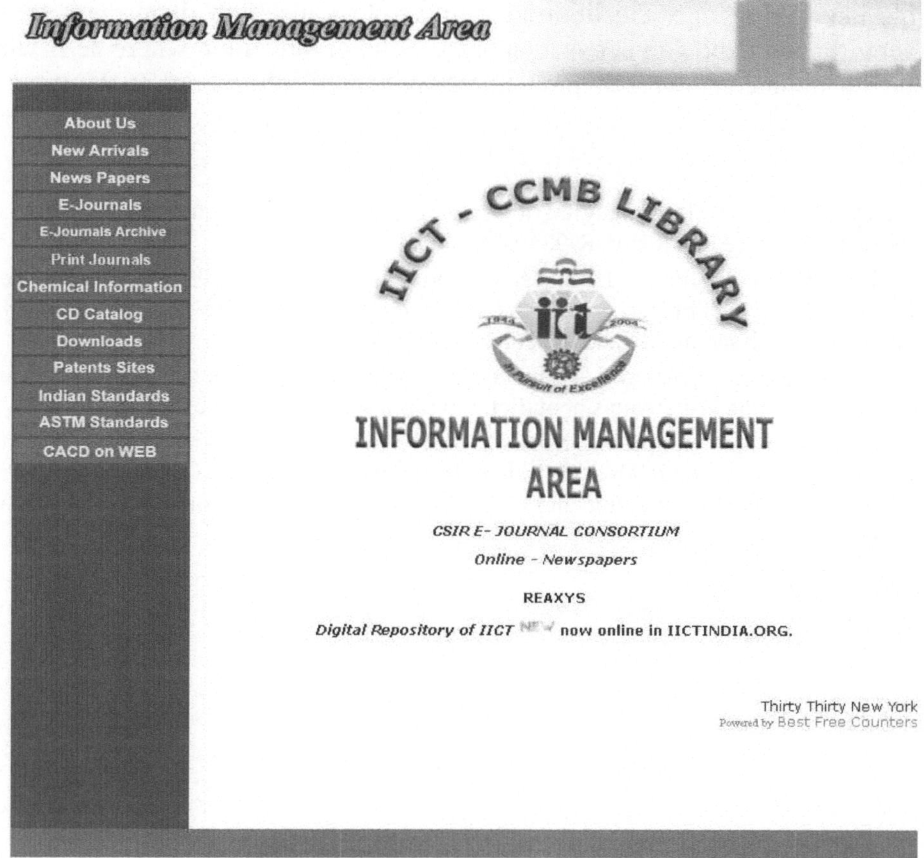

Fig. 2: IICT Library Home Page

3. Conclusion

Digital library programs seem to take on different complexions that reflect their host organizations' mission, leadership, available funding, and specific collection and service strengths. Most digital library project's objective is to generate, collect, store, and organize information in digital forms, and make it available to defined groups of users for searching, retrieval, and processing via communication networks and ultimately saving the time of the reader and providing right information to the right user. In a special library like IICT, managing digital repositories is essential as it satisfies the literature needs of the researcher. Researcher understands the type of research that was done earlier and research that is being done presently in a particular Institute and can choose the right problem for future research work. This helps avoiding duplication of research very easily and saves the time of the researcher. Also by connecting the digital repositories of a particular organization like CSIR, the uses for resource sharing and boosting the research are enormous. With the help of a repository and tools like home page, the librarian can mould himself to fit in the new era of Digital environment and can act as a catalyst to the organization where he is working in furthering the interests of it by proactive provision of information to the users.

References

[1] Gladney, H.M. *et. al.* (1994). Digital library: Gross structure and requirements: Report from a workshop. IBM Research Report RJ9S40, May 1994.

[2] Hill, L.L., Dolin, R., Frew, J., Janée, G. and Larsgaard, M (1999). Collection metadata solutions for digital library applications. *Journal of the American Society for Information Science,* Special Issue on Metadata, **50**(13), 1169–1181.

[3] Indian Institute of Chemical Technology. About the institution. Available online at http://www.iictindia.org/aboutus/aboutiict.htm [accessed 6June. 2012].

[4] Kumari, Lalitha and Varaprasad, S.J.D. (2003). Management of e-resources: Case study of Information Management Area at Indian Institute of Chemical Technology, Hyderabad. SIS2003 21st Annual Convention and Conference of Society for Information Science, Vol. 2, pp. 348–257.

Electronic Resources Management in Libraries, pp. 75–85

Knowledge Sharing among Agricultural Libraries in India: The Efforts of Indian Council of Agricultural Research

K. Veeranjaneyulu

ABSTRACT

The Indian Council of Agricultural Research (ICAR) is entrusted with knowledge sharing among agricultural library user community. To support this mission, the ICAR has initiated steps to support the agricultural libraries through innovative projects like National Agricultural Innovative Project (NAIP). The aim of the NAIP is to facilitate accelerated and sustainable transformation of Indian agriculture in support of poverty alleviation and income generation by collaborative development and application of agricultural innovation by the public research organizations in partnership with the farmers' group, the private sector, the civil society organizations and other stakeholders. This paper describes the various initiatives and projects undertaken by the NAIP to strengthen the agricultural information system in India. Among the various national projects are the Consortium for e-Resources in Agriculture, *Krishi Prabha*, and *e-Granth*, under NARS. This study examines the impact of all the above projects on the agricultural information generation and utilization is expected to help in strengthening of digital library and information management.

1. Introduction

The developments in Information and Communication Technologies (ICTs) have given a new lease of life to agricultural research and practice and to all the stake holders of agricultural knowledge producers and users, viz. agricultural scientists, entrepreneurs, farmers, policy makers and of course library and information professionals. Now, there is a sense of inter-connectivity or networking among all these players nationally and internationally giving rise to a revolution in agricultural knowledge. This in turn enhanced the extent, intensity and speed of agricultural knowledge production and use (Veeranjaneyulu and Rajagopal, 2001). The institutions under the Indian Council of Agricultural Research (ICAR) (http://www.icar.org.in) and their constituent libraries are playing a vital role in providing the required information to their users for education, research and extension. The capacity building of these libraries is the need of the hour for efficient and effective delivery of library and information services at national level through National Agricultural Research System (NARS).

2. Projects Initiated by NAIP

ICAR has sanctioned the following projects under NAIP (http://www.naip.icar.org.in) for sharing of Information among Agricultural Libraries in India:

- Consortium for e-Resources in Agriculture (CeRA).
- *Krishi Prabha*: Indian agricultural doctoral dissertations repository.
- *e-Granth*: Strengthening of Digital Library and Information Management under NARS.

2.1 *Consortium for e-Resources in Agriculture*

CeRA is the second largest Consortium (next to UGC-Inflibnet) covering basic, crops, dairy and animal and fishery sciences. All the consortium members are provided accessibility through respective IP addresses. Based on negotiation and discussion, subscription for more than 2800 journals including Annual Reviews, Indian journals, Springer Verlag, Elsevier, Taylor and Francis and open access journals were made accessible online on 24 × 7 basis to researchers in 131 institutions under NARS through CeRA platform (http://www.cera.jccc.in).

Background

The Council being an apex organization at the national level for promoting science and technology programmes in the agricultural research and education, an attempt has been made to make available the selected journals over the network of NARS institutions. The Consortium has commenced its operations since July 2008 through its headquarters at the Indian Agricultural Research Institute (IARI) New Delhi. The Consortium subscribes to full-text e-journals for 126 leading NARS institutions in India including 4 deemed universities, 3 ICAR headquarters, 47 ICAR institutes, 6 national bureaus, 9 national research centers, 19 project directorates, and 41 State Agricultural Universities (SAUs) (Visakhi, 2009). The expenditure on e-journals proposed for subscription under the consortium for these institutions are being met from the funds made available by the National Agricultural Innovation Projects (NAIP), a World Bank assisted agriculture project being executed by National Agricultural Research System (NARS) with the lifespan of six years, starting from 2006 to 2012.

Objectives

- To develop existing R&D information resource base of ICAR institutions/ universities, etc., comparable to world leading institutions/organizations.
- To subscribe e-journals and create e-access culture among scientists/teachers in ICAR institutes/agricultural universities.
- To study the impact of CeRA on the quality of research publications measured through SCI and NAAS ID.

Usage Level

During the past three years (2008, 2009 and 2010), the project was implemented through subscription to eight publishers for providing online access of subscribed journals to scientists, teachers and students. Accordingly, agriculture-based journals from CSIRO, Springer Verlag, Annual Reviews from 2008 onwards and Elsevier, Taylor and Francis and Indian journals from 2009 onwards were subscribed. In addition, *Nature* and *Web of Science* from Thomson Reuters (for evaluation of research publications) were subscribed for the lead institutes but catering to all researchers in NARS from October 2009 onwards. The tremendous usage from scientists/teachers from NARS was shown in the form of number of downloads of articles in CeRA during 2008–2011 (Figure 1).

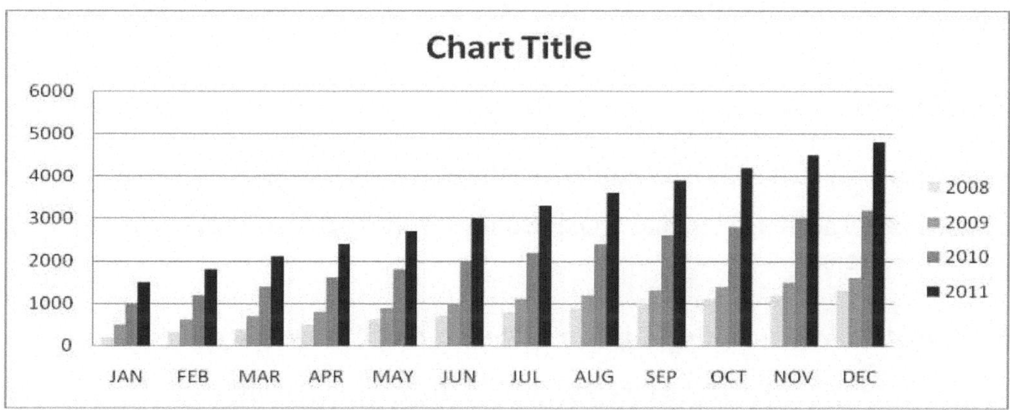

Fig. 1: Usage of E-resources in CeRA

The trend clearly showed that each year number of downloads were increasing, and the average cost of an article was reduced which means a good usage of e-journals provided by CeRA, and saving of huge amount of money of ICAR institutes/SAUs libraries, which now discontinued many of their subscriptions to journals because those are freely accessible to them through the CeRA. The figures for the usage of CeRA and cost reduction shows that more expenditure could be incurred on subscription of other e-resources like e-books, Hindi journals, periodicals etc. through the Consortium that will definitely provide access to useful information which was crucial for research.

2.2 *KrishiPrabha*

KrishiPrabha is an Indian agricultural doctoral dissertations repository. The title *KrishiPrabha* of the Project has its own significance; *Prabha* means morning; in other words "dawn of the day". Since, this project is first of its type in agriculture filed in India, hence the title *KrishiPrabha.*

Objectives

The following objectives were set for the project:

- To develop, organize and sustain knowledge base of Indian agricultural doctoral dissertations in digital form and make them accessible online.
- To develop a standard format for submission of e-theses by the SAUs/Data Centres (DAUs) to the Lead Centre.
- To upgrade skills of human resources of SAUs/DAUs/ICAR institutes.
- To publish a journal both in print and electronic formats.

Methodology

The Digital Repository was developed along with a distributed cooperative model. It consisted of the following components:

Lead Centre: Nehru Library, Chaudhury Charan Singh Haryana Agricultural University (CCSHAU), Hisar acted as national nodal agency for this Project (http://hau.ernet.in). University Librarian, CCSHAU, Hisar was the CPI and coordinates the work to establish, maintain and update the *KrishiPrabha* Database.

Data Centres: The 40 SAUs, and 5 deemed universities acted as data centres to provide data for the Project.

2.3 *Value Addition Including Software Support and Consultancy*

EQuest—a software developed and customized by Total IT Solutions, New Delhi – was used for e-content creation, organization, management, and uploading onto website for search over Internet.

3. Data Capturing

The Lead Centre hired Expedien e-Solutions, Noida, as Data Capturing Agency (DCA) for data capturing, editing, indexing and organizing the database.

The project was implemented in multiple phases. The Lead Centre purchased the digitization software, got it customized and launched (hosted) the same on the university website. Softcopies of theses already available with Data Centres were collected. The softcopies which were found in the standard format were uploaded on the website. The Lead Centre approached the Data Centres for permission to capture the data from those theses whose softcopies were not available. The DCA captured the data by scanning of the doctoral dissertations submitted during 2000–2007 at the Data Centres, and supplied the same in PDF format to the Lead Centre. The PDF files were thoroughly checked at the Lead Centre and converted into flash files if found in order, and uploaded on the CCSHAU maintained website. The Super Admin body again verified these records, assigned standard keywords using CAB Thesaurus, and finally submitted to the open access database for access to all the consortia partners. Files containing discrepancies were sent back to the DCA for correction which revisited the sites and returned the files to the Lead Centre after correction, which were uploaded with the database.

3.1 *Major Achievements*

A database of metadata and abstracts of about 7525 records, about 6000 full-text dissertations covering the period the period 2000–2007 has been created. IP-based access is provided to all the Consortium partners. University-wise distribution of dissertations uploaded in the *KrishiPrabha* Database is reflected in the given in Table 1.

4. *E-Granth*: Strengthening of Digital Library and Information Management Under NARS

The Council is an autonomous apex body responsible for organizing, conducting and managing research and education in agriculture and allied sciences in India. The ICAR also acts as a repository of knowledge and provide information on agriculture, horticulture, resource management, animal sciences, agricultural engineering, fisheries, agricultural extension and agricultural education. Digital technologies and online information resources have brought fundamental changes in how research is done, and also about what researchers expect from library and information services. The services that librarians and information professionals provide have also changed fundamentally over the past decade, and they now offer much more in providing leadership that brings improvements in research performance and effectiveness. New resources, services and technologies continue to create new opportunities, new challenges and new expectations.

Table 1: University-Wise Number of Theses Uploaded

Sl. No.	*University*	*Metadata and Abstract Count*	*Full-text Count*
1.	ANGRAU, Hyderabad	239	238
2.	AAU, Anand	121	110
3.	AAU, Assam	73	73
4.	BCKV, Nadia	190	190
5.	BAU, Ranchi	36	34
6.	CIFE, Mumbai	74	74
7.	CCSHAU, Hisar	1820	735
8.	CSAUAT, Kanpur	195	188
9.	CSK, Palampur	131	121

Sl. No.	*University*	*Metadata and Abstract Count*	*Full-text Count*
10.	BSKKV, Dapoli	48	48
11.	PDKV, Akola	90	90
12.	YSParmar, Solan	255	252
13.	G.B. Pant, Pantnagar	511	511
14.	GADVASU, Ludhiana	10	3
15.	IARI, Delhi	638	638
16.	IVRI, Bareilly	252	243
17.	IGKV, Raipur	28	28
18.	JNKV, Jabalpur	16	16
19.	KVAFSU, Bangluru	7	7
20.	KAU, Kerala	164	164
21.	MPUAT, Udaipur	285	108
22.	MAFSU, Nagpur	8	8
23.	MPKV, Rahuri	165	153
24.	MAU, Parbhani	79	78
25.	NDUAT, Faizabad	122	118
26.	NDRI, Karnal	160	155
27.	NAU, Navsari	5	5
28.	OUAT, Orissa	24	24
29.	PDDU, Mathura	5	5
30.	PAU, Ludhiana	489	437
31.	RAU, Bikaner	61	50
32.	RAU, Samastipur	114	91
33.	SBPUAT, Meerut	2	0
34.	SDAU, Dantiwada	28	27
35.	SKUAST, Jammu	26	1
36.	SKUAST, Kashmir	92	58
37.	SVVU, Triputi	4	3
38.	TNAU, Coimbatore	239	239
39.	TNVASU, Chennai	122	122
40.	UAS, Dharwad	251	130
41.	UAS, Bangalore	269	262
42.	UBKV, Cooch Behar	20	20
43.	WBUAFS, Kolkata	57	57
Total		7,525	5,914

The objectives of the *e-Granth* Project (http://www.egranth.ac.in) are:

- To create OPAC under Indian Agricultural Research Group Catalogue of all 12 library resources with OCLC partnership.
- To digitize important institutional repositories including rare books and old journals and make them open access under NARS.
- To strengthen capacity building for library and information management system.
- To implement the Koha library management software.

5. Union Catalogue of Agricultural Libraries (AgriCat)

It has been observed that in the past few years, subscriptions to journals by libraries of ICAR institutes/SAUs have been on the decline side mainly because of the financial crunch. Also, there is an increase in the cost of reputed relevant journals and books, due to which some of the research institutions in NARS are deprived of such journals and books. At the same time, the research/educational activities must always keep pace with the international competition for which all important journals and books should be made available to researchers/teachers in the NARS. Maintaining a traditional form of library with hardcopies is becoming labour-intesive and adds to the cost. Each and every library cannot be sustained with adequate funds. NARS must take advantages of sweeping changes taking place globally.

Duplicate records creation can be avoided by pooling the efforts through common electronic protocols. Union catalogs are useful to librarians, as they assist in locating and requesting materials from other libraries through inter-library loan service. The Indian NARS has a very large collection of institutional repositories in agriculture and allied sciences, in different libraries of ICAR institutes and state agricultural universities spread all over the country. Digitization of these valuable archives would allow online access to researchers, teachers and students to which they would not otherwise have access.

Keeping the above background in view, the project 'Strengthening of Digital Library and Information Management under NARS (e-Granth)' has been approved by NAIP, a World Bank funded initiative under ICAR. The Project has been approved as a pilot to be implemented by the consortium of the following 12 partner institutions comprising of libraries of ICAR, 4 deemed universities of ICAR and 7 SAUs:

- ICAR HQ, New Delhi
- IARI, New Delhi
- IVRI, Izatnagar, UP
- NDRI, Karnal, Haryana
- CIFE, Mumbai
- ANGRAU, Hyderabad, AP
- CCSHAU, Hisar, Haryana
- CSKHPV, Palampur, HP
- GBPUAT, Pantnagar, Uttarakhand
- MPKV, Rahuri, Maharastra
- TANUVAS, Chennai
- UAS, Bengaluru

The project aims at complete conversion of library catalogues into MARC-21 compliant union catalogue which enables sharing of the library resources; creation of Institutional Repository (IR) by digitization of rare books, journals and other important gray literature including all institutional publications with the view to serve as knowledge repository for whole NARS and capacity building of library professionals in NARS in managing these digital resources.

Strategy followed to develop group catalog, named AgriCat, was to adopt the OCLC's Connexion software for online cataloging and direct uploading of records to AgriCat and WorldCat in MARC-21. WorldCat is the largest Union Catalog in world held by OCLC. The existing catalogues were batch-uploaded which was processed by OCLC and added to AgriCat and WorldCat in batches.

AgriCat is a subset of WorldCat (http://www.egranth.ac.in or http://www.agricat.worldcat.org) and has been developed as a group catalogue of 12 partner libraries, intended to provide versatile search and retrieval facilities to share library resources which can be accessed on 24 × 7 basis. The patrons are able to search at three layers—global search (libraries worldwide), search group (AgriCat libraries) and search the individual library (local level). A user can also register and create his own mini library using the feature like MyList, MyWatch List, MySaved Searches for further use.

On searching a library one can see what has been recently added to the library and view it, an experience similar to visiting fresh arrivals section in a library. AgriCat may be used for resource sharing by article exchange and inter-library loans, acquisition planning to economize the shrinking funds. Practically, AgriCat virtualises the complete experience of physically visiting the library, searching through the catalog, going to stacks/racks, taking out the desired book and browsing it before deciding to get it issued. Sitting at the office desk or at your home, one can do this by a few clicks, using AgriCat.

For creation of IR, content has been identified mainly at four digitization partners by expert committee and harmonized at Lead Centre to avoid duplication. The digitization work and Integrated Content Management System has been outsourced to create IR. The IR digitally captures, preserves and provides easy access to the intellectual output of an institution and scholarly writings with open access mandate. The ICAR acts as repository of knowledge in agriculture and allied sciences, having very large collection of old and valuable books, records and various documents spread all over the country in different libraries of Research Institutions and SAUs in print format. Digitization of these valuable archives allows online access to researchers, teachers and students to which they cannot otherwise have access thus impacting the research.

Table 2: Institute-wise Total no. of Records in AgriCat as on 19-04-2012

Sl. No.	*Name of the Institute*	*Records*
1.	Indian Agricultural Research Institute (IARI), New Delhi	62,222
2.	Indian Veterinary Research Institute (IVRI), UP	23,958
3.	University of Agricultural Sciences (UAS), Bangalore	29,767
4.	GB Pant University of Agriculture and Technology (GBPUAT), Uttarakhand	44,935
5.	Ch. Charan Singh Haryana Agriculture University (CCSHAU), Hisar	79,055
6.	Acharya NG Ranga Agricultural University (ANGRAU), Hyderabad	27,910
7.	National Dairy Research Institute (NDRI), Karnal	34,950
8.	Central Institute of Fisheries Education (CIFE), Mumbai	14,498
9.	CSK Himachal Pradesh Krishi Vishwavidyalaya (CSKHPKV), HP, Palampur	29,623
10.	Mahatma Phule Krishi Vidyapeeth (MPKV), Maharashtra	26,674
11.	Tamilnadu Veterinary and Animal Sciences University (TANUVAS), Tamilnadu	30,754
12.	Directorate of Information and Publication of Agriculture (DIPA)/ICAR	7,453
	Total	4,11,799

Well equipped digitization facilities have been established at four locations of IARI, New Delhi; IVRI, Izatnagar; UAS, Bengaluru, and ANGRAU, Hyderabad. Digitization of identified valuable documents is progressing at these centers at about 50,000 pages per day. A Data Center facility to centrally host the repository consisting of 4 blade servers, Storage Area Network and 3 Terabyte Storage has been procured and installed at IARI, New Delhi.

6. *Krishi Kosh*

Krishi Kosh is an IR under NARS covering knowledge in agriculture and allied sciences, having collection of old and valuable books, records and various documents spread all over the country in different libraries of research institutions and SAUs.

Communities of *Krishi Kosh* are as given below:

- Acharya NG Ranga Agricultural University
- Central Marine Fisheries Research Institute
- ICAR-Indian Council of Agricultural Research

- Indian Agricultural Research Institute
- Indian Veterinary Research Institute
- *KrishiPrabha*
- University of Agricultural Sciences.

7. Capacity Building

Capacity building of the librarians in changing digital era is an important strategy to bring in sustainable change in the way information is collated, presented and accessed by the stake holders. To build capacity, five workshops/trainings have been held on Connexion, open source software DSpace, Koha, OJS and a national conference on contemporary issues related to library digitization. Further trainings and adoption of Koha as library management system is being taken-up to bring libraries on common standard platform with improved digital experience for users (Veeranjaneyulu, 2011).

Some of the major achievements and impact of the activities under the project till date are as under:

- Process for Online cataloguing using Connexion software, complying with MARC-21 International Standards, established and implemented, first time in the country. Required capacity has been built-in 12 partner libraries which can be replicated to other libraries of NARS.
- A software product, AgriCat has been created as subgroup of WorldCat to access combined holdings of 12 partner libraries. This serves as versatile virtual library interface.
- IR, digitally capturing, preserving and providing easy access to the intellectual output of NARS with open access mandate is being developed. DSpace has been configured and customized to meet the requirements. A mini data centre has been created at IARI, New Delhi for perpetual hosting of the contents.
- To strengthen the digital library initiatives, more advanced library management software, compliant to open international standards is necessary for easy data portability and data sharing. Koha has been identified for implementation with the help of an outsourcing agent for expert support, intensive training and in-house capacity building.

e-Granth project has catalyzed the enthusiasm of NARS librarians as well as user community to strive for the best in this digital world and synergies the efforts of our scientific community tirelessly working for the benefit of farmers, food security, nutritional enhancement and better place to live.

8. Conclusion

CeRA, *e-Granth* and *KrishiPrabha* are some of the initiatives taken up by the ICAR to create a knowledge sharing network of Indian agricultural information among agricultural libraries in India. A national consortium of agricultural libraries like CeRA is playing a vital role in providing research information to scientists located in all over India. All these activities will help increase the country's agricultural production and thereby achieve self-sufficiency in food.

References

[1] Veeranjaneyulu, K. and Rajagopal, T. (2001). Networking of agricultural information centres in Andhra Pradesh (AP-AGRINET): A model. *International Library Movement*, 23(3), 162–176.

[2] Veeranjaneyulu, K. (2011). Human resource development in information technology environment in Agricultural Libraries. *Indian Journal of Agricultural Library and Information Services*, 27(2), 31–34.

[3] Visakhi, P. (2009). Consortium for e-Resources in Agriculture. *DESIDOC Journal of Library and Information Technology*, 29(5), 24–30.

Electronic Resources Management in Libraries, pp. 86–101

Current Practices in the Management of Electronic Resources in University Libraries in Delhi: An Analytical Study

Margam Madhusudhan and Kanchan Rani

ABSTRACT

The present study examines the changing facets of e-resources and current practices with regard to acquisition, selection, mode of procurement, promotion, development policy, problems and future plans in university libraries of Delhi.

The findings shed light on the e-resources are: databases are very famous and subscribing e-resources based on easy to use, saving of space, and users demand. Users are given second preference in mode of procurement of e-resources. Currency and timeliness of the information is the first and cost of a resource is the last factor in collection development policy. Geographic parameter and remote accessibility is used in selection of e-resources. Through agent/vendor is highest and through exchange is lowest mode of acquisition. Providing links from library's home page is the higher order and trained staff is the top most problems associated with e-resources. The study also highlights the current practices in selection of e-materials and helps in efficient collection development policy of e-resources in libraries covered in the study.

1. Introduction

Electronic resources (e-resources) represent a significant and growing part of the academic library's offerings. E-resources are changing rapidly and leading to new generation of libraries. On one side, there is an increasing demand for good quality library collections in terms of large amount of information and on the other hand, the publishing media is striving hard to support the demand at lightning speed by way of e-publications as well as online access. But this has many implications in terms of cost, promotional activities, their management issues, etc. The perpetual job of libraries is collection development, preservation, retrieval of information and providing the required user services.

The basic functions of any library are collection, storage, and dissemination of information. Out of these three functions, "collection" occupies the most vital position and plays a significant role as it affects to a considerable extent the other two functions of the library. A representative collection is adequate in terms of both quality and quantity, if not properly and constantly nurtured will cease to be a live collection.

Hence, acquisition of information in its various forms should be done in a continuous process. In a developing country like India, different steps are being taken to disseminate information embedded in e-resources as emerged as quick sources of information.

1.1 *University Libraries*

A university library, therefore, inevitably becomes an intellectual arena and a place for knowledge. It acts as a meeting place of enquiring minds—those of researchers, faculty and readers. In a university, teaching is a part of research; and the latter is unthinkable without a good library and so occupies a place of significance in any university. Therefore, the library can enhance a university's reputation by providing access to world-class information resources and services and help to stimulate research by promoting collections and services widely and also play a pivotal role in ensuring the success of higher degree of research and success of university.

The users demand for electronic services is growing at a faster pace which has in turn compelled the library and information professionals to redesign and revamp the existing services by dismantling their conventional practices. Geller (2006) observes that the e-resources, at the selection stage, must meet a set criteria in addition to those we set up for print, and while it is still in the selection stage, this decision involves expertise and input from library staff members beyond the subject selector group. The need was felt that in depth on e-resources collection development and their current practices with particular reference to University Libraries in Delhi.

1.2 *Objectives of the Study*

The aim of the study is review of the recent developments related to current practices of e-resources and collection development policy in university libraries in Delhi. The specific objectives of the study are to:

- Find out the availability of different types of e-resources in University libraries in Delhi;
- Know the reasons for acquiring/subscribing e-resources;
- Study the different modes of procurement and acquisition of e-resources;
- Find out the current policies and practices followed for acquiring e-resources;
- Examine the different criteria for the selection of e-resources and collection development policy; and
- Identify problems associated with the e-resources and collection development in libraries under study.

2. Review of Literature

Much of the literature in this area is devoted to the use and impact of e-resources specifically in academic libraries, as well as the selection, acquisition, issues, and access of e-resources in general. Very little is found devoted to current practices and criteria related to online databases. The works of Kovacs and Robinson's (2004) and Gregory's (2006) are basically introductory books to e-resources collection development. The processes and criteria they provide could be applied to many a type of e-resources. Pilgrim and Dolabaille (2011) discussed about the provision and management of e-resources in academic libraries in developing countries and future plans for successful development of an increased e-resources. Noh (2010) proposed an improved evaluation mechanism specifically for e-resources in university libraries. Deng (2010) explored the pattern and trend of accessing e-resources in university libraries in Australia.

Some of the recent studies discussed very specific aspects, such as current and potential e-book use in research and instruction (2009–10); improve the current state of e-resources evaluation (2009–10), collections and collection-development policy (2007–10); major issues connected to the collection management in academic libraries (2010); changing trends in management of e-resources (2006–09).

3. Methodology

The Survey Method followed for this study with the help of structured questionnaire was designed keeping in view of the stated objectives and scope of the study comprising of dichotomous, multiple choice, rating, and opinion questions. However, a few open-ended questions were also included in order to gather qualitative data relating to the subject. Total 14 questions were included in the questionnaire under three major sections.

3.1 *Scope of the Study*

The present study is confined to all the eight university libraries in Delhi (both Central and State universities) namely: University of Delhi (UoD), Indira Gandhi National Open University (IGNOU), Jawahar Lal Nehru University (JNU), Jamia Millia Islamia (JMI), Ambedkar University (AU), Guru Gobind Singh Indraprastha University (GGSIPU), Delhi Technological University (DTU), and Jamia Hamdard (JH).

4. Analysis of Data

A survey was conducted through a structured questionnaire circulated personally among the eight university librarians in Delhi. All filled-in questionnaires were collected personally so the response rate is 100%.

The primary data was collected through structured questionnaire and the secondary data collected from the libraries covered in the study through library records, annual reports, plans, and other relevant documents/sources. On the basis of the responses received through questionnaires on various aspects of e-resources collection development and current practices, data is analyzed and interpreted in the following sections.

4.1 *Participating Libraries*

In India, the development of higher education is closely associated with the steady growth and development of the library in the institution of higher learning. A university library is a service component of its parent body. University library is the main channel of bringing information to cater the information requirements of the users. The overall functions of a university library include building up a comprehensive collection of academic and research literature, to organize and provide access to the information sources with the help of a variety of tools, and retrieve academic knowledge through multifarious information services. The participating university libraries were established between 1920 and 2008. The most recently established one is four years old (Ambedkar University) while the oldest one (Jamia Millia Islamia) is 92 years old. This information helps in determination of the collection development of the respective library and their practices since their inception.

4.2 *Availability of E-resources*

This is the most important and basic aspect related to e-resources collection development, the quality has replaced the quantity of library collection during the present days. The quality has direct link with the type of library collection as it depends upon the requirement of the users. University libraries need to procure a variety of documents not only in different subjects but also in types. Furthermore, the information explosion bringing in different types of information storage media calls for acquisition of information in various forms of documents. The data reveals that the libraries are also adding electronic media apart from print media. The e-resources include e-books, e-journals, databases, e-theses/dissertations, and CD/DVDs etc. Table 1 presents the availability of e-resources in libraries covered in the study.

Table 1: Availability of E-resources in Libraries Covered in the Study

Sl. No.	*E-resource Type*	*AU**	*DTU*	*GGSIPU*	*IGNOU*	*JH*	*JMI*	*JNU*	*UoD*
1.	Electronic books	✓	✓	✓	✓	✓	NA	✓	✓
2.	Electronic journals	NA	✓	✓	✓	✓	✓	✓	✓
3.	Databases	✓	✓	✓	✓	✓	✓	✓	✓
4.	Electronic theses/dissertations	NA	✓	✓	✓	NA	✓	NA	✓
5.	CD/DVDs	NA	NA	✓	✓	NA	✓	✓	✓

Note: NA = Not Available; *AU - Ambedkar University; DTU- Delhi Technological University; GGSIPU - Guru Gobind Singh Indraprastha University; IGNOU- Indira Gandhi National Open University; JH - Jamia Hamdard; JNU - Jawahar Lal Nehru University; and UoD - University of Delhi.

Table 1 reveals that databases are the most common e-resources possessed by all libraries covered in the study, followed by e-books and e-journals, e-theses/dissertations, and CD/DVDs. Surprisingly, AU library does not have many types of e-resources, whereas, GGSIPU and IGNOU libraries are having highest collection of e-resources. This data clearly indicates that the libraries covered in the study are having good collection of e-resources to cater the information needs of their information age users.

4.3 *Acquisition of E-resources*

Regular and continuous addition of e-resources by the university libraries help the users in accessing up-to-date information, thereby improving academic and research standards in the university. All libraries covered in the study have experienced a tremendous shift in e-content and deluged daily by offering e-resources in a myriad of forms (Table 2). It reveals that the UoD has the highest number of e-journals followed by central libraries of the JMI, JNU, GGSIPU, DTU, and IGNOU. The AU library being a recent origin has no e-journals. Thus, UoD, AU, IGNOU and JMI libraries have larger collections of databases, JNU, DTU and JH libraries have medium size collection and the GGSIPU library has small size of databases collection. Almost all libraries covered in the study, except JMI, possess fairly good collection of e-books. DTU has very good collection of e-books (15,523), whereas JH library has very small collection of e-books. The total databases held by libraries covered in the study are 415. Even the collection of Electronic Theses and Dissertations (ETDs) (except JNU, JH and AU) is moderate in most of the libraries covered in the study. It is surprisingly to note that in almost all libraries covered in the study are having CD/DVDs. The IGNOU library possesses more CD/DVDs (3,948), followed by JNU library with 3700. On the whole, the e-resources are moderate in number in all the libraries. Among the e-resources, e-journals account for 54.5%, followed by e-books with 32.3% and databases, ETDs and CD/DVDs account for 13.2%.

Table 2: E-Resources Collection in Study University Libraries

University Libraries	*Type of E-resources*				
	E-books	*E-journals*	*Databases*	*ETDs*	*CD/DVDs*
UoD*	11,284	43,209	84	5,805	2,000
JNU	2,409	14,500	47	NA	3,700
GGSIPU	13,963	9,000	03	22	2,399
JMI	NA	5,487	74	271	30
DTU	15,523	1,209	25	704	NA
IGNOU	555	4,539	77	1,403	3,948
JH	60	7,762	25	NA	NA
AU	7,000	NA	80	NA	NA

4.4 *Different Sources of Finance*

Finance is the crucial and vital factor that influences heavily and contributes much for the progress of any institution. Thus, finance is very essential element wherein the authorities and all concerned should take up necessary measures to provide stable, sound, and adequate financial support to meet the objectives of any given institution. It is often said that, universities exist for generations, dissemination and preservation of knowledge in the library are essential. To sustain, maintain and further flourish, library needs adequate finance.

The primary source of income of the universities is funding from the state/central government, UGC, and raising money by the universities themselves by way of fee and other charges. However, some universities receive donations from philanthropists and other agencies. The UGC provides grants to the university libraries under five year plan programme for purchase of e-resources for the plan period under certain conditions. It has also introduced special schemes to provide financial assistance for e-resources and for equipping libraries with necessary equipment and infrastructure to provide needed services to the academic community. The state/central government under the block grant releases funds to the university to meet expenditure on different heads of which the library is one. As the amount received both from the UGC and state/central government is inadequate, universities also contribute for the library from their own resources. Table 3 presents the different sources of finance of the libraries covered in the study.

Table 3: Different Sources of Finance

Sl. No.	*Sources of Finances*	*AU**	*DTU*	*GGSIPU*	*IGNOU*	*JH*	*JMI*	*JNU*	*UoD*
1.	UGC grants	✓	✓	✓		✓	✓	✓	✓
2.	University grants			✓	✓	✓	✓	✓	✓
3.	UGC special grants								✓
4.	Membership fee	✓	✓	✓	✓	✓	✓	✓	✓
5.	Library late fee	✓	✓	✓	✓	✓	✓	✓	✓
6.	Marketing of library products/services								
7.	Any other		✓						

Table 3 shows that all universities, except IGNOU are receiving grants from UGC. While, AU and DTU established in the year 2007 respectively and started receiving funds from the UGC recently and hence the percentage of university's assistance is very less. Furthermore, DTU library received financial assistance from the All India Council for Technical Education (AICTE) as special grant. No library is able to generate income from the marketing of library products and services.

It may be noted here that the amount received in the form of membership fee, late fee etc. goes to university account and the contribution made by the university/state government includes this amount. It is a well established fact that, the financial position of the university libraries is not so good. Many libraries are unable to carry out their objectives and goals like providing necessary e-resources highly needed for the improvement of the library services due to the financial crunch.

4.5 *Selection of E-resources*

Selection of e-resources is very important step in collection development process. If the right source is selected, the usage of such source will certainly be high. Librarian necessarily need not be the specialist in choosing the e-resources, but he has different selection tools to assist in selection process of e-resources. Several studies have shown that the users are the best judges in selecting the e-resources and as such, e-resources acquired on the basis of users' recommendations largely meet their requirements and also rate of their usage is more. In contrast, the Heads of the Departments recommend and select the e-resources for purchase in many universities in India. Table 4 presents the selection of e-resources in libraries covered in the study.

Table 4: Selection of E-resources

Sl. No.	*Responsibility*	*AU**	*DTU*	*GGSIPU*	*IGNOU*	*JH*	*JMI*	*JNU*	*UoD*
1.	Librarian		✓	✓		✓	✓	✓	✓
2.	Library Committee	✓	✓	✓	✓	✓		✓	
3.	Head of the Dept.		✓	✓				✓	✓
4.	Users		✓	✓				✓	✓
5.	E-resources Committee								✓

The table 4 shows that the selection of e-resources is primarily made by the Librarian and Library Committee in six universities. Surprisingly, Users and Heads of the Departments are given second preference in selection of e-resources in DTU, GGSIPU, JNU and UoD. In contrast, E-resources Committee gets subsequent positions in the process of selecting and recommending e-resources.

4.6 *Criteria for Selection of E-resources*

Many librarians believe that e-resources have changed the principles of selection radically; some believe that they will virtually eliminate selection. But, the selection of e-resources is still crucial for libraries. The four basic criteria for selection viz. quality, library relevancy, technical aspects, and cost remain the same in the electronic era of information. What they mean and how they are used has changed? But even quality and cost, the two most important criteria, carry great value for the responsible selection of e-resources.

The library aims to acquire information resources in support of teaching, learning and research. E-resources are selected on the basis of their subject content, courses, and ongoing research. The library will give priority to acquiring materials in e-format where this gives return on investment, enhanced service quality for users in terms of access and use of the material; value for money for the subject; and appropriate assurances of long-term access to the content. Where the principles set out above cannot be met through the acquisition of materials in e-format alone, a copy in print format will be acquired. Table 5 presents fourteen criteria for selection of e-resources in libraries covered in the study.

Table 5: Criteria for Selection of E-resources

Sl. No.	*Criterion*	*AU*[*]	*DTU*	*GGSIPU*	*IGNOU*	*JH*	*JMI*	*JNU*	*UoD*
1.	Quality	✓	✓	✓	✓	✓	✓	✓	✓
2.	Subject matter	✓	✓	✓	✓	✓	✓	✓	✓
3.	Currency and authority	✓		✓	✓				✓
4.	Uniqueness of content			✓	✓			✓	✓
5.	Geographic parameters								✓
6.	Relevance of material	✓	✓	✓	✓	✓	✓	✓	✓
7.	Cost	✓	✓	✓	✓		✓	✓	✓
8.	Network capability		✓	✓	✓	✓		✓	✓
9.	User friendly	✓	✓	✓	✓			✓	✓
10.	Strength of retrieval		✓	✓	✓			✓	✓
11.	Hardware compatibility	✓		✓	✓				
12.	Software compatibility	✓		✓	✓	✓			
13.	Service implications		✓	✓	✓				✓
14.	Remote accessibility				✓				

Table 5 reveals that the quality of a resource's content is a priority factor determining the decision making about subscription. The quality of digital content and that of printed content is determined according to a number of parameters, among which are the authoritativeness of a resource, its value, completeness, exactness, clearness, currency, uniqueness, and corresponding to academic standards. All the libraries covered in the study are maintaining the quality criteria for selection of e-materials.

E-resource must support the curricular and research needs of the university. There should be a target audience and an expected level of use. The resource will add depth or breadth to the existing collection. Collectively, a balance should be sought among the various disciplines and intellectual levels (post-graduate, research scholars and faculty) to meet the different needs. The currency and timeliness of the information is one of the important features of e-resources and 50% of libraries covered in the study are using the currency as the most important criteria in selection of e-resources. Content is the king of the e-resource and has a major influence in determining the search visibility of a particular e-resource. The content determines the utility of the e-resource and hence, the content of e-resource needs be unique, and relevant. Only 50% of libraries covered in the study are using this criterion.

It is interesting to note that UoD library has geographic parameter and IGNOU is using remote accessibility among libraries covered in the study for selection of e-resources. The criterion of the cost of a resource is the last in the list but by no means the last in practice. Price formation in the e-information market is rather flexible. Unlike printed journals which have a basic cost with a possible rebate, e-resources can change in price depending on the level of access to their content, the presence of additional options, the status of the selling organization, quantity of potential users, country, etc. The price can be changed as a result of negotiations or divided into several parts. At this point, it is necessary to remember once more the role of consortia. The level of membership in an organization helps to considerably decrease the expenditures for e-information. The majority of (87.5%) of libraries covered in the study are using this criterion.

Value addition factors of e-resources increase their utility and worth. These include the possibility of creating virtual interconnections, hyperlinks between different documents, article's bibliography equipped with hyperlinks; the possibility of combining several searches through a common interface; the possibility of creating a user's profile facilitating storage of sources, texts, searches (alerts), etc. Three-fourths of the libraries covered in the study are using network capability and user friendliness criteria. The conditions of access are the next important factor determining the efficiency of using a resource in an organization. At this point, two factors are taken into account: the limitations connected with copyright law (this is relevant to copying, transmission, and storage of electronic documents) and the method for identifying authorized users.

4.7 *Collection Development Policy*

The collection development policy provides general guidelines for allocating funds fairly and formulating objective selection criteria. The main purpose of the collection development policy is to establish guidelines for the planned development of e-resources to meet the academic and research information needs of the students and faculty at the university. From the mission statement of the university library, it is important to provide users with information and access to information in support of scholarly activity, research, student learning, teaching excellence and curricular development.

Primary users of the university library are the postgraduates, research scholars, faculty and staff. Its collection should serve instructional, curricular and research needs of all its primary users, including those with disabilities. At the same time, the ever growing production of books, periodicals, audio-visual material and e-resources, rising costs and a limited budget demand a prudent selection policy with the need to cooperative resource sharing. In this context, a question was asked regarding considerations under e-collection development policy and responses are presented in Table 6.

Table 6: Various Considerations under Collection Development Policy

Sl. No.	*Consideration*	*AU**	*DTU*	*GGSIPU*	*IGNOU*	*JH*	*JMI*	*JNU*	*UoD*
1.	Language to include	✓	✓		✓	✓	✓	✓	✓
2.	Language to exclude								
3.	Chronological limits	✓	✓	✓	✓		✓	✓	
4.	Geographical limits			✓	✓	✓		✓	✓
5.	Physical format	✓	✓	✓				✓	✓
6.	Physical condition	✓	✓	✓				✓	
7.	Whether translated or original language		✓	✓	✓	✓		✓	✓
8.	Whether work is in one format	✓	✓						

Table 6 reveals that the language is the top most consideration to be included in collection development policy with 87.5%, followed by chronological limits and whether translated or original language (75%), geographical limits and physical format of materials (62.5% each), physical condition of materials (50%), and whether work is in one format (25%); none of the libraries covered in the study consider excluding language in collection development policy.

4.8 *Modes of Procurement of E-resources*

There are different modes of procurement of e-resources based on the type and place of publication. The libraries may use simultaneously more than one mode of procuring e-resources. The data regarding mode of procurement adopted by the study university libraries is given in Table 7. It reveals that procurement of e-resources with the help of users' recommendations is followed by all libraries followed by using published catalogue (87.5%), through publishers websites (75%), and through aggregators/agents (62.5%).

Table 7: Mode of Procurement of E-resources

Sl. No.	*Acquisition Criteria*	*AU**	*DTU*	*GGSIPU*	*IGNOU*	*JH*	*JMI*	*JNU*	*UoD*
1.	Through published catalogue	✓		✓	✓	✓	✓	✓	✓
2.	Users recommendations	✓	✓	✓	✓	✓	✓	✓	✓
3.	Through publishers websites		✓	✓	✓		✓	✓	✓
4.	Through aggregators/agents		✓		✓		✓	✓	✓

4.9 *Modes of Acquiring of E-resources*

Mode of acquisition is an important part in collection development of e-resources. Subscription of e-journals and databases, especially foreign e-journals, involve more risk factors compared to Indian e-journals. Different libraries follow different modes of subscription to e-journals. Information from eight libraries covered in the study was sought on mode for acquisition of e-resources. Table 8 reveals that acquisition of e-resources through agent/vendor is the most popular followed by direct subscription and through consortia (87.5% each), open access (62.5%) and institutional repositories. Only one library acquires through exchange mode.

It is clear from Table 8 that foreign e-resources are being subscribed through Indian agents and Indian journals are being subscribed directly from the respective publishers. As e-journal subscription requires advance payment, the libraries covered in the study prefer agents who make payments first to the publishers on behalf of the libraries and claim the subscription amount from the libraries with a proof of payment. By doing so, the librarians are of the opinion that it is assured that the amount is reached to publishers enabling proper supply of journals; also they can fix the responsibility on agents from any transit loss ensuring regular and continuous supply of the journal issues.

Table 8: Modes of Acquiring of E-resources

Sl. No.	*Modes*	*AU*	*DTU*	*GGSIPU*	*IGNOU*	*JH*	*JMI*	*JNU*	*UoD*
1.	Through direct subscription	✓	✓	✓	✓		✓	✓	✓
2.	Through consortia based	✓	✓	✓	✓		✓	✓	✓
3.	Through agent/vendor	✓	✓	✓	✓	✓	✓	✓	✓
4.	Through exchange							✓	
5.	Free with printed subscription						✓	✓	✓
6.	Open access	✓	✓	✓	✓			✓	✓
7.	Institutional repositories		✓	✓				✓	✓

4.10 *Promotion of E-resources*

There are many ways to promote e-resources among the users as well as faculty members of the study university libraries so that users can aware about the e-resources and their features. Table 9 depicts the different steps of promotion of e-resources. It is evident from Table 9 that promotion of e-resources by providing links from library home page is followed by all libraries followed by conducting of information literacy programs (87.5%), e-mail/internal mailing lists (75%), and seminars and workshops (62.5%). Guides and tutorials and also posters account for 50% each.

Table 9: Promotion of E-resources

Sl. No.	*Steps of Use Promotion*	*AU**	*DTU*	*GGSIPU*	*IGNOU*	*JH*	*JMI*	*JNU*	*UoD*
1.	Links from library home page	✓	✓	✓	✓	✓	✓	✓	✓
2.	Information literacy programs	✓	✓	✓		✓	✓	✓	✓
3.	E-mail/internal mailing lists	✓	✓	✓	✓	✓			✓
4.	Guides and tutorials		✓	✓				✓	✓
5.	Seminars and workshops		✓	✓	✓			✓	✓
6.	Posters			✓		✓		✓	✓

4.11 *Problems in Development of E-Resources*

The demand for e-journals among the academic and research community has increased over the years. Due to decreasing budgets, libraries are forced to cancel subscriptions to important journals. The loss of journal subscriptions hampers access to scholarly research in Indian universities and limits researchers in global research opportunities. Table 10 presents the various problems associated with setting-up of e-resources in libraries covered in the study. It is observed data from Table 10 that the trained staff is the top most problem associated with setting-up of e-resources, followed by budget and networks, Internet bandwidth, infrastructure and problems with library websites.

Table 10: Problems in Setting-up of E-resources

Sl. No.	*Problem*	*AU**	*DTU*	*GGSIPU*	*IGNOU*	*JH*	*JMI*	*JNU*	*UoD*
1.	Budget		✓			✓	✓	✓	
2.	Infrastructure			✓				✓	
3.	Trained staff	✓	✓			✓	✓	✓	✓
4.	Networks		✓	✓				✓	✓
5.	Library websites							✓	
6.	Internet bandwidth		✓		✓			✓	

4.12 *Library Consortium*

Consortia-based approach has emerged as the hallmark of libraries to harness e-resources effectively. The shared subscription or consortia-based subscription to e-resources through the consortium of libraries permits successful deployment and desktop access to e-resources at highly discounted rates of subscription; it meets with the increasing pressures of diminishing budgets, increased user's demand and rising cost of journals.

The library consortia, on the basis of sheer strength of the number of institutions, offer healthy business growth opportunities to the electronic publishers and thus attract the best possible price and terms of agreements. With this, the libraries all over the world are forming consortia of all types and levels with an objective to take advantage of current global network to promote better, faster and more cost-effective ways of providing e-information resources to the information seekers. Table 11 reveals that majority of libraries covered in the study are members of the UGC-Infonet Digital Library Consortium and INDEST. Libraries have increasingly moved towards consortia as a way of brokering better prices and rendering rapid and efficient services to information seekers. However, library consortia is facing new challenges such as increasing expectations and a static budget, fair use, archiving of information, pricing strategies, measures of effectiveness and licensing e-resources.

Table 11: Membership in Library Consortia

Sl. No.	*University*	*Consortium*	*E-resources Accessible*
1.	AU*	NA	J-STOR e-journals
2.	DTU	INDEST	ASCE, ASME, Springer Link, Emerald, Science Direct
3.	GGSIPU	INDEST	IEL, ACM
		UGC- Infonet	ACS, APS, CUP, ISID, JCCC, JSTOR, Springer Link
4.	IGNOU	INDEST	5 Databases
		UGC-Infonet	6 Databases
5.	JH	UGC-Infonet	ACS, JCCC, CUP, Elsevier, JSTOR etc.
		DELNET#	Available to its members
6.	JMI	UGC-Infonet	ACS, JSTOR, Project Muse
		INDEST	IEL, ASCE, ASME
7.	JNU	UGC-Infonet	22 Databases
		INDEST	2 Databases
8.	UoD	UGC-Infonet	22 Databases
		NLIST^	Web of Science, LISA

*N-LIST—National Library and Information Services Infrastructure for Scholarly Content.

4.13 *Future Plans to Improve E-resources*

Libraries are the direct incentives to the development of educational, social and cultural activities of a nation. They transfer the knowledge and culture from one generation to other. They contribute a lot to the awakening of public in day-to-day life. In the words of Dr SR Ranganathan, libraries are not merely the store houses; they are rich springs from which knowledge flows out to irrigate the field of education and culture. So, libraries are an integral part of the academic mission of a university (2007). An open-ended question was asked the study university librarians about future plans to improve e-resources in their libraries. The responses received are as under:

- Implement a strategic plan for e-resources
- Improve the provision of e-resources (databases, e-journals and e-books)
- Continue the libraries' digitization programme and ensure current and long-term access to all digitized materials
- Expand the web-based online public access catalogues and improve theiraccuracy to facilitate access to all the Libraries' collections
- Promote workshops and information literacy programmes more frequently to enhance users' awareness of rich e-resources.

5. Conclusion

Today the university libraries are reorienting their collections and collection development policies in the light of e-resources. Not only collections are changing but also the role of librarians. The findings of the study revealed that tools and criteria used for selecting e-resources are different from those used for printed materials. It is useful to point out that relevancy of tools and criteria used is somewhat influenced by the typologies of the library. For example, of the fourteen criteria listed for selecting e-resources, the libraries covered in the study accepted four criteria fully and ten criteria partially.

The survey has also revealed that libraries covered in the study in Delhi are lagging behind in strategic planning of e-resources and collection development plan and its implementation. It is hoped that libraries at the universities in Delhi will attend to the lacunae and ultimately develop a set of "best practices" for librarians to effectively manage e-collections. For the good of the community and nation, university libraries in Delhi have to strive hard to improve accessibility and diversity in the digital age. They can do it provided they possess affordable technology, the power to negotiate through a cartel, and unwavering support from the authorities. Otherwise, they are liable to fall by the wayside, as traditional as they are now.

References

[1] Geller, M. ERM: Staffing, services, and systems. *Lib. Tech. Reports,* 2006, 42(2), 14–21.

[2] Kovacs, D.K. and Robinson, K.L. The Kovacs guide to electronic library collection development: essential core subject collections, selection criteria, and guidelines, ED. 2. New York, Neal-Schuman, 2004.

[3] Gregory, V. L. Selecting and managing electronic resources: a how-to-do-it manual for librarians. New York, Neal-Schuman, 2006.

[4] Pilgrim, M. and Dolabaille, A. Our journey from print to electronic resources: An acquisitions perspective at a Caribbean academic library. *Serials Librarian,* 2011, 61(1), 90–104.

[5] Noh, Y. A study on developing evaluation criteria for electronic resources in evaluation indicators of libraries. *Journal of Academic Librarianship,* 2010, 36(1), 41–52.

[6] Deng, H. Emerging patterns and trends in utilizing electronic resources in a higher education environment: An empirical analysis. *New Lib. World,* 2010, 111 (3–4), 87–103.

[7] Bierman, J., Lina, O. and Karen, R.S. E-book usage in pure and applied sciences. *Sci. and Tech. Libraries,* 2010, 29(1–2), 69–91.

[8] Cox, J. Developing model licenses for electronic resources: cooperation in a competitive world. *Lib. Consor. Manage: An Inter. J.,* 2009, 2(1), 8–17.

[9] Handman, G. License to look: evolving models for library video acquisition and access. *Lib. Trends,* 2010, 58(3), 324–34.

[10] Hanson, M. and Terese, H. Making the right choices: Pay-per-view use data and selection decisions. *Col. and Res. Lib. News,* 2010, 71(11), 586–8.

[11] Korah, A. *et al.* Off the shelf: trends in the purchase and use of electronic reference books. *J. Elect. Reso. Librarianship,* 2009, 21(3–4), 263–78.

[12] Flatley, R.K. and Prock, K. E-resources collection development: a survey of current practices in academic libraries. *Lib. Phil. and Prac.,* 2009, 11(2), 1–4.

[13] Lamothe, A.R. Electronic book usage patterns as observed at an academic library: searches and viewings. *Partnership: Can. J. Lib. and Inform. Pract. and Res.,* 2010, 5(1), 15.

[14] Wiersma, G. Collection assessment in response to changing curricula: An analysis of the biotechnology resources at the University of Colorado at Boulder. *Issues in Sci. and Tech. Librarianship,* 2010, 61, 61.

[15] Gutierrez, M.C.N. The use of electronic resources in the university libraries of the scientific area of the Universidad Nacional Autonoma De Mejico. *Ibersid: Revista de sistemas de inform. Doc.,* 2007, 117–22.

[16] Henry, E. *et al.* Collection analysis outcomes in an academic library. *Collection Building,* 2008, 27(3), 113–17.

[17] Khan, A. M. Managing collection development and organization in globalizing Indian university libraries. *Collection Building,* 2010, 2(1), 15–21.

[18] Morrisey, L. Data-driven decision making in electronic collection development. *J. Lib. Admn.,* 2010, 50(3), 283–90.

[19] Horava, T. Challenges and possibilities for collection management in a digital age. *Lib. Reso. and Techn. Ser.,* 2010, 54(3), 142–52.

[20] Kichuk, D. Electronic collection growth: An academic library case study. *Coll. Building,* 2010, 29(2), 55–64.

[21] Ciszek, M.P. and Courtney, L.Y. Diversity collection assessment in large academic libraries. *Coll. Building,* 2010, 29(4), 154–61.

[22] Sharma, C. Use and impact of e-resources at Guru Gobind Singh Indraprastha University (India): A case study. *Ele. J. Aca. and Spl. Librarianship,* 2009, 10(1).

[23] Di Mattia, S.S. Getting the money you need: relationships and fundraising. *Online,* 2008, 32(1), 22–6.

[24] Kusik, J. P. and Vargas, M. A. Improving electronic resources through holistic budgeting. *J. Ele. Res. Librarianship,* 2009, 2(3–4), 200–205.

[25] Price, A.C. How to make a dollar out of fifteen cents: tips for electronic collection development. *Coll. Building,* 2009, 28(1), 31–4.

[26] Shuling, W. Investigation and analysis of current use of electronic resources in university libraries. *Lib. Manage.,* 2006, 28(1), 72–88.

[27] Gowda, V. and Shivalingaiah, D. E-resources of information: A study of attitudes of research scholars. *In* Proceedings of the 5th International CALIBER, Chandigarh, 2007, 652–62.

Section–III

Electronic Publishing and Internet

Electronic Resources Management in Libraries, pp. 105–109

The Growth of E-books

A. Jack Meadows

1. Introduction

Looking backwards in time I remember first getting involved with e-journals in the 1980s. My first involvement with e-books came a decade later. When I ask myself the question-why this difference in time? Then the importance of prior expectations and custom becomes apparent. E-journals were particularly acceptable in STM (science, technology and medicine) subjects. People in these fields were often well-acquainted with computers, and with handling short pieces of text on them. Abstracts in these fields provided some of the earliest electronic text databases. The STM journal articles were fairly short and could be scanned on a computer screen without too much discomfort. E-books were of greater interest in the humanities, or to general readers, than to STM readers. Such readers expected books to be portable and properly legible. Portable reading devices were worked on during the 1980s, but it was only in the latter part of the 1990s that viable personal digital assistants (PDAs) became available (Wilson). These satisfied the portability requirement. The second requirement—legibility—also received attention. This meant satisfying the expectations derived from printed books. Readers typically expected to read black print on a white background, on a device that was no smaller than a standard paperback, and under all light conditions. Developments in both portability and presentation over the past few years have been sufficient to make e-book reading nowadays a generally acceptable substitute for reading the printed page.

2. Portable Devices

The problem with the word 'e-book' is that it is used in two senses: it can refer either to the material being read, or to the device on which it is read. I will look at the second connotation first. One of the continuing debates since the early days of the e-book has been whether what is required is a dedicated device, or a multi-purpose computer. It has been argued that PDAs with appropriate book-reading software have been improving to such a degree that they can satisfy book readers' needs. The obvious example is the iPad. This provides an iBooks application which several major book publishers have been willing to use. Perhaps more interestingly, both Amazon and Barnes and Noble have provided apps to allow their own systems (Kindle and Nook, respectively) to be used on the iPad. Arguments in favour of a

*Reprinted with permission from *DESIDOC Journal of Library and Information Technology*, 2012, 32(2), 83–86.

multi-purpose device have usually hinged on the belief that owners of hand-held computers will not want to carry around more than one such device. Hence, there will be a convergence of all the activities that interest them onto one gadget. The proliferation in the number of apps now available certainly suggests that there is some foundation for this belief. However, it has been argued in the past, and is still being argued today, that reading a book is a different kind of activity from, for example, playing computer games. This argument depends especially on readers' expectations of books. People have been brought up with printed books and still regularly read them. E-books, it is argued, should stick to this expected model, and this may lead to a device that is not optimised for other apps. It may be, however, that people's reading expectations will develop in the future so that convergence on a single hand-held device becomes acceptable. For the moment, providers of book-length material have to accept that it will be downloaded to a range of different devices.

A major problem raised by this variety continues to be that of compatibility. Whenever a new type of device appears this question raises its head. The usual assumption is that competition in the marketplace will soon produce a market leader which becomes the de facto standard. The often quoted example is the history of videocassette recorders (VCR) in the latter part of the twentieth century. After a number of years of competition, one format-VHS-became the market standard. However, competition does not always work this way. An example is the long-continued competition between Apple computers, with their own operating system, and windows-based computers. Part of the reason in this case for the continuance of both was that they had somewhat different capabilities. I can remember stocking teaching laboratories with computers when it became necessary to put on electronic publishing courses. To reflect what was happening in the publishing industry, it was necessary to provide two laboratories-one with Apple computers and the other with windows-based computers. This was because graphics-handlers in publishing preferred the former, while text-handlers preferred the latter. There is an important difference between this example and the VCR conflict, for the latter involved incompatible hardware. Nowadays, incompatibilities are more likely to be a software problem, and can usually be resolved by some kind of software fix on the original hardware. This makes it possible for different systems to coexist, though most people would agree that a universal standard is a better solution.

3. Content

Turning now to e-books in terms of their contents, material to be read electronically was available well before portable devices for reading it. Project Gutenberg, for example, was already providing book-length content in the 1970s. The growth in the number of books that the project archived electronically was, however, fairly limited until the early years of the present century. (When Project Gutenberg began, getting the text into machine-readable form was a fairly tedious process; this difficulty had eased by the latter years of the twentieth century). Over the past ten years, the number of books stored by the Project has soared to nearly 40,000 titles. During this period, other sites have appeared and grown. One that I find useful, for example, is the Internet Archive, which currently has well over two million users each day. One development in recent years has been the way the resources available have become multilingual. Project Gutenberg, for example, was essentially a source of English-language texts until the early years of the present century, when it became explicitly multilingual. The common characteristic of these free databases is that they are restricted to material that is either out of copyright, or has explicitly been licensed for use (Lebert).

Discussions of making the contents of printed books widely available, have been dominated by the question of copyright from the early days. The long-continued saga of Google Books in the United States reflects the difficulty of the problem. One of the big questions has been what to do with so-called ‘orphan’ publications. Many books are still in copyright but are out of print. Where the copyright is owned by an existing publisher it is straightforward enough to negotiate. But the copyright in many works resides with the author. (This contrasts with the typical position for journal articles, where there are correspondingly fewer difficulties with ‘orphan’ works). Tracking down each individual-sometimes even establishing whether they are still alive is a time-consuming process. But attempts to evade doing this soon run into legal problems: as happened with Google books (en.wikipedia.org/wiki/Google_Books). Even if negotiations with publishers over content go ahead, there are other pitfalls. For example, e-book platforms increasingly include a text-to-speech mechanism. From the viewpoint of the e-book provider this is part of an integrated package. However, publishers have traditionally seen audio editions as being distinct from the printed version, and expect to negotiate for them separately.

An equally difficult question is the pricing of e-book contents. Publishers receive manuscripts in electronic form from their authors, edit them in that form in-house, and then transmit them to the printers for paper-based production. For e-books, this last step is omitted, so one would expect the e-book version to be considerably cheaper than the printed version. This is often not reflected in the price. For example, Amazon has found publishers unwilling for major cuts to be made in the price of e-book material (one of the publishers’ arguments is that they cannot allow the printed version to be undercut by too much). In consequence, if the print version of a monograph on Amazon costs about £30, the electronic version is likely to be priced at only a bit less than £25. Even for popular fiction, the printed paperback version may cost £5 and the electronic version £4. It may be that publishers are correct in financial terms. The results so far from Springer e-books, for example, suggest that the print and electronic versions of their monographs are managing to coexist in terms of numbers of purchasers.

The situation for books has always been appreciably different from journals. Authors of journal articles are not paid for publication: indeed, they may have to pay for the privilege. So they are usually happy to see their work reproduced as widely as possible free of charge. Authors of books may receive royalties for their work, and they are often more hesitant about providing free access. This is less true of research monographs, where the likelihood of significant royalties is small. Moreover, authors in this field worry about the prices publishers are asking for their work. Research monographs costing £60 are not uncommon, and publishing runs are rarely more than a few hundreds. So academic authors naturally worry more about the restricted access to their work that is all this implies. One way round the problem is self-publishing. For example, using an on-demand publisher, such as Lulu in the United States, a monograph could be produced for £20 or less, while still including a royalty to the author. The problem with self-publishing lies, of course, in assessing the quality of the publication, since this typically relies on the author's own judgment. The problem is rather less important for books than for journal articles, since the value of books has traditionally been established via reviews after publication. Nevertheless, most authors of monographs like to be published by a body that is seen as having a good reputation for quality. One result is a current growing interest in institutional publishing. Most universities are now accustomed to handle online archives of journal articles produced by members of staff, often using their library facilities. It is not too big a step from this to including original book-length material in such archives. In fact, open access monograph publishing in the humanities and social sciences is currently on the rise, partly because of institutional collaborations of various kinds (observatory.jiscebooks.org).

4. Summary

The concept of an 'e-book' materialised over forty years ago. For many years, the problem lay in developing a portable device which readers found acceptable for reading text. Over the past decade, this problem has mostly been overcome. The argument has moved on to *whether readers will prefer to use a dedicated or a multifunctional device. Text for reading was already* available when the first portable devices came on the market, and the use of material that is out of copyright has been reasonably straightforward. The problem has been with material still in copyright, where it is necessary to trace the copyright owner and recompense them. Publishers fully recognise the significance of the move to e-books, but are reluctant to pass on the savings which electronic handling can provide. This is providing motivation for authors and their institutions to examine other channels for handling and distributing electronic texts. Considerable research on e-books, their problems and usage, has been done down the years: this now provides a solid background for detailed discussions of the points raised here (observatory.jiscebooks.org).

References

[1] Wilson, R. Evolution of portable electronic books.http://www.ariadne.ac.uk/issue29/wilson/

[2] Lebert, M. A short history of ebooks. http://www.etudesfrancaises.net/dossiers/ebookEN.pdf

[3] http://en.wikipedia.org/wiki/Google_Books

[4] Adema, J., Overview of open access models for e-books in the humanities and social sciences. http://bpnet.eclap.eu

[5] JISC National E-books Observatory Project: 2007–2010. http://observatory.jiscebooks.org

Electronic Resources Management in Libraries, pp. 110–126

Electronic Publishing: Domain of Chemistry

Siriginidi Subba Rao

ABSTRACT

The paper discusses briefly an overview of electronic publishing. An attempt has been made to group the selected electronic resources of domain of chemistry information into portals, patents and dissertations, full-text files (current and backfiles) and e-books, abstracting and indexing services, encyclopedias and handbooks, periodic tables, property databases and specialty databases. It concludes that in delivering electronic information two major developments are gaining momentum as archives from major publishers and preprints from academic circles as alternative methods of accessing research information. Also, scholarly publication of chemistry information in electronic form will continue to grow, adapting to meet changing needs of authors and readers alike.

1. Introduction

Electronic information or e-information products are revolutionizing publishing industry through rapid proliferation of electronic reading material in the marketplace. The growing popularity of the Web, public acceptance of new and improving easy-to-use technologies of e-information is paving way for their spread. The critical success factors for large-scale distributors of electronic texts are: a) finding a business model that works, one that is acceptable to users and generates money; b) reassuring publishers about their intellectual property rights by providing controlled access to texts, without making working environment too slow; c) providing reliable and speedy access; d) providing convenient user interfaces; and e) persuading academics to recommend using a service to students, in academic market. Authors, editors, publishers, librarians, most importantly, readers—all are witnessing a change from paper to electronic media for storage, dissemination and handling of information. The objective of this paper is to discuss briefly electronic publishing or e-publishing and lists various electronic chemistry resources to familiarize the community of chemistry related areas.

2. Overview of E-Publishing

A simple definition of e-publishing is not easy to identify as it covers a range of publications delivered through a variety of mechanisms. In essence, e-publishing is any form of presenting usable information in electronic, digitized or computerized form. The select definitions are listed below:

- An integrated production of documents using digitally stored documents, computerized composition and electronic printing systems (http://www.document management.org.uk/pages/glossary.htm).
- Industry involved with design, production and dissemination of information in electronic form. It includes a wide range of disciplines, such as multimedia, Website design, online services, CD-ROM, etc. (http://www.ite.poly.edu/55case/h4.htm).
- The use of electronic media, computers and telecommunications to deliver information to users in electronic form or from electronic sources (Hawkins *et al.*, 1994).

In rushing towards e-publishing and to achieve a presence on the Web, two major categories have emerged. The first one represents general Web publishing, which is typified by business/organizational web pages that are moving towards becoming an essential component of standard business operation. The second one represents education field, from general sites of universities and other academic institutions to scholarly information, which is offered through academic journals. The indexes from secondary publishers became searchable databases via Dialog in 1970's and on CDROMs in 1980's. When the Web became popular, primary journals began converting to Portable Document Format (PDF) for local printing or markup language formats for enabling users to hot links to other references for further study. Journals are commonly delivered by subscription over the Web; reference, legal and medical books are on CD-ROM or DVD-ROM and are becoming more Web savvy.

E-publishing has three significant advantages over print publications: (i) Access and distribution are faster, allowing quicker publication and feedback from both readers and authors, (ii) Interactive possibilities of e-publications enhance collaboration between individuals and disciplines, and (iii) E-publications offer greater scope for adoption of different publication models, access and easier searching. In this area multimedia capabilities offer most exciting possibilities for e-publications. Despite rosy glow that surrounds stampede towards e-publishing, disadvantages of e-publishing still exist. Electronic forms are not as portable as print. In addition, due to quality concerns, electronic formats are less acceptable in academic circles. And as technology available to Web developers for multimedia increases, so must the users' technical requirements.

3. Transitions of Publishing Industry

A brief overview of the transitions through which the publishing industry is passing is explained below (Clark, 1997).

3.1 *Conventional Publishing 1450–1995*

A very substantial industry emerged from the innovations of Gutenberg and Caxton. It evidences many of the hallmarks of the industrial age. It has naturally resisted, and then sought to accommodate, the various forms of Information Technology (IT).

Fig. 1: Desktop Publishing 1985–2000

During the mid-1980s, it became feasible to prepare quite sophisticated layouts, using a PC of the kinds affordable by small businesses and by individuals. This substantially increased the speed of production, enabled higher quality presentation, and began to undermine the justification of large publishing houses' dominance of the publishing process.

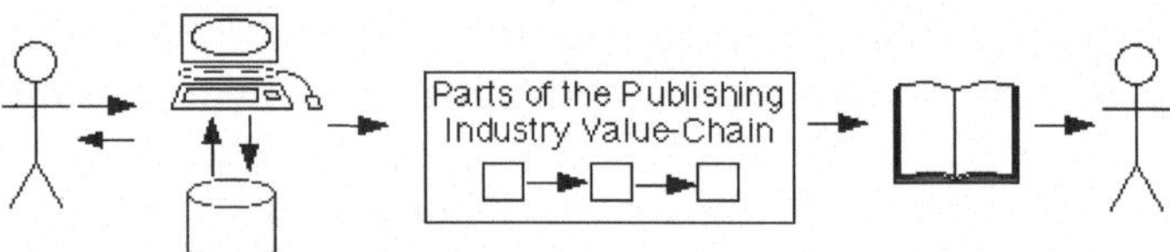

Fig. 2: Electronic Publishing 1990–2000

Desktop publishing essentially electronised aspects of the production process for conventionally printed materials. During the early-to-mid-1990s, it became increasingly feasible to publish materials using electronic media. CD-ROMs were an early mover, but various forms of Internet-reticulated soft-copy emerged, and the explosion of the World Wide Web, commencing in 1993, quickly settled the argument about the medium of choice.

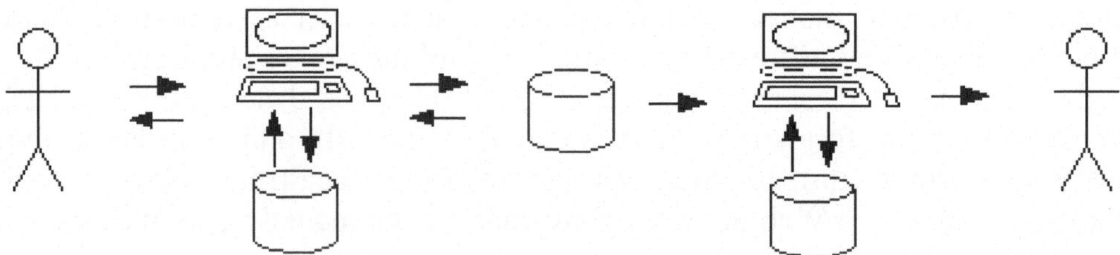

Fig. 3: Cross-Media Publishing 1998–2000

During the latter part of the 1990s, maturation has been taking place at both ends of the production chain. At the content-originator's end, there is a drift away from specialized software in which electronic publications are prepared, as mainstream 'word processing' packages are migrated towards 'document processing' tools. Meanwhile, the infrastructure is being developed to enable storage in one, master-format (XML), with delivery to the consumer in any of multiple formats (HTML, Word, PDF, Postscript, XML).

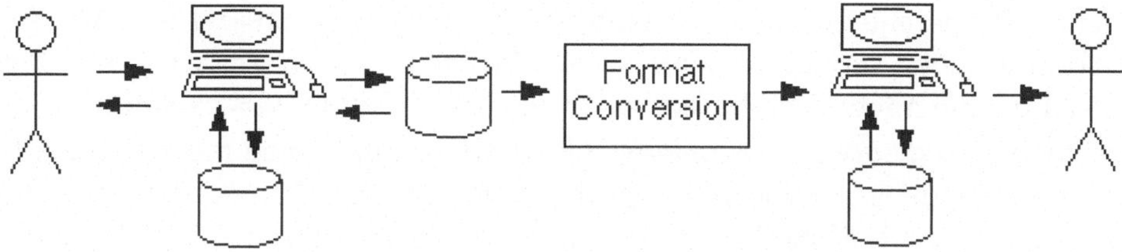

Fig. 4: Interactive Publishing 2000–2100

The conventional models described above provide a valuable basis for analysis. But they represent recent and current conventionalism, and miss the revolutionary impacts of the channels and media on which electronic publishing is built. Each model described so far has involved a production-line or industry value-chain, with a series of providers passing materials to an ultimate consumer of content. Publishing has assumed a mass medium, broadcast, and one-way.

Technologies that are already available embody the capability for recipients to interact with the content, variously by changing it in place, or by spawning new versions of it. The process can therefore become one of re-cycling; of component-based, ongoing re-creation or cumulative creativity; and of intentional collage rather than (nominally) original creation. As a result, the model changes from a sequence to a cluster, 'like bees around a honey pot'. This emergent model has enormous implications, and throws into serious doubt the survival of the term 'publishing' in anything like its contemporary meaning.

4. Types of E-Publications

The broader types of e-publications are discussed below:

- ***Informal Publishing:*** It will be in the form of "frequently asked questions" files that are usually attached to electronic mailing lists and newsgroups. In the traditional print world this sort of information is considered as grey literature, unpublished material that is difficult to identify and even harder to locate. Publication of this material via the Web has made this information widely available but has brought with it a plethora of additional problems relating to issues such as quality and authority of information.
- ***Newspapers and Magazines:*** Many mainstream print newspapers and magazines have established websites to offer a range of electronic services that are intended to mirror and complement to the existing print publications, either in part or in whole. Many popular magazines across the whole gamut of subjects can be located by using a search engine such as Google or AltaVista.
- ***Self-published Magazines or 'Zines:*** Originally best described as small-scale publications frequently with an underground flavour. Producers of 'zines are quick to get them into electronic form and encompass a range of subjects from

science fiction and computer hacking to art, politics and television. Many 'zines perform a public service of some type, while the majority of 'zines are originally text-based and a few Web-based 'zines now offer multimedia capabilities.

- ***Electronic Journals or e-Journals:*** These are scholarly and more frequently peer reviewed journals produced by professional societies or academics. The first electronic journal, Mental Workload was established in the late 1970s and failed to ever publish a single issue, but made a useful contribution in documenting time, effort and procedures required to produce a successful e-journal. The 1990s saw an explosive spread and acceptance of technology that combined the massive advances in computer processing power and increases in affordability, leading to an enormous increase in e-publications on the Web.
- ***Pre-print Archives:*** These provide a previewing service for research information while waiting for print versions to be released. Pre-print archives allow for faster discussion and feedback on content between researchers.
- ***Online Books:*** Full-text e-publications are an important form of e-publishing. Many electronic versions of print materials are being transferred via the Web.

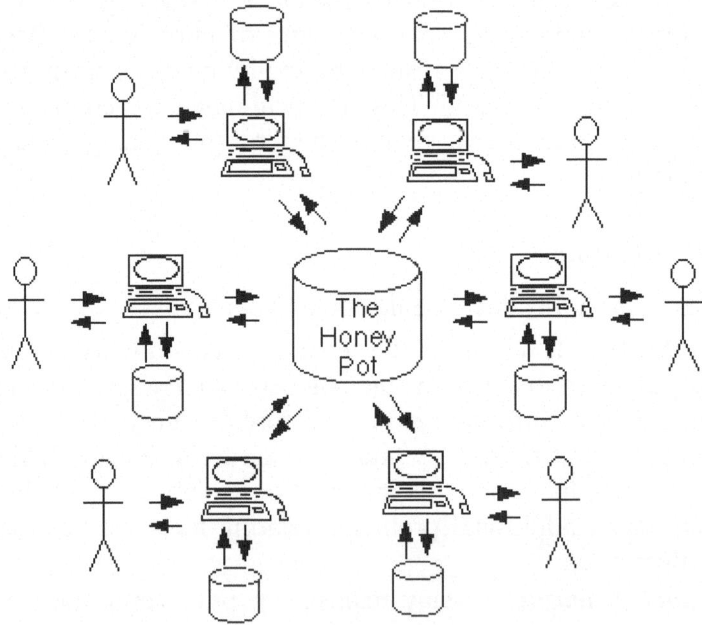

Fig. 5: Honey Pot Model of E-publishing

5. Domain and Chemistry Information

Domain means a particular environment; a walk of life; a distinctive group of people with some shared interest; a knowledge domain that one is interested in or communicating about; a closed area of employment (http://www.cogsci.prince ton.edu/cgi-bin/webwn). Accordingly, Chemistry fits into this. The information needs of chemists are well catered by the Internet and became an instrument to improve accessibility and quality information for chemists. Printed media are able to present only a one-dimensional approach to chemistry information whereas the very nature of which is three-dimensional. Chemists communicate in structures that are difficult to represent in two dimensions and in processes, which are impossible to represent on printed page. The Internet also facilitates making available of sophisticated molecular modeling programs to scientists who do not possess extensive training or expensive graphics equipment, for visualization of molecular surfaces (Drey, 2002). An attempt has been made to group the selected electronic resources of chemistry information into portals (Glander-Hobel, 2002), patents and dissertations, full-text files with back-files and e-books (Town *et al.*, 2002), abstracting and indexing services, encyclopedias and handbooks, periodic tables, property databases and specialty databases.

5.1 *Portals*

The word portal means gateway and for a Website one that is, a major starting site for users when they get connected to the Web or one that users tend to visit as an anchor site that hosts content from multiple Websites. In other words, portal is a framework for a Website that aggregates information from a variety of sources; provide access to an information network and a set of services through the Web. The following select Websites act as a single gateway to access chemistry related information through a variety of resources (publications: full-text journals, archives, patents, abstracting and indexing services, monographs; databases and directories; meetings; careers; etc.) in a seamless way. The idea is to offer everything that the user needs under one roof, so that the user is trapped forever.

ChemCenter (http://www.chemistry.org/portal/a/c/s/1/home.html): It is the portal site of the American Chemical Society (ACS) that includes major Web resources of the Society, ACS Publications and Chemical Abstracts Service (CAS). ACS serves as a host to several sites in a fragmented manner (Warr, 1998). Access to journals: Chemical and Engineering News, Chemist at Work and Modern Drug Discovery require paid membership to ACS.

The ACS hosts the following databases: ACS Web Editions (ACSWEs), ACS Journal Archives (ACSJAs) and Reagent Chemicals.

ChemPort (http://www.chemport.org/html/english/general.html): A linking technology developed by the CAS, offered as a free service to CAS electronic services customers and its publishing partners. ChemPort is also available with CA on CD and CA Selects on the Web. It offers two main services: ChemPort Connection and ChemPort Reference Linking.

ChemSoc (http://www.chemsoc.org/): An electronic network of the Royal Society of Chemistry's (RSC) societies numbering 30. It acts as a portal for RSC journals, books and conferences, and supports teaching of chemistry at all levels. It hosts ChemBytes ezine that comes from Chemistry in Britain.

RSC Web Editions (http://www.rsc.org/): Available from 1997 to present and contain full-text articles to more than 7 publications. The journal articles are available on the Web 4–6 weeks in advance of being published in print. The RSC hosts the ***RSC Journals Archive*** (http://www.rsc.org/is/journals/retrodigitisation.htm).

ChemWeb (http://www.chemweb.com/about/): The largest online chemical community that was launched in 1997. It provides a range of information for those in research chemistry, chemicals industries and related disciplines (Warr, 1998; Warr, 2002; Culp, 2002). The membership to ChemWeb is free and members are entitled to access more than 400 journals and 20 databases from different publishers (owned by Elsevier Science).

ChemFinder (http://chemfinder.cambridgesoft.com/about/): Offers access to scientific databases such as reference, chemical, reaction and safety, on complimentary basis to individuals and on subscription basis for enterprises.

The reference databases include: *ChemFinder Free Edition* and *ChemINDEX Subscription Edition*: Both facilitate searching on chemical structures (2-D and 3-D models), physical properties and hyperlinks; and *The Merck Index*: An authoritative Web resource for chemicals, drugs and biologicals with over 10,000 monographs on single substances or groups of related compounds. The chemical databases include: *ChemACX Net* and *ChemACX Pro*. The reaction databases include: *Organic Syntheses*, *Compendium of Chiral Auxiliary Applications*, *ChemReact* and *ChemSynth*.

Other Portals**:* ***Chemdex (http://www.chemdex.org): A web based directory from the University of Sheffield that has 7196 links organized under 13 categories; ***ChemIndustry*** (http://www.chemindustry.com/info/aboutus.asp): The most visited portal serving over 2.5 million searches per month (Fishman and Brattkus, 2002; Warr, 2002) that serves both professionals (acts as a directory, search engine and hosts full-text of 45,000 entities) and advertisers (promotes their products and services); ***SpectroscopyNOW*** (http://www.spectroscopynow.com/Spy/basehtml/SpyH/1,1181,0-8-1-0-1-about_this_site-0-0,00.html), a freely accessible spectroscopy portal from John Wiley and includes: mass spectrometry, x-ray spectrometry, NMR, etc., ***Chemical Analysis.com*** (http://www.chemicalanalysis.com/) brings together individuals and organizations in need of chemical analysis, free of cost, by hosting a database of laboratories, consultants from around the world; and ***Links for Chemists*** (http://www.liv.ac.uk/Chemistry/Links/links.html) indexes about 8,400 chemistry resources from over 75 chemical categories on the Web.

5.2 *Patents and Dissertations*

A patent is a document issued by a national government granting the patentee (inventor) the exclusive right to manufacture; use or sell the invention (original products, processes, or composition of matter) described in the patent for a prescribed interval of time and protection against copying or unauthorized use.

A dissertation is a substantial work of independent original research completed in partial fulfillment of the requirements for a master's or doctoral level that makes a contribution to the current body of knowledge in a scholarly field. The selected list includes:

- ***WIPO PCT Database*** (http://pctgazette.wipo.int/): Covers 1978 to present with weekly updations from 177 state members of WIPO. It permits free searching and viewing front page. ***Europe's Network Patent Databases*** (http://ep.espacenet.com/): Covers 1997 to present, from members states and permit free full-text searching. The esp@cenet facilitates to find English language abstracts of patents from EPO's in-house databases from over 50 countries.
- ***IBM IP Network*** (http://www.delphion.com): Offers free full-text searching including front pages display of US patents, EP-A and B, WIPO PCT and JP. The ***IBM IP Network for Business*** (http://www.delphion.com), a fee-based one offers the advantages of IBM IP Network with added business needs.
- ***Derwent World Patents Index*** (http://www.derwent.com/worldpatentsindex/index.html): A fee based database that covers chemistry since 1963 from 40 international patent offices/organizations.
- ***MicroPatentWeb Full-text*** (http://www.micropat.com/0/new_fulltext29809.html) and ***Front Page*** (http://www.micropat.com/0/new_wps9809.html): These are fee-based full-text and front pages only accessible databases. Both contain PCT (WO) patents (1978-current for full-text and front page), EP (1988-current for full-text; 1978-current for front page), US (1836-current for full-text; 1976-current for front page) and Japanese patents abstracts (1976-current update).
- ***WIPS Patent Search Database*** (http://www.wipsglobal.com): Contains data from patent offices all over the world that has been saved in a uniform format for easy access through an integrated Web-based search system.

Patents by individual countries include: ***USPTO Web Patent Database*** (http://www.uspto.gov/patft/index.html) covers 1976 to present, offers free full-text searching; ***UK Patents*** (http://gb.espacenet.com) covers 1996 to present, offers free searching and abstracts display; ***Japan Patent Office*** (http://www.jpo.go.jp/index.htm); ***German Patent and Trademark Office*** (http://www.dpma.de/index.htm), etc.

The patents can also be accessed through several online hosts including STN (http://www.stn-international.de), Questel-Orbit (http://www.questel.orbit.com), Dialog (http://www.dialog.com), CAS (http://info.cas.org), etc.

The dissertations are available through:

- ***ProQuest Digital Dissertations** (PQDD)* (http://wwwlib.umi.com/dissertations/): Provides citations from 1861 to present and about 2 million doctoral dissertations and masters theses from 1000 graduate schools and universities. The full-text comprises about 1.7 million titles available both in paper and microform formats. Institutional subscribers receive online access to complete file of dissertations from 1997 forward. The visitors are offered free access to the current two years of citations and abstracts.
- ***Networked Digital Library of Theses and Dissertations*** (http://www.theses.org/): Provides access to theses and dissertations in electronic format throughout the world.

5.3 *Full-Text Journals, Backfiles and E-Books*

Full-text journals are published directly by societies or commercial publishers or via third party aggregators who offer a common interface and search system for accessing several journals simultaneously at a single website. The backfiles provide retrospective information that forms the foundation for today's breakthroughs, *i.e.* provide in-depth background data essential for research success. The e-books contain text in digital form or book converted into digital form or digital reading material, images with unique identifiers, displayed on computer screen or read on a computer through a network or view or read on all types of computers or formatted for display on e-book readers (Rao, 2001). The select list includes:

- ***Internet Journal of Chemistry*** (http://www.ijc.com/IJC/statepurp2.html): Focuses on use of the Internet by chemists in both presentation of chemical research and developments of Internet resources. It publishes peer-reviewed articles in HTML format and offers archival retrieval. It takes advantage of special attributes of the Internet and distributed computing environment that are difficult or expensive to include in traditional publications. These include chemical structures, hyper-molecules, video/movies, VRML, spectra in downloadable files, interactive programs using Java or CGI scripts, etc. The access to full-text is on subscription basis since 2000 however, access to table of contents and abstracts are free.
- ***Ingenta*** (http://www.ingenta.com): Launched as s subscribed database in 1998 and became the leading Web infomediary to exchange academic and professional content online. It provides access to more than 6,000 full-text online publications from about 260 academic and professional publishers, and contains over 16,570,495 articles. It facilitates purchase of articles from over 28,572 publications on a pay-per-view basis, deliverable by fax or Ariel delivery.
- ***ScienceDirect*** (http://www.info.sciencedirect.com/about_us.shtml): It is a Web delivery system form Elsevier and covers 1996 to present. It provides access to full-text of more than 1800 scientific, technical and medical peer-reviewed

journals; links to articles from over 170 other publishers, over 11 million articles and 60 million abstracts. It includes MedLine, Exerpta Medica, Academic Press's IDEAL system, information from CRC Press, the American Institute of Chemical Engineers (AIChE). ScienceDirect is equipped with science-specific search engine, scirus.com (Spedding, 2002; Warr, 2002). This also hosts backfiles collection.

- ***Backfiles on ScienceDirect*** (http://www.info.sciencedirect.com/backfiles/index.shtml): Initiated as part of Elsevier's ongoing commitment to knowledge preservation that spans over 180 years. These full-text searchable backfiles consists of about 8 million articles with HTML summaries and reference lists, enabling direct linking to cited and citing articles. The first backfile collection was chemistry comprising of 87 journals covering 1939–1995.
- ***Wiley InterScience*** (http://www3.interscience.wiley.com/): Provides Web access to publications of John Wiley and Sons Inc., since 1997. The coverage includes over 1,000 journals, major reference works, online books, current protocols laboratory manuals, databases, etc. The visitors are permitted to browse and search journals tables of contents and article abstracts regardless of their subscription status. The licensed users view enhanced abstracts with references along with full-text. The journals are grouped under 14 main subject areas including chemistry. InterScience make available its content through EBSCO gateway; deliver an end-to-end solution to life science researchers through LabBook; link articles or references or abstracts on Wiley Interscience with the Celera Discovery System (Spedding, 2002). The non-subscribers use the pay-per-view mode to access the collection. It also hosts.
- ***Wiley InterScience Polymer Backfile Collection*** *(PBC)* (http://www3.interscience.wiley.com/cgi-bin/collectionhome/PBCOL/HOME): An online backfile of 636,000 pages from journals of Polymer Science and Engineering area, from volume 1 and issue 1. The articles are formatted in PDF for article body, in HTML for header material and references, thus facilitating linking both internal (within Wiley InterScience) and external (CrossRef/DOI, ISI Web of Science, CAS, etc.) resources.
- ***Dekker*** (http://www.dekker.com/index.jsp): Offers journals, e-books and encyclopedias in S&T and medicine. About 40 journals in chemistry are available online via ***ChemWeb.com*** (http://www.dekker.com/misc/releases/ChemWeb.jsp). The users have free access to browse journals tables of contents and view abstracts on ChemWeb. The access to full-text articles is available at http://www.dekker.com/to users from institutions or libraries with Dekker journal subscriptions. Individual users can also purchase single articles by online pay-per-view transactions. Dekker in association with OverDrive, Inc., has launched two innovative e-book sites offering over 500 titles. The institutional site (http://www.ebooks.lib. dekker.com) allow libraries to purchase titles for perpetual access that includes multiple and concurrent viewing. The other (http://www.

ebooks.dekker.com) serves the individual consumer. Dekker e-books are also available through netLibrary.

- ***Blackwell Synergy*** (http://www.blackwell-synergy.com/info): An online journals service from Blackwell comprising about 840 journals. It provides free access to guest and registered users to search articles, read abstracts, download citations and purchase single articles. The subscribers are entitled to access full-text articles (in both PDF and HTML format), enable link to abstracts of cited articles in other journals, link forward to articles that cite this article and OnlineEarly articles access, where available.
- ***HighWire Press*** (http://highwire.stanford.edu/): Develops and maintains the Web versions of important journals in Biomedicine and other disciplines. It produces 362 HighWire hosted journals and became one of the largest archives of free full-text science. It assists in online publication of 2,126,487 free full-text articles from 203 journals. The access is through personal subscriptions or institutional access or consortia or national access; pay-per-view accesses to 284 other journals; plus free access to all abstracts and free access to full-text of selected journals for readers in developing countries.
- ***SpringerLink*** (http://www.springerlink.com): Provides electronic and printed literature from Springer-Verlag since 1996, from over 2720 peer-reviewed journals and more than 50,784 books online. It is divided into 11 online libraries including chemical sciences. It facilitates free access to search functions, tables of contents, keywords and alerts. The subscribers to a specific journal title receive online access also. Currently, it offers a pay-per-view option for journal articles and chapters in Lecture Notes in Computer Science for its registered users.
- ***Knovel*** (http://www.knovel.com/knovel2/Overview.jsp) online books and databases: Provides full-text access to 500 titles and 20 million data records in science and engineering. It facilitates access to about 900 tables of physical and chemical data from McGraw-Hill, CRC Press, Reed Elsevier, ASME, SPE, ASM International, Butterworth Heinemann, US Govt. agencies, etc. The tables are easy to navigate and full-text searchable (Culp, 2002). The e-books from Knovel include: *International Critical Tables of Numerical data, Physics, Chemistry and Technology*; *Knovel Critical Tables*; *Smithsonian Physical Tables*; and *Thermochemistry of the Chemical Substances*.

5.4 *Abstracting and Indexing Services*

An abstract is a brief summary of an article that often appears at the beginning of a scholarly or technical article. An index provides the source information you need to find each article, usually the periodical title, issue number and page numbers. The periodical indexes and other databases often contain abstracts that can help you decide whether an article is relevant for your purposes. The selected list includes:

- ***Chemical Abstracts Service*** (CAS) (http://www.cas.org/about.html): Provides digital literature of chemistry and other scientific disciplines, since beginning of 20th century. It facilitates access to summaries and indexes of chemistry-related articles from more than 40,000 scientific journals, in addition to patents, conference proceedings and other documents. From January 1, 2010, Chemical Abstracts and other print-based products (except CA SELECTS) are no longer available in printed format. CAS with advanced search and analysis technologies, delivers the most complete, cross-linked, and effective digital information environment for scientific research and discovery through such products as SciFinder, STN, STN Express, and STN AnaVist, as well as services, such as Science IP.
- ***ISI Web of Science*** (http://thomsonreuters.com/products_services/science/science_products/a-z/web_of_science): Provides researchers, administrators, faculties, and students with quick, powerful access to the world's leading citation and full-text databases. Authoritative, multidisciplinary content covers over 12,000 of the highest impact journals worldwide, including Open Access journals and over 150,000 conference proceedings. Offer access to current and retrospective coverage in the sciences, social sciences, arts, and humanities, with coverage to 1900 and more than 250 disciplines. It facilitates access to: *Science Citation Index Expanded*; *Social Sciences Citation Index*; *Arts and Humanities Citation Index*; *Index Chemicus* and *Current Chemical Reactions*.

5.5 *Encyclopedias and Handbooks*

An encyclopedia is a reference source containing authoritative information, either general or subject specific, available as a book, or set of books, or digital version of such, which provides background information and specific facts. The handbook is a concise reference document that provides factual information on a specific subject or subjects, organized for easy access by practitioners. The select list includes:

- ***Ullmann's Encyclopedia of Industrial Chemistry*** (http://as.wiley.com/WileyCDA/Section/id-407379.html): First published in 1914 and facilitates access to more than 1050 articles and search through indexes such as full-text, author, CAS registry number and subject.
- ***Kirk Othmer's Encyclopedia of Chemical Technology*** (http://as.wiley.com/WileyCDA/WileyTitle/productCd-0471484962.html): Designed by scientists for scientists and published since 1949. The latest edition (fourth) is available online only and supports search in both query-based and menu-driven modes. It facilitates search by keywords, author, company, brand, CA Registry Numbers, physical and chemical properties, safety factors, uses, derivatives, etc.
- ***e-EROS Encyclopedia of Reagents for Organic Synthesis:*** Reference source for reagents used in organic chemistry. It provides access to 50,000 reactions and 3,800 frequently consulted reagents.

- ***Registry of Toxic Effects of Chemical Substances*** (http://www.cdc.gov/niosh/rtecs.html): Provides access to more than 152,970 toxic chemicals. The data are organized by prime chemical name and each file includes six types of toxic data: primary irritation, mutagenic effects, reproductive effects, tumorigenic effects, acute toxicity and other multiple dose toxicity. This is available in three formats: online, CD-ROM and tape.
- ***Industrial Chemical Additives Handbook*** (http://www.synapseinfo.com/indexfr.htm): Provides information on functional additive chemicals and materials used in the formulation of chemical products. It facilitates access to trade name additive products about 40,000; generic additive products about 7,500 equipped with cross-referenced synonyms about 16,000; functional/application categories about 36,000 in an index format; CAS, EINECS/ELINCS number, Chemical Formula index; international manufacturers. It is fully searchable by structure, substructure, reagent, reaction type, experimental conditions, etc.

5.6 *Periodic Tables*

A periodic table presents the arrangement of chemical elements, according to their atomic numbers, in vertical columns having similar properties and rows showing shifts in properties. The select list includes:

- ***WebElements*** (http://www.webelements.com/webelements/index.html): Provides detailed information about elements in the periodic table that include atomic information, physical properties, isotopes, compounds, crystal structure and uses. It is extensively illustrated, and available as scholar and professional editions.
- ***Chemicool Periodic Table*** (http://www-tech.mit.edu/Chemicool/): An interactive periodic table useful for high-school chemistry classes. In addition to general information about elements, it includes states, energies, oxidation and electrons, appearance and characteristics, reactions, conductivity, abundances, etc.

5.7 *Property Databases*

These include a basic or essential attribute shared by all members of a class; *i.e.* a study of the physical properties of atomic particles. The selected list includes:

- ***CrossFire*** (http://www.mimas.ac.uk/crossfire/docs/bcs101.html): An integrated chemical information system comprising of Beilstein Database for Organic Chemistry, Gmelin Database for Inorganic Chemistry and Beilstein Commander software to access and search the two databases. The Beilstein database provides Organic Chemistry literature from 1771 to date, covering over 8.7 million structures, 10 million reactions and more than 600,000 author abstracts (added from 1980). It also provides chemical names, properties and methods of preparation of compounds. The Gmelin Database provides inorganic, organometallic and coordination compounds, alloys, etc., literature from 1772 to date (bridging the gap from 1995 onwards) covering about 1.8 million compounds and 1.5 million reactions (Culp, 2002).

- ***CHEMnetBASE*** (http://www.chemnetbase.com/): A gateway to Web versions of Chapman and Hall/CRC chemical information resources. It contains information on physical property data, structural representations and chemical synonyms. It is available on annual subscription mode, on a site license basis only to multi-user organizations, wherein access to individuals is by IP recognition. The products of CHEMnetBASE include:
  - *Combined Chemical Dictionary* (http://www.chemnetbase.com/scripts/ccdweb.exe): A structured database on chemical substances and provides access to descriptive and numerical data on chemical, physical and biological properties of compounds; systematic and common names of compounds; references; structure diagrams; etc. The online version facilitates access to records of about 266,000 in Dictionary of Organic Compounds, 181,000 in Dictionary of Natural Products, 102,000 in Dictionary of Inorganic and Organometallic Compounds, 45,000 in Dictionary of Drugs and 14,000 in Dictionary of Analytical Reagents.
  - *The Handbook of Chemistry and Physics* (Ed 84) (http://www.hbcpnetbase.com): Provides access to physical constants of more than 11,000 organic compounds, chemical carcinogens data and critical constants to 858 fluids.
  - *Polymers* (http://www.polymersdatabase.com/): A property database of polymers.
  - *Properties of Organic Compounds* (http://www.chemnetbase.com/scripts/pocweb.exe): Helps in identifying unknown compounds and for known compounds to find additional data and references. It offers access to physical data, spectral data and structures of over 29,000 organic compounds.
- ***ATSDR's Toxicological Profiles*** (http://toxprof.crcpress.com/): Provides access to 162 profiles (about 40,000 pages) of toxicological and epidemiological information. Each profile includes an examination, summary and interpretation of available data evaluations on hazardous substances, chemicals and compounds. The data was organized by route of exposures: inhalation, oral and dermal.
- ***DIPPR*** (http://dippr.byu.edu/products.html): Provides searchable textual and pure component numeric physical property data for commercially important chemicals and substances about 1743, since 1982. The DIPPR file consists of 29 constant properties and 15 temperature-dependent properties.

5.8 *Specialty Databases*

Specialty databases are dedicated to collecting relevant sites for a particular subject. The selected list includes:

- ***Protein Information Resource*** (PIR) (http://pir.georgetown.edu/pirwww/aboutpir/aboutpir.html): A freely accessible and integrated bioinformatics database that supports research in genomics, proteomics and science studies. It maintains annotated Protein Sequence Database that offers about 283,000 sequences covering total taxonomic range.

- ***Research Collaboratory for Structural Bioinformatics*** (RCSB) (http://www.rcsb.org/index.html): A non-profit consortium devoted to understand the functioning of biological systems through 3-D structure of biological macromolecules. RCSB maintains the following databases:
  - *Protein Databank (PDB)* (http://www.rcsb.org/databases.html): An international repository for processing and distribution of 3-D biological macromolecular structure data and includes over 24,080 structures.
  - *Obsolete Structures* (http://pdbobs.sdsc.edu/index.cgi): An archive with obsolete entries from PDB, for history perspective and to test new versions of software.
  - *Nucleic Acid Database* (http://ndbserver.rutgers.edu/): A repository for 3-D structural information about nucleic acids and includes 2,444 structures.
  - *TargetDB* (http://targetdb.pdb.org): A weekly updated sequence target database that provides registration and tracking information for worldwide structural genomics and proteomics projects.
  - *Structural Homology* (http://cl.sdsc.edu): Facilitates to find similarities in 3-D protein structures by deploying compound likeness and incremental combinatorial extension.
  - *Protein Kinase Resource* (http://pkr.sdsc.edu/html/index.shtml): Web based resource on protein kinase family of enzymes and includes tools for structural, computational analyses and links to related information.
  - *Biological Macromolecule Crystallization Database (BMCD) and the NASA Archive for Protein Crystal Growth Data* (http://wwwbmcd.nist.gov:8080/bmcd/bmcd.html): Offers access to 3547 crystal entries from 2526 biological macromolecules for that diffraction quality crystals obtained. BMCD hosts the NASA Protein Crystal Growth Archive that includes crystallization data generated from micro-gravity studies.
  - *BioMagResBank* (http://www.bmrb.wisc.edu/): Provides access to NMR spectroscopy data on proteins, peptides and nucleic acids.
- ***Entrez*** (http://www.ncbi.nlm.nih.gov/Database/index.html): A text-based search and retrieval system for National Center for Biotechnology Information's public databases. It integrates and interlinks scientific literature, DNA and protein sequence databases, 3-D protein structure and protein domain data, population study data sets, expression data, assemblies of complete genomes and taxonomic information.
- ***Cambridge Structure Database*** (CSD) (http://www.ccdc.cam.ac.uk/products/csd/): Serves as a repository with more than 233,218 entries and offers bibliographic, chemical and crystallographic information for organic molecules and metal-organic compounds, whose 3-D structures determined from diffraction studies of X-ray and neutron.

- ***Inorganic Crystal Structure Database*** (ICSD) (http://icsd.ill.fr/icsd/): Provides access to numeric database of inorganic crystal structures, with atomic coordinates and contains 73,519 entries, since 1913. It has future plans to cover metals and inter-metallic compounds.
- ***BRENDA*** (http://www.brenda.uni-koeln.de): A comprehensive Enzyme Information System covering about 3,500 different enzymes, since 1987. It is available free to academic, non-profit users over the Internet and as an in-house database to commercial users.
- ***Solvents Database*** (SOLVDB) (http://www.syrres.com/esc/solvdb.htm): Assists in identification of alternative solvents and provide data on physical/chemical properties, environmental fate, health and safety, and regulations (137 data fields) of chemicals.
- ***Integrated Spectral Data Base System for Organic Compounds*** (SDBS) (http://www.aist.go.jp/RIODB/SDBS/intro-en.html): A free, integrated spectral database system for organic compounds that includes 6 types of spectra: EI mass, ^{1}H decoupled ^{13}C NMR, ^{1}H NMR pattern (90 and/or 400 MHz), ^{1}H NMR parameter (300 MHz), FT-IR, laser-Raman and ESR, in a directory database of compounds (Culp, 2002).
- ***SPRESI^{web}*** (http://www.infochem.de/eng/index.htm): InfoChem's SPRESI^{web} is basically structure and reactions database, provides access to 4.5 million compounds, 3.5 million reactions from 380,000 references including 98,000 patents over the Internet and intranet. It facilitates links to document delivery services: FIZ AutoDoc, CISTI and Subito; patent offices: Espacenet, US Patent and Trademark Office and MicroPatent, other databases like ChemNavigator and company in-house databases. Apart from structure and reactions data, it offers over 20 million chemical, physical and biological property data.
- ***Chemical Reactivity Worksheet*** (http://response.restoration.noaa.gov/chemaids/react.html): A free database that offers data about reactivity of substances or mixtures of substances, covering more than 6,000 common and special hazardous chemicals.
- ***Orbitron*** (http://www.shef.ac.uk/chemistry/orbitron/): Provides access to images representing atomic and molecular orbitals; animated plots of wave functions and electron density; dot-density plots of electron density; plots of radial distribution functions, etc.

6. Conclusions

All the chemical information resources are good in their own way and certainly offer flexibility as they all serve a different purpose. The electronic era is well established and most of what used to be available in print and now available in electronic form. What we are witnessing is a transition between traditional publishing and new. Online journal publishers are allowing users to click through to cited papers from other publishers. They are also making available their material to portals and aggregators and allowing them to facilitate single-article downloads on a pay-per-view basis. Alliances between publishers and database producers are enabling researchers to download both articles and data behind them at the same point.

The true value of electronic delivery of information is being experienced, as major new developments in archiving (ACS, RSC, Polymer Backfile Collection, HighWire Press, Elsevier ScienceDirect backfiles) and preprints (CPS), are gathering momentum. Major publishers are investing in making their archives available online and academic circles to produce alternative methods of accessing research information. The Open Archives Initiative (http://www.openarchives.org) facilitated author/institution self-archiving of institutional research output, both pre and post peer review. The ePrints (http://www.eprints.org) potentially enables institutions to become part of a fully interoperable archive. Preprint servers are inevitable outcome of events.

In the current electronic era, publishers in addition to peer review function, also offering distribution and electronic delivery, links from references to other articles and decreasing costs per downloaded articles appropriately to the current trends. The scholarly publication of Chemistry information in electronic form will continue to grow, adapting to meet the changing needs of authors and readers alike.

References

[1] Clarke, R. (1997). Electronic publishing: A specialised form of electronic commerce, 10th Int'l EC Conf., Bled, Slovenia (June 1997). Available: http://www.rogerclarke.com/EC/Bled97.html

[2] Culp, B. (2002). The chemical handbook: Glorious past, parlous present, no future? Available: http://www.infonrtics.com/chemical/ch02/files/culp.pdf

[3] Drey, J. (2002). Chemistry online: An ideal formula for chemists. Available: http://www.researchinformation.info/riaut02chemistry.html

[4] Fishman, Y. and Brattkus, K. (2002). The chemist's query: A session level analysis of search. Available: http://www.infonrtics.com/chemical/ch02/files/fishman.pdf

[5] Glander-Hobel, C. (2002). Internet portals for chemists. *Online Information Review,* 26,(3), 146–163.

[6] Hawkins, D. *et al.* (1994). Shaping the electronic publishing industry. *In* The Electronic Publishing Business and Its Market, Blunden and Blunden, PIRA.

[7] Rao, S.S. (2001). Familiarization of electronic books. *The Electronic Library*, 19(4), 247–256.

[8] Spedding, V. (2002). Journal cross-linking: The Web's potential untangled. Available: http://www.researchinformation.info/feature1a.html

[9] Town, W.G. *et al.* (2002). Chemical e-journals, chemical e-Preprints. *Online Information Review*, 26(3), 164–171.

[10] Warr, W.A. (1998). Communication and communities of chemists. *Journal of Chemical Information and Computer Science*, 38(6), 966–975.

[11] Warr, W.A. (2001). A report on the presentation chemistry preprint server: A revolution in chemistry communication. National ACS Meeting (CINF Division) in San Diego, USA.

[12] Warr, W.A. (2002). From vertical communities to portals in the post-dotcom era. Available: http://www.infonrtics.com/chemical/ch02/files/warr.pdf

Electronic Resources Management in Libraries, pp. 127–135

Collection Development in the e-Content World: The Challenges of Procurement, Access and Preservation

N.V. Sathyanarayana

I have known Dr. A. Lakshmana Moorthy for over two decades since his early DESIDOC days with the senior Dr. S.S. Murthy. The Senior Murthy transformed DESIDOC to a role model during his time. The junior Moorthy has left his indelible foot prints in his own unique style and passion for the profession, taking DESIDOC to digital mainstream and spreading the digital access impact all across the DRDO scientific community. A brilliant writer and a passionate speaker that I know of him, Dr. Moorthy's writing and editorial skills have earned him respect and position of an excellent science editor also. This little piece is a small tribute to Dr. Moorthy's deep commitment to LIS profession and his leadership achievements.

1. Introduction

Collection Development is one of the most demanding professional functions of a Library that involves deeper understanding of the users' needs, organizational eco-system in which a library functions, and the supply-chain of information and publishing industry. The importance of this function to library's usage value continues to be more demanding in the E-Content world. However, the multitude of choices offered and controls exercised by the content creators and providers such as authors, publishers, aggregators, distributors and the laws that regulate the ownership, pricing and usage rights of e-Content makes the collection development process one of the most challenging functions in the libraries of digital world today. It is a very different process demanding the libraries to redefine their purpose and functions. This article is a broad sketch of emerging challenges of e-collection development and the changes it will bring in other key functions of the libraries. The scope of discussion is limited to journals and books in the digital format.

2. A Fundamental Change

In the print world of educational and research content, the collection development function revolved around the library's philosophy of ownership and preservation for perpetual use. When the libraries purchased the content from the publishers, the lending and perpetual usage rights came by default under the first-sale right doctrine of the Copyright Laws. Purchase for permanent retention was the only business model available for print collections. However, publishers continued to own the intellectual property (IP) rights of the content often without even keeping a single copy of books that have gone out-of-print and the back volumes of journals. It is well known that when publishers decided to come out with digital archives of their older journals form volume 1, many of them had to fall back on the preserved collection of library's bound volumes! Evidently, the publishers did not directly control the method of access and preservation of print material after it was sold to the libraries.

In the e-Content world publishers have taken direct and strategic control of content, its IP ownership, and its delivery and usage through the entire legal life-cycle of the content until the copyright period expires. Technology will facilitate them to maintain just one copy of the content, and a few mirror copies if need be, to serve the needs of all the global users through Internet. What the libraries buy will be *right-of-access* to this copy for limited or unlimited usage, for a limited or unlimited period, but by a limited number of users defined as authorized users of the library (members of the library). The process of obtaining and maintaining the *right-of-access,* which is known as *licensing*, is gradually replacing the traditional procurement model of content buying. Earlier in the print world publishers did not control and manage the usage. In the e-world, they will be completely controlling and managing this function through structured levels of rights, licenses and pricing models.

3. Redefining the Purpose of Collection Development

With the publishers taking direct control of managing the access and preservation, the selection of content that adequately serve the needs and purpose of library's user community at affordable costs *today* becomes more important than its needs in a distant future. The new mission of collection development may have to be—*Just-in-time access to the relevant and required content accessible by the user from anywhere.* This imperative mission will force the following changes in the collection development practice:

- Collection development will become a short-term, need based plan. It will move from purchase for permanent retention to licensing for a definite or indefinite (perpetual) period of access and usage.
- Investment focus will shift from content ownership for preservation to the provision of technology infrastructure that will enhance the access, delivery and usage value of the licensed content.
- Libraries will have to engage the publishers to develop content licensing models that will be more affordable and serve the needs of the user community for content at a global level.
- A new kind of user awareness program will have to be created for the user community to understand and appreciate the new content licensing models,

associated copyright compliance requirements, and the price value of the content in addition to its usage value.

4. Business Models

Many business models are evolving in various permutations and combinations around the new licensing process for e-Content procurement. These models may control the access by content volume, duration of access, size of the user population and the computing devices used for access. They generally fall into a variant of one or many of the following general models.

4.1 *Perpetual Access Rights*

This model is similar to libraries buying books and journals in the print-model. The library can license the content that grants access rights by its user community for an unlimited period. Technically this means that the library has the *access rights* for its (organizational) life. The questions that arise around this model are:

- Will the library have local archiving rights for the content? If so, how and when will the publisher deliver the content and at what cost?
- How does the publisher or the service provider guarantee the continuation of access in the event of closure of his organization?
- Will this model provide the ownership privilege under the doctrine of first sale right that the libraries have under the copyright laws? Or, will it reduce ownership to the state of virtual reality forever?
- Is this right transferable in the event of the library or its parent organization merging into another entity?
- How is this right shared in the event of a split? For example, if the University is split into two Groups or Campuses, or the library is split into two independent blocks in the same campus.

4.2 *Limited Period Access Rights*

This model is similar to renting or leasing the access rights for a limited period which could vary from one month to one year or more. Consumer models are available, directed to end-users where a user can license access rights on a monthly payment/usage model which of course will not be appropriate for libraries. Normally, the libraries sign the license agreement for a period from one to three years. By general understanding, library will cease to have right of access to the content once the lease period expires. Following are some of the issues and questions that need to be addressed under this model:

- This model is popularly used by Aggregators who license the content from the publishers. The Publishers generally grant limited period of license to the

Aggregators. Hence, Aggregators are constrained by the business compulsions of limited options in dealing with licensing period and pricing terms. While delivering the content to libraries Aggregators need to have a common licensing and pricing model for the content of all the publishers that their Aggregation platform provides. For this reason, Aggregators are not able to guarantee perpetual access rights to the content they deliver. There are a few exceptions in Aggregation models which have tried to offer perpetual access rights which are complex to manage.

- Many publishers offer this model as an alternative. Some publishers offer this model only as conditional and refuse to make available content for perpetual access.
- Libraries develop collections for meeting the educational and research needs of their users. While licensing the content under this model may restrict the library's access by the period of lease, what happens to the usage rights of a user who has downloaded a portion of the content for his study or research that may lost beyond the library's lease period? User has downloaded the content, like he takes a photocopy of an article form a journal under the fair-use doctrine which permits him to use the article for the entire duration of his academic or research needs. Does it amount to infringement if the end-user retains the downloaded copy even after the library's subscription has expired and not renewed?

4.3 *Subscription Model*

This model is perceived to be similar to libraries subscribing to print journals with many variants in the right of access. It is the most confusing model due to too many varied practices by publishers in setting the terms of licensing. It is a hybrid model of both perpetual access rights and limited access rights. Following practices and issues concerned with this model need the attention of libraries for engaging with publishers to fine-tune this model for reducing the ambiguity.

- In the initial days of e-Journals, publishers offered free access to e-version, limited to the current year of subscription as part of the print subscriptions. E-access was for limited content (current year's content only) and for a limited period (one year). This was a business strategy to promote e-journal usage. Most publishers have dropped this model but some still continue to offer.
- As a standard term of subscription model, when libraries subscribe to e-version of the journal either independently or as part of the print subscriptions with additional payment for e-version access, libraries get access to e-version of the content for the current year (subscription year) with archival access to a few years of back-files depending upon the period for which the publisher maintains the back-files on his site. The current year's (subscription year) content will be made available for perpetual access, but the back-years' content will not be available for perpetual access. This means:
  - If the publisher has his collection available for 15-years;

- If the library has subscribed to e-version for 5-years, with or without print subscription;
- If the library stops renewing after 5-years; and
- The access will be perpetual for the 5-years of paid subscription content, and will be stopped for the rest of the 10-years content.

- Some publishers provide back file access as part of current subscription for rolling period of 3–5 years. Rolling period is one of the most confusing and least practical models.
- Of late publishers are optionally applying subscription model for e-books also. They are applying this model largely for selling their complete collection or subject collections which will include their back-lists. Besides finding new market for their books, they have brought in a fundamental change by digitizing their back-lists. The concept of out-of-print or out-of-stock will no longer be applicable for books. Subscription model for books has raised a serious issue of long-term affordability of this mode to libraries.

4.4 *User Population*

Within the business models discussed above, publishers exercise different levels of access control as a means of inventing new business models and to manage price-flexibility in product pricing. In the print world, the content had inherent access disadvantage. A copy could be available for one user at a time and the libraries had to buy multiple copies where demands were more. A fundamental change that the e-Content has brought in is the feasibility of 24/7 access to all the content that a library licenses to all its users, and simultaneously. This will never happen in reality and in any situation only a small part of the library's content will be under use by a small section of the users. Taking advantage of this fundamental change, publishers have replaced the multiple copy purchase concept by concurrent access model. It is like saying three concurrent users are equivalent to licensing three copies. This model is particularly relevant for text books. The model has opened up two distinct pricing options:

- Pricing based on number of users in the Campus (FTE or Full-Time-Equivalent Model) with no limit on the number of concurrent users.
- Pricing based on number of concurrent (simultaneous) users accessing the content irrespective of the user population of the library.

4.5 *Pay-per-View Model*

This model is equivalent to paid document delivery service. Publishers never offered this model in the print world. Digital content has made this model a new, though very limited, revenue opportunity for the publishers and a deterrent strategy to protect the stable revenue from the subscription model. This model has all the potential to bloom as a cost-affordable option to both libraries and end-users. But, neither the libraries due to practical problems nor the Publishers due to revenue considerations are willing to give a serious chance to this model. One of the reputed e-Journal aggregators admitted to this author in a recent conversation that his system is recording around 100 million turned-away users every year. Even charging $1 per article would have brought him revenue three times more than his current subscription based revenue. Turned-away users refer to users landing for full-text in a publisher portal from discovery services like J-Gate or Google or any abstracting and indexing services that provide links to full-text.

4.6 *Subscription based Article Delivery Model*

Libraries rarely buy all journals due to affordability constrains even from speciality publishers in their subject area. Users approach to published content is rarely by journal but more by their topics of interest and study needs. Every publisher knows that subscription model limits the access to users for articles from his other non-subscribed journals by the library, but has rarely ventured into develop article delivery model as a parallel and equally remunerative business model comparable to subscription model. Of late, as a means of making the article delivery (Pay-per-view) model affordable, a few publishers have started bundling article delivery through subscription model. For example: a library serving the needs of users in the Chemical research group subscribes to five journals from the Royal Society of Chemistry (RSC) which publishes about 30 journals. Its users have definite and regular need for articles from the rest of the RSC journals but the library can't afford to subscribe them all. RSC's subscription based offer for a pre-defined bundle of articles in the range of 100–1,000 from the non-subscribed journals can meet the library's needs as an alternative and affordable model to subscribing the journals.

4.7 *Platform Fee*

In the print world the cost of delivery medium and the technology (printing, binding, paper, etc.) were inclusive in the final product price. Usage and preservation did not require publisher's technology intermediation. In the e-Content scenario, technology is present in every stream from content creation and delivery to usage, archiving and preservation all of which provided and mediated by the publisher. The back-end technology infrastructure for large scale delivery and management of the content is significant and requires constant up-gradation year after year. Publishers rarely develop or own the technology. They will be licensing technology as a service from various technology providers. Most of the publishers will be hosting their content on the technology platforms provided by third-party service companies. Publishers pricing for the E-Content generally includes the technology platform fee (cost of using the technology for access, delivery and usage management) also. E-Content licensing raises several technology related issues when publishers license the content to libraries. Some of the key issues are:

- Library will be buying e-Content from several hundred publishers, year-after-year. Will the publishers agree to make available the bare content to the library in a portable format for the library to aggregate and host the content in a platform of its choice instead of using multiple access platforms?
- When a library subscribes to e-journals on perpetual access model paying an annual subscription fee for the content the platform usage fee is included in that fee for the year of subscription. When the library stops subscribing to these journals, what happens to its rights to use the platform for the content which is licensed for perpetual access since the publishers may not be licensing the platform separately? There is a payment issue for continued use of publisher's technology platform for the content library has subscribed for a few years but no longer continues to subscribe.
- In case of content that is licensed in a non-subscription model (one-time-purchase) for perpetual access, how does the publisher determine the platform fee for perpetual access to content through his platform?
- For the e-book collection licensed by the library for perpetual access, once the copyright expire the Publisher need not and is not obliged to provide any delivery support thorough his technology platform as he no longer owns the copyright. How will the library manage such e-collection for continued access by its patrons?

5. Rights and Licenses

When a library buys a book or a journal, it acquires the *right* to make it available for unlimited and unrestricted use by its user community and retain the acquired copy for ever. In effect, it acquires unlimited lending rights to its users. This right is called the first-sale-right which includes the right to protect the copy for ever, circulate among its members any number of times, or re-sell that copy to anybody. The implicit right in protecting the physical copy for ever will also extend the right to take a backup copy for use in the event of the book suffering mutilation. The only limitation imposed on the library by the copyright law is—*total restriction from copying for any purpose* other than limited copying of a small portion (not substantial portion) of the book required by an authorized user of the library for his/her own individual educational or research and study purpose. This concession is given under the fair use doctrine.

5.1 *Managing the Rights and Licenses*

When the library moves to e-Content what it acquires is the *right-of-access* to the content wherever the publisher is hosting the digital copy. Since the library doesn't get a physical copy and the medium limits the right to access only, limited or perpetual, it opens up a new world of controlled or managed access. Due to the fear of the fact that the copyright laws do not adequately cover the situations and implications of content acquisition and access in the digital medium, publishers started the practice of *licensing* the copyrighted content with additional terms to protect their IP rights and economic interest. With every purchase of e-content, signing a license agreement has become a normal practice now. The digital collection of content that libraries will be developing in future and their ownership patterns will be represented by two elements:

- Rights acquired for access based on the business model of the publisher chosen by the library
- A Licensing document describing terms of contract under which the *rights* are acquired.

These two elements will control and manage the access all through the perpetual contract. Hence, all the systems, functions and services of the library such as the library automation system used by the library, circulation of e-Content, access through discovery services like J-Gate or Library's OPAC or a federated search systems, renewal tracking, local archiving etc. will have to be redefined to work through controls of these rights and licenses.

6. Perpetual Access vs True Ownership

The print world has created an ownership myth for the libraries which is a result of the social responsibility that the libraries assumed as social memories of the civilization. It was a limited ownership of the physical copy that the library acquired through purchase. The real owner remained the IP rights owner (Author represented by his Publisher). The physical ownership guaranteed perpetual access to the content by virtue of the provisions of first sale right doctrine of the copyright law as mentioned earlier in this paper. With that came the perpetual maintenance responsibility to the library and the associated costs.

When the library purchases digital copy of a book, the privilege of perpetual access should be applicable to this purchase also through this doctrine of first sale right. But, there is a serious technology bottleneck for exercising this right at the usage level, particularly in the function of lending the digital book. Copyrighted works do not comfortably fit within the constraints of the first sale doctrine (en.wikipedia.org/wiki/First-sale_doctrine). Copyright laws completely restrict substantial copying of the copyrighted material. When the library loans a printed book to its patrons, it involves no copying. But, when it lends a copy of the digital book, the lending process creates additional digital copies at the delivery and usage point. The library retains the source copy unless deleted/deactivated temporarily from its digital content repository through some special technology and restores only after the user returns the digital copy. There must be a control at the user's end to permanently delete the copy from the user's machine once the loan period is expired. While the Digital Rights Management (DRM) technologies exist to manage this process, it is expensive and often proves to be an irritation to the user.

Perpetual access is highly desirable to libraries from the century-old mind set of retention for re-use. However, in the E-Content world libraries have an opportunity to bring in a paradigm shift in the pricing models for digital content as service rentals. Some disruptive economic model like Google needs to emerge for the paid content to make this happen.

7. End Notes

Nothing explains the implications of the changes the digital technology and the internet are driving, better than the recent uproar in the massive digital lending of e-books. When a library buys a print book, by the doctrine of first sale right it acquires unlimited lending privilege except that the nature of the medium puts a restriction on lending to one-user-at-a-time and only until the copy gets mutilated through circulation to a point of non-use. Normally a book survives 20–50 circulations depending on the quality of paper and binding. This system of lending is undergoing fundamental change with e-books. Overdrive is a company that provides a platform for facilitating and managing lending of e-books as a technology service to the libraries. In just one year (2011), American Libraries checked out 350 lakhs digital titles, with 170 lakhs reservations pending (overdrive.com/news/eBook-Discovery-and-Sampling-Skyrocketing-at-Public-Libraries)! Threatened by potential loss of new sales due to the massive upsurge in digital lending by libraries, several publishers have withdrawn selling e-books to libraries. In an open letter to librarians explaining its switch to limit the number of check-outs a library can offer on an e-book, HarperCollins said that its previous policy of "selling e-books to libraries in perpetuity, if left unchanged, would undermine the emerging e-book eco-system, hurt the growing e-book channel, place additional pressure on physical bookstores, and in the end lead to a decrease in book sales and royalties paid to authors (Open Letter to Librarians, 2011). When a library now buys (licenses) an e-book with perpetual access rights, technically it can use one copy (one license) to lend the book to any-number-of-its-members-at-at-time with no fear of loss or mutilation. Extend this concept to the public library system of a country. The implications could be disastrous to the publishing system of the world. Obviously, the E-Content access and delivery system needs to invent a new model for library buying.

Libraries will be increasingly buying the E-Content through new form of licensing for a fee. But, what may not change is: Library's users will continue to access the content free unless the libraries also shift to commercial eco-system of charging for usage.

References

[1] First-sale-doctrine. Wikipedia. http://en.wikipedia.org/wiki/First-sale_doctrine

[2] eBook discovery and sampling skyrocketing at public libraries. http://overdrive.com/news/eBook-Discovery-and-Sampling-Skyrocketing-at-Public-Libraries

[3] Open letter to librarians. HarperCollins, Library Love Fest blog. 3 March 2011. http://harper library.typepad.com/my_weblog/2011/03/open-letter-to-librarians.html.

Electronic Resources Management in Libraries, pp. 136–143

Collection Development in the Libraries in Puducherry Region

U. Nagalingam and Ramesha

ABSTRACT

This paper presents the collection development of libraries in Puducherry region. Describes the Electronic collection development in libraries, also discusses about the collection development policy and opinion of the respondent libraries where the state-of-the art ICT applications and collection development and resource sharing is taking place. Suggest the ways and means to adopt need based collection development policy which best suits for providing effective information services to the user's community viz, Cooperative collection development and resource sharing.

1. Introduction

Development, organisation and management of collections are essential for satisfying users' needs in all types of libraries. During old days, little or no importance was given to users of libraries. Many libraries now realised that simply collection of materials for the sake of collection would neither fulfill the objectives nor enhance the image of the library. Dr SR Ranganthan's trinity concept of library, *i.e.*, user, documents and staff, are clearly explain the significance of library collection development that is heart of overall functions and activities. Therefore, librarians have to give much importance for the collection development. While developing collection librarians have to keep in mind the objectives of the organisations/institutions as well as needs and requirements of the user community. The present study was conducted in Puducherry region with different types of libraries to know and understand the growth and development of library collection through years and analyse the collection development policy adopted by the participant libraries and information centres.

2. Puducherry: A Brief Historical Perspective

The Union Territory (UT) of Puducherry comprises of four scattered regions namely Puducherry (formerly Pondicherry), Karaikal in Tamil Nadu, Yanam in Andhra Pradesh on the east coast and Mahe in Kerala on the West coast. The UT of Puducherry offers quality education with excellent physical infrastructure and almost cent percent literacy level. The UT is giving more importance for developing higher education. Many academic and research institutions have been established in Puducherry region to promote better quality education. Several courses are being offered by these institutions.

3. Development of Higher Education Institutions in Puducherry

The first Indian government institution namely Jawaharlal Institute of Post Graduate Medical and Research (JIPMER) was established in 1964 and another research institution namely French Institute was established 1956 by the French Government. The first and foremost college, namely the Tagore Arts College was established in 1961. This is followed by a number of colleges established by the UT Government, Central Government, French Government, and government-aided and self-financing managements. At present there are 48 educational institutions (Table 1) in the region, out of which 29 colleges represent "self financing" category. These institutions have established libraries to support education, learning and research interests of the academic community. These institutions are providing many services for the betterment of the users of libraries besides providing ICT-based services to the users. These institutions provide adequate information on various subjects such as arts and humanities, science and technology, medicine and agriculture.

Table 1: Classification of Educational Institutions in Puducherry

Sl. No.	*Type of Institution*	*Number*	*%*
1.	Universities	2	4.17
2.	Government Institutions	13	27.08
3.	Government Aided Colleges	2	4.17
4.	Self Financing Colleges	29	60.41
5.	Research Institutions	2	4.17
Total		48	100

4. Objectives of the Study

The study has been conducted with the following objectives:

- To study the growth and development of different types of libraries in Puducherry region.
- To examine the resources available in the libraries under study.
- To survey the quantum of collection development in the libraries of Puducherry Region.
- To analyse the collection development policy adapted by the libraries in Puducherry Region.
- To analyse and interpret the opinion of the respondent libraries with the state-of-the art collection development.

- To suggest the ways and means to adopt need based collection development policy which best suits for providing effective information services to the user's community.

5. Collection Development

5.1 *Size of Book Collection*

The data in Table 2 presents the size of books collection in different institutions. The collection is highly concentrated below 10,000 books in three-fourths of the libraries. The reason being most (70.83%) of the libraries were established during 1990's and the collection slowly progressed in these libraries. On the other hand, 4 (8.33%) libraries have collection between 50,000 to 1,00,000 and in one library the collection has gone beyond one lakh, since it is the Central University library established two decades ago.

Table 2: Size of Book Collection

Sl. No.	*Category*	*Volumes*					*Total (%)*
		Below 10,000	*10,001–20,000*	*20,001–50,000*	*50,001–1 lakh*	*> 1 Lakh*	
1.	University	1	–	–	–	1	2 (4.17)
2.	Government	7	–	5	3	–	15 (31.25)
3.	Government aided	2	–	–	–	–	2 (4.17)
4.	Self-financing	26	2	–	1	–	29 (60.41)
Total (%)		36 (75.01)	2 (4.17)	5 (10.41)	4 (8.33)	1 (2.08)	48 (100)

5.2 *Subscription of Periodicals*

Periodicals are the back-bone to do research to get latest information in their respective areas of interest. The libraries under the survey with regard to the subscription of periodicals are presented in Table 3. About 70% of the libraries subscribing to less than 100 journals, on the other hand, only 2 (4.17%) libraries

Table 3: Periodicals Subscription

Sl. No.	*Category*	*Titles Subscribed*				*Total (%)*
		< 100	*101–200*	*201–500*	*> 500*	
1.	University	–	–	1	1	2 (4.17)
2.	Government	10	3	2	–	15 (31.25)
3.	Government aided	1	–	1	–	2 (4.17)
4.	Self-financing	23	5	–	1	29 (60.41)
Total (%)		34 (70.83)	8 (16.67)	4 (8.33)	2 (4.17)	48 (100)

subscribe to more than 500 journals. The analysis clearly reflects that universities and higher education institutions required more journals for extensive study and research.

5.3 *E-Resource Collection*

Developments in the area of information and communication technologies (ICT) impact on all walks of human life and the society. The emerging trends in ICT, more particularly e-resources in libraries, are changing entire library environment. How the libraries are moving towards building of e-resources to fulfill the changing needs of user community is presented in Table 4. The majority of the self financing colleges (60.41%) are subscribing to electronic resources followed by Govt. Colleges *i.e.*, 31.25%. It is interesting to note that majority of the higher educational institutions in Puducherry region moving towards print to the electronic due user demand and institutions encouragement in the changing technological environment.

Table 4: Collection of E-resources

Sl. No.	*Category*	*Number*				*Total (%)*
		<100	*101–500*	*501–1000*	*>1000*	
1.	University	–	–	1	1	2(4.17)
2.	Government	11	3	–	1	15(31.25)
3.	Government aided	1	1	–	–	2(4.17)
4.	Self-financing	24	4	–	1	29(60.41)
	Total (%)	36 (75.00)	8 (16.67)	1 (2.08)	3 (6.25)	48 (100)

6. Collection Development Policy and Committee

The well structured collection development policy plays a crucial role in the overall collection development of the institutions. There are associations, organisations and institutions which evolved a collection development policy for different types of libraries to adopt and execute the same. In many cases libraries are not strongly following any national standard collection development policy due to various reasons. The survey showed that in the Puducherry region, 31 (68.75%) libraries are adopting their own institutional policy for the collection development; in 33 (64.58%) libraries, some times it was approved by the library committee or organization or institute management.

Book selection can be done by faculties, students, librarians, heads of the Institutions and the Library Committee. A judicial selection of books in any library is one wherein different people shall involve and it should not be vested with one or a few individuals. Therefore, in this survey, the librarians were asked to indicate the authority for book selection. It is found that (Table 5) in majority of the libraries 44 (91.66%), faculties of institutions are responsible for the book selection. Role of librarians is noticed in 43 (89.58%) libraries. Further it is observed that in many libraries more than one person is involved in the book selection. But it is interesting to note that students are also participating in the book selection in 2 (4.17%) libraries.

Table 5: Book Selection Procedure in Libraries

Sl. No.	*Description*	*Libraries*	*%*
1.	Library Committee	30	62.50
2.	Heads of departments	30	62.50
3.	Faculty	44	91.66
4.	Students	2	4.16
5.	Librarian views considered	43	89.58
6.	Heads of institutions	29	60.41

It was found that more than one book selection tool has been used in selecting the books which is a sound practice. The book selection tools used in these libraries including publishers' catalogue (97.91%), publishers' website (87.50%), publishers' circulate e-mails (83.33%), book reviews (83.33%) and national bibliographies (18.75%). From the analysis it is clearly reflects that all most all the libraries under the survey they are following locally developed collection development policy based on the nature and type of institutions. Further it is noticed that the active library users also involved in library collection development.

7. Mode of Book Procurement

Book procurement is done by several modes. The obtained from the libraries reveals that books approval basis (48, 100%) is followed by all libraries followed by from local book shops (44, 91.66%), directly from publishers and through appointing vendors (43, 89.58%) each, inviting quotations (42, 87.50%), and by organising book exhibitions (40, 83.33%). The data also reveals that more than 80% of the libraries are following all the above stated methods in acquiring books. It is observed from the analysis it is good to note that different libraries following different methods of book procurement according to the local needs and approved by the library committee and authorities of the management.

8. ICT Applications and Collection Development Policy

The reasons for the impact of IT applications on collection development policy have been analysed. Six different variables have been considered for this purpose and the analysis is shown in Table 6. It is observed from the Table that a majority of the respondents (81.25%) felt that "IT application affects the regular budgeting provision". Three-fourths (75%) of the sample felt that "IT takes major share form budget" and "operational cost will exceed year after year". The least impact factor is that "IT applications higher salaries for the trained staff that affect the collection development policy".

Table 6: ICT Applications Affecting Collection Development

Sl. No	*Description*	*Institutions (%)*					
		University	*Govt.*	*Govt Aided*	*Self-Financed*	*Total (%)*	*Rank*
1.	Affects regular budgeting	2 (4.17)	12 (25.00)	2 (4.17)	23 (47.91)	39 (81.25)	1
2.	ICT takes major share of budget	2 (4.17)	12 (25.00)	1 (.08)	21 (43.75)	36 (75)	2
3.	Operational costs exceed year by year	1 (2.08)	11 (22.91)	2 (.17)	22 (48.83)	36 (75)	2
4.	AMC cost affects collection development	1 (2.08)	9 (18.75)	1 (2.08)	14 (29.16)	25 (52.08)	4
5.	Higher salaries for trained staff	–	8 (16.66)	1 (2.08)	12 (25)	21 (43.75)	5
6.	Imbalanced collection development	2 (4.17)	9 (18.75)	2 (4.17)	18 (37.5)	31 (64.58)	3

In order to identify the significance of the variables that affect the collection development policy, chi-squire test has been conducted and presented in Table 7. It is interesting to note that there is significant relationship between the variables affecting collection development and the IT applications with respect to the different types of libraries, since the calculated chi-square value is less than the table value (11.070). Further, it is interpreted that the ranking of the variables did not change much from the frequency distribution analysis and chi-square test (Table 8). From the analysis (Table 7) and Chi-square values (Table 8) clearly exhibit that the ICT strongly influencing on collection

Table 8: Chi-square Test on Collection Development and ICT Applications

Sl. No.	*Variable*	*Chi-square Value*
1.	IT affects the regular budgeting provision	1.907
2.	IT takes major share from the budget	3.165
3.	Operational costs are exceeding year by year	2.359
4.	AMC costs affect the collection development	1.612
5.	Higher salaries for a trained staff affects the collection development	7.008
6.	Balanced collection development	5.770
7.	Adequate fund are provided	2312

Note: Degrees of freedom is 5. Table value at 95% level of significance is 11.070.

development of different higher educational institutions under the study area and at the same time it was noticed that higher the impact of ICT higher benefits to the libraries and information centers.

9. Changing Dimensions of Library Resources: Library of the Future

With the changing dimensions and directions of ICT fast approaching the library and information centres (LICs) around the world, the electronic information sources have become integral part of the library. Electronic and web resources play crucial role to in the teaching, learning, research and extension activities of the institutions and organisations. The impact of electronic information resources on LICs has been widely reported in the literature with change dramatically impacting higher education, change that focuses on and enabling array of technologies and networks to advance teaching, learning, and research. This vision encompasses a new library that blends the best traditions of the past—those of structure, service, and subsidy—with an electronic or virtual learning one which transcends time or a place.

10. Suggestions

The following two suggestions are given for adopting need-based co-operative collection development for the libraries:

10.1 *Collection Development Policy*

One of the major factors affecting library effectiveness is the size and nature of the collection which needs direct attention by administrators and the library managers. It is necessary to develop the collection to satisfy the information needs of the designated users of the respective libraries. In view of the changing scenario in the ICT and changing needs of users, it is suggested that libraries in Puducherry shall strive a right choice between printed and electronic publications. In case of difficulty to acquire the necessary information resources due to financial constraints, it is suggested that they can enter into resource sharing arrangements with the other libraries at local, regional or national level. Further, it is suggested that they should draft and implement a workable collection development policy which shall be objective and need based.

10.2 *Digital Resources-based Organisations*

Considering the significance and utility of digital resources, it is suggested that libraries, in addition to print resources, shall build digital resource collection in conformity with the vision and mission of their parent organisations. Further it is suggested that librarians should draw the e-resources from other institutions and also tap the freely available e-resources over the net. The recent advances in ICTs, networking, Internet and electronic products have brought about a revolutionary change profoundly affecting the selection, acquisition and information transfer processes in libraries. The technology is mainly being used for communication, database searching, bibliographic and full-text searching. It has also changed the concept of archiving.

11. Conclusions

The recording and communicating the human knowledge through the years changed enormously; but more changes are taken place after the invention of printing technology which has given birth for new avenues and avatars in the society and even the educational institutions and libraries. From the inception of the libraries the collection development is an important activity for all types of libraries. With strong influence of ICT, libraries are seeing a sea of changes in terms different form of DVD-ROMs, e-journals, e-books and e-databases. These resources are more user friendly with multimedia capabilities for greater understanding of thought content and also can be accessed any time anywhere. But there are challenges before the LIS professionals in building and management of e-resources in a networked environment. The present study gives a clear cut opinion and trend in collection development with e-resources by the participated libraries in Puducherry region. The study proves that users still prefer printed resources for their study, learning and research purpose. But there is a growing trend in moving slowly to electronic and online resources, more particularly by younger generation and also those who are studying technology related subject areas. Therefore it is the need of the hour that libraries under the study need to have strong and appropriate collection development policies to satisfy all types of user community as well as to acquire more electronic and online resources which will lead the networked information society.

References

[1] Desphande, K.S. (1999). The Librarian, the book trade and collection development: random reflections. *Library Science with a Slant to Documentation and Information Studies*, 36(4): 249-256.

[2] Maharana, B, Choudhury, B.K. and Dutta, S (2004) Collection development of electronic information resources in the R and D libraries of Kolkatta city: a survey. Library Herald, 42(3): 225–246.

[3] Seetharama, S. (1997). Collection development/management in an information technology based environment: current initiation and issues. DESIDOC Bulletin of Information Technology, 17(1):11–20.

[4] Ramesha (2006). Changing dimensions of electronic information sources and services in the networked environment: Paradigm shift from physical place to virtual space. *In* Library Resources and Services in the Digital Era. SRM University, Kattankulathur, pp. 134–141.

Electronic Resources Management in Libraries, pp. 144–163

Building Digital Libraries using Greenstone

M.G. Sreekumar

ABSTRACT

Digital Libraries (DLs) have been gaining increasing attention as well as academic interest over the years worldwide, owing to the growing demand for improved information and knowledge management solutions in universities, institutions as well as enterprises. Advancements in technology in recent years and its resultant diffusion into society are just the natural offshoots which propelled this movement. DLs are structured storage environments of digital data with a consistent format for index and content abstraction. DLs do enable the seamless integration of the scholarly electronic information, help in creating and maintaining local digital content, and strengthen the mechanisms and the capacity of the library's information systems and services. Considering the fact that currently the penetration of electronic content into our libraries and information centers is gone upto 70–80 percent, it unequivocally prompts us to leverage on the latest digital technologies towards building practical digital libraries and in setting up dynamic electronic information systems. Without proper understanding of the complexities, procedures and practices involved in content building, content management, collection building, metadata harvesting as well as collaboration, and the long term preservation strategies, individual DLs will remain islands of structure in an unstructured Internet sea. Developing world standard digital libraries demand deployment of costly software solutions which are obviously beyond the reach of most of the universities/institutions and this is more so in the Asian and the African region. This paper therefore aims at portraying the unlimited potential of DLs in real world perspective by trying out open source solutions. It attempts to unleash and demystify the plethora of features and functionalities of the open source software Greenstone. For the information professionals who subscribe to continuing education and to those who value and nurture the spirit of life long learning, Greenstone is close to their hearts, and needs no introduction. Greenstone is a top of the line and internationally renowned software system for developing digital libraries, promoted by the New Zealand Digital Library project research group at the University of Waikato. It is developed and distributed in cooperation with UNESCO and the Human Info NGO. The aim of the software is to empower users, particularly in universities, libraries, and other public service institutions, to build their own digital libraries. One of the key features of Greenstone is that it is quite easy to install, configure, customize and administer, even by the novice. It also facilitates seamless aggregation and integration of the digital content possessed by the library. More details of the software and examples of building digital libraries using the Greenstone software are available at http://www.greenstone.org.

1. Introduction

Libraries all over the world are in the constant business of providing their clientele nascent as well as legacy information and in the process they buy, subscribe, license and accumulate information in an unprecedented array of content categories or publication types, and in a rapidly proliferating mix of formats (digital as well as print). There is a great deal of cultural divide and philosophical deviation between the traditional information resources being handled by libraries for centuries now and the new genre of electronic and digital information being sourced and accessed. In the traditional paradigm, the books and journals bought and subscribed to by the libraries were naturally owned by them, allowing them to make the best use of the resources within the 'fair use' clause of Copyright Act. Whereas in the electronic publishing scenario all the traditional belief, approach and understanding about the digital documents that the library purchase/subscribe to, have a world of difference. Libraries get only a license to use the electronic information (books, journals, databases, softwares etc.) against purchasing, and even this license is issued only for a prescribed period of time. Librarians at the same time, have the professional responsibility to assure uninterrupted as well as perpetual access to the information subscribed to by the library. Issues of copyright, intellectual property, and fair use are very much important to libraries (Orsdel, 2002).

In the current practical library setting there is an amazing penetration of digital information through a variety of publication forms such as books, journals, portals, vortals, reports, CBTs, WBTs, cases, databases etc. The penetration level of electronic information in the special libraries and libraries belonging to centers of higher learning are supposed to be 70% against their print counterparts. To make matters more complex the vast array of different formats, standards and platforms in which documents are published, pose a multiplicity of threats to the librarian who is supposed to be the custodian and service provider of these information products once it has found its way into the library. As librarians, we are sometimes the stewards of unique collections too.

2. Digital Libraries

Digital Libraries (DLs) are emerging as a crucial component of global information infrastructure, adopting the latest information and communication technology. DLs are networked collections of digital texts, documents, images, sounds, data, software, and many more that are the core of today's Internet and tomorrow's universally accessible digital repositories of all human knowledge. According to the Digital Library Federation (DLF- http://www.dlf.org), digital libraries are organizations that provide the resources, including the specialized staff, to select, structure, offer intellectual access to, interpret, distribute, preserve the integrity of, and ensure the persistence over the time of collections of digital works so that they are readily and economically available for use by a defined community or set of communities.

Currently in vast majority of instances, the concept Digital Library is being practiced by and large loosely or even confused by many information systems. It is therefore imperative that the concept is properly understood so that there is no ambiguity while we progress with the work of designing or developing a DL which is fully justified in the technical sense of the word. It is important that embarking on a digital library project is something which will take away substantial amount of time, energy, manpower and of course the hard earned money being pumped into it – be it for system development or towards development and maintenance of the collection, in a meaningful way. There is consensus all over that there exists a very large quantum of digital information, scholarly as well as trade, which are scattered and distributed throughout the Net and also being stored in numerous other databases and repositories spread across the world. Also there is an unprecedented technology support and availability of infrastructure for digital libraries.

3. Digital Library Features

Digital libraries offer new levels of access to broader audiences of users and new opportunities for library and information science field to advance both theory and practice (Marchionini, 1998). They contain information collections predominantly in digital or electronic form. Electronic publications have some special management requirements as compared to printed document. They include infrastructure, acceptability, access restrictions, readability, standardization, authentication, preservation, copyright, user interface etc.

DLs enable the seamless integration of scholarly electronic information, help in creating and maintaining local digital content, and strengthen the mechanisms and capacity of the library's information systems and services. They increase the portability, efficiency of access, flexibility, availability and preservation of digital objects. DLs can help in moving the nation towards realizing the enormously powerful vision of 'anytime, anywhere' access to the best and the latest of human thought and culture, so that no classroom, individual or a society is isolated from knowledge resources. DL brings the library to the user, overcoming all geographical barriers (ICDL, 2004).

4. Digital Library Software

Undoubtedly it is essential to have a robust and flexible digital collections management and presentation software for creating and delivering digital collections. The preservation of digital objects is currently intimately tied to software that presents those objects. Complete preservation of complex digital objects, especially, is likely to require preservation of the software needed to use those objects (Borgman, 1996). The complexity of the situation is that DL technologies and contents are not static. Continual evolution and investment are required to maintain the DL. Commercial DL products are comprehensive and extensible enough to support this evolution, but in many cases they are beyond the reach of most of the libraries in India. Some of the popular commercial DL software in the Indian libraries including VTLS (http://www.vtls.com) from the international market and ACADO (http://www.transversalnet.com/acado/index.htm) as an Indian initiative. The latter is definitely less costly when compared but still striving its best to get a critical mass of users. The whole lot of associated issues include initial purchase fee, licensing fee, upgrade fee, annual maintenance contacts (AMCs) and so on. The best available choice for the librarian now is to turn to an Open Source Software (OSS). OSS has grown tremendously in scope and popularity over the last several years, and is now in widespread use. The growth of OSS has gained the attention of research librarians and created new opportunities for libraries (Frumkin, 2002). According to Stallman and others OSS is a Free Software uses the 'free' from 'freedom', not the one from 'free beer' (http://www.opensource.org/docs/definition_plain.html).

"OSS is software for which the source code is available to the end-user so that they can modify as per their requirements. The licensing conditions are intended to facilitate continued re-use and wide availability of the software in both commercial and non-commercial contexts. The cost of acquisition to the end-user is often minimal. According to the proponents of OSS, 'Open source is a development methodology; free software is a social movement'. There are number of other notable features to OSS. Firstly, it has no secrets and innards are available for anyone to inspect. It is not privately controlled hence it is likely to promote open access approach rather than proprietary formats. It is typically maintained by communities rather than corporations and hence bug fixes and enhancement are often frequent and free. It is usually distributed free of charge (developers make their money from support, training, and specialist add-ons; not marketing). It is also essential to clear up some of the misunderstandings about OSS. Open source software may or may not cost money. The cost of ownership often bears little relation to the cost of acquiring a piece of software. Open source software has a copyright holder and conditions of legal use. Open source software does not mandate exclusivity. One can use open source programs under Windows. Also one should not choose software solely on the basis of open source. Interoperability and open standards for data are equally important" (OSS Watch, 2005).

According to Altman, for the library fraternity there are other set of reasons too for preferring OSS over commercial software. Long term preservation, assurance of privacy, provision for auditing, facilitating community resources, and conformity to open standards are hallmarks of OSS. Since commercial software is usually distributed only as a binary that will run only on a single hardware platform (and often only under a single version of a particular operating system) commercial software is very difficult to preserve over the long run without developing hardware emulation (and possibly OS 'emulation', as well). OSS, in contrast, can often be recompiled, or at least ported, to new hardware and operating systems (Altman, 2001). In order to get a picture about the availability of OSS for DL applications, it is encouraged to visit the directories of OSS projects, such as GNU (http://www.gnu.org) and SourceForge (http://www.sourceforge.net) open source directory which lists over fifty-thousand projects, and the numbers continuously growing.

5. Digital Library Objectives and Workflow

The primary objective of a DL is to enhance the digital collection in a substantial way, by strategically sourcing digital materials, conforming to copyright permissions, in all possible standards/formats so that scalability and flexibility is guaranteed for the future and advanced information services are assured to the user community right from the beginning. The DL library should also be able to integrate and aggregate the existing collections and services mentioned above with an outstanding client interface. This implies that the DL system should also have a strong collection interface capable of embracing almost all the popular digital standards and formats and software platforms, in line with the underlying DL technologies in vogue. This is crucial in the case of multimedia integration, which is again important as we planned to also host a digital audio and video library as part of the core library collection. Emphasis should also be given to maximize the efficiency and effectiveness of the information access and retrieval capabilities of the system by deploying Resource Description Framework (RDF) supplemented with popular descriptive metadata standards. The Internet also possesses, in addition to its mammoth proprietary information base, an invaluable wealth and a vast collection of public domain information products such as databases, books, journals, theses, technical reports, cases, standards, newsletters etc., scattered and distributed across the world. This treasure should also be explored to its maximum for collection building, based on the source and quality. Standard workflow patterns are to be identified for the system which include 'content selection', 'content acquisition', 'content publishing', 'content indexing and storage', and 'content accessing and delivery'. The system should also concern about such related issues, viz., preservation, usage monitoring, access management, inter-operability, administration and management etc.

It is always desirable to have crosswalks between the digital catalogue of the library (OPAC) and the DL, as the OPAC in most cases, acts as a stepping stone for effective information discovery in the library. It also facilitates a healthy bridging between the traditional and the DL. MARC or any of its variant forms is the desired bibliographic standard recommended for the OPAC, for want of interoperability. Dublin Core (DCMI), MODS (Metadata Object Description Schema) or METS (Metadata Encoding and Transmission) are the recommended metadata format for the digital collection, and XML is the desired encoding scheme (XML). The XML encoding schemas and the related DTDs (Document Type Definitions) strengthen the digital library on strong footing and the XSL (Extensible Stylesheet Language) transformations acts as dynamic gateways between the diverse data streams and the HTML front-end.

6. Selection of the Digital Library Software

The software selection based on set parameters is an uphill task, as the technology itself is still emerging. In general, what is desirable is a system that is flexible enough to fit the current digital information system as above and to accommodate future migration. It should be robust in technical architecture as well as the content architecture. The system should address all major DL related issues such as 'design criteria', 'collection building', 'content organisation', 'access', 'evaluation', 'policy and legal issues' including 'intellectual property rights'. That the system should be in a position to embrace almost all predominant and emerging digital object formats and capable of supporting the standard library technology platforms, should be the major focus. It should provide two important user interfaces: a public user interface for presentation and a metadata creation interface for administration. The system should also provide a powerful search engine and the interface should be easy to navigate and there should be provision for customization.

There are many DL softwares available, proprietary as well as open source, and most of them conform to international standards. As mentioned earlier, VTLS and ACADO are the commercial ones available and popular in the Indian market. Some of the popular Open Source Softwares for digital libraries, which are in use internationally, are 'DSpace', 'Dienst', 'Eprints', 'Fedora', 'Greenstone', etc. In line with the subject thrust of this paper, the Greenstone features are discussed in this paper.

7. Developing Digital Libraries Using Open Source Software

Digital libraries do enable the creation of local content, strengthen the mechanisms and capacity of the library's information systems and services. They increase the portability, efficiency of access, flexibility, availability and preservation of content. A state-of-art DL shall give a real boost to the library's modernization activities and its endeavours to launch innovative digital information services to the user community. Once the information is made digital, it could be stored, retrieved, shared, copied and transmitted across distances without having to invest any additional expenditure. Value added and pinpointed information at the click of the mouse will become a reality if there is a Library Portal to provide access to the invaluable collection hosted by the DL.

World over there is increasing appreciation of the Open Access (OA) movement and the Open Source Software (OSS) philosophies and for may a libraries it is a chosen decision, be it technical or financial reasons, not to go for a proprietary digital library software. One needs to evaluate some of the popular OSS for DLs, which are in use internationally. 'Dienst', 'Eprints', 'Fedora', 'Greenstone', etc. are among the candidates for the preferred software. Obviously Greenstone outscores the group as a general purpose DL software from the point of view of a multi-publication type, multi-format, multimedia and a multi-lingual practical DL (Greenstone). And once finalized, it could be formally adopted as the software for creating the DL.

The Greenstone Digital Library Software (GSDL) is a top of the line and internationally renowned OSS system for developing digital libraries, promoted by the New Zealand Digital Library project research group at the University of Waikato, led by Dr. Ian H. Witten, and is sponsored by the UNESCO. Greenstone software uses three more additional associated softwares namely, Java Run Time Environment (JRE), ImageMagick and Ghostscript. The software suite is available at the open source directory 'Sourceforge.Net'.

8. Greenstone Fact Sheet (www.greenstone.org)

Greenstone is a suite of software for building and distributing digital library collections. It is not a digital library but a tool for building digital libraries. It provides a new way of organizing information and publishing it on the Internet in the form of a fully-searchable, metadata-driven digital library. It has been developed and distributed in cooperation with UNESCO and the Human Info NGO in Belgium. It is open-source, multilingual software, issued under the terms of the GNU General Public License. Its developers received the 2004 IFIP Namur award for "contributions to the awareness of social implications of information technology, and the need for an holistic approach in the use of information technology that takes account of social implications."

There are presently two versions of Greenstone going around, Version 2 and 3, and they are generally represented as Greenstone2 and Greenstone3. The latest in Greenstone2 as on June 2012 is V.2.85 and that of Greenstone3 is V.04. Greenstone2 will be there for some more years, but ultimately Waikato/Greenstone see that Geenstone3 will replace it.

8.1 *Technical Features*

Platforms: Greenstone runs on all versions of Windows, and Unix, and Mac OS-X. It is very easy to install. For the default Windows installation absolutely no configuration is necessary, and end users routinely install Greenstone on their personal laptops or workstations. Institutional users run it on their main web server, where it interoperates with standard web server software (*e.g.* Apache).

Interoperability: Greenstone is highly interoperable using contemporary standards, It incorporates a server that can serve any collection over the Open Archives Protocol for Metadata Harvesting (OAI-PMH), and Greenstone can harvest documents over OAI-PMH and include them in a collection. Any collection can be exported to METS (in the Greenstone METS Profile, approved by the METS Editorial Board and published at http://www.loc.gov/standards/mets/mets-profiles.html), and Greenstone can ingest documents in METS form. Any collection can be exported to DSpace ready for DSpace's batch import program, and any DSpace collection can be imported into Greenstone.

Interfaces: Greenstone has two separate interactive interfaces, the Reader interface and the Librarian interface. End users access the digital library through the Reader interface, which operates within a web browser. The Librarian interface is a Java-based graphical user interface (also available as an applet) that makes it easy to gather material for a collection (downloading it from the web if necessary), enrich it by adding metadata, design the searching and browsing facilities that the collection will offer the user, and build and serve the collection.

Metadata Formats: Users define metadata interactively within the Librarian interface. These metadata sets are predefined: Dublin Core (qualified and unqualified), RFC 1807, NZGLS (New Zealand Government Locator Service), AGLS (Australian Government Locator Service). New metadata sets can be defined using Greenstone's Metadata Set Editor. Plug-ins are used to ingest externally-prepared metadata in different forms, and plug-ins exist for XML, MARC, CDS/ISIS, ProCite, BibTex, Refer, OAI, DSpace, METS.

Document Formats: Greenstone basically supports all popular file formats and media. Plug-ins are also used to ingest documents. For textual documents, there are plug-ins for PDF, PostScript, Word, RTF, HTML, Plain text, Latex, ZIP archives, Excel, PPT, Email (various formats), source code. For multimedia documents, there are plug-ins for Images (any format, including GIF, JIF, JPEG, TIFF), MP3 audio, Ogg Vorbis audio, and a generic plug-in that can be configured for audio formats, MPEG, MIDI, etc.

9. User Base

***Distribution*:** As with all open source projects, the user base for Greenstone is unknown. Tens of thousands of installations of Greenstone are estimated across world as is evidenced by the increasing volume of messages being exchanged in the various fora, especially the Greenstone E-lists. It is distributed on SourceForge, a leading distribution centre for OSS.

Greenstone Example Collections: Examples of public Greenstone collections (see http://www.greenstone.org for URLs) can be found at:

- Association of Indian Labour Historians, Delhi
- Auburn University, Alabama
- California University at Riverside
- Chicago University Library
- Detroit Public Library
- Gresham College, London
- Hawaiian Electronic Library
- Illinois Wesleyan University
- Indian Institute of Management Kozhikode (IIMK)
- Kyrgyz Republic National Library
- LeHigh University, Pennsylvania
- Mari El Republic, Russia
- National Centre for Science Information, Bangalore, India
- Netherlands Institute for Scientific Information Services
- New York Botanical Garden
- Peking University Digital Library
- Philippine Research Education and Government Information Network
- Secretary of Human Rights of Argentina
- Slavonski Brod Public Library, Slovenia
- State Library of Tasmania
- Stuttgart University of Applied Sciences
- Texas A&M University Center for the Study of Digital Libraries
- University of Illinois
- University of North Carolina Bibiblio project
- Vietnam National University
- Vimercate Public Library, Milan, Italy
- Washington Research Library Consortium
- Welsh Books Council

10. Languages

One of Greenstone's unique strengths is its multilingual nature. The reader's interface is available in the following languages: Arabic, Armenian, Bengali, Catalan, Croatian, Czech, Chinese (both simplified and traditional), Dutch, English, Farsi, Finnish, French, Galician, Georgian, German, Greek, Hebrew, Hindi, Indonesian, Italian, Japanese, Kannada, Kazakh, Kyrgyz, Latvian, Maori, Mongolian, Portuguese (BR and PT versions), Russian, Serbian, Spanish, Thai, Turkish, Ukrainian, Vietnamese. The Librarian interface and the full Greenstone documentation (which is extensive) is in: English, French, Spanish, and Russian.

11. Training

Training is a bottleneck for widespread adoption of any digital library software. Greenstone's Waikato site http://www.greenstone.org; the Greenstone Wiki http://g reenstone.sourceforge. net/wiki/index.php/GreenstoneWiki. The Greenstone Support for South Asia http://greenstonesupport.iimk.ac.in give many training materials and guidance on the software. It is observed that Greenstone training and workshops are quite common in digital library conferences and seminar all over the world and this itself speaks volumes the importance of Greenstone.

12. E-mail Support

There are many E-Lists and E-Groups available for Greenstone support. For subscribing to the main Greenstone lists, visit https://list.scms.waikato.ac.nz/mailman/listinfo/greenstone-users, for User's List (greenstone-users-request@list. scms.waikato.ac.nz) and https://list.scms.waikato.ac.nz/mailman/listinfo/greenstone-devel for Developer's list. There is also an E-List for supporting the South Asian Greenstone users greenstonesupport@iimk.ac.in. You can join the South Asia Support E-List by filling the form at http://eprints.iimk.ac.in/mailman/listinfo/greenstonesupport.

13. Greenstone: Features

The salient features of Greenstone are basically taken from two of the official publications of the software development team appeared in D-Lib Magazine during the year 2001 (Witten, 2001) and 2003 (Witten, 2003). Greenstone builds collections using almost popular and standard digital formats such as HTML, XML, Word, Post Script, PDF, RTF, JPG, GIF, JPEG, MPEG etc. and many other formats which include audio as well as video. It is provided with effective full-text searching and metadata-based browsing facilities that are attractive and easy to use. Moreover, they are easily maintained and can be augmented and rebuilt entirely automatically. The system is extensible: software plug-ins accommodate different document and metadata types. Greenstone incorporates an interface that makes it easy for people to create their own library collections. Collections may be built and served locally from the user's own web server, or (given appropriate permissions) remotely on a shared digital library host. End users can easily build new collections styled after existing ones from material on the Web or from their local files (or both), and collections can be updated and new ones brought on-line at any time. The Greenstone Librarian Interface (GLI) is a Java based GUI interface for easy collection building. Greenstone software runs on a wide variety of platforms such as Windows, Unix/Linux, Apple Mac etc. and provides full-text mirroring, indexing, searching, browsing and metadata extraction. It incorporates an interface that makes it easy for institutions to create their own library collections. Collections could be built and served locally from the user's own web server, or (given appropriate permissions) remotely on a shared digital library host. The other set of features include OAI plug-in (introduced since the 2.40 version) and DCMI compliance, UNICODE based multi-lingual capabilities and a user-friendly multimedia interfacing (Unicode). Further more, it has a powerful search engine 'Managing Gigabyte' Plus-Plus ('MG' PP) and metadata-based browsing facilities. A very interesting feature of Greenstone is its exhaustive set of well documented and articulated manuals (http://www.greenstone.org/cgi-bin/library?e=p-en-docs-utfZz-8&a=p&p=docs) such as 'Installer's Guide', 'User's Guide', 'Developer's Guide', and 'From Paper to Collection' a document describing the entire process of creating a digital library collection from paper documents. This includes the scanning and OCR process and the use of the Organizer. There is one more interesting documentation 'Inside Greenstone Collections' which clarifies most of the trickier parts of using Greenstone, especially dealing with configuration file for the collection in question.

The primary objective of any digital library will be to enhance the digital collection in a substantial way, by strategically sourcing digital materials, conforming to copyright permissions, in all possible standards/formats so that scalability and flexibility is guaranteed for the future and advanced information services and are assured to the user community right from beginning. The digital library has to be planned in such a way that it will integrate and aggregate the existing collections and services with an outstanding user interface. Accordingly, necessary strategies are to be adopted towards working out the digital library system. This implies that the digital library system should have a strong collection interface capable of embracing almost all the popular digital standards, digital formats and software platforms, in line with the underlying digital library technologies in vogue. This is crucial in the case of multimedia integration, which is again important as it is planned to host digital audio and video library as part of the core library collection.

14. Greenstone Installation

The GNU Public License version Greenstone can be downloaded from http://www.greenstone.org or http://sourceforge.net/index.php. You can download the binaries for Linux or Windows. The associated softwares such as Java Runtime Environment (JRE) and the Imagemagick are also to be downloaded. A graphical tool is used for collection building and configurations and customization. This is called the Greenstone Librarian Interface (GLI) and it requires the Java Runtime Environment (JRE). The latest version pertaining to Volume 2 release of Greenstone as on June 2012 is V.2.85. Here is what you need to do to install Greenstone:

- Select the language for this installation. We choose **English**
- Welcome to the Greenstone Digital Library Software Installer. It is recommended that you uninstall any previous installations of Greenstone2 before running this installer. Click <**Next**>
- License Agreement. Click <**Accept**>
- Choose location to install Greenstone. Leave at the default and click <**Next**>
- Components. Click the question mark button on the right of each component will display the description of this component in a popup window. Leave at the default (all components are selected) and click <**Next**>
- (For older installers you must now select collections. Leave at the default, Documented Example Collections, and click <**Next**>)
- Enable administration pages. Read the description on this page, if you check to enable, click <**Next**> to set admin password. Choose a suitable password and click

<**Next**> (If your computer will not be serving collections online, the password doesn't matter)

- Click <**Install**> to start the installation. Click <**Show Details**> to show the details of this installation
- Files are copied across.

15. Collection Building and Configuration

Greenstone used to have three modes for collection building, viz., Command Line, Web Interface and the GLI. Among these GLI is the one getting more prominence as far as the librarian/information professionals are concerned?

15.1 *Greenstone Librarian Interface*

The GLI was introduced recently, progressing with the version 2.4x. Soon the GLI got strengthened as well as popularized, and the Web Interface mode has been withdrawn temporarily, while it could also be reinforced if one wishes so. The GLI based collection building is quite easy and simple a method. Collection developers can activate the GLI software and use the 'Gather', 'Enrich', 'Design', 'Create', and the 'Format' panels for making, configuring, customizing and managing collections.

(a) The 'Gather' Panel facilitates putting the relevant files from the 'workspace' to the 'collection building' area. The 'Enrich' Panel explains how metadata is created, edited, assigned and retrieved, and how to use external metadata sources. Help for this is provided in the GLI Interface. The 'Design' Panel facilitates customizing your interface, once your files are marked up with metadata. Using the Gather Panel, you can specify the fields that are searchable, allow browsing through the document, facilitate the languages that are supported, and provide the buttons that are to appear on the page. Help for this is provided in the GLI Interface. The Create Panel facilitates creation of your collection.

To build a typical collection, say MyTest collection, first go to File section, select New and then give the collection name as MyTest. Select OK from the panel and then you will get another panel popped up where you will select the appropriate Metadata Set. You may also give the description about the collection here. By default, the system will prompt Dublin Core metadata set. Click on OK button and you will get the collection create panel made ready for accepting the file(s).

The 'Gather' Panel is activated now. From the 'Workspace' provided, identify the document to be put in the collection by locating it in the local folder. Drag and drop the file to the Collection Area using the mouse. The necessary plug-in for the creation of the collection is to be tick marked and enabled in the 'Design' panel, which is the next step in the collection building process. If the collection has objects for which plug-ins are not provided in the default set, a new dialog box for adding the required plug-in will appear and it has to be the added to the default set.

(b) Go to the **Enrich** panel and give necessary values for the Dublin Core element sets.

***Manage Metadata Sets*:** This feature allows you to add, configure and remove the Metadata Sets in your collection and what Elements they contain.

(c) **Design Panel:** The next step is to give necessary values and arguments for the **Design** panel which include (Note: GLI Design Panel's own language is used below i. to x., for want of clarity and to avoid any ambiguity in usage):

- ***General Options:*** In this section, give the e-mail address of the 'collection creator', 'collection maintainer', 'collection title' (will be supplied by the system), collection folder (will be supplied by the system), Image file location for the Collection icon and the Image file location for the Document icon. Click on the Tick mark for making this collection publicly available.
- ***Document Plug-ins:*** This section facilitates adding, configuring or removing plug-ins from your collection. To add one, choose it from the combobox and click Add Plug-in. To configure or remove one, select it from the list of assigned plug-ins and then: i) Change its position in the plug-in order by clicking on the arrow buttons. (Note: The position of RecPlug and ArcPlug are fixed). ii) Configure it by clicking Configure Plug-in, iii) Remove it by clicking Remove Plug-in. Plug-ins are configured using a pop-up design area with a scrollable list of arguments. Enable arguments and enter or select values as necessary.
- ***Search Types***: Defining the search type is an advanced feature, only available when enabled (by checking the Enable Advanced Searches box). Once enabled, further controls for selecting and changing the order of search types become available. See the 'Search Type Selection and Ordering' section of the 'Design' Panel for more information on this.
- ***Search Indexes:*** The required number of searchable indexes the collection must have, is to be selected here. To add a new index, enter a unique name for the index, select material/metadata is to be indexed, and click 'Add Index'. If you wish to add all of the available sources so as to have indexes built on them, then click Add All.
- ***Partition Indexes:*** This feature helps to refine index creation. This facility is disabled in the GLI mode.
- ***Cross-Collection Search:*** This feature facilitates cross-collection searching, where a single search is performed over several collections, as if all the collections were one. Specify (Tick Mark) the collections to include in a search by clicking on the appropriate collection's name in the list below. The current collection will automatically be included. (Note: If the individual collections do not have the same indexes (including sub collection partitions and language partitions) as each other, cross-collection searching will not work properly. The user will only be able to search using indexes common to all collections).

- ***Browsing Classifiers:*** This feature allows the A to Z browsing of the collection and by default if takes the Dublin Core. Title You can more data elements in the A to Z classify list as deem fit for the collection using this feature.
- ***Format Features:*** The web pages you see when using Greenstone are not pre-stored, but are generated 'on the fly' as they are needed. Format commands are used to change the appearance of these generated pages. Some are switches that control the display of documents or parts of documents; others are more complex and require html code as an argument. To add a format command, choose it from the 'feature' list. If a True/False option panel appears, select the state by clicking on the appropriate button.
- For example, to get the Cover Image displayed in the document while building the collection, go to the Choose Features dropdown box and enable the DocumentIMages, *i.e.*, make its value to True.
- ***Translate Text:*** Use this feature to review and assign translations of text fragments in your collection. The translated text will appear in a different box in the browser.
- ***Metadata Sets:*** This feature allows you to add, configure and remove the Metadata Sets in your collection and what Elements they contain.

(d) Now go to the **Create** panel and click on the **Build Collection**. Greenstone will start creating the collection. You can see the built collection by clicking on the Preview Collection.

Please remember you have to save your collection development process from time to time. It is not mandatory that you need to comply with the entire set of formalities for a building a collection in a single stretch. You can do it in different sessions too. What is important is saving the sessions from time to time. In the GLI mode of collection building, the various panels to be used are illustrated in Figure 1.

(e) Format Panel

- ***General:*** This section explains how to review and alter the general settings associated with your collection. First, under the Format tab, click General. Here some collection wide metadata can be set or modified, including the title and description entered when starting a new collection. First are the contact email addresses of the collection's creator and maintainer. The following field allows you to change the collection title. The folder that the collection is stored in is shown next, but this cannot be altered. Then comes the icon to show at the top left of the collection's About page (in the form of a URL), followed by the icon used in the Greenstone library page to link to the collection. Next is a checkbox that controls whether the collection should be publicly accessible. Finally comes the Collection Description text area as described in Creating a New Collection.
- ***Search:*** This section explains how to set the display text for the drop down lists on the search page. Under the Format tab, click Search. This pane contains a table

listing each search index, index level (for MGPP or Lucene collections), and index or language partition. Here you can enter the text to be used for each item in the various drop-down lists on the search page. This pane only allows you to set the text for one language, the current language used by GLI. To translate these names for other languages, use the Translate Text part of the Format view (see Translate Text feature in the Format panel).

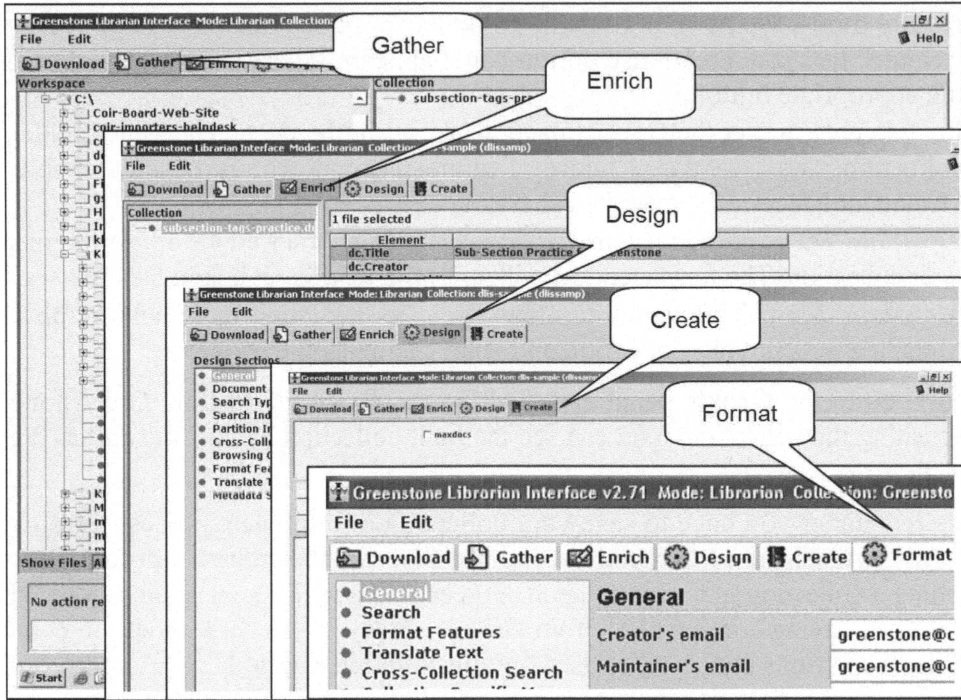

Fig. 1: GLI Panels for Gather, Enrich, Design, Create and Format

- ***Format Features:*** The web pages you see when using Greenstone are not pre-stored, but are generated 'on the fly' as they are needed. Format commands are used to change the appearance of these generated pages. Some are switches that control the display of documents or parts of documents; others are more complex and require html code as an argument. To add a format command, choose it from the 'feature' list. If a True/False option panel appears, select the state by clicking on the appropriate button.

  For example, to get the Cover Image displayed in the document while building the collection, go to the Choose Features dropdown box and enable the DocumentI Mages, *i.e.*, set its value to True.
- ***Translate Text:*** Use this feature to review and assign translations of text fragments in your collection. The translated text will appear in a different box in the browser.

- ***Cross-Collection Search:*** This feature facilitates cross-collection searching, where a single search is performed over several collections, as if all the collections were one. Specify (Tick Mark) the collections to include in a search by clicking on the appropriate collection's name in the list below. The current collection will automatically be included. (Note: If the individual collections do not have the same indexes (including sub collection partitions and language partitions) as each other, cross-collection searching will not work properly. The user will only be able to search using indexes common to all collections).
- ***Collection Specific Macros:*** Under the Format tab, click Collection Specific Macros. This view shows the contents of the collection's extra.dm macro file. This is where collection specific macros can be defined. To learn more about macros, see Chapter 3 of the Greenstone Developer's Guide.

15.2 *Hierarchy Structure*

To create indexes for section and sub-section, the pre-requisite is that the document should be in HTML format. Therefore your collection files in other formats like PDF, Word, etc. are first to be converted into HTML format. Also in the Collection Configuration file (for GLI, in the Design Panel, in the Document Plugin section, while configuring the Arguments in the HTML Plugin, click and enable the 'description_tags'), the HTML plug-in has to be modified to 'plug-in HTMLPlug – description_tags'. Corresponding changes have to be made in the 'indexes' and the 'collectionmeta' lines. Obviously now the Source File has to be edited as a HTML file structure. For the section and sub sections, you need to edit the source file as follows, giving XML tags as comments in the body of the HTML file. The Figure 2 shows a hierarchy structured E-Book.

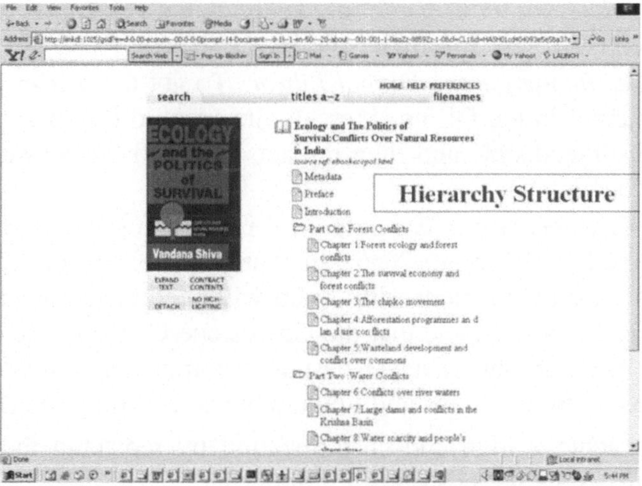

Fig. 2: An E-book with the Hierarchy Structure

15.3 *Customization of User Interface (MyLibrary)*

In order to change the look and feel of the Greenstone user interface, you need to work on the Collection Configuration (Collect.cfg) files. Customising the User Interface requires a certain degree of knowledge on HTML and some level of Web Designing skills are pre-requisites for this.

1. *Collect.cfg:* This is the collection configuration file. You can find this file in the Program Files\Greenstone\collect\etc directory. Details on how to create this file can be found in the Developer's Guide, 1.5 Collection configuration file and 2.3 Formatting Greenstone output.
2. *Macro Files:* Macro files have an extension '.dm'. All macro files are stored in the macros directory. Details on how to create macros and macro files can be found in the Developer's Guide 2.4 controlling the Greenstone user interface.
3. *Image Files:* All images files can be found in the Program Files\Greenstone\ images directory.
4. *Main.cfg:* This file contains a list of all macro files used for the User Interface. If you created a new '.dm' file, you need to add it to this file. The main.cfg file is stored in the Program Files\Greenstone\etc directory.
5. *Getting the Cover Image:* For you to get the Cover Image of your input document, you need to put the image file and the source file (document) into a single folder. They both should bear the same name also. While building the collection, Greenstone will take both the files to Program Files\Greenstone\collect\<collection name>\archives\Hash. The collection thus built will display the Cover Image along with the document. Also in the Design Panel, in the Document Plugin section, while configuring the Arguments for the HTML Plugin, give the custom argument as 'cover_image'.
6. *Getting the Collection Icon:* Click on Design panel ->General Option -> URL to home page icon (Browse for image and locate it).
7. *Getting Header Image for the Digital Librar:* To get the header image which says MyLibrary banner in the DL head, create the graphic file (preferably a GIF file), name it as 'gsdlhead.xxx' and then replace it with the file available in Program Files\Greenstone\images.
8. *Deep Level Customization:* By default, Greenstone's collection icon area is a matrix grid (the N × 3 format). You can change the collection icon area by editing the '_content_ macro' in 'home.dm'. You will need to remove the '_homeextra_ macro' (this is the N × 3 table that the Greenstone C++ code automatically creates for you) and can then put whatever design customization you want into this area. You will need to put the icons and links to the collection yourself.

You can also achieve high end customization by replacing the 'home.dm' with 'yourhome.dm' in the \greenstone\etc folder.

16. GSDL: Helpline, Archives

Greenstone's E-Mail list is a very useful and active listserv which shares and clarifies user experiences and stories dealing with real life situations. To subscribe or unsubscribe to the list via the World Wide Web, visit https://list.scms.waikato.ac.nz/mailman/listinfo/greenstone-users or, via email, send a message with subject or body 'help' to greenstone-users-request@list.scms.waikato.ac.nz. Greenstone has started one more List recently, for the Greenstone 3 Version (the latest Beta version) user group, and the details are available at https://list.scms.waikato.ac.nz/mailman/listinfo/greenstone3.

UNESCO has initiated a Greenstone support organization for South Asia in 2006, supported by a group of experts in the region, and it is coordinated by IIM Kozhikode http://greenstonesupport.iimk.ac.in. The site is rich with many of the Greenstone support materials. In addition, an E-list greenstonesupport@iimk.ac.in offers online support to professionals on Greenstone.

For those looking for quick solutions for their real-time or on-the-job trouble shooting while using the software, 'Greenstone Archives' is a treasure house. It is a database of the email messages circulated in the List, and is searchable. The mails generated from the List and its threads are archived and made available for the user community. The archive is available at http://www.sadl.uleth.ca/nz/cgi-bin/library?a=p&p=about&c=gsarch-e. This is the major list used worldwide for Greenstone and the content of the messages is usually global in nature. Developers and Greenstone users can avoid a great deal of unwanted labour by carefully going through the archive before they start working on problem solving, or before shooting a mail to the List.

17. Conclusions

The ever changing landscape of the information paradigm poses a host of new IT and information challenges not only to the library and information professionals, but to the users, patrons and scholars and the publishing community as well. Indeed the new environment throws up a host of unprecedented features and avenues, and interestingly enough, if we know how to tap them well, we find there is a plethora of opportunities, and most of them even for free. The 'free things', so belovedly called world wide the Open Source Softwares, many of them could even be compared against their commercial counterparts in terms of their strength, efficiency, power and the ever increasing user base. Among the major challenges include the information professionals' emergent need to acquire the necessary skill sets and working knowledge on the cutting-edge information science and information technology areas and in leveraging them in a contextually relevant manner.

Working on a Digital Library project in general, especially working with the Greenstone Digital Library Software in particular has been highly exhilarating, enriching as well as rewarding. The treasure of knowledge, skills, experience, expertise, and exposure we have achieved and accomplished during the past four years have been extremely enjoying and simply terrific. It is also important sharing the real life experience of a particular software as a an application user, as there exist a great deal of difference in view points when it comes from the software developers themselves. Frankly, we also have grown with the software from strength to strength. We have every appreciation to Greenstone as far as its usability, extensibility and flexibility are concerned. We are also indeed pleased with its consistent technology catch-up strategies and their untiring extension activities. One should appreciate the dynamic Greenstone team for their selfless open source philosophy, and their relentless work in this regard just for the cause of science. We have been closely watching the world scenario in the area of digital library research and we are quite convinced that Greenstone is a fast growing community coupled with deep commitments from the developers in taking this software to further heights and making this an outstanding open source model for digital library development. The Wiki and the OAI features of Greenstone and the ambitious Greenstone 3, released already and running in its version 3.04, which draws its strength from the open source family of Web Services technologies facilitating configurable, extensible and dynamic digital libraries are all testimony to their commitment to excellence in digital library software development. In the meanwhile UNESCO came forward to support them unconditionally and it is a proud privilege to announce that we have the Greenstone Support for South Asia already launched with their support, to take care of the DL needs of this region.

Acknowledgement

This review article on digital libraries is for the promotion of open source softwares by information professionals.

References

[1] Orsdel, Lee Van; Born, Kathleen (2002). Doing the digital flip. *Library Journal,* 127(7), 51–55.

[2] OCLC Report on five-year information format trends. 2003. http://www.oclc.org/reports/2003format.htm

[3] Marchionini, G. (1998). Research and development in digital libraries. Allen Kent (Ed.) *Encyclopedia of Library and Information Science*, 63: 259–279.

[4] Sreekumar, M.G. and Sunitha, T. (2005). Essential Strategies and Skill Sets Towards Creating Digital Libraries Using Open Source Software [Proceedings of NACLIN 2005, DELNET, Bangalore, India].

[5] Borgman, Christine L. (1996). Social Aspects of Digital Libraries,pp170 [Proceedings of the first ACM international conference on Digital libraries Bethesda, Maryland, United State, March 20–23, Organised by Association of Computing Machinery].

[6] Frumkin, Jeremy (Ed). (2002). Special issue on open source software. *Information Technology and Libraries* 21(1).

[7] Stallman, Richard http://www.opensource.org/docs/definition_plain.html

[8] OSS Watch http://www.oss-watch.ac.uk/talks/2003-09-24-csg/index.xml

[9] Altman, M. (2001). Open source software for libraries: from greenstone to the virtual data center and beyond. *IASSIST Quarterly*. Winter: 1–7.

[10] SourceForge.Net (world's largest Open Source software development website) http://www.sourceforge.net

[11] RDF (Resource Description Framework). http://www.w3c.org/RDF

[12] DCMI (Dublin Core Metadata Initiative). http://dublincore.org

[13] Greenstone Digital Library Software. htttp://www.greenstone.org

[14] Witten, Ian H. *et al.* (2001). Greenstone: Open-Source Digital Library Software. *D-Lib Magazine,* 7(10), 1–16.

[15] Witten, Ian H. (2003). Examples of practical digital libraries: collections built internationally using Greenstone. *D-Lib Magazine* 9(3), 1–15.

[16] Unicode Consortium htttp://unicode.org

[17] IIMK Digital Library http://iimk.ac.in/gsdl/cgi-bin/library

[18] Greenstone Support for South Asia http://greenstonesupport.iimk.ac.in

Electronic Resources Management in Libraries, pp. 164–171

Open Access Scholarly Publishing in Economics: An Analytical Survey

K.P. Singh

ABSTRACT

Open access movement is gaining momentum around the world and more and more publishing houses are coming forward in providing the peer reviewed scholarly literature in Economics. The study aim to investigate the open access scholarly literature in the field of Economics published worldwide. The study also focuses on the growth in various facets of open access literature in Economics such as chronological growth, continent and country wise distribution, frequency and language wise distribution and the role of major publishing houses in the movement of open access.

1. Introduction

The killing technology of the 21st century, *i.e.*, ICT has shrink the physical boundaries of the world and brought many revolutionary changes in the entire process of accessing and acquiring, storing and retrieving, downloading and distributing, and consolidation and communication information throughout the world. Moreover, increasing prices of research journals by the publishers has posed a major threat to libraries and information centers. To communicate the work published in the form of scholarly literature to the world-wide community of researchers and scientists, the Open Access (OA) Initiative emerged as an ultimate solution that promotes free access to scholarly publications over the Internet, removes the price and permission barriers and ensures the widest possible dissemination of research. Singh and Negi (2011) discussed the collective movements by the international organisations, decelerations, conventions and various key issues in the movement of OA journals worldwide.

1.1 *What is Directory of Open Access Journals?*

The Directory of Open Access Journals (DOAJ) was first conceived by the Nordic Conference on Scholarly Communication in Lund/Copenhagen (http://www.lub.lu.se/ncsc 2002) about the idea of creating a comprehensive directory of OA journals. It was felt that it would be a valuable service for the global research and education community. With the result, the directory came into the existence in the same year. The directory covers open access scientific and scholarly journals in different disciplines in all languages, having a quality-controlled system. It has nearly 8,000 journals.

1.2 *What is Open Access?*

Open access is simply the free online availability of digital data, figures, contents, scholarly journal articles, research results which authors/researchers publish without expectation of payment and is based on an ethical argument that research funded by the public should be available to the public on public domain as natural resources such as light, air, water, etc. The OA operates within the legal framework and own the original copyrights to for their work. Authors can transfer the rights to publishers to post the work on the web or else can retain the rights to post their work on the archives. The following points are worth to mention in the context of understanding about open access (Singh and Negi, 2011):

- OA is the ultimate convergence (new avatar) of an age old tradition and the new technology, to make impossible to possible an unprecedented public good;
- An old tradition—forwardness of authors and scholars to publish the fruits of their research in scholarly journals without payment, for the sake of wider use and application by the public freely on Internet (*i.e.* a public information footpath to all);
- For the public good and they make possible as far as possible for world-wide electronic distribution of the peer-reviewed journal literature and completely free and unrestricted access to it by all scientists, scholars, teachers, students, and other curious minds; and finally
- OA is a technology's answer to the scholarly journals crisis or popular as serial crisis, the world face today.

1.3 *Aim and Objectives of the Study*

The study aims to identity the OA scholarly literature in Economics indexed in DOAJ. In addition to this, the specific objectives of the study include to know the (a) chronological growth and development, (b) the world wide distribution, and (c) Asian contributions; and to investigate (d) the languages and frequency wise distribution, (e) the contribution of different types of publishers, and (f) to compile a directory of OA scholarly literature in economics.

1.4 *Scope of the Study*

The study covers the scholarly literature in the Economics published worldwide and indexed in OA system such as DOAJ in the entire domain of economics and their allied fields. Library is a growing organism which is truly applicable to DOAJ also. At present, about 8,500 peer-reviewed scholarly journals are accessible in OA mode through DOAJ. The study covers 173 peer-reviewed journals published by the various R&D organisations, academic bodies, commercial publishers and professional associations throughout the world. Further, the study also covers the literature being published in other than English language such as Spanish, Portuguese, Dutch, Italian, Russia, Serbian and German.

1.5 *Research Methodology*

For the purpose of the present study, literature review on the various aspects of OA movement/initiative has been done from the major leading databases namely *Library and Information Science Abstracts (LISA), Library, Information Science and Technology Abstracts (LISTA), Emerald database* and print journals. After reviewing in the area of OA and scholarly publishing at the website of DOAJ, the required data needed for the study was collected. To know the actual position and other statistical data which is not available at DOAJ website, the website of the each journal was accessed and gaps were filled in. In the final stage the data is analyzed and interpreted with the help of MS-Excel based on a set of parameters to get the right picture to OA scholarly literature in the area of economics.

2. Review of Literature

Sangeeta and Sonbham (2008) feels that OA initiative emerged as a revolutionary movement that promotes free access to scholarly publications over the Internet, removes the price and permission barriers and ensures the widest possible dissemination of research. OA exists where there is free, immediate and unrestricted availability of digital content. While Kingsley (2009) argues that the traditional scholarly journal system is outdated and in need of re-organization and that the new Internet technologies provide opportunities for change. Ylotis (2005) finds that OA archives and OA journals as steps forward towards the democratization of information and knowledge by removing access restrictions. McCulloch (2006) also argues similar to Ylotis that the OA initiative is dramatically transforming the process of scholarly communication, bringing great benefits to academic world. Haider (2007) argues that OA as a way to connect the developing world to the system of science, by providing access to scientific literature published in the developed world. Arunachalam (2008) stresses the need for OA mandate by various research organizations in India for their own research output and for projects funded by them, Keisham and Sophiarani (2008) pointed out that OA initiative emerged as a revolutionary movement that promotes free access to scholarly publications over the Internet, removes the price and permission barriers and ensures the widest possible dissemination of research. Singh and Negi (2011) investigated the contribution of Indian premier research organization such as CSIR, DRDO, ICAR, ICMR, INSA, etc. in publishing and making available scholarly information and made available in OA mode. The study analyzed and presented the data in many dimensions such as OA journals according to subject wise, institutions wise, and others dimensions such as language, frequency, mode, formats and coverage.

3. Data Analysis and Interpretation

The collected data from the DOAJ has been thoroughly analyzed using the MS-Excel and discussed in the following sections. The following tables give the overall picture of OA scholarly publishing literature in economics. As per the DOAJ, 173 OA journals are being published in the field of economics worldwide. Table 1 shows the top 10 leading countries in the contributing to the filed of economics. It is found that Romania is on the top rank with 25 journals, followed by United State of America and Spain having 17 journals each, Brazil having 15 journals, Mexico and Canada having 7 journals each, UK, Italy and Colombia having 6 journals each respectively. Therefore, the study indicates that more than 64% literature is being contributed/ published by these ten countries representing the entire Western World.

Table 1: Top 10 Countries Contributions to Economics in DOAJ

Country	*Journals*	*%*	*Rank*
Romania	25	22.52	1
USA	17	15.31	2
Spain	17	15.31	3
Brazil	15	13.51	3
Mexico	7	6.30	4
Canada	7	6.30	4
UK	6	5.40	5
Italy	6	5.40	5
Colombia	6	5.40	5
Germany	5	4.50	6
Total	111	100.00	

Table 2: Asia's Contribution to OA Journals in Economics

Country	*Journals*	*%*	*Rank*
Pakistan	04	57.14	1
India	01	14.28	2
China	01	14.28	2
Indonesia	01	14.28	2
Total	07		

The Asian countries have contributed the least to OA journals in economics, *i.e.*, only 7 journals. Table 2 shows that Pakistan occupies the top position with 4 OA journals constituting 57.14% of the total contribution. Unfortunately world's large populated countries like India and China have only one journal each to their account. Therefore, these countries should come forward and improve its contribution to OA journals in economics.

Table 3: Year-wise Growth of OA Journals in Economics Indexed in DOAJ

Year	*Journals*	*%*	*Cumulative Total*
2003	04	2.31	04
2004	06	3.46	10
2005	10	5.78	20
2006	17	9.82	37
2007	16	9.24	53
2008	13	7.51	66
2009	16	9.24	82
2010	40	23.12	122
2011	08	7.74	170
2012*	03	1.73	173

* Up to March 2012.

The Table 3 reveals chronological growth of OA scholarly publishing in economics. Since the inception of DOAJ in 2003, during the last ten years (2003–2012 up to March), 173 journals were indexed to DOAJ in OA category. Further, the study also found that during the year 2012, the highest number of journals (40 journals, 23.12%) have been added to DOAJ, followed 17 Journals in 2006, 16 Journals in 2007.

Table 4: Frequency of Distribution of OA Journals

Issues/Year	*Journals*	*%*	*Rank*
1 issue (annual)	11	7.69	4
2 issues (biannual)	69	48.25	1
3 issues	18	12.58	3
4 issues (quarterly)	34	23.77	2
5 issues	02	1.39	7
6 issues (bimonthly)	03	2.09	6
12 issues (monthly)	06	4.19	5
Total	143		

Note: Due to some technical problems 30 journals were not accessed over Internet, therefore, the interpretation is based on the 143 journals that are accessed at the time of conducting this study.

It is evident from Table 4 that 69 journals (48.25%) are being published half-yearly, followed by 34 journals quarterly (23.77%), 18 journals (12.58%) 3 issues per year, and so on. Only 3 bimonthly journals are being published. Table 5 shows the journals published in various languages. It can be viewed that the most of the economics journals are being published in English Language, *i.e.* 78 journals (76.47%) followed by 13 journals in Spanish (12.74%), 6 journals in Portuguese (5.88%), one journal in Dutch, Italian, Russia, Serbian and Germany (0.98%) languages respectively. At the initial stage of Internet, almost all the literature was only available and accessed in English language. Today a large amount of literature is also available in other languages and the same can be read and downloaded in English by using advanced translation applications/services which are available freely on Internet.

Table 5: Language-Wise Distribution of OA Journals

Language	*Journals*	*%*	*Rank*
English	78	76.47	1
Spanish	13	12.74	2
Portuguese	06	5.88	3
Dutch	01	0.98	4
Italian	01	0.98	4
Russia	01	0.98	4
Serbian	01	0.98	4
Germany	01	0.98	4
Total	102		

It is shown in Table 6 that out of the 173 OA journals in economics, 102 (58.95%) titles are being published in monolingual followed by 57 (32.94%) titles in two languages, 11 in three languages, and two journals in five languages and one title in four languages. Thus, the study found that multilingual publishing of the content is no problem on Internet and the trend of multilingual publishing is increasing.

Table 6: Distribution OA Journals According to Language (Bilingual)

Language	*Journals*	*%*	*Rank*
One Language	102	58.95	1
Two Languages	57	32.94	2
Three Languages	11	6.35	3
Five Languages	02	1.15	4
Four Languages	01	0.57	5
Total	173		

Table 7 provides information about the availability of downloading options available in OA scholarly journals in economics. It is viewed from the Table 7 that 146 journals (97.33%) are available in PDF followed by 2 journals (1.33%) in HTML and PGY/HTML, respectively. Twenty-three journals could not be accessed at the time of conducting this study; therefore, the above figures are based on 150 journals only.

Table 7: Downloading Formats of OA Journals

Format	*Journals*	*%*
PDF	146	97.33
HTML	02	1.33
PDF/HTML	02	1.33
Total	150	

Publishers are the most important channels of communicating and dissemination of scholarly information worldwide. The Table 8 gives information on the types of publishes involved in contributing to the OA initiative/movement. It is found from the study that academic publishers are contributing 83 journals, followed by professional associations (31), commercial publishers (27) R&D publishers (12) and others contributing 12 journals. The nature of other 12 is that these are being published in the name of the journal as publisher.

Table 8: Publisher-wise Distributions of OA Journals

Publishers	*Journals*	*%*	*Rank*
Academic publishers	83	47.97	1
Professional associations	31	17.91	2
Commercial publishers	27	15.60	3
R&D publishers	20	11.56	4
Others	12	6.93	5

4. Findings of the Study

On the basis of the data collected from the DOAJ on the OA scholarly literature in economics the following inferences has been drawn:

- There are 111 scholarly OA journals contributed by top 10 countries of the world in the field of economics. Romania tops the list with rank 1 followed by USA.
- Only 7 journals are contributed from the Asian region; Pakistan tops the list and India has only one OA journal in the field.

- A total of 173 journals (up to March 2012) in the field of economics have been indexed worldwide. The highest number (40 journals) were indexed in the year of 2012.
- From the frequency point of view 69 journals are being published biannually.
- Seventy-three journals are published in English language. However, a sizable number of journals are also published in Spanish, German, Portuguese and Dutch.

5. Conclusion

In the changing context of the traditional commercial publishing system, due to their policies, limitations etc. have become less effective. On the other hand the new system of scholarly communication, *i.e.*, OA system is gaining momentum due to the collaboration of international scholars/associations in overcoming the problem of escalation of prices of journals and dwindling budgets. OA movement is much more popularized in developed countries like USA, UK etc. but the countries like Romania also contributing a lot in the field of economics. When we look into the overall contribution to OA in economics, we find very little contribution from the Asian countries like, India, China, Russia, Japan, Korea, etc. It is worth to mention that India contributing 312 journals to OA movement especially in the field of science and technology. Therefore, all government sponsored publishers should seriously come forward to provide scholarly information in OA to the world communities for the progress of research and academic endeavours.

References

[1] Arunachalam, S. (2008). Open access to scientific knowledge. *DESIDOC Journal of Library and Information Technology,* 28(1), 7–28.

[2] Haider, J. (2007). Of the rich and the poor and other curious minds: On open access and development. *Aslib Proceedings*, 59(4/5), 449–461.

[3] Kingsley, D. (2009). The journal is dead, long live the journal. *On the Horizon,* 15(4) http://dspace.anu.edu.au/bitstream/1885/44522/1/OnTheHorizon%20Submitted.pdf. (accessed in April 2012).

[4] McCulloch, E. (2006). Taking stock of open access: progress and issues. *Library Review*, 55(6), 337–343.

[5] Sangeeta, Keisham and Soubam, Sophiarani (2008). Open access journals and open access Initiatives in India. *In*: PLANNER-2008. Ahmedabad, Inflibnet, 2008. pp. 205.

[6] Singh, K.P. and Negi, Nandi (2011). Open access and scholarly communication: role of public funded research and development organizations in India. *IASLIC Bulletin*, 56(4), 211–238.

[7] Ylotis, K. (2005). The open access initiative: A new paradigm for scholarly communications. *Information Technology and Libraries*, 2(4), 157–162.

Electronic Resources Management in Libraries, pp. 172–176

Open Access to *Defence Science Journal*: A Case Study

V. Senthil

ABSTRACT

Defence Scientific Information and Documentation Centre (DESIDOC) is a nodal centre for information communication and dissemination in the Defence Research and Development Organization (DRDO). As the publication wing of DRDO, DESIDOC brings out regular publications including Defence Science Journal, DESIDOC Bulletin of Information Technology, DRDO Newsletter, DRDO Samachar and Technology Focus. These periodicals cover a wide variety of topics in various subject areas targeting different user communities situated all over India. A project was undertaken with an aim to provide open access to the full text of these periodicals to the users world-wide. The project also aimed at facilitating the users to directly submit the manuscript into the system and carrying out the entire editorial process. The open source software Open Journal System (OJS) is used and customized according to the user requirements. This software was tested for nearly six months before made it available to the user community. This paper discusses the experience in using OJS, various processing steps and statistics on user, usage and various features of the model.

1. Introduction

There is an exponential growth in the volume of published information. In recent times electronic publishing became more popular. The reasons for this include the availability of technologies for easy creation and management, difficulties in retrieving information from print publications in libraries, literature seepage and scattering, need to control and provide access to ever increasing volume of information, faster rate of increase in the costs of raw materials used in publishing leading to the escalation of manufacturing costs of books and journals, the need to reduce the time required for conventional publishing, and the realization of the potential and unique features of electronic media. Although many types of publications are in vogue, e-journals gained a lot of acceptability and gradually these gave way to online journals (Senthil and Moorthy, 2006).

2. DRDO Publications

Defence Scientific Information and Documentation Centre (DESIDOC) is bringing out two peer-reviewed journals namely *Defence Science Journal (DSJ)* and *DESIDOC Journal of Library and Information Technology (DJLIT)* formerly known as

DESIDOC Bulletin of Information Technology (DBIT) on bi-monthly basis. These journals are published only on print media till the year 2007. During the year 2008 open access policy has been adopted by DESIDOC and all DRDO publications are brought in print and electronic versions and are made available on Internet. At present, the entire collection of *DSJ* and *DJLIT* since volume 1 onwards is made available on Internet through open access mode.

2.1 *Defence Science Journal*

Defence Science Journal is a bi-monthly peer-reviewed journal. The journal publishes research papers in various disciplines of basic and applied sciences, engineering and technology having direct defence applications. Review papers, short communications, research notes and scientific correspondence on defence are accepted for publication in the journal. The articles published in the Journal are indexed/reviewed in over a dozen abstracting and indexing periodicals.

2.2 *DESIDOC Journal of Library and Information Technology*

It is a bi-monthly publication bringing out the current developments in library and information technology to its readers. It publishes original research papers and review articles and current developments in Library and Information Science (LIS) and technology. It also covers professional developments including literature and book reviews, conferences, etc. for the benefit of the LIS professionals.

3. Open Journal System

Open Source Software is software created by programmers who want to share their source code, which is part of a program that is readable by anyone who might find the program, or a variation of the program. In the other words the term open source refers to software in which the source code is freely available for others to view, amend and adapt (Rama Reddy, 2004). The Open Journal System (OJS) is open source software developed by the Public Knowledge Project and released under the GNU General Public License for the management of peer-reviewed journals. The OJS is designed to facilitate the development of open access, peer-reviewed publishing, providing the technical infrastructure not only for the online presentation of journal articles, but also an entire editorial management workflow, including article submission, multiple rounds of peer-review, and indexing. OJS relies upon individuals fulfilling different roles, such as the Journal manager, editor, reviewer, author, reader, etc. (http://www.dwheeler.com/oss_fs_why.html).

3.1 *Use of OJS for DRDO Peer-Reviewed Journals*

To provide better accessibility globally, a study was carried out to publish e-versions of the two journals viz. the *Defence Science Journal* and the *DESIDOC Journal of*

Library and Information Technology. Since most of editorial processing requirements are fulfilled by the Open Journal System, the software was tested and implemented to publish the journals. Although OJS comprises many publishing routines used in publishing peer-reviewed journals, it was customized and limited procedures/routines are only implemented in publishing the two journals. The important roles adopted are Journals Manager, Editors, Section Editors, Reviewers, Authors and Users. The roles of Layout Editor and Proof Reading activities are not used. The System also has the facility of RSS feeds, simple and advanced search facility, browsing the contents by authors, issue, and title. Figure 1 shows interlinking of OJS adopted in publishing the journals. Some of the routines are explained in the succeeding paragraphs.

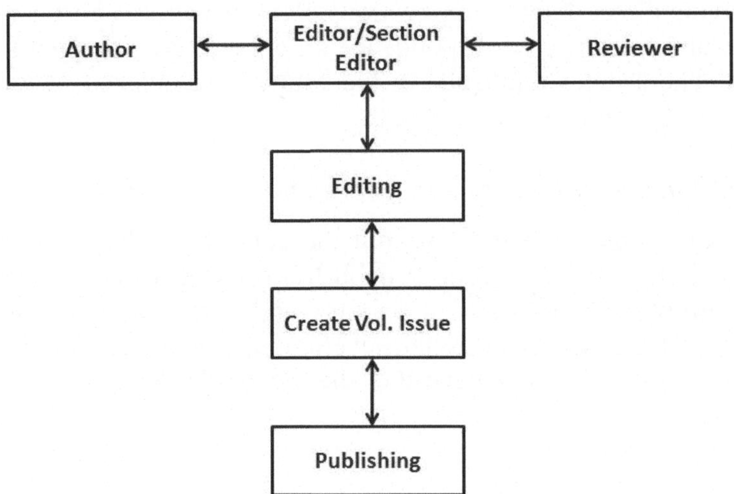

Fig. 1: Workflow Adopted in Publishing of OJS

- ***Journal Manager:*** This plays an important role in managing the manuscripts and sets up journal by filling in templates and checking options; it manages users, reading tools, indexing, prepared emails, and assigns roles.
- ***Authors:*** This is mandatory to register with the system for submission of the manuscripts. An email alert with a unique control number is automatically generated and sent to the author after submission of the manuscript. Authors can trace the status of their submission after logging into the system using the with a unique control number. Once the manuscript is vetted by the reviewer, the comments of the reviewer are sent to the author for modifications, if any. 3922 authors are registered with the system (October 2012).
- ***Editors/Section Editors:*** Editors or Section Editors are allowed to oversee the entire editorial process and publishing issues. Editors usually check the manuscripts after receiving from the authors and send to the reviewers for vetting the manuscript. The reviewers add their comments on the system which helps the editor to take a

final decision on the paper. Once the manuscript is accepted, the Editor decides the issue in which the manuscript has to be published and allots the manuscript to the particular future issue. The Editor can also create the volume, issue, year etc through OJS.

- ***Reviewers:*** As on September 2012, *DSJ* has 1794 reviewers; most of them registered by themselves in the system. The reviewers cover various fields of science and technology and their areas of interest also mentioned against each individual in micro-level. This helps the editors to decide to whom the manuscript has to be sent for reviewing. Review process is partially blind, *i.e.*, the names of authors are known to reviewers (as biases are negligible to nil) names of reviewers are not revealed to the authors to avoid any undue controversy (in case of adverse comments). The entire reviewing process is carried out using OJS and no manual process is involved. This reviewing process using OJS reduced the time delay from submission to publishing to a great extent (from 18 to 8 months).

4. Open Access

As per the DRDO policy and also as required by OJS, the journals are made accessible on Open Access. Both *DSJ* and *DJLIT* were hosted on Internet (http://publications.drdo.gov.in) for open access by subscribers, scholars, researchers, peers and public at large. Both the titles are registered wit the Directory of Open Access Journals (http://www.doaj.org). There was better visibility for the contents of the journals which are highly used with full text articles are downloaded by the international research community. Month-wise usage details for the year 2011 are given in Table 1. The statistics reveal that the usage of special issues is more than general issues (for *DSJ*). Table 2 shows the number of reviewers, authors and readers as of October 2012. Analysis of the user statistics revealed that many users are registered as reviewers or/and authors and vice versa.

Table 1: Usage Statistics for 2011

Journal	*Jan*	*Feb*	*Mar*	*Apr*	*May*	*Jun*	*Jul*	*Aug*	*Sep*	*Oct*	*Nov*	*Dec*
DSJ	485	595	1230	1163	2130	1124	300	1604	2183	962	1785	1777
DJLIT	7933	7637	7015	8398	4625	6643	9594	10373	8428	3485	3605	4198

Table 2: Users of Journals

Users	*DSJ*	*DJLIT*
Reviewers	1794	297
Authors	2533	1354
Readers	3287	1812

Country-Wise Users: The details are compiled and presented in Table 3. Only those users enrolled with the system having more than two digits are taken into consideration to prepare this list. Predictably India has most users followed by Afghanistan. More than 2000 users are registered from each of these two countries; remaining users from various countries are enrolled with two digits. It is also noted that the users from almost all Asian countries are enrolled with the system and actively using Defence Science Journal. Interestingly there was only one user from the country Yemen.

Table 3: Country-wise Users Enrolled for *DSJ*

No.	*Country*	*Users*
1.	India	2391
2.	China	66
3.	United States	42
4.	Iran	34
5.	Central African Republic	24
6.	Malaysia	18
7.	Nigeria	17
8.	Taiwan	17
9.	South Korea	13
10.	Bangladesh	11
11.	Serbia and Montenegro	11
12.	Russia	11

5. Conclusion

The use of OJS definitely improved the currency of the content by reducing the time taken for publishing after submission, visibility, and overheads leading to enhanced impact factor and frequency (both for *DSJ*) and publication of increased number of papers per year. Open access made *Defence Science Journal* and *DESIDOC Journal of Library and Information* more popular among international users as observed by the registration of users. Open Journal System is effectively used by users as well as DESIDOC for the online submission, reviewing and the entire editorial process to bring out Defence Science Journal.

References

[1] Senthil, V. and Moorthy, A.L., Online Access to DRDO Periodicals using Open Source Software, *International Conference on Digital Library (ICDL),* 5–8 December 2006, New Delhi.

[2] Reddy, E. Rama, Open Source systems in the library and on the Net, International workshop on "Democratization of Information: Focus on Libraries", 18–19 January 2004, Mumbai.

Electronic Resources Management in Libraries, pp. 177–186

Cloud Computing as Value Addition and Cost Effective Solution to Library and Information Centres

C. Sasikala

ABSTRACT

Cloud computing is a new technology model for IT services which many businesses and organizations are adopting. It allows them to avoid locally hosting multiple servers and equipment and constantly dealing with hardware failure, software installs, upgrades and compatibility issues. For many organizations, cloud computing can simplify processes and save time and money. This article defines cloud computing and shows how it is different from traditional type of computing. It also discusses types and how cloud computing applications could be beneficial to Library and Information Centres.

1. Introduction

The phrase Cloud Computing is steadily gaining momentum in the last few years. After Web2.0, it became one of the most hyped technology buzzwords. The term has become ubiquitous with varied definitions. Gartner Group (n.d.) defined cloud computing as "a style of computing in which massively scalable and elastic IT-enabled capabilities are delivered as a service to external customers using Internet technologies". As per the Educause (2011) it refers to the delivery of scalable IT resources over the Internet, as opposed to hosting and operating those resources locally, such as on a college or university network. Those resources can include applications and services, as well as the infrastructure on which they operate. In a simple sense, cloud computing means using web services for computing needs which could include using software applications, storing data, accessing computing power, or using a platform to build application (Kroski, 2009).

Cloud computing is a new technology model for IT services which many business and organizations are adopting. It allows them to avoid locally hosting multiple servers and equipment and constantly dealing with hardware failure, software installs, upgrades and compatibility issues. For many organizations, cloud computing can simplify processes and save time and money (Jordan and Goldner, 2011). Anyone connected to the Internet (Figure 1) is probably using some type of cloud computing on a regular basis. Whether they are using Gmail, organizing photos on Flickr or searching the web with Bing they are engaged in cloud computing. One interesting aspect of the origin of cloud computing is that ii did not start as a technology for the business enterprise, but was driven by the public with services like Facebook and Flickr (Moore, n.d.). Cloud computing is essentially of four different types: infrastructure, platform, applications and Services. According to Jordan and Goldner, computing serves different requirements of the clientele (Table 1). As the Table illustrates, varied definitions of cloud computing are seen in the literature due to varied applications. Many cloud services may provide more than one solution or a combination to the end users. For example, Google docs provide both infrastructure services and applications.

Table 1: Types of Cloud Computing Solutions

Type	*What it is?*	*Examples*
Infrastructure	Praying space/time on external, servers	Amazon A3 Bungee
Platform	An existing software platform to build your own applications on	Facebook
Applications	Software applications accessed with a web browser	Google docs. Salesforce.com
Services	Ready-to-use services accessed with a Web browser	ADP Mint.Com

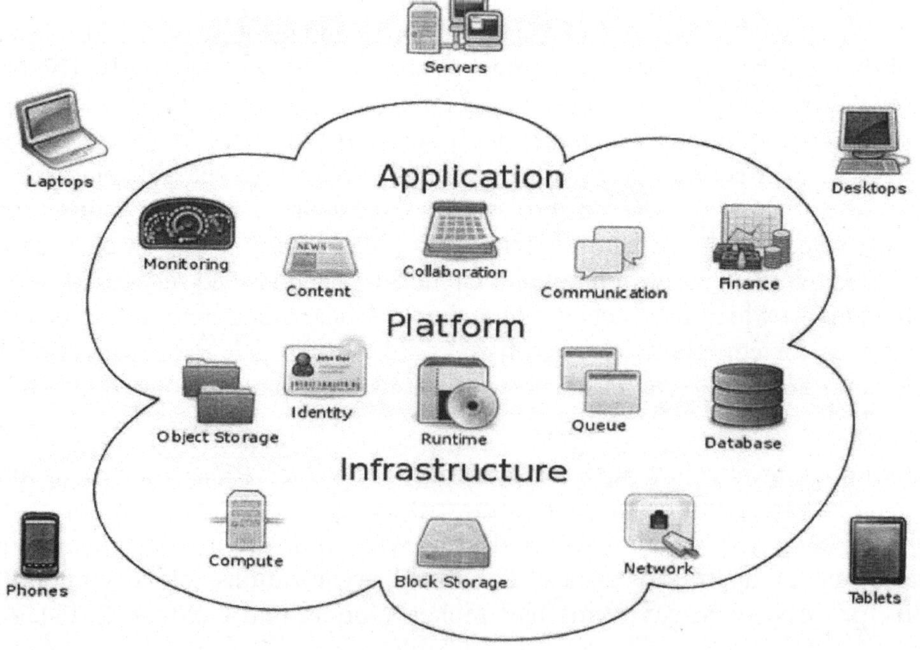

Fig. 1: Cloud Computing (Warren, n.d.)

1.1 *Types of Cloud Computing*

Kroski (2009) described three major types of cloud computing. These include:

- ***Infrastructure as a Service (Iaa S):*** This is a model in which organizations outsource the equipment used to support operations, including storage, hardware, servers and networking components. The service provider owns the equipment and is responsible for housing, running and maintaining (SearchcloudComputing.com). This type of cloud computing is also sometimes referred to as Hardware as a Service (Haa S); it involves both storage services and computing power. For example, Amazon's Web Services, one of the major players in this area, offers two main products including the Elastic Compute Cloud (EC2) which provides computing resources, and Single Storage (S2) for data storage. The main advantage of Infrastructure as a Service is that it allows the institutions to hand off commodity or non-differentiating services so that staff can focus on things that do differentiate the institutions.
- ***Platform as a Service (Paa S):*** With Paa S, a computing platform is provided which supplies tools and development environment to help companies build, test, and deploy web-based applications, Businesses don't need to invest in the infrastructure required for building web and mobile applications but can rent the use of platforms such as Windows Azure, Google AppEngine, and Force.com. Applications which are built using these providers' services however are usually locked into that one platform.
- ***Software as Service (Saa S) or Applications as a Service (Aaa S):*** Application or Software is delivered as a service to the customer who can access the program from any online device. Some of these web-based applications are free, such as Hotmail, Google Apps, Skype and many Web 2.0 applications, while business-oriented Saa S, such as Sales Force, is leased on a subscription basis. There is usually little customization or control available with these applications. However, subscribes benefit from low initial costs, have access to (usually 24 × 7 basis) support services, and need not worry about hosting, installing, upgrading or maintaining the software.

1.2 *Cloud Computing vs. Conventional Computing Methods*

The evolution and development of IT solutions clearly shows that during the last 25 years, most part of the research in IT focused on software development and system engineering primarily on the personal computer environment. This era was characterized by monolithic, proprietary operating systems and programs that had lengthy development time and release cycles. Further, the application software was used to be developed in isolation with main focus on single application. Clustered computing, distributed computing and parallel processing are the predecessors to the cloud computing. The latter enables the installation and running of hardware and functionality on a network/Internet cloud traditionally performed in a local environment. In essence, the Internet cloud becomes the development platform and the operating system to which programmer writes reusable, constantly updated software components that are delivered over the network and that can be embedded or loosely coupled with other web application.

2. Cloud Computing and Libraries

Cloud applications, platforms and services are being embraced by libraries, librarians and library users around the world. The logic behind opting for cloud computing by libraries lies in seeking solutions to many issues and problems faced by them in the contemporary electronic environment. Chris Anderson (2011), Editor of the *Wired Magazine* rightly pointed out that the web is all about scale, finding ways to attract the most users for centralized resources, spreading those costs over larger and larger audiences as the technology gets more and more capable. It's not about the cost of the equipment in the racks at the data centre; it's about what that equipment can do.

We all know that libraries are always serving the society in different ways. They are changing rapidly. Even cost and time requirements are exploding. They are facing challenges in coping up with the changing and increasing demand from users to have faster and cost effective services. In a distributed environment, through multiple local servers each one supporting different application libraries are trying to reach out the end-users. However, a number of ways in which the information is accessed is making the computing infrastructure very complex. While the IT access is fragmenting, the user needs to access required information at any point or place is growing. Such an environment creates tension for the user between how to manage the information and its accessibility and availability in his/her day-to-day life. To tackle these issues, the capabilities of existing computer infrastructure in libraries have to be reviewed and enhanced. The library needs a platform which offers easy scalability along with redundancy and security. Achieving this aim with traditional in-house servers is not possible since it is cost-prohibitive. Cloud computing helps in such situations with cost-effective technology solutions. It refers to a wider field which includes hosted applications, web-based client services, and a distributed, platform-independent server architecture.

Another important issue bothering libraries is safe and secured data storage. Cloud computing offers custom solutions to this issue. Implementing cloud-based data storage became considerably easier in recent years. Services such as Dropbox (http://dropbox.com) and Mobile Me (http://www.me.com) have made this process as simple as saving user data to a local folder on his hard drive. Contemporary hi-fi environment has brought radical change in the ownership patterns of information and information sources. We have already experienced big shifts in how libraries manage resources with the move from print-journals subscriptions to database—subscription and electronic/online journals purchasing models. This transition really helped the libraries to scale their resources and provide better services. In the same manner, current cloud computing initiatives allow technologists to think and plan about how a library can handle its computing resources. Adopting cloud solutions provides libraries an opportunity to save time and resources and also re-allocate resources to improve services. Cloud computing enables the libraries in:

- Subscribing to high quality services as and when needed
- Choosing best value, not choosing piece by piece technology
- Saving costs on IT infrastructure and its management
- Improving service quality in terms of performance and availability
- Improving visibility and accessibility of the services offered
- To focus on core activities, grow, and innovate, and
- Collaborating, aggregating and sharing.

Since cloud computing works on a cooperative platform, it has to adhere to certain key principles like (Hua, 2010):

- *Data richness:* Offer data tools and integrated work flows for all purchased, licensed and digital content.
- *Collaboration:* Share data and services with other libraries and partners in a controlled way.
- *Designed for the cloud:* Responsive, massive scalable, highly fault tolerant, suitable for public consumption.
- *Openness:* Support interoperability between cloud-based solutions, with library developed or 3rd party applications/services.
- *Extensibility:* Platform can be extended by applications, provided by the supplier, libraries or partners.

From practical point of view, the platform offers an infrastructure for developing and sharing applications. A service platform with architecture capable of supporting all the above mentioned features enables libraries to develop their own custom applications for library management activities. At the same time, they can expose and share those applications as web services on the platform for others to find and reuse. While sharing and applying the available applications, all of them can innovate new applications, techniques and tools collectively.

Just like, business organizations, libraries can also use cloud computing services to host or backup their websites, for content delivery, to run high performance computing simulations, to host media collections, and much more. Most of these cloud services are available on a pay-per-usage basis, enabling customers to scale up or down depending on their need at any given time and place and only pay for what they have used. This scaling facility can provide significant cost savings and effective deployment of capital resources. Instead of investing on purchase and maintenance of servers, software and infrastructure, all these are rented by the libraries. Libraries will be able to scale instantly and on-demand paying only for the processing power, bandwidth or storage space they use. Cloud services make data and computing capabilities portable, sharable, and accessible from any online device; they are OS-neutral, and usually easy to use. If libraries are cautious in availing the cloud services from a major provides (reputed agency), the risk involved in down time or data loss will be low as these providers usually have redundancies and backups in place, as well as tested security measures.

The review of literature on the use of cloud computing in libraries for alleviating their ICT applications and increasing the efficiency reveals good number of examples of libraries adopting cloud based services (Kroski, 2009; Mitchell, 2008; Kroski, 2011; EDUCAUSE Spotlight on Cloud Computing Services, 2010; Jordan and Goldner, 2011; Breeding, 2007). Libraries have quietly been on the forefront of cloud computing technology for a number of years. Mitchell (2012) narrates some of the examples of different types of cloud computing applications in libraries. The use of Saa S in libraries reaches back into early 2000 with the establishment of companies like SerialsSolutions (http://serialssolutions.com). Much of the work in migrating to e-journals has focused on Saa S platform and recent companies such as LibGuides (http://www.libguides.com) have shown that libraries are willing to invest in Saa S solutions. In the Iaa S arena, Amazon's EC2 offers IT infrastructure for organizations to launch differently sized servers using a variety of operating systems, including several flavors of Linux and Windows. EC2 provides organizations with essentially unlimited storage using their S3 service, the ability to take snapshots of both data and servers, and the ability to include EC2 servers in an organization's private network. A full catalog of EC2 features is available on the EC2 website (http://aws.amazon.com/ec2).

Jordan and Goldner (2011) identified seven potential areas where application of cloud computing technology could bring improvement. They are:

- Most library computer systems are built on pre-web technology
- Systems distributed across the Net using pre-web technology are harder and more costly to integrate
- Libraries store and maintain much of the same data hundreds and thousands of times
- With library data scatter across distributed systems the library's web presence is weakened
- With libraries running independent systems collaboration between libraries is made difficult and expensive
- Information seekers work in common web environments and distributed systems make it difficult to get the library into their workflow
- Many systems are only used to 10 percent of their capacity. Combining systems into a cloud environment reduces the carbon footprints, making libraries greener.

Jordan and Goldner (2011) further regroups the above areas of improvement under three headings viz. technology, data and community. It facilitates improvements in the use of state of art technologies. Cloud computing solutions are built on current technology and are architected to allow for technology shifts. For example, in the contemporary highly competitive consumer market, the businesses and organizations operating in a cloud environment are able to adapt and deliver their services through mobile devices much more quickly and less expensively.

3. Challenge of 21st Century

The literature also warrants five major challenges that every librarian will face in the 21st century (Matthews, 2011). In order to survive, the library professionals have to overcome the following challenges:

- ***Broadest Spectrum of Library Customers in History:*** The six generations (including the Gen Next of adolescents) that comprises 21st century library customers create significant differences in library service demands, with the most drastic difference between the Great Generation and the Millennial. This difference creates a heavy demand on librarians to continue traditional library services for some patrons, while creating new technology based services for digital native customers. Digital fugitive and digital native customers are at opposite ends of the customer services spectrum, but both deserve excellent library services.
- ***Information Literate Millennial Customer:*** Information literacy became a point of concern for many nations in the contemporary information age. For example, to ensure that future America is capable of participating in the global economy, American government gave a major priority to teach information literacy to young people to be able to use all the technology effectively to access and manage information. The role of librarian as expert researcher handing information to a waiting patron is the antithesis to the collaborative, participative mindset of the emerging millennial customer. Even Gen Y customers are more technologically literate than most librarians, because the vast majority is digital natives, but very few of them are pursuing a career in librarianship. In order to prepare for the increasingly more information literate millennial customers, librarians need to become guides for information literate participants.
- ***Computers that Replace Librarians*:** The world's literature growth shows that research is progressing at an exponential rate because of the massive quantities of data available to researchers in the contemporary society. Computers are a million times faster than they were 10 to 15 years ago. We have the computing capacity now to deal with … one trillion calculations a second. Research is going on to develop what they expect will be the world's most advanced "question answering" machine, able to understand a question posed in everyday human elocution—natural language, as computer scientists call it—and respond with a precise, factual

answer. All these developments have lot of implications for libraries and librarians. To cope up with these challenges, librarians have to change their mind set, adopt the appropriate technology and creatively implement them into the existing environment.

- ***Transition to Digital Content:*** The publishing trade is showing a steady increase in the dominance of electronic format over the print format of information. Since the digital media providers are providing greater access to e-books, audio books, music and video than a local library can afford to offer from its own collection, traditional circulation is overshadowed by electronic formats. This is clearly evident from the sales report' of Amazon (2011) that from the beginning of the year 2011, for every 100 paperback books it has sold, the Company has sold 115 kindle books. Overdrive, industry leader among digital content media provider in order to satisfy the preferences of Millennial library customers who wants to access more digital content rather than owning them so it developed custom downloadable websites, or Virtual Branches which in look and feel like one of the local library branches for 10,000 libraries worldwide.
- ***Devaluing of the Library's Benefit to the Community:*** Another frightening issue of concern to the library professionals in the recent years is devaluating of the library's benefit to the society by cutting down the funds drastically resulting in the lay-off of staff and closure of local branch libraries. These developments pose big threat to the very existence, survival and role of the libraries in the 21st Century. Further with such backdrop, the libraries have to face major challenges and also they have to compete with,
  - Commercial information providers like Google, Netfix and Amazon
  - Digital technologies like smart phones, tablets and geosocial networking, and
  - Decide the strategies to be followed to retain its relevance in its local community which is a part of global community.

4. Conclusions

The 21st century library and information centers can best answer and face the above five challenges by adopting latest technology solutions like cloud computing. Whether it is meeting the wide spectrum of information needs of end users or providing more advanced and high quality information services to satisfy information literate millennium user or the need to employ the most advanced systems with extraordinary computing power to answer and satisfy the online queries in the place of a reference librarian or to facilitate seamless and wider access to the digital content available to the users across the globe or for enhancing their technical and managerial capabilities to compete with the commercial information providers and digital technologies to remain relevant and survive in the society, the library profession has no other option except embracing the potential of technologies like cloud computing.

In spite of the value addition and solutions offered, there are certain critical issues of concern to the librarians before moving to cloud based services. The most important is to check whether cloud computing is in any manner improving the efficiency and effectiveness of the existing system cost effectively to offer better services to users. To ensure this, the other aspects like built-in scalability, reliability, security, privacy and multi-tenancy of the cloud computing services have to be studied. Issues like ownership of data stored on the cloud and the rights the library will have on extraction and use of their data for other services or purposes have to be taken care of by the library while shifting over to cloud solution. Both technical and legal aspects of security and privacy must be examined. Multi-tenancy is crucial for scalability of any cloud service. This is one of the features of software architecture adopted in cloud computing services where a single instance of the software run on a server enables serving multiple client organizations simultaneously.

There are ample opportunities for libraries in the contemporary information age to prove their relevance to the society. Cloud computing is one such technology and services which offers not only a bundle of benefits but also enhances the capabilities of libraries to march ahead to meet the global challenges in the information world.

References

[1] Anderson, Chris (n.d.). http://www.wired.com/techbiz/it/magazine/16-03/sffree?current+page=all Accessed on 5 September 2012.

[2] BBC Technology News (6 August 2012). Amazon selling more Kindle ebooks than print books. http://www.bbc.co.uk/news/technology-19148146 Accessed on 5 September 2012.

[3] Breeding, Marshall (2007). It's time to break the mold of the original ILS. *Computers in Libraries*, 27(10), S. 39–41.

[4] Educause (2011). 7 things you should know about cloud computing. Educause Hearing Initiative. http://www.educause.edu/resources/spotlightoncloud, Accessed on 5 September 2012.

[5] Gartner Group. http://www.gartner.com/it/page.jsp?id=1035013, Accessed on 5 September 2012.

[6] Hua, Nie (n.d.). Cloud Computing: A China view. http://www.oclc.org/multimedia/2010/files/aprc/september2010/hua.pdf, Accessed on 5 September 2012.

[7] Jordan, Jay and Goldner, Matt (2011). Winds of Change: A taxonomy of clouds for libraries. Lecture presentation, OCLC.

[8] Kroski, Ellyssa (2009). Library cloud atlas: A guide to cloud computing and storage. *Library Journal*. http://www.libraryjournal.com/article/CA6695772.html

[9] Kroski, Ellyssa (2011). 21 Useful cloud computing resources for librarians. http://oedb.org/blogs/librarian/2011/21-useful-cloud-computing-resources-for-librarians, Accessed on 5 September 2012.

[10] Matthews, Steve (2011). Two rules for 21st century librarianship success in 21st century library organisation. http://21stcenturylibrary.com/2011/10/12/five-challenges-every-librarian-must-face, Accessed on 5 September 2012.

[11] Mitchell, Erik (2012). Using cloud services for library IT infrastructure. *Code {4}lib Journal*, Issue 17. http://journal.code4lib.org/articles/2510.

[12] Moore, Geoffrey. Core content and the cloud. http://www.youtube.com/ watch?v=0swJCYL H2C, Accessed on 5 September 2012.

[13] SearchcloudComputing.com. http://searchcloudcomputing.techtarget.com/ Accessed on 5 September 2012.

[14] Warren, Christi. Cloud Computing: The Layperson's Guide to Distributed Networks. (Buzzword Breakdown services. support by The Network, Cisco's Technology news site).

[15] Wikipedia. http://en.wikipedia.org/wiki/Multi-tenancy, Accessed on 5 September 2012.

Electronic Resources Management in Libraries, pp. 187–198

Cloud Computing in Libraries: Trends and Future Prospects

Usha Mujoo Munshi and Sanjay Garg

ABSTRACT

Looking at the metamorphism of the computing technology, cloud computing has emerged as the front runner underlining a thin line between the term Internet and Cloud Computing. In this article one will observe a brief overview of what is cloud computing, how it got started and who are the leading nations as far as the cloud computing is concerned. Through this article, we would like to shed light on the emergence and use of cloud computing in libraries, the areas where cloud computing can be better utilized in the libraries especially in the developing countries like India.

1. Introduction

The Information and Communication Technology (ICT) has become pervasive in all walks of life. The convergence of various information and communication technologies has enabled us to manage business in an environment that is open to be navigated and cruised round the clock. At the same time technology has also facilitated us in maximizing the use of resources through cooperative endeavours. While this cooperative culture was somewhat prevalent in some service organizations, with technology it is becoming more viable and feasible to employ and adapt it in many sectors for efficiency and efficient use of resources.

In libraries, the technological innovations and applications started with retro-conversion, accessing CD-ROM databases (primarily bibliographic in nature), eventually the DIALOG databases laid the road for online access. Further, circulation through automated systems, employing bar code technology or RFID technology in the library has come into vogue. The migration of libraries from print to digital was buttressed by the availability of the technology, along with the systems and solutions for creating digital resource bases particularly open access repositories. Cooperative acquisition through licensing of e-resources with the help of consortia, availability and access to full text databases and the like all roped up to enhance the application of ICT in libraries. Now the libraries are involved world over heavily in crowd sourcing using social networking tools and thus being closer to their users all along. It is evident that the technologies developed find place in library applications much quicker then one could imagine. Similarly the emergence of technologies like cloud computing have already been initiated to be used for library services. This paper focuses on a general scenario of Cloud computing and its application for libraries given in the proceeding paragraphs.

1.1 *What is Cloud Computing*

In a common parlance cloud computing uses computing resources (hardware and software) that have been delivered as a service via over a network which is commonly as Internet. Cloud computing relies on sharing of resources to achieve coherence and economies of scale over a network.[1] At the foundation of cloud computing is the broader concept of converged infrastructure and shared services. Cloud computing entrusts remote services with a user's data, software and computation. There are many types of public cloud computing.[2] For instance, one can have infrastructure as a service or, platform, software, storage, security, data, test environment, etc as a service. A schematic representation of an abstraction of a typical cloud computing set-up which otherwise contains a complex infrastructure is given in Figure 1.

1.2 *Cloud Computing Genesis*

It may be appropriate to indicate how cloud computing actually started. The term cloud computing does not have its definite history, but it has been seen that the term have been derived from the practice of using drawings of stylized clouds to denote networks in a diagram of computing and communication systems.

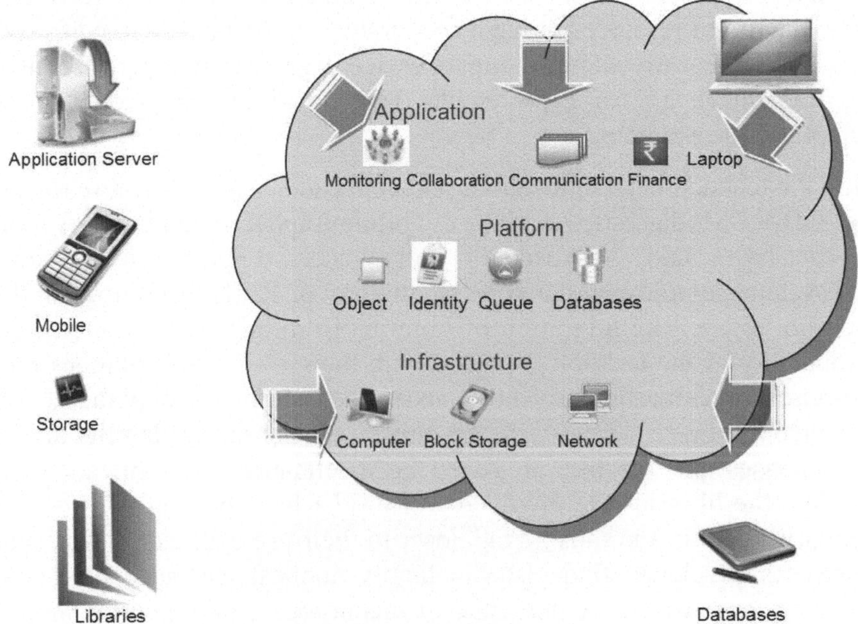

Fig. 1: Cloud Computing

In 1990s some private telecommunication companies who used to provide point to point data circuits started providing VPN (Virtual Private Network) with good quality services and low cost[3]. The cloud symbols has been used extensively which denotes the demarcation point where the responsibility was fixed both for the provider and the user.

The actual concept of cloud computing got underway in 1950s[4] when large scale mainframes became available in academics and corporate sectors, and in turn was available via thin client/terminal computers. Cloud computing started to gain ground because mainframe was not a viable option as far as the cost is concerned, so institutions and corporate sectors started to look out for more viable and cost effective methods. In the year 2007 Ben Dorsi-Todaro[5] demonstrated in his Tech Me Out blog post titled We Are Obsolete—a crude yet affordable method for an average computer user to achieve the basic concept of cloud computing from the comfort of a person's own home. In the early 2008 Eucalyptus[6] became the first open source AWP API compatible platform which was used for deployment in the privately managed cloud computing platforms. After the dot-com bubble, Amazon played a key role in the development of cloud computing by modernizing their data centers. Amazon initiated a new product development effort to provide cloud computing to external customers, and launched Amazon Web Service on a utility computing basis in 2006.[7–8]

IBM in the year 2011[9] launched the Smarter Computing framework to support Smarter Planet among the various components of the *Smarter Computing Foundations.* Recently, in the year 2012, Dr. Biju John and Dr. Souheil Khaddaj propounded the cloud as a Virtualised, Semantic source of information.[10] The ubiquitous availability of high-capacity networks, low-cost computers and storage devices as well as the widespread adoption of hardware virtualization, service-oriented architecture, autonomic, and utility computing have led to a tremendous growth in cloud computing.[5,3]

2. Models of Cloud Computing

There are primarily three models for cloud computing.

- ***Software as a Service (Saa S):*** A single application through the browser to thousands of users is used in this type of cloud computing. There is no upfront investment is needed as far as the customer is concerned in servers and software's, but on the other hand on the provider side just one application is needed keeping the cost low as compared to conventional hosting.
- ***Platform as a Service (Paa S):*** This is basically another form of Saa S Variation. In this form cloud computing delivers development environment as a service. The basic function of this service is to build one's application which would run on the providers infrastructure and which is in turn delivers to the users via the internet from the providers servers.

- ***Infrastructure as a Service (Iaa S):*** This is the basic cloud service model which provides physical as well as virtual and other resources. In this the virtual service act as a guest by a hypervisor such as Xen or KVM. Other resources in Iaa S cloud include images in a virtual machine image library, IP addresses, VLN's and other software bundles.

2.1 *Deployment Models*

Besides the structural models, there is categorization based on the deployment models also, as given below. Some of the key deployment models are[5]:

- ***Public Cloud:*** In a public cloud applications, storage and other resources are made available to the general by a service provider. These are offered either free or on a pay-to-use model. In this model service providers such as AWS, Google own and operate offer access via internet[11].
- ***Community Cloud:*** Sharing of infrastructure between several organization from a specific community with a common concerns such as security, compliance, jurisdiction are part of the community cloud model.
- ***Hybrid Cloud:*** Hybrid cloud is a composition of two or more clouds (Private or Public) that remain unique entries but are bound together, offering the benefits of multiple deployment.
- ***Private Cloud:*** Private cloud is cloud infrastructure operated solely for a single organization, whether managed internally or by a third party and hosted internally or externally. While opting for a private cloud project will require a significant level and degrees of engagement to virtualize the business environment.

3. Applications

The application which are being used in the cloud computing solutions practically have not limit to it. In a cloud computing environment, everything from generic such as normal word processing software to more sophisticated customized software/programmes which primarily designed for a specific task/company are deployed. The following are some of the various applications which are available as a cloud computing solutions:

- ***Gmail*** is basically is freely available application which is providing its services since February 2007.
- ***Google Calendar*** is a time management web application which is offered by Google since July 2009.
- ***Google Groups*** application was designed by Google as a cloud computing solution which supports discussion groups.

- ***Dropbox*** is basically file hosting service which is totally web based and used cloud computing solution to enable users to store and share files and folders with others through internet using the synchronization process.
- ***BaseCamp*** features are To-Do-List, Milestone Management, Forum like messaging, File Sharing and Time Tracking
- ***HighRise*** is another cloud computing solution which is a shared collection development web application supports CRM tasks.
- ***BackPack*** is a web based personal information manager and intranet for small businesses. This application has features—User Created Page which include text, images etc., and an iCalendar format calendar.

3.1 *Pros and Cons of Cloud Computing*

The goodies of the cloud computing lie in its economically viable and technically feasible offerings. The following are some of the advantages that cloud computing facilitates:[14]

- ***Unlimited Storage:*** In a cloud computing environment, there is no need of infrastructural expansion or adding new servers to the existing one, one just need to access its data from cloud when needed.
- ***Environment Friendly Technology:*** Since the services in cloud based computing largely depends on telecommunications, and work at home programs, organization can largely reduce carbon emissions caused by traditional computers.
- ***Unlimited Processing Power:*** Under the cloud computing, all the computers whether it is, in public domain or private domain or in a hybrid cloud, there is no need more CPU's or in-house IT infrastructure for the same
- ***Flexible Workforce:*** The major advantage of cloud computing is one can be employed for work even from home or can work while travelling thus thereby improve the productivity of the organization/companies.
- ***Less Maintenance:*** While working in traditional office whenever transformation in storage, power or software applications was carried out, renovation of the whole infrastructure becomes inevitable, but with the advent of cloud computing, organization has to pay for whatever its being used thereby reducing cost on maintenance.
- ***High Scale Dynamism:*** While comparing the traditional businesses where organization are leg behind in the market as they cannot afford the ever-changing dynamism, but on the other hand cloud computing provides cost effective approach to enterprises by providing centralized infrastructure.
- ***Excellent Real Time Access:*** Central storage for all data, platforms and infrastructure in a cloud environment easily enables the sharing of information and online collaborations which is needed by knowledge workers.

The cloud computing does have some inherent weaknesses that are supposedly treated as its advantages; some of these are enumerated below.

- ***Totally Dependent on Providers:*** All the services of the cloud solution are solely provided by the service providers and in this way the organizations are totally dependent on the providers for data controlling and responsibility.
- ***Complexity of the Cloud Nature:*** Major issues arise in complexity of cloud nature as all functionality, reluctance to process visibility, and transportability. Organizations that rely fully on these systems and services have to take into account extra responsibility of understanding the services and to changes in contracted services.
- ***Compliance Monitoring:*** In order to maintain the fluency of the business of the organization, QoS (Quality of Service), SLAs (Service Level Agreements), are required to be monitored regularly.
- ***Limitations of Freedom and Creativity:*** Several experts have pointed out that cloud computing has totally finished the freedom of users and has affected the implementation of innovative ideas and creativity.
- ***No Privacy:*** In a cloud computing environment it becomes quiet for users to place their private data on a cloud solution. The private data and personal details of an individual become known or in other words are disclosed to a third party.

3.2 *Issues Related to Cloud Computing*

There are several issues that need to be paid attention to while considering the application of cloud computing as a service model in organizations. Some of the core ones are[5]:

- ***Privacy:*** The cloud computing models have been criticized by the law keepers and law makers who advocates that the ease with which the companies control services and monitor it at their own free will
- ***Compliance:*** In order to obtain compliance from regulators and credit card industry and other agencies, the users may to adopt community or hybrid deployment modes that are typically more expensive and more restricted benefits.
- ***Legal:*** Any revolutionary changes in the landscape of global computing, certain legal issue does arises in the areas of trademark infringement, security concerns with regard to sharing of propriety data sources
- ***Open Standards:*** It has been that many cloud computing providers expose APIs which are typically well documented, but are unique in their implementation and thus are not interoperable.
- ***Security:*** Due to widespread popularity of the cloud computing, concerns are being raised with regard to the security issues which has been introduced through the adoption of new model. The efficiency and effectiveness of the traditional

protective mechanism are being reconsidered as the characteristic of this innovative deployment can differ from those of the traditional architecture.

4. Cloud Computing in Libraries

Libraries all over the world have been using the concept of Cloud Computing over the last decade or so. As one of the types of cloud services is data, as such libraries have initiated this service in their systems. For instance databases in the libraries are accessible as cloud application, Union catalogue can also be considered under the cloud computing umbrella.

4.1 *Potential Areas of Cloud Computing Applications in Libraries*

- Pre Web Technologies are used by most library computer systems
- Systems distributed across the net using pre-web technology which are harder in nature and costlier
- There is a large scale duplication of the data
- Due to scattered and distributed data, the library web presence is very weak
- Collaborations between libraries are difficult and expensive as libraries run their own independent servers
- Information seekers gather information through common web interface whereas distributed systems makes it difficult to get the library into their workflow
- Most of the systems installed 10% of the their total capacity. Cloud computing can reduce the carbon footprints, making the libraries more greener.

The improvements listed above can be grouped into three categories:

Technology Improvements: Libraries need to add more systems to manage their collections both in terms of physical forms as well licensed digital collections. Libraries have to ponder on two of the major issues regarding this.[15]

- Libraries have to find ways for open service architecture Many clouds offer this type of openness with published Applications Programme Interfaces (APIs) that any programmer can take advantage of, that means for any emerging service or technology, libraries will not always be dependent on vendor or third party to start taking advantage of these services or technology.
- Libraries can get rid of the technology and focus more on collection, patron services and innovation. Servers can be decommissioned and staffdo not have to maintain the complex software stack necessary to run the local systems, instead technical skills can be re-employed for extending cloud services into their environment and vice-versa (their environment into the cloud services).

Data Efficiencies: Keeping in view the advantages of technology deployment under the cloud solution, data storage in cloud computing can bring cheers in the libraries. However, some points that need to be borne in mind to bring about data efficiencies are:[15]

- One of the first thing a library under cloud solution should recognize the same data which have been stored hundreds and thousands of times across the libraries need to be identified.
- Secondly cloud solutions can greatly benefit libraries by collaborating and cooperative intelligence, and through such methods libraries can share pools of data for cooperative collection building, preservation and digitization and sharing of materials. Search engines like GOOGLE, YAHOO, bing, etc. can utilize large stored data, this will enable library collection be more relevant to search engines.

Community Power: Cloud solutions can create an online information community network; such a community can be of two categories viz.[13] (a) internal community of libraries collaborating within a single institution and across institutions, and (b) external community of libraries and information seekers.

4.2 *Major Libraries with Cloud Computing Solutions*

There are a number of libraries across the globe where Cloud computing Solutions have been either implemented or at the implementation stage. The following paragraphs focus on some of the initiatives in this direction. It may be indicated here that while library clouds or *Cloud computing* in libraries currently facilitate Web-based applications that change the way one works and collaborate online, focusing on two key areas of providing data and *services*:

- ***OCLC's WebCart***[13] is one of the first examples which is nearly 40 years old and which pre-dates both web and Cloud Computing. Other similar union catalogue came into existence with the help and support from national libraries and large union catalogues such as National Library of Australia, Bayerische Staatsbibliothek in Germany and Bibsys in Norway.
- ***National Library of Australia (NLA) Trove***[13] which has used the web to accomplish two tasks, one combining the collection of Australian Libraries with other important Australian and international collection and information sources, second to open up much of this content for the use of the public, who in turn can tag it, edit it, collect it by themselves and review it as per their opinion.
- ***HathiTrust:***[14] Building repository of digitized books and Journals from major research libraries which are situated in United States. The main focus of the HathiTrust is preservation of cultural record which can be accessible over a long period.

- ***OAISTER:***[14] First started by University of Michigan and now managed by OCLC whose main aim is to harvest all major digital repositories around the world. OAISTER is a union catalogue of millions of records which have been collected worldwide using the Open Access Initiative Protocol for Metadata Harvesting (OAI-PMH), as of today OAISTER includes more than 25 million record collected from 1,100 contributors.
- ***Europeana:***[15] Gathering the digitized collections from Europe's galleries, libraries, archives and museums which usually covers books, paintings, films, museum objects and archival records. The aggregations of the content will most importantly allow the content to be meshed up with other services and which in turn can be re-used. Europeana is definitely an opportunity which enhances its presence and reaches out more to its users, increases their web traffic, shares the users experience through Europeana and also envisages new partnerships.

4.3 *Cloud Computing Service Providers in Libraries*

- ***Ex-Libris:***[16] Ex-Libris is the best and well known cloud computing service providers of USA. Ex-Libris caters to all types of Libraries. The software is built on open architecture with support for interoperability standards and the software has number of features like compatibility with Unicode font, data migration flexibility, customization, etc.
- ***Polaris Library System:***[16] This is another cloud computing service provider software which provides solutions with regard to library automation. The company provides solutions in acquisition and processing systems of a library, it Polaris ILS Client License to integrate various PC's and print management systems of the library. The system adopts various library standards such as MARC 21 for bibliographic details, data XML, Z39.50 for information retrieval, Unicode, etc.
- ***Dura Cloud:***[16] Dura Cloud comes into picture with regard to the digital library services. Dura Cloud is basically a sister concern company of Duraspace which is a collaboration of Dspace Digital Library Software and Fedora Commons. Dura Cloud provides Open Source Code and codes that needs to be installed on the library machines. If a library cloud storage and software for the use in the library then one must have to subscribe to Dura Cloud services at a very nominal cost.

5. Cloud Computing in Indian Libraries

Looking at the present scenario, though many Indian Libraries have adopted and assimilated the emerging technologies fairly well, but not many of them have even initiated, implementation of cloud computing concepts. However, Indian libraries strength lies in synergetic and consolidated efforts in adopting new technologies.

5.1 *Major Libraries in India Using/Initiated the Process for Cloud Computing Solutions*

Academic Libraries in Orissa: In the libraries of Odisha, Department of Library and Information Studies have at the university has proposed to set up a cloud computing as their backup methodology. In this proposal, it has been proposed that a external hard drive will be passed on to the faculty to back up their data, which is in fact a tedious process, the method proposes that the department should create their own cloud computing servers.

The feature of cloud computing can be accomplished by the purchase of pogoplug device that will connect to the network; Pogoplug is an Internet enabled product that will allow the LIS department to connect their own external hard drives. With Pogoplug, staff and students will be able access the cloud hard drives through the web portal.

6. Caveat Emptor

If the Libraries and information centres, University Libraries are considering and deciding to move from the traditional library system to the more modern technology systems such as cloud computing solutions. There are certain questions that need to be pondered over. Foremost, whether this service will make the library more efficient and help to offer better service to its organization. If it is recognized or in other words if it is determined that cloud computing cannot accomplish its tasks then the libraries have to further take into account into certain considerations:[13]

- Whether there is scalability, reliability and security in-built factor in the cloud computing service.
- Is it multi tenancy.
- Who is the owner of the data stored in the system.
- What all rights are there for the library for extracting their own data and what will happen to the data while leaving the service entirely.
- Whether this service is an open system where the external data and services can be economically integrated into this service and its services can be economically integrated into external services.
  - These are some of the questions that libraries might need to ponder over before offering large chunks of data and services via cloud computing systems.

7. Conclusions

No technology is permanent in this world today, and no solution is perfect for any software or services but still efforts are made to make them fit in order to enhance the benefits and reduce the demerits. On the one hand, cloud computing is a great technology that provides unlimited storage, environment friendly technology, unlimited processing, mobile workforce, increased flexibility, dynamic scalability etc, but on the other hand it has certain demerits such as total dependency on providers, compliance monitoring, endangered liberty and privacy etc.

Libraries have the opportunity to improve the services in today's challenging information society. Cloud computing can be a good avenue which can move them towards a new future, which in turn can bring several benefits to the libraries. Looking at it in a holistic manner, cloud computing technology needs a lot of research work which will bring more advancement and customer satisfaction.

References

[1] National Institute of Science and Technology. Definition of cloud computing. http://csrc.nist.gov/publications/nistpubs/800-145/SP800-145.pdf. Accessed on 13 October 2012.

[2] Monaco, Ania (7 June 2012). A view inside the cloud. http://theinstitute.ieee.org/technology-focus/technology-topic/a-view-inside-the-cloud. Accessed on 21 September 2012.

[3] Working Group of the IETF. (July 1993). Meeting report from the IP over ATM, Chapter: Switch. http://mirror.switch.ch/ftp/doc/ietf/ipatm/atm-minutes-93jul.txt. Accessed on 21 September 2012.

[4] Ryan, Falvey Merchant. Regulation of the cloud in India. *Journal of Internet Law,* October 2011, 15(4), http://ssrn.com/abstract=1941494

[5] Corbató, Fernando J. An experimental time-sharing system. SJCC Proceedings. MIT. http://larch-www.lcs.mit.edu:8001/~corbato/sjcc62. Accessed on 22 September 2012.

[6] Rochwerger, B. *et al.* The RESERVOIR model and architecture for open federated cloud computing. *IBM Journal of Research and Development*, 2009, 53(4).

[7] Jeff Bezos' Risky Bet. *Business Week.*

[8] IT Knowledge Exchange, Tech Target. Amazon's early efforts at cloud computing partly accidental. http://itknowledgeexchange.techtarget.com/cloud-computing/2010/06/17/amazons-early-efforts-at-cloud-computing-partly-accidental. Accessed on 22 September 2012.

[9] Proceedings of the International conference on Cloud computing and Service Engineering (CLUSE2012), Bangalore, India.

[10] Launch of IBM Smarter Computing. https://www-304.ibm.com/connections/blogs/IBM SmarterSystems/date/201102?lang=en_us. Accessed on 1October 2012.

[11] Defining Cloud Services and Cloud Computing. IDC. 2008-09-23. http://blogs.idc.com/ie/?p=190. Accessed on 2010-08-22. Accessed on 22 August 2010.

[12] Emergence, Performance and Computing and Issues Challenging Cloud Computing by Rajesh Nawal, Ashish Gupta, Pragya Nayyar, Rajesh Gurjar—Proceedings of the NCNTE 2012, Third Biennial conference on Nascent Technologies.

[13] Winds of Change: Libraries and Cloud Computing by Matt Goldner, OCLC.

[14] OAister - http://www.oclc.org/oaister

[15] Europeana - http://pro.europeana.eu/web/guest/about

[16] Cloud Computing for Libraries: A SWOT Analysis by Miteshkumar Pandya, Planner 2012, INFLIBNET, Gujarat.

SECTION–IV

Electronics Resource Management Systems

Electronic Resources Management in Libraries, pp. 201–212

Electronic Resource Management

V. Vishwa Mohan and Achala Munigal

ABSTRACT

Electronic resources are growing at a tremendous rate and collections of electronic resources in libraries are growing exponentially both in size and use. ERM becomes essential under such circumstances. The paper presents a brief history of the development of ERM, description of the available ERM technologies that are available in open source and commercial. It attempts to find out whether ERM systems are integrated with the existing popular library automation software by conducting an online study. It concludes with a note that integration of ERMS in library automation software is imperative in the present digital era.

1. Introduction

Management is a universal phenomenon. In the modern society, we do not merely talk about business management or financial management; it permeates all spheres and activities of human life. Today we talk about time management, self management and so on. This being the situation, the importance of management of electronic resources need not be emphasised.

Electronic resources are growing at a tremendous rate therefore these collections in libraries are growing exponentially both in size and use. It is estimated that the world's information is doubling every two years. In 2011 the world will create a staggering 1.8 Zeta bytes of information. By 2020 the world will generate 50 times the amount of information. Such growth would certainly lead to chaos. Under such circumstances management comes into picture (Digital Universe).

Management of electronic resources is a very wide concept that deals right from their generation/production, organisation and control, storage and retrieval, etc. The credit goes to the Internet and Web technologies that are so efficient to ensure organisation and control of electronic resources worldwide on the World Wide Web.

However, it is the libraries that have the direct impact of the exponential growth of electronic resources. Tull *et al.* (2005) observed, "Libraries have struggled to manage the burgeoning number of electronic resources…" With this tremendous growth, some complications are faced by libraries in evaluation, selection, acquisition/subscription, maintenance, organisation, storage and retrieval/provision of the resources. Here comes the need for electronic resource management.

2. History

It was Tim Jewell (see NISO) who developed the idea of Electronic Resource Management (ERM) in 2001–2002. The roots of ERM can be traced with the development of MARC in the mid-1960s a project by the Library of Congress. The later developments include the creation of Dialog database in 1966 followed by the WorldCat in 1971 by OCLC. CD-ROM technology and online databases changed the way information was managed in the mid 1980s but searches were usually mediated by a librarian. Finally it is the Web and Web-related technologies revolutionised the organisation and control of electronic resources in other words the management of electronic resources at global level.

As far as the role of libraries in the management of electronic resource is concerned, at times it looks to be elusive because of the very nature of their availability and accessibility. For instance when a library subscribes to the access to online electronic resources, the library need not really bother about storage, organisation, and maintenance of these resources because the vendor of the resources maintains the resources and the library or its users will simply access these resources. Similarly, in case of open access resources there is no need for subscription of the sources also.

But at the same time when the terms of access are different and number of vendors increases, the complexity also increases. When libraries make subscription to e-resources with permission to download and archive the resources then the management of electronic resources arises. It is also because of the availability of different types of electronic resources that might form the collection of e-resources in the libraries. Different types of resources need to be handled with different technologies and software. It is well known that electronic resources are categorized broadly into two types from their availability point of view: they are open access sources and subscribed sources. Other categorization/categories include(s) full-text and bibliographic databases; online and offline sources, and so on. According to Tessa Minchew (2012) "Electronic resources include not only music and video CDS or DVDs but also include software, databases, institutional repositories, websites, e-books, e-journals, playways, podcast, vodcasts etc. As a rule of thumb, e-resources are items that require the use of a computer (See, AACR2 appendix D, electronic resources)."

Further when libraries endeavoured to develop their own collection of e-resources in the form of institutional repositories they need to resort to electronic resource management. Until recently, hardly any tools available to manage electronic resources, so libraries used databases which were developed in-house, spreadsheets, file folders, e-mail file folders to manage the electronic resources. So a need for developing standards for ERM was felt.

In this context a clear idea relating to what constitutes ERM is needed. According to Wikipedia ERM is "the practices and software systems used by libraries to keep track of important information about electronic information resources, especially Internet-based resources such as e-journals, databases, and e-books. The development of ERM became necessary in the early 2000s as it became clear that traditional library catalogues and integrated library systems were not designed to handle metadata for resources as mutable as many online products are" (Electronic Resource Management).

The above definition of ERM clearly denotes that it is not merely a software system, but it is also the set of practices used by libraries to keep track of important electronic information resources. Thus the concept of ERM is a generic and wider one. However, the main problem is how to count usage and who sets the standards or the practices?

The Digital Library Federation and National Information Standards Organization (NISO) (2012) began work in May 2002 to develop standards for ERM data. NISO, a non-profit association accredited by the American National Standards Institute (ANSI) identifies, develops, maintains, and publishes technical standards to manage information in changing and ever-more digital environment. NISO standards apply both traditional and new technologies to the full range of information-related needs, including retrieval, re-purposing, storage, metadata and preservation.

ERM systems in library and information centres (LICs) are supposed to deal with acquisition and management of licensed e-resources, tracking electronic resources right from ordering through licensing and final access. Linking license documents to resource records, providing descriptions of resources, information about the data providers, consortia arrangements, access platform, displaying licensed rights, contact information for all content providers etc is also very significant. Logging problems with resources and providers/suppliers/publishers and providing customizable e-mail alerting systems (e.g. notices to managers when actions are expected or required) etc. is also pertinent. These functions cannot be performed manually as they are machine based therefore, it is the technology alone that would ease and facilitate the librarians. The ERM System may be integrated into the library automation system modules or may be a standalone system, preferably with a public interface, either separate or integrated into the OPAC.

In August, 2004, the Digital Library Federation published its final report, Electronic Resource Management: Report of the DLF ERM Initiative (DLF ERMI). After reviewing the features of the existing ERM systems (http://www.carolsmith.us/downloads/663ERMSPaper.pdf), the study identified seven key areas of ERMS functionality: i) descriptive bibliographic data, ii) licensing details, iii) financial information, iv) order status information, v) administrative/technical activities, vi) support information, and vii) usage statistics.

The above indicate a narrow and prevailing sense of ERMS and/or functionality of ERMS. Therefore, to handle various aspects of e-resource management, some institutions themselves had developed in-house ERM systems in the absence of commercial solutions. Most of the present ERM Systems used by libraries deal with tasks of keeping track of important information about electronic information resources, especially Internet-based resources such as e-journals, databases, and e-books. They endeavour to track individual electronic resources like either the e-journals or e-books right from ordering through licensing and final access, linking license documents to resource records etc. There is no single interface that manages all the electronic resource as defined by Tessa.

3. Management of E-Resources

With various publishers/providers devising their own standards in producing electronic resources, libraries were finding it increasingly difficult in managing these electronic resources. Since there were no established patterns, various studies were conducted on standardisation of terms, definitions, compatibility of data etc. listed below:

- ***COUNTER*** (Counting Online Usage of Networked Electronic Resources) initiative facilitates in recording online usage statistics. The use of online information resources is growing rapidly. It is widely agreed by producers and purchasers of information that the use of these resources should be measured in a more consistent way. Librarians want to understand better how the information they buy from a variety of sources is being used; publishers want to know how the information products they disseminate are being accessed. An essential requirement to meet these objectives is an agreed international set of standards and protocols governing the recording and exchange of online usage data. The COUNTER Codes of Practice provide these standards and protocols and are published in full on their website (COUNTER).
- ***Creative Commons*** is a non-profit organization that enables the sharing and use of creativity and knowledge through free legal tools. Our free, easy-to-use copyright licenses provide a simple, standardized way to give the public permission to share and use creative work—on conditions of the user choice. Creative Commons licenses let you easily change your copyright terms from the default of "all rights reserved" to "some rights reserved." Creative Commons licenses are not an alternative to copyright. They work alongside copyright and enable the user to modify his/her copyright terms to best suit his/her needs.
- ***The Digital Rights Expression Languages (DREL) Workgroup*** within the IEEE Learning Technology Standards Committee is gathering requirements that a standardized DREL must meet to support learning, education, and training. DREL standardization efforts exist, are well advanced, and are supported by large industry groups (multimedia, consumer electronics, telecommunications, the IT industry, etc.). The workgroup assumes that such languages will be incorporated into technology in the present decade. Their goal is not to create another DREL standard but to ensure that existing standards can be effectively used by the educational community (WG4).

- ***indecs*** (an acronym of "interoperability of data in e-commerce systems; written in lower case) was a project part funded by the European Community Info 2000 initiative and by several organisations representing the music, rights, text publishing, authors, library and other sectors in 1998–2000, which has since been used in a number of metadata activities. indecs was built from a simple generic model of commerce (the "model of making"): a model of the life cycle of any kind of content from conception to the final physical or digital copies. indecs provided an analysis of the requirements for metadata for e-commerce of content (intellectual property) in the network environment, focussing on semantic interoperability. For example, instead of treating sound carriers, books, videos and photographs as fundamentally different things with different (if similar) characteristics, they are all recognised as creations with different values of the same higher-level attributes, whose metadata can be supported in a common environment (indecs).
- ***A Data Dictionary*** is a set of terms, with their definitions, used in a computerized system. Some data dictionaries are structured, with terms related through hierarchies and other relationships: structured data dictionaries are ontologies. An *interoperable* data dictionary contains terms from different computerized systems or metadata schemes, and shows the relationships they have with one another in some formal way. The purpose of an interoperable data dictionary is to support the use together of terms from different systems. The DOI system uses an interoperable structured data dictionary: the indecs Data Dictionary (iDD). DOIs need not make use of this, but it is envisaged that many will: any DOI intended to allow interoperability (*i.e.* which has the possibility of use in services outside of the direct control of the issuing Registration Agency) is subject to DOI metadata policy, which is based on the registration of terms in the iDD (DOI and Data Dictionaries).
- ***Liblicense*** is a standard or model licensing agreement. The LIBLICENSE Project was created in January 1997, comprising two parts. The LIBLICENSE website provides resources (including model license language and detailed discussion of licensing terms) through an extensive series of links and menus. LIBLICENSE-L is a continuing discussion forum for licensing issues and related contemporary concerns in the domain of scholarly communication. These materials will serve as a useful starting point toward providing librarians with a better understanding of the issues raised by license agreements in the digital age. The LIBLICENSE Project has been hosted since November 2011 by the Center for Research Libraries (Libicense).
- ***The Exchange of Serials Subscription Information*** a whitepaper by Ed Jones was prepared for the NISO, with support from the Digital Library Federation. This study was undertaken in order i) to identify current and potential applications in which serials subscription data are exchanged, ii) to identify the formats currently in use for such exchange, and iii) to ascertain the perceived utility of standards to

support such exchange, including standard identifiers for subscribers and services (NISO).

There are a number of ERM Systems like Open source ERMS, In-house developed ERMS by universities and commercial ERMS.

4. Open Source ERM Systems

The following is a sample of the open source ERM Systems:

- ***Calibre*** is a free and open source e-book library management application developed by users of e-books for users of e-books. It has a cornucopia of features divided into the following main categories: i) library management, ii) e-book conversion, iii) syncing to e-book reader devices, iv) downloading news from the web and converting it into e-book form, v) comprehensive e-book viewer, and vi) content server for online access to the users' book collection (Calibre).
- ***Esciurus*** is (or rather, will be) a desktop application that allows the users to build and maintain their personal collection of e-books, in particular scientific publications. It will store not only these papers, but also associated metadata (author, title, bibliographic information, etc.), allowing for fast and intuitive retrieval. It handles e-books in the upcoming ".epub" format (OCF/OPF), as defined by the International Digital Publishing Forum. The program is being developed in Java. It, therefore, runs on all major platforms.
- ***FreERMS*** is an electronic resource management system for libraries. It is written in PHP using the symfony framework (1.4). It requires PHP 5.3, and has been tested on Ubuntu Linux systems (FreERMS).
- ***Custom Summon Searches*** is a tool for creating scoped searches in Serial Solutions' Summon Discovery service written in Javascript to provide a lightweight solution to a common problem. Released under the GPL, one can download the source and customize it to reflect his/her library's specializations (http://gvsulib.com/labs).
- ***SUSHI Py*** is a short Python class that allows libraries and other organizations to harvest COUNTER statistics via the NISO SUSHI protocol. SUSHI Py is capable of reading a list of SUSHI services from a CSV file or a MySQL database, and it can likewise write the resulting COUNTER report to a CSV file or a MySQL database. SUSHI Py was developed because there is a notable lack of usable and well documented SUSHI harvesters. The few projects listed by NISO are several years old, appear abandoned, and are unnecessarily large. The goal of it is not just to be simple to use but also to be simple to understand. It is a proof of concept. SUSHI Py is for the following people (SUSHI Py):
  - Librarians and other electronic resource managers who want to implement SUSHI without paying big bucks for a commercial ERM client.

  - Librarians and electronic resource managers who want a clear and documented example of how SUSHI works so that they can build their own custom implementation.

- ***The Home Library Archive*** (http://sourceforge.net/projects/phphomelibrary) categorizes and keeps track of books by Library of Congress format. Automatically adds new information from the Library of Congress or Amazon whenever we add a new book. It has plain output appearance, but robust functionality under the hood.
- ***Open Digital Rights Language (ODRL) Initiative*** is an international effort aimed at developing and promoting an open standard for policy expressions. ODRL provides flexible and interoperable mechanisms to support transparent and innovative use of digital content in publishing, distribution and consumption of digital media across all sectors and communities. The ODRL Policy model is broad enough to support traditional rights expressions for commercial transaction, open access expressions for publicly distributed content, and privacy expressions for social media (ORDL).
- ***PRISM:*** The Publishing Requirements for Industry Standard Metadata (PRISM) is an IDEAlliance Specification that defines an XML metadata fields and controlled vocabularies for managing, aggregating, and delivering publishing content for magazines, journals and more.
- ***Project RoMEO:*** The RoMEO Project (Rights MEtadata for open archiving) was a JISC funded project (2002/3) at the University of Loughborough to investigate the rights issues surrounding the self-archiving of research in the UK community under the Open Archive Initiative Protocol for Metadata Harvesting (OAI-PMH). Through surveying the academic community it ascertained how give-away research literature and metadata was used and how it should be protected. From this work, the RoMEO project created a list of publishers' conditions for self-archiving (RoMEO).
- The Shibboleth System is a standard based, open source software package for web single sign-on across or within organizational boundaries. It allows sites to make informed authorization decisions for individual access of protected online resources in a privacy-preserving manner. The Shibboleth software implements widely used federated identity standards, principally OASIS' Security Assertion Mark-up Language (SAML), to provide a federated single sign-on and attribute exchange framework. Shibboleth also provides extended privacy functionality allowing the browser user and their home site to control the attributes released to each application. Using Shibboleth-enabled access simplifies management of identity and permissions for organizations supporting users and applications. Shibboleth is developed in an open and participatory environment, is freely available, and is released under the Apache Software License (Shibboleth).
- ***OLLARA*** is a free, open source, web-based electronic resource manager (ERM) written in PHP and MySQL. It was developed at the Ferris Library for Information,

Technology and Education, and is based on University of Wisconsin-La Crosse's ERMs (Ollara).

5. Types of ERMS

The following are some of the in-house ERMS developed by libraries to handle their electronic resources.

5.1 *In-house ERM Systems*

E-Matrix is the locally developed serial and electronic resource management system in use at the NCSU Libraries. This tool acknowledges that the issues associated with electronic resources mirror those that face their serial collection as a whole, regardless of format. E-Matrix therefore supports the effective management of the NCSU Libraries serial collection by managing print and electronic journals and databases (E-Matrix).

reSearcher is an award-winning integrated suite of open source products for locating and managing electronic information resources, designed for use by students and researchers in academic libraries. The four main modules of reSearcher include CUFTS, the open source serials management; GODOT, the open source link resolving; dbWiz, the open source federated searching; and the Open Knowledgebase.

reSearcher enables libraries to provide students and researchers with streamlined access to an integrated array of information resources. Together, reSearcher's components deliver rich portal-type functionality, presenting a unified interface to research databases, library and union catalogues, internet search engines, and other electronic information sources (reSearcher).

5.2 *Commercial ERM Systems*

Of late, a number of vendors introduced various commercial ERM packages to handle e-resources effectively and in a standardised manner. Some commercial systems include:

- ***ERM as a Solution from SwetsWise*** includes comprehensive list of features and benefits included, with an integrated A-Z listing of all acquired content available to end users, swift access set-up for new e-journal subscriptions and automatic, pro-active claiming of missing content. With the ability to browse and purchase content also included, the potential and capabilities of the full package begin to realize themselves (SwetsWise).
- ***ERM from Innovative Interfaces, Inc.*** (http://www.iii.com/) assists in centralizing and assimilating all of the technical and administrative details of digital resources, Innovatives ERM saves staff time, improves collection analysis, and makes the most of scarce budgetary resources. Used in tandem with Innovative's WebPAC Pro or Encore, ERM makes it easy for patrons to find the e-resources they need, elegantly

presenting important information such as renewal dates, authentication, proxy data, and complete content descriptions. Libraries can use Electronic Resource Management as a stand-alone solution or as an integrated module of the Millennium ILS. As a stand-alone system, libraries can enjoy the benefits of ERM's ability to maintain resources, track licenses, and manage coverage data.

- ***Endeavor Meridian*** 1.5 is designed to help librarians and information professionals efficiently manage electronic resources as well as the licenses and packages associated with those resources (Endeavor).
- ***360 Resource Manager from Serials Solutions*** is the complete solution for reducing the time and effort required to manage the entire lifecycle of e-resources. 360 Resource Manager offers a full set of features to control complex subscription management issues, from tracking license terms of use to managing renewal dates, all integrated with the authoritative Serials Solutions KnowledgeWorks knowledgebase. 360 Resource Manager works for libraries of all sizes and types and is also offered in a Consortium Edition for library groups (360 Resource Manager).
- ***Verde from Ex Libris*** is a centralized repository through which all e-resource workflows—acquisitions, trial, usage, cost, access and administrative data are managed. Built-in workflow management capabilities enable the library to define consistent and replicable processes, helping staff keep track of task assignments throughout the e-resource life cycle (Verde).

5.3 *Open Source and Commercial ERM Systems*

When there is availability of many open source and commercial ERMSs it appears as if ERM is not a serious problem in the libraries but its felt that the existing library automation packages, electronic resources available in the library are all not integrated with ERMS. As a result the librarians have to depend on more than one different software systems to handle e-resources. The following are some of the most popular and widely applied library automation software which are also used for ERM.

- ***NewGenLib*** is completely web based solution and uses Java Web Start™ Technology and has compatibility with international metadata and interoperability standards like MARC-21, MARC-XML, z39.50, SRU/W, OAI-PMH. It allows digital attachments to metadata etc. But it does not imply that it has integrated electronic resource management (NewGenLib).
- ***Virtua of VTLS*** is a full-function library management system, providing management of circulation, cataloging, serials, acquisitions, course reserves and more (VTLS). All functions are fully integrated, allowing any staff user to access any function at any time according to their library-assigned permissions VITAL from VTLS builds on core Fedora™ capabilities to provide every feature—ingesting, storing, indexing, cataloging, searching and retrieving—required to handle large text

and rich content collections. Workflows have been adapted to meet the specialized requirements of libraries and archives. Beyond capabilities provided in VITAL, VTLS offers services including metadata conversion, digitization of content, and customization of Web interfaces. It is quite clear that Virtua needs to be integrated with VITAL (VITAL).

- ***LibLime Koha*** is the most advanced open-source Integrated Library System in use today by hundreds of libraries worldwide. Though it is considered to be a completely Web-based solution. However it is not an ERM integrated Library Automation Software (Koha).
- ***LibSys*** is a popular integrated commercial LA software in India. It doesn't seem to have integrated with ERMS. Its LSDigital is a document digitization software used by libraries for the purpose of easy management, multi-access, reduction of storage space of the document and the preservation against spoilage of rare books, research papers, important documents and archived newspapers, maps, etc. The software has been designed to facilitate easy searching of text in the document. LSDigital is a complete Digital Resource Management System (DRMS) which can be integrated with any twain compliant scanner. However, this DRMS is not an ERMS in its real sense (LSDigital).
- ***SOUL*** is none other than a software than is developed by Inflibnet with a significant feature consisting of UNICODE based multilingual support for Indian and foreign languages. It supports cataloguing of electronic resources such as e-journals, e-books, virtually any type of material. It is also Compliant to International Standards such as MARC21, AACR-2, MARCXML. It supports requirements of digital library and facilitate link to full-text articles and other digital objects and still it lack integration of ERMS (SOUL).

The above shows that almost all the popular library application software, though endeavour to meet the requirements of cataloguing electronic resources, developing and maintaining digital libraries/institutional repositories. But they are not full-fledged ERMS or LA software with integration of ERMS. In view of the e-resource revolution, it is imperative on the part of the LA Software to integrate ERMS so that ERM becomes easier to the libraries.

6. Conclusions

E-resources are dynamic in nature. With the advent of open access resources that are freely accessible over the Web, the rate of use of e-resources is increasing day-by-day. Consequently management of these resources is turning out to be more difficult. As open access resources are always on the web, but accessing the same resources may not be possible as some of the resources may be lost and the number of resources increases day-by-day thus, leading to difficulties in retrieval. Even in case of subscribed sources retrieval of specific sources earlier consulted may not be remembered by the user relating to his/her work therefore certain important electronic resources may need to be downloaded or archived and preserved in the library. And keeping track of important information about electronic information resources, especially internet-based resources such as electronic journals, databases, and electronic books, proves to be cumbersome. Under such circumstances the need for ERMS arises in the librarians to manage the collection of their electronic resources.

Although there are so many open source and other commercial ERMS available in the market, and a lot of progress has been made, there are many more obstacles or hurdles to cross like copyright issues and establishment of standard identifiers for subscription data exchange. With libraries handling license agreements and e-books there may be more to come. So, an effective ERM strategy needs to be urgently devised and integrated with every LA software coming into the market.

References

[1] 360 Resource Manager from Serials Solutions http://www.serialssolutions.com/en/services/360-resource-manager (accessed on 16 September 2012).

[2] Calibre. http://calibre-ebook.com/about (accessed 16 September 2012) COUNTER. http://www.projectcounter.org/ (accessed on 16 September 2012).

[3] Creative Commons. http://creativecommons.org/about (accessed on 16 September 2012).

[4] Digital Universe. http://www.emc.com/leadership/programs/digital-universe.htm (accessed 02 September 2012).

[5] DOI and Data Dictionaries. http://www.library.cornell.edu/elicensestudy/doi/040310DOI DataDictionaries.pdf (accessed on 16 September 2012).

[6] E-Matrix. http://www.lib.ncsu.edu/e-matrix/ (accessed on 10 September 2012).

[7] Electronic Resource Management. http://en.wikipedia.org/wiki/Electronic_resource_manage ment (accessed on 14 September 2012).

[8] Electronic Resource Management. http://www.iii.com/products/electronic_resource.shtml (accessed on 16 September 2012).

[9] Electronic Resource Management. http://en.wikipedia.org/wiki/Electronic_resource_manage ment (accessed on 22 August 2012).

[10] Electronic Resource Management System. http://www.carolsmith.us/downloads/663ERMS Paper.pdf (accessed on 25 August 2012).

[11] Esciurus. http://esciurus.sourceforge.net/ (accessed on 06 September 2012).

[12] FreERMS. https://github.com/yitznewton/freerms#readme (accessed on 10 September 12).

[13] indecs Content Model. http://en.wikipedia.org/wiki/Indecs_Content_Model (accessed on 16 September 2012).

[14] Jones, Ed. The Exchange of Serials Subscription Information http://www.niso.org/publications/white_papers/Serials-WP.pdf (accessed on 15 September 2012).

[15] Koha. http://www.koha.org/about (accessed on 07 September 2012).

[16] Liblicense http://liblicense.crl.edu/(accessed on 14 September 2012).

[17] Libsys. http://www.libsys.co.in/companyprofile_milestones.html (accessed on 09 September 2012).

[18] LSDigital. http://www.libsys.co.in/offerings-lsdigital.html (accessed on 17 September 2012).

[19] Minchew, Tessa. Electronic Resource Management http://www.slideshare.net/tminchew/electronic-resources-management-a-day-in-the-life (accessed on 11 September 2012).

[20] NewGenLib. http://www.verussolutions.biz/web/content/features (accessed on 02 September 2012).

[21] NISO. http://www.niso.org/about/ 1(accessed on 02 September 2012) 6.09.2012 12:17 IST.

[22] ODRL Community Group. http://www.w3.org/community/odrl/ (accessed on 12 September 2012).

[23] Ollara. http://ollara.ferris.edu/ (accessed on 14 September 2012).

[24] PRISM http://www.prismstandard.org/ (accessed on 08 September 2012).

[25] reSearcher. http://researcher.sfu.ca/ (accessed on 13 September 2012).

[26] RoMEO: Publisher copyright policies and self-archiving 1 http://www.sherpa.ac. uk/projects/sherparomeo.html (accessed on 12 September 2012).

[27] SUSHI Py. http://sourceforge.net/projects/sushipy/ (accessed on 16 September 2012).

[28] Shibboleth http://shibboleth.net/ (accessed on 12 September 2012).

[29] SOUL http://www.inflibnet.ac.in/soul/downloads/SOUL2.0.pdf (accessed on 04 September 2012).

[30] Swets launches ERM as a service. http://www.swets.com/swets-launches-erm-as-a-service (accessed on 15 September 2012).

[31] The Home Library Archive. http://sourceforge.net/projects/phphomelibrary (accessed on 15 Sept. 2012).

[32] Tull, L., Crum, J., Davis, T., and Strader, C.R. (2005). Integrating and streamlining electronic resources workflows via Innovative's Electronic Resource Management. *The Serials Librarian*, 47(4), 103–124.

[33] University Libraries: Library Labs http://gvsulib.com/labs (accessed on 09 September 2012).

[34] Verde. http://www.exlibrisgroup.com/category/VerdeOverview (accessed on 12 September 2012) 12.09.2012 09:42 IST.

[35] VTLS. http://www.vtls.com/products/virtua (accessed on 07 September 2012).

[36] Vital. http://www.vtls.com/products/vital (accessed on 07 September 2012).

[37] WG4: Digital Rights Expression Language. http://ltsc.ieee.org/wg4/index.html (accessed on 16 September 2012).

Electronic Resources Management in Libraries, pp. 213–228

Need for Digital Media Systems in Media Industry

Sarminah Tamsir and C.K. Ramaiah

ABSTRACT

Media content companies find themselves with a wealth of analogue materials to be archived and managed. In this digital age, an obvious goal for these media companies is to commercially exploit their media content. However, before they could do this, they first have to digitise their media content so that they could offer their customers an opportunity to browse and preview their assets online. And for some media content companies, the ultimate goal is to allow customers to purchase and download content directly from the company's website. In order to achieve this, they must first digitise, log, index, store, and organise the content. In short, media companies must think about using the Digital Content Management system (DCM) for manage their media centres. These companies should strategically plan a business model for their assets, in terms of how the company plans to organise, to use, and to commercialise their media content. Embarking on DCM requires huge investment and therefore it is necessary to balance it with the potential revenue that it could bring in for the company. This paper attempted to provide an overview of latest technologies related to DCM for organising, managing and exploiting the content in terms of revenue.

1. Introduction

The most dynamic area of the media industry especially the broadcasting industry is not the programming, the stars, corporate maneuvering, or the ratings battles, but it is the technology used to make all of these and other exciting challenges possible. The three camera methods of shooting situation comedies (sitcoms) has changed very little in 40 years, but the equipment used to record, edit, and distribute a programme has undergone multiple generations of evolution. In many cases the introduction of new technology has been the enabling force behind any dramatic change that has taken place. For example, the use of robotic mount cameras in television news production has replaced human operators in the studio. As a result, one of the biggest challenges faced by media industries at any level is to keep up with the latest technologies. The media industry is in the midst of a 40-year metamorphosis from analogue to digital technology. Digital technology is sweeping its way through the media industry. Digital technology represents an improved method of capturing sound and images as pure data processing ones and zeroes in a torrent of data transmitted over-the air and through cables of many types.

1.1 *Trends in Media Industry*

The most important trends sweeping through the media industry can be divided into two categories: technological and organisational (Seel and Grant, 1997).

Technological Trends

There are two aspects of technological trends. Firstly, is there increase in the number of channels available to viewers? The increase is due to a combination of several factors, with the most important being the introduction of new distribution technologies including cable television and Direct Broadcast Satellite (DBS) services. This combined with the fact that digital compression can increase the number of channels offered by a service by a factor of four to eight, will allow many broadcaster to avoid the "either/or" decision. Instead, they will deliver "both".

Secondly, is the transition from analogue to digital technology in the process of producing media products? In the early days, virtually all equipment used in media production created, stored, or manipulated continually varying analogue waveforms. These analogue waveforms were subjected to electronic interference, and no re-production was a perfect copy of the original waveform. The digital revolution began with the introduction of computers, which converted analogue signals into digital, allowing us the manipulation of pictures using mathematical algorithms. Nowadays, these "digital video effects" devices are inexpensive and had the capability of creating a range of video effects, which is not possible using the analogue technology. The next step was the introduction of digital videotape recorders that allowed perfect reproduction of images through 100 or more generations (copies of copies).

Today, every piece of equipment used in the media production are digital. In fact, we cannot find any more analogue video recording and recording of the content is on different type of magnetic storage: DVD, erasable discs, fixed hard disks which are used for computer storage. In essence, the move to digital technology has fully introduced computers to virtually in all areas of media production. Nearly every piece of digital television equipment has a computer as its heart to control and manipulates the digital data according to pre-programmed parameters.

Together with Internet technology, data broadcasting or web casting and streaming media has further improved the distribution/delivery of services. These activities have created the evolution in media production. For example, in the television industry, data broadcast is a concept whereby a combination of video, audio, software programmes, streaming data or other digital/multimedia content are transmitted continuously to intelligent devices such as PC, digital set top boxes and hand-held devices like mobile phones where these can be manipulated. The broadcast concept means that although a return path might be available, it is not required. Content is received without being requested. This in turn has created a new business model for the media industry.

In fact, it will change the whole spectrum of media industry management and operation. Together digital technology and Internet have brought a new form of entertainment and information. New opportunities in media industry will mean new business models, new forms of advertising, new kinds of interactive programmes, and many other changes benefiting both the consumer and stakeholders alike (Janik, 2001).

Organisational Trends

There are two aspects of organisational trends. First development is the introduction of digital technology in the integration of media industries with competent communication and electronic industries. On the technological front, computer manufacturers are providing equipment used in the media production process.

The second organisational trend is the direct response to the fact that other industries have set their sights on media industries especially the broadcasting industries. The radio and television industries are experiencing an unparalleled era of mergers and buyouts as broadcasters position themselves to compete in the new media landscape. This consolidation has also been driven by the deregulation of ownership limitations that is a direct response to the desire of the policymakers to create a more competitive media marketplace. For example the telecommunication industry has shown great interest in the media industry and a merger is likely to take place wherever possible. Taken together, these four trends suggest that:

- The number of media outlets is increasing (and will continue to increase).
- The increase is fed by cheaper media production costs, economies of scale with consolidations of the media/television industry and the entry of new companies, most notably computer and other microelectronics companies, into the media/television industry.

In general, media industry around the world is approaching a crossroads. New devices give the broadcaster more operational choices. The old model of operation is going away and a new model is needed to address the future requirements of broadcasting facilities (Reuter, 2000). Organisational factors as well as technological, are now causing—or will soon cause revolution virtually in every area of the media industry. Correll (n.d.) states that the World Wide Web has dramatically changed the way businesses and consumers access and consume media. This technological convergence has not only had an impact on the telecommunications and media industries but also on the consumer electronics, entertainment and computing industries.

2. Digital Content Management

The advancement of digital technology does not spare media content. According to Dan Agan, the media content is the fundamental raw material on which any broadcaster's business-critical operations are built (Tassel, 2001). It is the foundation on which their businesses are laid and the key resources required for realising value. In the case of broadcasters, it is the inherent desirability and availability of these assets that determine the ultimate viability of the real products *i.e.* the viewers' eyeballs. In the case of cable casters, they too need eyeballs to sell advertisement, but the ongoing availability and desirability of the content itself also ensures continued and expanded distribution by cable operators who pay for the content. Digital technology has changed the way of managing the media content for the past ten years.

2.1 *What is Digital Content Management System?*

Sun Microsystems defined Digital Content Management (DCM) system as the systems and processes for digitising, storing, accessing and securing digital media in a distributed network environment (Rosenblatt, 1997). According to Harris (2000), DCM is a system that manages the creative asset and ingest it into a system, log it in, catalogue it (identify the metadata), create database of that information, provide tools that may allow browsing (like Internet search engine) and shows the results of searches on a workstation. In full, it is an enterprise wide system application which is able to create a signals path from the storage work location and automatically transfer the materials in the proper form at the destination in a "just-in-time" for delivery. Artesia Technologies (2002) defined DCM as a set of coordinated technologies and processes that allow the quick and efficient storage, retrieval and re-use of digital assets.

Tassel (1998, 2001) on the other hand, defined DCM as a complex combination of hardware, software and business practices that allows companies to produce, market and manipulate information products more efficiently. Basically, there are two types of systems related to DCM, namely, the Media Asset Management System (MAMS) and Content Management System (CMS). But a complete DCM has another two attributes, *i.e.*, the Metadata Link and the Digital Right Management (DRM) system. MAM offers operational efficiencies and cost savings, Content Management (CM) supports and new opportunities to generate revenue. DRM is the central piece of media distribution systems that will enable a return on the investments made in creating digital media content. However, in order to realise these returns a company or organisation must generate detailed metadata at some point. Whether it is through a MAM system or an ingest to CM process, the metadata is the key link that ties MAM, CM and DRM together to maximise the benefits from DCM operations. When the equipment is an end-to-end system handling the range of tasks of MAM and CM, it will be called as DCM system as shown in Figure 1. It is necessary at this point to define certain terms in order to understand this emerging digital technology properly. To begin, media "asset" is generally understood to be text, graphics, photos, drawings, video, audio, sounds and music, or any combination of these elements. However, media "content" usually refers to a finished product.

2.2 *An Overview of DCM System*

According to Tassel (2001), DCM system comprises of various steps and processes. Table 1 shows an overview of DCM system. It shows various details of the steps and processes that are involved in DCM system.

2.3 *Benefits of DCM System*

Artesia Technologies (2002) and Sun Microsystems (n.d.) have highlighted two major benefits that can be derived by implementing DCM. It is believed that DCM is the most efficient and profit generating procedure in a networked world. It allows re-purposing of media content and mass-production of the content so that they can be distributed in many different platforms. DCM also makes it possible to track and retrieve various versions of the asset as they were produced.

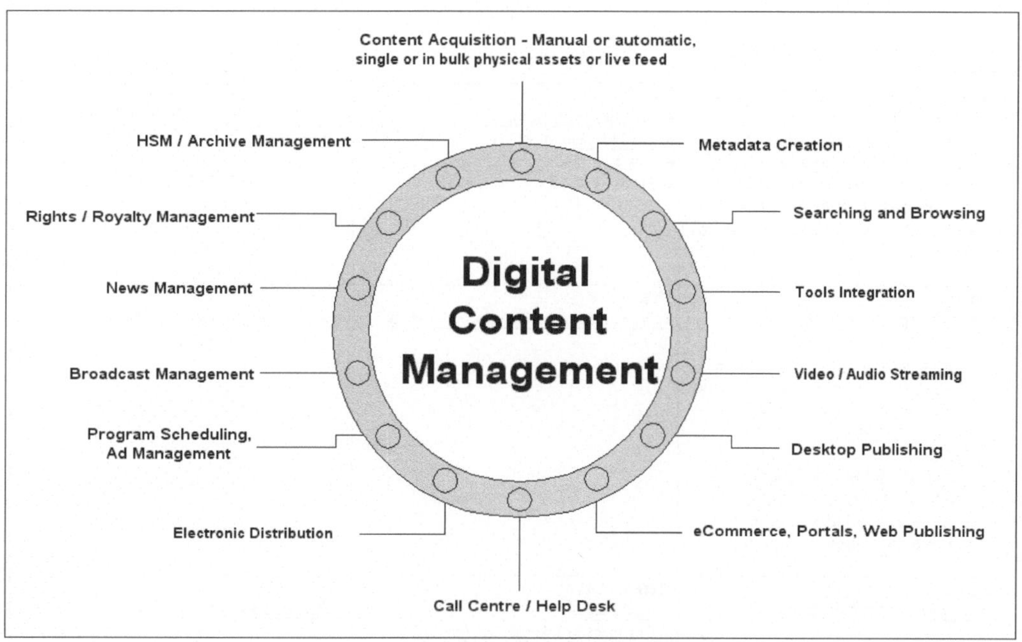

Fig. 1: Components of DCM System

3. Media Asset Management System

The MAM systems handle media-based content in the production and postproduction side. The term "asset" includes all the elements that make up programmes such as video, audio, graphics, drawing and text. It also includes the documents that guide the completion of the finished product such as scripts, rundowns and even Edit Decision

Table 1: Steps and Processes in DCM System

Media Asset Management Create Assets and Programs	**Content Management Distribute Content**		**Relationship Management Monetize Content**
Original and Repurposed Material	Wholesale (B2B)	Retail (B2C)	Backoffice Administration
Step 1 • Capture or acquire assets • Generate metadata	**Step 1** • Encode: *Apply appropriate markup language: HTML, SGML, XML	• Encode: Language, user player types, bit rates, end-user devices	• Process Payments
Step 2 • Ingest 1. Digitize assets, if analog 2. Parse (by text keyword, scene change, lighting, change lyrics, key change, etc.) 3. Capture existing metadata 4. Generate metadata that describe asset 5. Filename, name, number, informal handle • Brief description in natural language • File format detail • Creation software detail • Attach descriptive meta-tags • Generate lowresolution proxies for search, browse and retrieval (If ingested material is a finished program, encode for distribution)	**Step 2** • Intellectual property protection (IP) *Digital watermark *Encryption • Digital Rights Management (DRM) *Embed business rules in content (Subscription, pay-per, ad-supported, etc.)		• Track content and usage • Collate and report session data per partnership aggrement
	Step 3 • Format for consumption • Enable customization • Link to metadata database • Embed callouts for target ads		• Calculate referral payments to affliates and other sources
Step 3 1. Assemble rough cut by browsing lowresolution proxies 2. Edit and assemble program (includes repurposing and re-expressing of existing assets and programming) • Collect session data 1. User information 2. Content request information 3. Authenticate ser ID* /account status (*authorized users to retrieve assets via metatags)	**Step 4** • Apply distribution wrapper or format *SOAP *ICE		• Refer merchandise to fulfillment partner(s) and allocate payment
Step 4 • Check out asset from storage **Step 5** • Check-in asset into storage • Invoice version control	**Step 5** • Insert ads • Transport to playout server • Publish to edge servers • Modulate and encode, as needed for channel • Broadcast/push content • Monitor transmission *Quality of service data		• Aggregate royalties
Step 6 • Store new asset or program, as well as previous version	**Step 6** • Automated intake by receiving sites	• Serve to user(s) *On-demand *Opt-in push or pull/push	• Pay content provider royalties

Source: J. Van Tassel

Lists (EDLs). The basic MAM technology consists of computers, software, storage systems and an integrated network to interconnect all of the technology. An MAM system takes in digital materials categorises it and tracks the media assets. It allows employees at workstations to store, locate, retrieve, edit and alter, format and restore both individual media assets and the entire programmes. Companies can choose to store all of the versions of a particular asset as it progressively changes. MAM is a quantum leap beyond document and image management. MAM allows companies to manage all of their documents which include photographs, audio files, videos files, images, text etc (Hess, 1998). Some of the systems are: MediaStore (www.si-media.tv); Elvis Digital Asset Management system (www.elvisdam.com), and Razuna, the Open Source Digital Asset Management system (www.razuna.org).

3.1 *Benefit of MAM*

The following are the major benefits of a MAM system (Tassel, 1998; Lindstrom, 1999; Hess, 1998; Kerschbaumer, n.d.):

- ***Collaboration:*** It allows collaborations among employees, suppliers, vendors, and customers. It enables people to work in parallel on the same project or to multiple projects at the same time without having to wait for someone else to finish their work and free up the original material.
- ***Efficient Rights Management:*** It allows the contractual rights and other obligations to be attached to the contents. This in turn allows rapid determination of what the company owns how it is allowed to use, and how much should be paid for it.
- ***Cost Saving:*** MAM can save considerable amounts of money as it reduce the number of times the content is digitised and costs of transporting the content from one location to another for the duration of a project. Gistic Inc. (1997), a research firm has done a study on MAM and found that it is an efficient system saves time. The study found that individual media users who adopt MAM would spend: a) 36% less time transferring files, b) 28% less time reorganising files, c) 14% less time locating files, and d) 13% less time tracking multiple—version files.
- ***Search Locally or Globally*:** It allows employees outside the corporate headquarters to access files through a simple web interface for searching.
- ***Return of Investment:*** MAM allows user to preview each hit and select the appropriate media asset via thumbnail pictures and not just the filename. The company could then get the returns on its initial investment in the form of creative time.
- ***Bottom Line:*** Re-use and re-expression of content means that creative firms can deliver client work significantly faster and also at marginal costs. Getting more work done and at a faster rate will enables a creative firm to complete more projects means more revenue to the company.

- ***Business Values:*** The strategic application of MAM systems builds shareholder value. It shows the investors and the potential corporate partners on how a re-expressible media assets and leveraged metadata can help create competitive advantage in delivering faster cycles, lower costs, license revenues and boost the valuation of their companies.
- ***Business Diversity:*** MAM has created much other business activities out of the same media content such as those associated with rights management.

3.2 *Barrier to MAM*

According to Tassel (1998), cost and corporate culture are barriers to MAM systems in that the cost of large-scale MAM systems is very expensive in both money and time. Departmental rivalries may also act as barriers to the adoption of MAM. These systems have profound effects on workflow. Streamlining of workflow that will result in the flattening of office hierarchies or the elimination of intermediaries who package and format information for other parties are unavoidable. Thus the adoption of MAM system is likely to face with great resistance from staff in the company.

4. The Metadata Link

The road to a well organised production, storage and exchange of digital multimedia is madc possiblc only with Mctadata. Mctadata arc thc singlc most important to active an effective and consistent A-V production environment (De Jong, 2000).

4.1 *What is Metadata?*

CasaBianca and Okon (n.d.) defined metadata as data about data, or information about the information that follows in the same video bit stream. It gives structure to the value of the media assets, which is vital for the re-purposing of media content. Metadata can be generated both through automated process or human notation. Automated metadata generation usually occurs at "ingest" or when materials come into the digital system.

4.2 *Importance of Metadata in MAM and DCM Systems*

Both MAM and DCM systems depend on metadata to identify retrieve/searching the assets and elements that compose a shot, sequence or programme. The metadata quality, quantity, granularity, descriptiveness, search ability and availability are at the heart of DCM organisational systems. Peter DeVries feels that the worst thing that can happen to content is to have no metadata attached to it. It means that it is *data* and not *information* where no one can find it or use it (De Jong, 2000). There is so much effort made to standardise metadata. There are also meta-metadata efforts to make these languages compatible with one another particularly across related industries. For example, in broadcasting industry, MPEG2 has a limited metadata vocabulary but expanded in MPEG4. MPEG7 is a standard that specifically addresses metadata and MPEG21 is an attempt at an "ubber" meta-standard designed to address all the standards for end-to end DCM. In SMPTE/EBU formulation, individual assets *i.e.* the video, audio, text and data are referred as "essence". Information about "essence" is called "metadata".

5. Digital Right Management System

A DRM system is a key enabler for the distribution of digital media content. It is primarily is an anti-piracy technology and presents a far bigger revenue generating and content control opportunities for both existing and new businesses, especially through metadata management. Normally it comes as part of the DCM system but also available as independent unit.

According to Sun Microsystems, DRM is a series of enabling technologies and services that together control, create, market and maintain business rules for the use of any digital content in public or private networks. Today, DRM products can be leveraged to address issues including the control of rights, the usage permissions of the content and digital information. DRM is an integrated part of DCM and it is a key and critical tool for copyright owners when they wish to distribute their valuable digital content.

5.1 *Benefits of DRM*

Several studies (Rosenblatt, 2000; Tassel, 2000) have highlighted the benefits of DRM as given below:

- ***Comprehensive Rights Management:*** It is important for media company to identify materials to a company do not have the rights so as to avoid costly litigation problems. MAM system protects and tracks the rights and the interests of all participants in the value chain be it the content creators, producers, aggregators, publishers, distributors, traders and brokers, enterprises, governments, institutions and consumers.
- ***Distribution:*** DRM system could prevent large-scale unauthorised distribution and track the users and track their usage of the content purchased.
- ***Easy Payment:*** DRM system enables electronic payments and gathers information about consumers in an automated process and networked environment.
- ***Wider Market:*** DRM system provides assurance to media content owners to market their assets widely. It collects information about those who receive the content and the companies could use the data to generate additional revenue streams. Current DRM software also allows content distributors to embed the explicit terms and conditions of the transaction of the media content and tie these rules permanently to the content as it moves from creation to consumption.

5.2 *DRM Implementation Issues*

According to Sun Microsystems, content identification, authentication and digital signatures are some of the technologies that can be considered when implementing DRM system.

- ***Content Identification:*** Every DRM system begins with identifying the media content *i.e.* the unique material identifier need to be applied.
- ***Authentication:*** This is necessary if content providers want to know whether their content has been altered in any way.
- ***Digital Signatures:*** This means "signing" the image by embedding an encrypted hidden "signature" code in each frame of a video in a picture.

5.3 *DRM Protection Technologies*

Tassel (2001) and Rosenblatt (1997) have identified the protection technologies that can be applied before and after the distribution of contents.

Before Content Distribution

- ***Secure Containers*:** This method aims at keeping the content encrypted at all times except when it is inside a secure perimeter of some kind.
- ***Encryption*:** Combined with the need for authentication and authorisation for access, encryption ensures that content is available only to those who have the rights to it and no one else. In order to make the content visible, the receiver is provided with a way to de-crypt the message.

After Content Distribution

- ***Digital Watermarking:*** The purpose is to forge an unbreakable link between content and one or more participants in the content value chain.
- ***Digital Fingerprinting:*** It is related to watermarking. In this approach, each customer receives a copy of the digital content that has slightly different fingerprints. This is accomplished by embedding slightly different marks or codes in a file each time a new copy is made or downloaded.
- ***Traitor Tracing:*** It extends the capability of content owner to track down the person responsible for large-scale theft of intellectual property.
- Tracking Media Content: The capability to track the usage of media content across all platforms.

5.4 *DRM—Content Distribution Methods*

According to Tassel (2001), four methods are being used to distribute content:

- ***Conditional Access:*** This is the easiest method to implement. The content is encrypted and moved to a conditional access set-top box. The box will decode the contents and deliver it to a display or playback device.
- ***Extract and Watermark:*** Extraction refers to the removing of content from a secure container and the wrappers that hold the content and the business access that limit the use of the content. The content may also be digitally watermarked as it is being extracted from the container.
- ***Content Protection via Consumer Device:*** This method could be applied to devices such as DVD players where the content is protected and extracted to analogue outputs such as TV sets.
- ***DRM-Enabler Device:*** This method requires a device that has full computer functionality in order to handle full DRM functions. This method is still at the developing stage.

6. An Overview of Digital Media Content Industry

In the media industry, the media companies or organisations can be categorised as commercial libraries, television companies and production companies, distributors, government agencies, archives, educational institutions, libraries and museums and the associations, corporations, foundations, historical societies etc. In this paper, only the media centres categorised under the commercial libraries and the TV companies were studied. The TV companies and the media centres run by the commercial media content libraries in term of their overall business management are listed here. It is because, the commercial media content libraries were most appropriate who are the real users of these systems. Major media centres of broadcasting organisations include Australia Broadcasting Corporation, British Broadcasting Corporation, Canada Broadcasting Corporation, Nippon Hoso Kyokai International Inc., and TV New Zealand. Commercial media libraries include Budget Film Inc., Cinenet (Cinema Network Inc), Film and Video Stock Shots Inc., Image Bank, and the Source Stock Footage Library Inc.

Five out of the ten selected media centres/oraganisations are the media centres or archives within TV companies, while the other five media centres/organisations are commercial libraries specialising in stock footages business. The five media centres within TV companies are selected based on their business nature that is broadcasting. The five commercial libraries are selected based on their business profile. The method for identifying their business profile is by identifying their client list. The fact that they are being patronised by well known filmmakers, advertisers, movie makers, TV stations etc, shows that they have a reasonably impressive business profile which is a sound reflections that they are established companies with good collections. The sources of information of their clients' profile were extracted from their respective websites.

6.1 *Business Issues*

Like any other business sector, the media content owner is not only being affected by digital video technology but is also being dramatically transformed by the Internet. Tariot of Footage.net feels that with the advance digital video technology and the increase Internet access speeds, more companies will devote money towards developing on-line catalogues and digitising images. Once these images are digitised, the whole process of storing, managing and controlling access will be integrated into their sale (Keenlyside, 2000).

6.2 *Selling Content Online*

Sun Microsystems produced a tool to facilitate for web commerce that enables digital content providers such as broadcasters, music companies and film studios to build a stronger relationship with their customers by providing:

- The ability for viewers to personalise the content.
- A flexible technology for content providers (which allows them to transform content into multiple products and services that generate multiple revenue streams).
- Enhanced data communications for corporate usage, including video training and internal corporate communications.
- Superior controls over content consumption and distribution.

This new, integrated solution set provides functionality, which covers all facets of content development, management and distribution. It provides the most secure form of content delivery available over the Internet. The availability of the Internet and the demand for speed has jointly created an accelerated trend towards the so-called "disintermediation", where middlemen are cut out of the products/services value chains. The transparency of the markets reduces many players to commodity providers facing pure price competition. While many companies are initially dragged reluctantly into this market scenario, there will be more and more who chooses to actively endorse the new era and build their strategy largely or entirely around "visual e-business".

Today's streaming technology can provide these media companies the possibility of communicating electronically with their clients using a combination of powerful video, audio and electronic transactions. This process makes it important for companies to find ways of reaching their business partners and end users with an electronic communication form that is not only as powerful and emotional as TV but also allows people to transact electronically.

6.3 *Business Challenges*

By breaking down the barriers to content distribution, the selling of content on-line and streaming of digital content creates unique business challenges that revolve around several basic issues, including:

- ***Security and Rights Management:*** This is to ensure that all players in the value chain, including content owners, content providers, and content distributors, are fairly compensated for their intellectual property and services.
- ***Audience Tracking:*** A key to the successful e-commerce strategy is to track how well the product or service meets the market demand. For digital content to be assessed, content providers and distributors need to know who is watching or listening to their content and which portions are most popular etc. They also need to track viewership or listenership and compile statistics differentiate by the transmission channels. The requirement to protect the rights of content owners makes audience tracking even more critical. To be compensated fairly for the use of their content, content distributors must know which customers to bill and on what they consume as well as how to allocate subscriber fees to a specific content owner.
- ***Personalisation:*** For digital content, clients are already gaining the ability to build their own personalised music and video channels. This is a value-added feature compared to the conventional methods of content distribution such as broadcast, screening in theatres, or sales via CDs, videocassettes or DVDs.
- ***Targeted Advertisements:*** Sponsored content by the advertisers requires a feedback mechanism in order to prove that advertising works for such programmes.
- ***The Right Service at the Right Price:*** The Internet's huge popularity has created bottlenecks. The emergence of rich media as popular form of using the web could exacerbate the problem. The spread of broadband which promises to ease congestion along the "last mile", has raised the bar on customer expectations for service. Consequently, the quality of service is becoming a competitive necessity for digital content providers.

7. Conclusions

This paper has reviewed the various media technologies those has or could change the operations of media companies. It shows how digital delivery is changing the way media content is created and distributed. The exponential growth of digital technology has caused all the media industries to transform their analogue content to digital format. The obvious reason for this move is to improve access (Keenlyside, 2000). Combined with management systems, numerous benefits can be derived and amongst which the most important is the generation of revenue.

Much has been discussed about the technology that are available leverage the media content business and management. However, the cost involved in engaging the use of such technology should not be neglected. For example, the cost of purchasing DCM, MAM equipment's is one factor that cannot be ignored as the cost falls between the range of a few thousands dollars to few million dollars (Lindstrom, 1999). Since media companies especially the broadcasters require a broad range of functions and demands high levels of quality and reliability, they usually find themselves looking at very high-end systems available in the market. Such systems requires huge amount of cash investment, so careful planning is necessary. Opting for the 'right' mix is of great concern for media businesses. This is because of the fear that the technology might go in another direction, rendering their considerable investment obsolete (Keenlyside, 2000). According to Correll (n.d.) and Castle and Ivey, (2000) the future media trends are as follows:

- ***Technological Convergence:*** The highly hyped 'convergence' of television and the Internet and a long-term divergence of content delivery on a variety of digital platforms. Convergence has long-term implications on how future 'internal' production systems and workflow are organised and operated. Divergence represents the marketplace of tomorrow or the external applications of content management to satisfy the demands of the next generation of wired or more likely wireless consumer. Wakelin (2000) observes that this trend is very prevailing.
- ***Bandwidth:*** Broadband infrastructure and digital television platforms rapidly being deployed and this will realise the promise of revenues and viewership gains.
- ***Traditional Media Evolves and Adapts:*** With the World Wide Web becoming a mass medium, the traditional media companies have to re-evaluate the way they develop, manage and distribute their content. The media companies have to keep abreast with the latest technology in order to remain competitive in the business. Smyka (2000) feels that TV is evolving rapidly into a new landscape that is catalysed by interactive technology that extends way beyond the old one to many streams of broadcasting.
- ***Technological Product Development:*** The technological product developers will constantly provide content creators and distributors with the necessary platform and tools to navigate the minefield of competing standards and business models. They will become the media moguls of the next millennium.

It is important to have a clear directive or a business plan that indicates a clear message to all users of target implementations. There is no such thing as 'one-size-fits-all' approach but it is important to develop a consistent strategy that aligns the media business with the future of content delivery. It is also important to pick a vendor who can offer a proven system that meets the requirements. Walker (2000) sees that there are huge pressures on suppliers to get things right and justify the investments made by the media companies.

References

[1] Artesia Technologies. (n.d.). What is digital asset management system? Artesia Technologies. http://www.Artesiatech.com/what_dam.html (accessed on 22 August 2010)

[2] CasaBianca, L., Okon, C., M. (n.d.). Metadata and content: A guide for video pros. Digital television. http://www.digitaltelevision.com/dtvbook/appecdixb.shtml (accessed on 24 July 2010)

[3] Castle, G., Ivey, K. (2000). The Future of television: content management. *Broadcast Engineering*. www.broadcastengineering.comm/html/2000/dec/features/futuretv4.htm (Accessed on 12 April 2010).

[4] Correll, B. (n.d.). Media trends: The Internet effect. http://www.sun.com/media/mt.interneteffect.html (Accessed on 10 August 2010).

[5] De Jong, A. (2000). Metadata in the audiovisual production environment: an introduction. Vienna, International Federation of Television Archives (FIAT/IFTA).

[6] Hess, E. (1998). In on the ground floor. *Business Solution*. http://www.businesssolutions mag.com/Articles/1998_08/980802.htm (Accessed on 23 July 2010).

[7] Janik, C. (2001). Here in the future. *Sound and Video Contractor*. http://indus.../ magazinearticle.asp?magazinearticleid=116583&mode=prin (Accessed on Aug. 28, 2001).

[8] Kerschbaumer, K. (n.d.) Appendix B: Storage and archiving/asset management. The guide to digital television. http://www.digitaltelevision.com/dtvbook/appecndixb.shtml (Accessed on 24 July 2010).

[9] King, A. (2000). Archiving and content. *Broadcast Engineering*. http://www. broadcast-engineering.com/html/2000/dec/features/archivingcontent1.htm (Accessed on 12 April 2010).

[10] Keenlyside, S. (2000). Special report: Stock footage. *Boards Magazine*. http://www.boards mag.com/articles/magazi.../stockfootage.html?word=digital&word=media&word=librarie (Accessed on 25 May 2010).

[11] Lindstrom, L.R. (1999). Multimedia mayhem can media asset management save the day? *Presentation Technology*. http://www.presentatuibs.com/techno/soft/1999/01/31f1_mm_01. html (Accessed on 23 July 2010).

[12] Rosenthal, E.M. (1997). It's a small world: global networking shapes the stock footage business. *Millimetre*. http://www.mil.../magazinearticle.asp?magazinearticleid=107648&magazineid= 124&mode=prin (Accessed on 4 July 2010).

[13] Seel, P.B. and Grant, A.E. (1997). The future of broadcasting. *Broadcast Technology Update: Production and Transmission*. Boston, Mass.; Focal Press.

[14] Sun Microsystems. (n.d.). Digital rights management: Managing the digital distribution value chain. White paper. http://www.sun.com/media/index.html (Accessed August 2010).

[15] Sun Microsystems. (n.d.). Streaming media workflow: An overview. White paper. http://www. sun.com/media/index.html (Accessed in April 2010).

[16] Sun Microsystems. (n.d.). EMEDIA@SUN: content management. http://www.sun.com/media/ sol.content.html (Accessed on 27 July 2010).

[17] Tassel, M., J. (2001). Digital content management: creating and distribution media assets by broadcasters. Washington, DC: NAB Research and Planning Department.

[18] Tassel, M., J. (1998). Media asset management. *Technology Futures Inc.* http://www.tfi.com/pubs/ntq/articles/view/98Q2_A3.html (Accessed on 23 July 2010).

[19] Walker, G., M. (2001). Asset management part 2: finding and sending media. *World Broadcast Magazines*. http://www.industryclick.com//magazinearticle.asp? magazine articleid=105309 &mode=print (Accessed on 2 August 2010).

[20] Wakelin, S. (2000). Broadband: its prophetic grasp on advertising. *Boards Magazine*. http://www.boardsmag.com/articles/magazine/2…m1?word=media&word+content&word=intern (Accessed on 27 July 2010).

Electronic Resources Management in Libraries, pp. 229–240

Electronic Resources in Print and Television Media Libraries: A Case Study

Sunita Koya

ABSTRACT

This paper is an overview of how the different electronic resources are created used and organized in Ramoji Knowledge Centre which caters to the needs of the print and electronic media namely *Eenadu*, ETV and the information requirements of the entire Ramoji Group.

1. Introduction

- Today there is an earthquake in Indonesia? Is there going to be a Tsunami? Will it affect India?
- New CM announced in Karnataka.
- Presidential elections, we require biodata of probable candidates.
- Devanand is no more, require his visuals, movies, songs biography highlights of his professional life and real life.
- Today is international no smoking day.
- Rupee exchange rate falling.

And anything under the sun, which an alert media knowledge centre, which is attached to the print or electronic media, has to provide information in all formats such as text, pictures, video clips sometimes even write-up which covers the topic etc. The pressure will be more for those working for an electronic media. Some issues are predictable, others not. So an alert media knowledge centre, an information centre has to deal with all what is happening and immediately for this a digital library with all its collection in electronic format is required. An information provider/Librarian is no more just doing the regular work of cataloguing, classification, procuring books, magazines either in physical or electronic formats but is more than that they need to work on that and provide immediately authentic correct information which is relevant to both the layman and the expert. In India still newspapers are much in demand whether in English or other languages and this we know from the increasing circulation released from time to time. The requirement in newspaper library will be all types of information—pictures, backgrounders, digesters and chronologies etc.

While detail information is not required like in academic libraries but pictures and video clips are a must and these clippings are organized in such a way for electronic news, they can make big impact on the organization's image. They can control their costs and improve and expand the newspaper content available to their researchers in electronic form by being discerning in their acquisition of digital resources, and by having a tie-up with other organizations these are having an interest in maintaining news content including some libraries, the news industry, and database vendors. Therefore, again, informal library collection development and preservation requires reliable metadata to access the contents of electronic news collections and access to digital libraries both available on the Internet and with other libraries.

2. Definition of Electronic Resources

According to AACR2, 2005 Update, an electronic resource is 'Material (data and/or program(s)) encoded for manipulation by a computerized device'. This material may require the use of a peripheral directly connected to a computerized device (e.g., CD-ROM drive) or a connection to a computer network (e.g., the Internet). *Though this is a good definition but does* ***not*** *include electronic resources that do not require the use of a computer, for example, music compact discs and videodiscs.*

Resources on the research databases, web pages are drawn from records in the Electronic Resources Module (ERM). For the purpose of the research databases, these web pages are defined as online information resources which include bibliographic databases, electronic reference books, search engines for full-text collections, digital collections of data and data sets. *(Even this definition does not cover all the aspects).* Electronic resources refer to those materials or services that require a computer for access, manipulation, or reproduction including, but not limited to, numerical, graphical and textual files, electronic journals, bibliographic or full-text databases and Internet resources.

3. Electronic Resources/Digital Formats

3.1 *Philosophy*

The Libraries' goal is to provide a rich array of electronic resources that are accessible through university library via the web page, at times and locations convenient to the users. Management of electronic resources is more complex than traditional print resources and involves analyzing a variety of issues that are cross-jurisdictional in nature. Issues concerning technology, access, maintenance, vendor support as well as licensing terms must be considered. For this reason, a separate statement of guidelines is necessary for these materials. The library staff should base their decisions on the principles outlined in this policy. Traditional fixed medium resources will be converted to digital format as they become available online.

3.2 *General Selection Principles*

- Digital resources must contribute to the Libraries' mission of providing support for instruction and research. They must support identifiable current or future needs of the institution or organization.
- Electronic or digital formats are considered in context with the needs of appropriate disciplines.
- Electronic formats are preferable to fixed media when the content and coverage is equivalent or when the digital format offers value-added enhancements over the print.
- Service implications, technical support and licensing requirements must be given careful consideration prior to commitment and may determine the feasibility of acquiring a new electronic resource.
- A minimum of duplication between formats will be allowed.
- Resources housed on remote servers are preferable to locally mounted products.
- Electronic products should have the ability to be archived, if necessary.

3.3 *Evaluation Criteria*

The evaluation criteria formulated by the University of Texas at Arlington is given below (http://www.uta.edu/library/ir/files/policy-er.pdf):

- The resources are easy to use and include such features as tutorials, more than one search level, context-specific help screens, index browsing, etc. The product's coverage must be stable—older information doesn't drop off when updates occur.
- If currency is important, the content should be updated regularly without significant lag time that would limit the product's usefulness.
- Data should be platform-independent and available in a variety of formats.
- Licensing terms are adequate for the libraries' needs or vendor is willing to negotiate for terms favorable to the library.
- The vendor/producer is reliable and offers customer support and training.
- The documentation is clear and complete.
- Information providers control access by Internet protocol addresses.
- Providers make products available on a trial basis, at no cost to the Libraries.
- These electronic resources may be acquired by OSU libraries, as well as other libraries if licensed for the entire Columbus campus provided via OhioLINK.
- Free resources evaluated by the collection manager and deemed to meet the above criteria. Free resources must have a bibliographic record added to the online catalog before they will be added to the ERM and appear on the [Research Databases Web] page.

Reference library is the heart of the organisation and acts as a center for the collection of literature in different fields and topics and develops a comprehensive collection of information that is useful for reference purpose. IT is the amalgamation of both traditional as well as the modern elements of a library. The reference sources are available in print as well as digital format. The digital resources/services at the library are growing day by day with the addition of more resources like digesters, backgrounders, photographs video file shots etc., news alerts of different events and days, indexes of magazines and newspapers which is an in house information resource created by the librarians and researchers. Ninety percent of the resources are stored in electronic format in databases. Electronic resources include those available on the net which keep growing day-by-day.

To cater to the needs of the diverse group of users from different television channels, newspaper and the group companies' information is culled out of the traditional information sources such as journals, monographs, reports, and the specific information and reference services is provided. This is in the form of newspaper clippings, pictures, visuals backgrounders and ready to use digesters for editorials, special articles, news, health women and general programmes, graphics etc. Authenticity is maintained and it is also seen that the copyright is not infringed as it effects the media organization. The points to be followed while using electronic resources:

- To ensure the highest level of user satisfaction.
- To support media with authentic information.
- To provide effective access to various resources available.
- To keep the Newspaper, TV Channels on par and ahead of the other channels by providing the latest information.
- To provide effective and timely services to meet the needs of the media irrespective of personal intervention.
- To provide a range of books, periodicals and electronic resources in keeping with the Organization's needs.
- To acquire best resources and facilities to suit organization's present, future and anticipatory needs.
- To excel in the field of information delivery.
- To provide required information at all hours.

The following resources, most of them now are available in electronic format, are maintained in the knowledge centre:

- Newspapers with national and international coverage
- Newspaper clippings (both online and offline)
- Journals, monographs
- Budget documents
- Reference books
- Statistical reports
- Backgrounders

- State and central government reports, and
- Bound volumes of magazines and other reference materials which are required for the different channels depending on their immediate needs.

4. Services Offered in Ramoji Knowledge Centre

Newspapers of different languages are all available on the net and some of them with their web IP addresses are given; these include regional, national and different language editions and also international papers. The following services are provided in the Ramoji Knowledge Centre (RKC):

- ***Newspaper Clippings:*** In this, all the important topics from different newspapers, related to different subjects, are taken and filed according to the subject. A separate section is being started especially for newspaper clippings
- ***Abstracting:*** Abstracting services are provided to the users. Abstract is prepared in a card format by taking data from journals.
- ***Current Awareness Service:*** The contents, abstract and page number of the articles from different magazines which are being subscribed are also sent. This will enable people from different desks to know about the topics of their interest, covered in different magazines of the week/month etc.
- ***Indexing Service:*** Indexing of important news items from different magazines are prepared. These indexes are prepared on a card. Details covered in these indexes are: (a) title of the story/item, (b) abstract of the item, (c) magazine's name, (d) date and issue number and (e) page numbers. After preparation these, index cards are arranged alphabetically.
- ***Table of Contents Service:*** TOC of different journals is taken and sent to different desks of media.
- ***User Orientation Programmes:*** User orientation is provided to the people from different desks of print and electronic media. In this, the users are orientated for use of OPAC. A tour of library is conducted to educate the users about the use of Digital Library, and other sources available in the library. Further, the users are informed about the future plans of the library and their suggestions are collected in this regard.
- ***Library Automation:*** The traditional library work *i.e.* Acquisition, technical processing, and serial control entail lot of time when the operations are done manually. So, the RKC library chose to switch over to automation of the library operations to provide faster information services and to set profession-wide standards. After making a survey of the existing automation softwares, it was decided that the library will adopt the KOHA: an Integrated Library Management System, which is an open source and freely available over the Internet. We look forward to maximize the benefits of automation by spreading computer use to all the aspects

of library operation. We have developed in-house software for journals cataloguing and integrated into the intranet as per the existing software in the organisation to facilitate smooth operation. Similarly for general information, we use DSpace and WinISIS for off-line content which is mostly used by the library staff for giving on demand reference services.

Similarly, for the content we have adopted a similar system for all online operations of content processing since a lot of the information is in language and it has to be integrated with the news production and television production and the format of contents should be compactable with the systems and technology used. Again it is in-house developed software and much of the content is picked up from the production and archived. This is available at the news desks of media department.

- ***Video Library:*** This is the web interface of WinISIS which we use for our offline video tapes, online visuals are stored on servers which run to several hundreds of terabytes and directly accessed from news desks. Offline visuals are searched and provided by the library to the research staff.
- ***Web Interface to News Video Tape Database:*** World Wide Web Integrated Set of Information System (WWWISIS) has been developed by a commercial company called BIRME. It provides the web interface to Computerized Documentation System/Integrated Set of Information System (CDS/ISIS). Here in Knowledge centre, WWWISIS is being used for providing web interface to the data stored in Bibliographic Database developed with CDS/ISIS. In CDS/ISIS, the data related to Visuals of important personalities, incidents, or important structures like parliament building, assembly etc. are entered and backup is taken onto CDs/DVDs or in DVCs. The following are the fields of the data provides in the WWWISIS database. These fields are used to enter the data regarding the News Video Tapes in CDS/ISIS.

Field No.	*Field*
10	Tape Number
20	Subject
25	Description
30	Personality
35	Language
40	Place
50	TCR in-out
60	Sound Bite
70	Date of VT
80	Time

If a simple search is done on Abdul Kalam, then various details like Tape No., Subject of the tape, description etc. will be displayed in the following format:

Tape No	DVC66/1468 TELUGU
Subject	ABDUL KALAM, BHARATA RATNA
Description	Former Defence Adviser Kalam visited to Hyderabad
Personality	Abdul Kalam, A.P.J.
Language	English
Place	Hyderabad
TCR in-out	01:22:00:14 to 01:25:28:22
Sound Bite	Where we can have knowledge and do hard work, we achieve bigger things of life
Date of VT	07/05/2002
Time	03 Min 28 sec

Besides these, the relevant information file shots (video files) pictures are put in the relevant folder in the server which is accessed by the journalists and users as and when the event happen. For example, in case of accidents, terrorist attacks, assembly parliament sessions, etc. relevant inform is culled out and make ready to use the information by placing on the server.

5. Important Websites Heavily Used by Media/Libraries

5.1 *Newspapers and Magazines*

In the 21st Century, many newspapers are providing their services in electronic format, some have paid service and most of them have free service. From the newspapers, we can clip the most important articles and news for the future use. Some of the useful resources are:

Press Release : http://pib.nic.in
Newspaper websites : http://www.getfreeebooks.com
Epapers Hub : http://www.epapers-hub.com
Hindustan Times : http://paper.hindustantimes.com
Times of India : http://epaper.timesofindia.com/index.asp
DNA : http://epaper.dnaindia.com
The Hindu : http://epaper.thehindu.com
The Tribune : http://epaper.tribuneindia.com
Pioneer : http://dailypioneer.com
Indian Express : http://epaper.indianexpress.com
Telegraph : http://epaper.telegraphindia.com

Eenadu	: http://epaper.eenadu.net
Dainik Jagaran	: http://in.jagran.yahoo.com/epaper
Dainik Bhaskar	: http://epaper.bhaskar.com
Rajasthan Patrika	: http://epaper.patrika.com
Online Magazines	: http://www.onlinemagazineshub.com
Tehelka	: http://emagazine.tehelka.com
Open Access Journals	: http://www.doaj.org
BBC	: http://www.bbc.co.uk
India Today	: http://indiatoday.intoday.in
Outlook	: http://www.outlookindia.com/index.asp

5.2 *E-books*

Nowadays large numbers of e-books are published by the different agencies including publishers, which are free to everyone. Anyone can read and download the book. Examples of this category include:

http://www.scribd.com
http://www.gutenberg.org
http://www.onlinefreeebooks.net
http://www.getfreeebooks.com

5.3 *Reference Websites*

The following sites are ready reference sites, which caters the information needs quickly and they are basically meant for reference purpose.

http://www.wikipedia.org
http://www.thefreedictionary.com
http://www.google.co.in
http://answers.yahoo.com
http://www.about.com
http://www.answers.com
http://www.ehow.com
http://www.reference.com
http://hubpages.com
http://www.wikihow.com/Main-Page
http://www.wikia.com/Wikia
http://archive.org/index.php
http://www.howstuffworks.com
http://www.bl.uk/eresources/newspapers/colindale2.html

5.4 *Important Government Websites*

Some of the important government's official websites are given below:

Government Website Directory : http://goidirectory.nic.in
Parliament of India : http://www.parliamentofindia.nic.in
President of India : http://presidentofindia.gov.in
Prime Minister's Office : http://pmindia.nic.in
Planning Commission : http://planningcommission.nic.in
Central Bureau of Investigation : www.cbi.nic.in
Central Vigilance Commission : www.cvc.nic.in
Election Commission of India : http://eci.nic.in
Census of India : http://censusindia.gov.in
Human Rights Commissions : http://nhrc.nic.in
National Crime Record Bureau : http://ncrb.gov.in
Comptroller And Auditor General of India : http://cag.gov.in
Finance Commission : http://fincomindia.nic.in
Meteorological Department : http://www.imd.gov.in
Ministry of Statistics and Planning : http://mospi.nic.in
Reserve Bank of India : http://www.rbi.org.in/home.aspx
Budgets : http://indiabudget.nic.in
Districts of India : http://districts.nic.in

5.5 *Websites of International Organisations*

UNO : http://www.un.org/en
Food and Agriculture Organization : http://www.fao.org
International Labour Organization : http://www.ilo.org
International Monetary Fund : http://www.imf.org
UNESCO : http://www.unesco.org/new/en
World Bank : www.worldbank.org.in
World Health Organization : www.who.int
UNDP : www.undp.org
Atomic Energy : http://www.iaea.org

5.6 *Legal Websites*

Supreme Court of India : http://supremecourtofindia.nic.in
Indian Courts : http://indiancourts.nic.in
Indian Kanoon : http://www.indiankanoon.org
Law Commission of India :
http://www.lawcommissionofindia.nic.in
Bar Council of India : http://www.barcouncilofindia.org

Legal Information Institute of India : http://liiofindia.org
Law Ministry : http://lawmin.nic.in
National Consumer Disputes Redressal Commission
: http://ncdrc.nic.in
Central Information Commission : http://cic.gov.in

5.7 *Free Image Websites (Personal and Commercial use)*

The media library collects the images from its reporters, photographers and the agencies. It stores the information in a server for the future use. Apart from these it uses some the free copyright licensed websites for the use of photographs.

http://images.google.com
http://www.sxc.hu
http://www.photos8.org
http://www.morguefile.com
http://www.photoeverywhere.co.uk
http://freerangestock.com
http://www.imagebase.davidniblack.com/main.php
http://www.photogen.com/free-photos/cat15.html

5.8 *Audio and Videos*

In-house video archives are provided access to the news Desk in which users can search the newsfeed 24 × 7 basis. Apart from this, it uses Youtube, Dailymotion etc keeping in view that copyright is not infringed upon.

5.9 *Official Websites of Political Parties*

Indian National Congress (INC) : http://www.aicc.org.in/new
Bharatiya Janata Party (BJP) : http://www.bjp.org
Bahujan Samaj Party (BSP) : http://bspindia.org
Dravida Munnettra Kazhagam (DMK) : www.dmk.in
Telugu Desam Party (TDP) : www.telugudesam.org
Samajwadi Party (SP) : www.samajwadiparty.in
Nationalist Congress Party (NCP) : www.ncp.org.in
Communist Party of India (Marxist) : www.cpim.org
Communist Party of India : http://www.communistparty.in
Trinmool Congress : https://aitmc.org

6. Conclusions

Ranganthan's Fourth law is Save the time of the Reader. Keeping an eye on time saving principle, the media library prefers to provide electronic information services to its users in shortest possible time. An electronic resource not only save the time but also saves space. A librarian and users can search the required information within a short time span. Media library clients do not have sufficient time, they are busy with framing stories, and news. They need right information at the right time. As per the requirements, the librarian sends the electronic information to the user quickly to complete the task in hand on times. The media library collects and provides the information which is perused for the total electronic and print media; it is mainly using the 2 Is viz. Information and Ideas. It provides Information and Ideas to the Users.

The recent and ongoing contraction in the newspaper industry and the emergence of the Internet as a venue for real-time news broadcast suggest that preserving newspapers will become less effective strategy for long-terms needs. A combination of both the newspaper in soft copy and micro format is the best way to preserve which most of the major newspapers are doing. Though television is a newer media but its format keeps changing from AVI, MPEG, MPEG 2, MPEG 4 and so on and it is a tough task for the electronic media librarian to preserve video file shots with frequently changing video formats.

Audiovisual library is the part and parcel of our electronic media library which has a huge amount of information that needs to be preserved for future use. The rich variety of media expressions in society has been reflected in the services offered to users by the libraries. There is a sea of information available electronically on the Internet, but the library and librarian uses the electronic information sites which are more reliable and authentic. They also keep attention on copyright when they provide the information, pictures etc. to their media production team members.

Libraries have to judiciously deal with all sorts of material, including print, audiovisual, electronic (including Internet) and multimedia. Librarians should be aware of the potential of audiovisual and multimedia formats as resource materials and include them in their collections. The range of audiovisual and multimedia materials acquired by a library must depend, as it does for printed materials, upon the needs of its users, upon the extent of its activities, and upon its ultimate users as this is very specific in media libraries but the range of information to be catered is tremendous alert media librarian will keep in touch with the news events which is current and will happen many things can be predicted to some extent. It is only the instant spot news which cannot be predicted.

Acknowledgements

My special thanks are due to Mr. Duryodhan Nahak and P. Yadaiah of RKC, for helping in getting the required information and compiling websites URLs required for this article.

References

[1] http://ctlonline.net/webreadyplus/lesson10_elecinfo.asp

[2] http://www.westga.edu/~distance/ojdla/spring151/finamore_hochanadel_hochanadel_millam_reinhardt.html

[3] http://www.crl.edu/focus/article/5514

[4] Guidelines for audiovisual and multimedia materials in libraries and other institutions. IFLA, Audiovisual and Multimedia Section, March 2004.

[5] Avasia, Maya. Electronic resources: Collection development

[6] Venkadesan, S. Digital preservation of electronic resources at JRD Tata Memorial Library, Indian Institute of Science, Bangalore. Available at http://www.medialibraryinc.com

[7] http://www.electroniclibrarian.com/presenters/tracks

[8] ERME-2010: National Workshop on E-Resources Management for Excellence

[9] E-resources for media and communications (http://www.londonmet.ac.uk)

Electronic Resources Management in Libraries, pp. 241–248

Mobile Agents and their Role in Proliferation of E-Resources

Chaynika Taneja and Sumit Goswami

ABSTRACT

The gaining popularity of e-resources and need for their efficient distribution and access led to emphasised the requirement for new technologies and approaches for information dissemination. Mobile agent technology is one such promising technology that uses mobile code to perform the designated task. This paper presents an overview of the mobile agent technology and its role in the growth of electronics resources. Mobile agents as a development platform for implementing digital libraries have been discussed. E-transaction systems and information retrieval using mobile agent technology are also described. Finally, a mobile agent model for e-learning and evaluation has been proposed as a substitute for traditional models.

1. Introduction

The growth of Internet and the World Wide Web (WWW) has led to an explosion in the field of information services. These technologies have revolutionised the growth and proliferation of electronic resources. Intangible sources of information and media have replaced the traditional tangible sources. Digitisation of sources has been extensively carried out and organisations today have built their own digital libraries, institutional repositories and web portals. An E-Resource may be defined as a document or data source in electronic format which may be accessed digitally. The data may be text, image or multimedia. E-resources may be accessed either directly through a peripheral storage like CD/DVD or over the Internet. E-resources may take the form of e-books, e-journals, databases, newsletters, conference proceedings, white papers and so on.

E-resources have several advantages over print resources, primary being convenience, ease of access and reduced cost. An e-resource may be accessed by multiple users simultaneously. The same resource may contain multiple forms of data like audio, video, image and text. These inherent benefits have led to considerable growth in the available e-resources which makes their distribution and proliferation a demanding but challenging task. Several technologies have been proposed to achieve this task. Mobile agent technology is one such approach which is widely been used for implementing e-resources distribution and access systems. The paper discusses the mobile agent technology and its role in the growth and proliferation of e-resources.

2. Mobile Agents: An Introduction

Mobile agent is a program that performs a predefined computational task on behalf of a user by moving autonomously from one node to the other in a network (Tripathi, Ahmed and Karnik, 2001). It is a software agent that contains data and code. The phenomenon of creating a code and transporting it to another machine to execute the code is also referred to as Remote Evaluation (Sahinkoz and Erdogan, 2003). Mobile code technologies like Java enable creation of mobile agents that can move across heterogeneous entities and perform various functions. The increasing pervasiveness of Internet in our daily lives and development of scripting languages like Perl and TCL have made mobile agents a promising technology. The technology is now a widely accepted design paradigm used in implementation of applications requiring distributed control.

Since the computation code moves closer to nodes, use of mobile agents helps reduce the network bandwidth requirements and latency (Tripathi, Ahmed and Karnik, 2001). The approach is a step ahead of the traditional client server model. These features make mobile agent technology a useful alternative when dealing with various distributed systems such as e-commerce. The applications of mobile agents are diverse ranging from network management to Internet services. Mobile agents have been contributing in the proliferation of electronic resources by providing a platform to implement digital libraries, information filtering and retrieval systems (Tripathi, Ahmed and Karnik, 2001). Some of these applications have been explained in this paper.

3. Architecture and Framework

A mobile agent has a task encapsulated in it. The managing station dispatches the agent to a remote site. On reaching the site, the agent executes the code and performs the designated task. The agent can either return to the originating site or it may send the results in a message (Sahinkoz and Erdogan, 2003). Since each agent performs its function independently, a number of agents are deployed across the different entities in a system to achieve a target. Since the computation is now performed parallely, the task can be performed in lesser time. A mobile agent may be characterised by the following features (Deng, *et al.*, 2002):

- Ability to execute the code automatically on reaching a remote site
- Ability to communicate with other agents
- Perform the functions delegated by the user
- Should function autonomously
- Capable of asynchronous functioning.

As depicted in Figure 1, a mobile agent comprises of two parts and various stages in the execution of life cycle (Al-Sakran, 2006):

- ***Code*:** This comprises of the instructions that define the agent, its functions, behaviour and intelligence.
- ***Data:*** Agent data comprises of the global variables that characterize the behaviour of the agent.
- ***Execution State:*** The agent may reside in one of the several states. These states are stages in the life cycle of the agent.

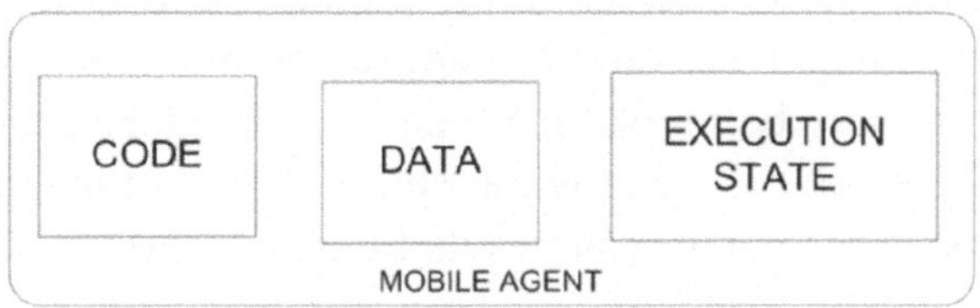

Fig. 1: Representation of a Mobile Agent

The mobile agents require a network to communicate with each other. This network is often referred to as the Agent Communication Network. An agent communication network comprises of the following components (Deng, *et al,* 2002):

- *A host station*—defined as a network node that houses an agent. A station may have multiple hosts at any instant of time.
- *A society*—a group of agents that have a common goal.
- *A query station*—interface for a user to specify a task which in turn is broken into several smaller goals.
- *A species*—a society that has a common goal of same priority.

4. Mobile Agent Life-Cycle

A mobile agent undergoes transition from its birth to termination. This evolution is represented by the mobile agent Markovian chain which is explained in Figure 2.

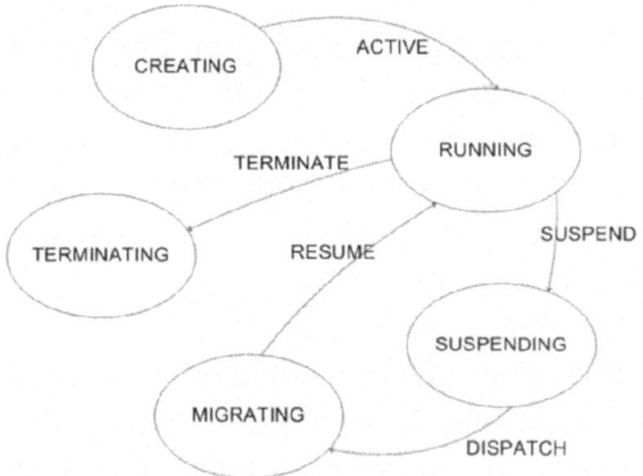

Fig. 2: Markovian Chain Representing Mobile Agent Life-cycle

At any instance, a mobile agent can be in any of the states of the Markovian cycle and their state transition diagram can be explained as:

- In the creating state, agent is created.
- Once activated, transition occurs to the running state. The agent executes the code and performs its functions in this state.
- The agent may be deleted in the running state to enter into the termination state.
- A running agent may be suspended in the running state to enter in the suspending state. The agent sits inactively on the agent server and waits to be activated again.
- A suspended agent may be revoked. When it is dispatched to a host, it enters the migrating state in which the agent is travelling between the hosts.
- On reaching the site, the agent resumes its functions and enters running mode.

5. Applications

Mobile agents find their applications in a plethora of fields some of them being network management and engineering, scientific computing, distributed data applications etc. We discuss some of the potential areas in which they can play an important role in proliferation of electronics resources.

5.1 *Digital Libraries*

A digital library is a collection of data objects which are maintained by independent sources. It comprises of files, images, databases, web servers etc. A digital library is characterised by the following features:

- Stores large amounts of data; both structured and unstructured.
- Ability to store and modify both the stored data as well as the structure.
- Support for multimedia data formats like audio and video.
- Ability to identify user profiles and provide access to data depending on access rights.

Mobile agents in the implementation of digital libraries have to cater to these requirements. A mobile agent based digital library comprising of various independent agents each of which has a specific task to perform. There are agents for both users and servers. The exact architecture of a mobile agent based digital library may vary with the platform and specific requirements. Some of the agents which may be a part of a digital library including:

- ***User Presentation Agent:*** A user presentation agent is responsible for handling the presentation of the retrieved results depending on the user preferences. It can process and refine the results according the user's environment and choice of language.
- ***Database Query Agent:*** A database query agent may be created to run queries on the collection of objects in the digital library. Since a digital library usually

comprises on a number of independent databases, this agent acts as an interface between the users of the library and the e-resources.

- ***Query Management Agent:*** A query management agent manages the user queries, translates them and performs information retrieval by handing over the query to the query management agent.

5.2 *E-Transaction Systems*

The growth of Internet and Web technologies has led to the development of several e-transaction systems. Transaction systems function on structured blocks of data, filtering and utilising required data fields from distributed sources to complete a transaction. Mobile agents help in the execution of tasks autonomously without the need of client interference. They can interact with multiple servers and make transaction execution flexible and simple (Mohamad, 2005). Most of the transaction systems use a distributed database management system (DDMS) to store and retrieve data. Traditional approaches exert heavy load on the DDMS systems due to their centralised nature of execution. Use of light weight and portable mobile agents for database connectivity makes the transactions faster and reduces the load on the servers.

5.3 *Information Retrieval*

Information retrieval is an inherent capability of most of the applications today. Applications require some data to be extracted from sources and thereafter processed. Mobile agent technology is now widely being used for implementing information retrieval systems. Some of the potential areas where the deployment has been practiced are enlisted (Glitho, Olougouna and Pierre, 2002):

- ***Search Engines:*** In mobile agent based search engines, a master agent is created which process the user query, and creates a list of potential servers. The master agent then creates multiple clone agents, each of which is dispatched to the servers to look for information which matches the searched query. The results are collected back and analysed by the master agent and finally displayed to the user in suitable format.
- ***Medical Systems***: In medicine, agents collect data about and the patient's health. The data is then recorded, previous history is retrieved and the compiled information sent to the medical practitioner for diagnosis and treatment.
- ***Weather Forecasting and Modelling:*** Meteorological services employ mobile agent approach to forecast weather conditions. The user creates an agent with policies defined to create an alarm if certain criteria are met. The agent periodically polls the weather sensors like temperature, humidity, pressure etc. It analyses the received results and sounds an alarm if the measured values exceed the thresholds set by the user.

- ***Scheduling Applications:*** Schedulers and e-organizers use an agent to visit different servers and compile information about availability of the participants to finalize the most suitable data and time for a meeting. The agent uses data field from electronic calendars and may also require that the agent of some participants re-schedule some other meetings.

Performance analysis of such applications have illustrated that there is a significant increase in performance and reduction in latency when these applications are implanted using mobile agent technology rather than the client server paradigm (Glitho, Olougouna and Pierre, 2002).

5.4 *E-Learning and Evaluation*

The mobility and flexibility of mobile agent technology makes it the perfect candidate for implementing e-learning systems. Traditional classroom teaching systems have given way to virtual lecture rooms and e-learning portals. Such approaches have score over the traditional systems in several aspects. They make the content available anywhere and anytime. Course content can be customised according to individual preferences. Performance can be regularly monitored. The mobile agent technology uses software agents to emulate human instructors. A typical e-learning system may consist of the following components (Al-Sakran, 2006).

- ***Agent Server:*** It creates, distributes and coordinates with other agents. It performs negotiation between the various agents to enable efficient distribution of control.
- ***Instructor Agent:*** A human instructor may configure the instructor to perform the various teaching tasks. It frees the human instructor from a number of tasks like releasing and monitoring course content and evaluating the progress.
- ***Learner Agent:*** This agent assists the students by searching smartly the availabl E-resources, obtaining feedback and performing assessment of the performance.
- ***Interface Agent:*** This agent assists the users in various tasks like filtering the received information, creating user profile based on behaviour, interacting with other agents and similar activities (Yan, 2006).

Figure 3 shows a typical set up comprising of a teacher, student, a resource creator, database and web server all connected by mobile agents (Yan, 2006).

Mobile agents based e-learning systems have been empirically proved to be superior to traditional systems based on the client server model (Al-Sakran, 2006). The mobile agent technology can have several potential applications in e-learning domain. Intelligent agents help to refine search engine results and hence provide more relevant resources. They may help customise the course content to suit the users' interest and preferences.

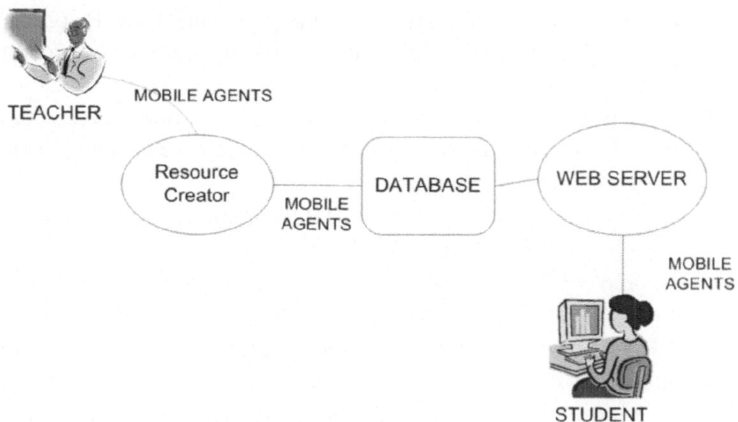

Fig. 3: A Typical Mobile Agent Based E-Learning System

6. Challenges

Mobile agent technology has been widely accepted as a design approach in implementing distributed systems. However, there are certain challenges that the technology faces. Complexity in design and maintenance as compared to traditional approaches is one such road block. Security of mobile agent based systems is another major concern that hampers their widespread deployment. Mobile agents are susceptible to attacks from malicious users during transition. Host machines are also vulnerable to ghost agents which may masquerade as genuine mobile agents. Integration and interoperability with existing applications are some other issues that need to be addressed to make the technology widely acceptable (Mohamad, 2005).

7. Conclusion

The paper discussed only some of the potential applications of the mobile agent technology in the growth of e-resources. As electronic resources continue to expand and volume of information being handled by current systems further increases, the technology will extend itself to newer areas and domains. Agent-based Electronic Resource Management Systems could soon see the light of the day. The ability of mobile agents to function efficiently in heterogeneous environment is ideal for e-resource access and disseminations systems. As advances continue in this promising technology, it will prove to be a boon for information and library resources.

References

[1] Al-Sakran, Hasan (2006). Developing e-learning system using mobile agent technology. IEEE Information and Communication Technologies—second ICTTA 2006. Damascus, 2006, pp. 647–652.

[2] Deng, L.Y., Shih, T.K., Huang, T., Liao, Y., Wang, Y. and Hsu, H. (2002). A distributed mobile agent framework for maintaining persistent distance education. *Journal of Information Scence and Engineering,* 18(4), 489–506.

[3] Glitho, R.H., Olougouna, E. and Pierre, S. (2002). Mobile agents and their use for information retrieval: A brief overview and an elaborate case study. Ericsson Research, Montreal, *IEEE Network*, 16(1), 34–41.

[4] Mohamad, Hassan Ayman (2005). Trends in mobile agent applications. *Journal of Research and Practice in Information Technology*, 37(4), 323–351.

[5] Sahinkoz, O. K. and Erdogan, Nadia (2003). A two-levelled mobile agent system for electronic commerce. *Journal of Aeronautics and Space Technologies*, 1(2), 21–32.

[6] Tripathi, Anand R., Ahmed, Tanvir and Karnik Neeran M. (2001). Experiences and future challenges in mobile agent programming. *Microprocessors and Microsystems,* 25(2), 121–129.

[7] Yan, Wenqing Cheng (2006). Mobile agents in e-learning resource management, 36th ASEE/IEEE Frontiers in Education Conference, 28–31October 2006, San Diego, CA.

Section–V

Access and Use of Electronic Resources

Electronic Resources Management in Libraries, pp. 251–258

Access to Government Generated Digital Data and Information: Gazette of India and Other Resources

P.R. Goswami

ABSTRACT

The purpose of this paper is to briefly discuss the availability of digital government information in India with special reference to Gazette of India, which is considered to be in the category of grey literature. The Gazette is published in an inexplicable format. Taking into account its use pattern one can say that it has a high reference value for the government functionaries as well as for the researchers in the field of public policy and governance.

1. Introduction

The use of the term Information Age signifies advances that have taken place in information technologies. Our society has always been based on information exchange and libraries have been rich sources of vast quantities of readily available information. It is basically Information Technologies (IT) that has changed rapidly since the invention of digital computers. Now a days creation of digital content and making it available on the web has become easier primarily due to decreasing storage costs and cheap computing facilities. Electronic journals with the ability to provide full text searching and hyperlinks continue to become the accepted norm for the publishers. It has been said that the amount of digital information produced annually is by some estimates more than thirty-five thousand times the complete contents of the Library of Congress and it is growing at a faster rate.

Government is considered to be the largest publisher in a country like India. It functions through a number of interactive formations known as Departments, Ministries, Commissions, Bureaus, etc. They produce a vast quantity of data and information as results of their activities. The published versions of their information are made available in digital form on their websites. However, flagship publications (including Annual Report) of most of the government agencies are also released through normal publishing channels in print form.

1.1 *What is a Gazette*

The Oxford English Dictionary (OED) defines Gazette as a newssheet or a periodical publication giving an account of current events. It has been mentioned in the OED that Gazette was first published in Venice about the middle of the 16th century. Later similar newssheet appeared in France and England in the 17th century. The first official journal published in England was the Oxford Gazette, the first number of which appeared in November 1665 when the Court was at Oxford due to outbreak of plague in the country. In England, the three official journals were the London Gazette, the Edinburgh Gazette and the Dublin Gazette. They were issued by the authority twice in a week containing lists of government appointments and promotions, names of bankrupts and other public notices.

2. Gazette of India

It is evident that Gazette of India is a tradition bound publication having a strong bond with the British official Gazette. At present this publication is recognised as the most authentic record of government rules and regulations, orders, notifications, pertaining to constitution of Committees, Commissions, etc.

The following are the main sections and sub-sections of Gazette of India, which is published every week by the Department of Publications, Government of India. The orders, notifications etc. released by the Government organs, *i.e.*, Ministries, Departments, and statutory bodies are published in a chronological order.

- ***Part-I - Section 1:*** Notification relating to Non-statutory Rules, Regulations, Orders, and Resolution issued by the Ministries of the Government of India (other than the Ministry of Defence) and by the Supreme Court.
- ***Part-I - Section 2:*** Notifications regarding Appointments, Promotion, Leave etc. of Government Offices issued by the Ministries of the Government of India (other than the Ministry of Defence) and by the Supreme Court.
- ***Part-I - Section 3:*** Notifications relating to Resolution and Non-Statutory Orders issued by Ministry of Defence.
- ***Part-I - Section 4:*** Notification regarding Appointments, Promotions, Leave etc. of Government Officers issued by the Ministry of Defence.
- ***Part-II - Section 1:*** Acts, Ordinances Resolutions.
- ***Part-II - Section 1A:*** Authority Texts in Hindi languages of Acts, Ordinances and Regulations.
- ***Part-II - Section 2-*** Bills and Reports of Select Committee of Bills.
- ***Part-II - Section 3:*** Sub-Section I—General Statutory Rules including Orders Byelaws etc. of general character issued by the Ministries of the Government of India (other than the Administration of Union Territories).

- ***Part-II - Section 3:*** Sub-Section II—Statutory Orders and Notifications issued by the Ministries of the Government of India (other than the Ministry of Defence) and by the Central Authorities (other than the Administration of Union Territories).
- ***Part-II - Section 3:*** Sub-Section III—Authority texts in Hindi (other than such texts, published in Section 3 or Section 4 of the Gazette of India) of General Statutory Rules and statutory order (including Bye-laws of general character) issued by the Ministries of the Government of India (including the Ministry of Defence) and by Central authorities (other than administration of Union Territories).
- ***Part-II - Section 4:*** Statutory Rules and Orders issued by the Ministry of Defence.
- ***Part-III - Section 1:*** Notification issued by the High Courts, the Comptroller and Auditor General, Union Public Service Commission, the Indian Government Railways and by Attached and Subordinate Offices of the Government of India.
- ***Part-III - Section 2:*** Notification and Notices issued by the Patent Office, relating to Patents and Designs.
- ***Part-III - Section 3:*** Notification issued by or under the authority of Chief Commissioners.
- ***Part-III - Section 4:*** Miscellaneous Notifications including Notifications, Orders, Advertisements and Notices issued by Statutory Bodies.
- ***Part-IV:*** Advertisements and Notices issued by Private Individuals and Private Bodies.
- ***Part-V:*** Supplements showing statistics of births and Deaths etc. both in English and Hindi.

Gazette of India is a bi-lingual publication compiled by the Government Press on the basis of notifications/orders issued by the Ministries and Departments. The subscribers or libraries receive loose issues of this publication every week.

3. Digitization Project

Central Secretariat Library (CSL), Ministry of Culture is considered to be the repository of all government publications. CSL previously known as Imperial Secretariat Library also has a vast collection of official publication of British era. A project was initiated by the CSL in 2003 to digitize a part of its collection comprising Annual report, Performance Budget. Demand for Grant, Expenditure Budget (all pertaining to Ministry/Department of Culture) and Gazette of India. One of the most widely used groups of publication is the serial Gazette of India, which is released in different parts and sections.

It was experienced that users generally ask for Gazette of India issues citing any one or combination of subject, part number, section, sub-section, date, GSR number etc. A retrieval system was designed keeping in view the nature of query received from the users. The following types of search facility was provided in the database created by the CSL.

- Full text search
- Searchable on various metadata such on title, chapter, paragraph, etc.
- All or a few words
- Proximity search
- Boolean search.

In addition to this, a strong retrieval mechanism was also developed with the help of proprietary software. The retrieval was possible by document by date of publishing, by Ministry/Department and also by organization under each Ministry/Department. An extension search was also possible with pre-determined or pre-defined keywords. The project was completed in 2005 and the entire database containing the issues pertaining to the years 1950 to 2002 were made available to the users through the internet of the library. Later the publisher *i.e.* Department of Publications decided to provide access to digital version of this serial against payment. This facility was started with effect from the issues of the year 2010 and continued for a year or so.

4. Recent Developments

Recently, the publisher of the Gazette of India has decided to make it available on the web free of cost. This is a policy decision prompted perhaps by the National Data Sharing and Accessibility Policy (NDSAP), 2012 issued under the aegis of the Department of Science and Technology (DST). It has been observed that a large quantum of data generated using public funds by different agencies in the country remains inaccessible to the civil society or general public. Most of these data is non-sensitive in nature and could be used by public for research or development purposes. NDSAP has been promulgated primarily to promote data sharing and to enable access to government data for national planning and development. It also aims to promote a technology-based culture of data management and data sharing and access. For data to be re-used, it needs to be properly described (Metadata) and linked to services that disseminate the data to other researchers and stakeholders. The present method of data storage is as diverse as the organizations or disciplines that generate it. There is a need to develop institutional repositories and data centers at national levels so that users can access it easily.

The following are the benefits of the data sharing policy.

- Maximising use: Ready access to government data will facilitate extensive use of a valuable public resource.
- Avoiding duplication: The data sharing policy is aimed to eliminate the chance of collection of same data by different bodies.

- Maximised integration: By adopting common standards for the collection and transfer of data, integration of individual data sets seems to be feasible.
- Ownership information: The identification of owners for the principal data sets would enable the users to identify. Those responsible for implementation of priotitised data collection programmes and development of data standards.
- Decision Making: Easy and ready access to existing data on important variables is essential for many decision making tasks like protecting the environment, development planning, managing assets, improving living conditions, national security and controlling disasters.

Regarding implementation, of the policy, DST will serve as the nodal agency for coordination and monitoring of NDSAP in close collaboration with all central ministries by creating data.gov.in through National Informatics can be (NIC). All sharable data will be made available on 'as-is where-is' basis. Guidelines for implementation will be brought out by the DST incorporating the technology to be used and standards for data and metadata. This project would entail expenditures for both data owners and data managers for analog to digital conversion, data refinement, data storage, quality up-gradation etc. Budgetary support would be necessary for each Department/Ministry.

5. Preservation and Access

A part of government produced information in the form of annual reports, proceedings of meetings/conferences, expert committee recommendation, committee and commissions reports etc. are now made available in published form and quite a few of them are for limited use or 'restricted use' for official purpose only. One way to preserve these sources is to retain them in digital from or digitize the old volumes. However, proper preservation and providing access to these born digital or digitized material is a challenging task. The digital format of the contents is various and they are generally dictated by short term needs of the officials who initially create them for their own use. Their motivation to use only 'good' standard digital format is very low. Libraries and archives in the government sector will have to deal with this material and they have to find whether there are well-understood ways to keep it usable over time. Needless to say, management of digital content in a library or archive requires new technological infrastructure, new policies and procedures as well as new core competencies of staff. Government libraries and archives with still function in a traditional way and they need significant change or transformation to deal with the digital content.

Recently announced NDSAP (2012), aims at the promotion of technology based culture of data management as well as data sharing and access. In 1992, UNESCO started the Memory of the World Programme (MOW) to protect and promote the world's documentary heritage through preservation and access. These two tasks complement each other, for access encourages protection and preservation ensures access.

The programme has three main objectives:

- To facilitate preservation of the world's documentary heritage through all appropriate means. The making of access copies, to relieve pressure on the use of original materials is encouraged.
- To assist universal access to documentary heritage including making digitized copies and catalogues widely available while respecting legislative and other limitations.
- To raise awareness would wide of the significance of documentary heritage through such means as the memory of the World Register, the media and promotional and informational publications.

Later in 2003, UNESCO adopted the charter on the preservation of the Digital Heritage a non-binding international instrument that draws attention to the preservation of a new type of source material *i.e.* digital heritage. It has been defined in the charter as 'cultural, educational, scientific and administrative sources as well as technical, legal, medical and other kinds of information created digitally or converted into digital form from existing analogue resources that have lasting value and significance. The charter has rightly explained that digital heritage is particularly vulnerable due to hardware and software obsolescence and also due to organizational uncertainties. The charter has asked for immediate action, development of strategies and international cooperation.

6. Government Information and Reference Service

Professional bodies of librarians have issued guidelines for references service. According to the guidelines reference service considers availability of current and accurate resources and easy access to these resources. So far libraries have relied on cataloguing and classification for providing easy access. It has been rightly emphasized that value added services in a library has been in cataloguing to provide a uniform record of a document and in classification to provide a subject arrangement and finding tool.

After a close scrutiny of content and structure of various categories of government publications, one can raise a question whether all types of publications need to be classified and arranged according to the subject order enumerated in the schemes like DDC or UDC. Most of the prominent libraries in India have a fragmentary collection of government publications. Since there is limited bibliographical control of this category of publications, it is difficult to say which library has got a near exhaustive collection. Government is the largest publisher in India and at all levels of state, *i.e.* union, sate, municipal and district. A wide array of books, reports, proceedings, serials etc. are released in a diffused manner all over the country. Major publishers include the Planning Commission, Reserve Bank of India, Ministry of Commerce, Ministry of Agriculture and Ministry of Statistics and Programme Implementation. One has to critically examine the archival memory of these organizations to prepare on exhaustive list of their publications. In most of the libraries reports or serials released by government organs are arranged in a classified order. The call number of a report consists of classification number and book number. One has to consider whether 'provenance method' is more appropriate for the purpose of arranging these publications. This method is generally used by the archivists for arranging records. According to this, information sources/records are organized according to the body that created the sources. For example, all reports originated from the Ministry of Agriculture and its organs are to be kept at one place in a particular order. This will enable a Reference Librarian to keep a track of all publications originating from a particular organ of the government.

7. Digital Sources and Reference Service

Reference service has changed a great deal. Libraries are now using Internet to access a variety of sources both free and licensed. Librarians are also using new Internet based technologies as potential ways of interacting with people who have short range or long-range queries. How does the Internet based technology responds to the needs of a librarian? This was asked to a group of professionals working in public and academic libraries in USA. The purpose was to know about their experience and also to elicit their opinion and altitude about the use of technology in reference service.

The following are the major findings of the study:

- Ready reference questions can be answered with digital resources.
- Personal and private questions as well as research questions are not answered property with digital sources.
- Questions requiring a quick answer are poorly served by digital sources. However most of the questions can be attempted with the help of digital sources.

It is difficult to say whether librarians in India have similar type of experience with digital sources. Indian content on the Internet is limited though it is growing rapidly National Informatics Center (NIC) has developed websites of many government agencies. Most of the Ministries/Departments have put their current data and information on the website.

8. Concluding Remarks

Digitization of government data and information and their proper upkeep with retrieval facility is now considered important. Several policy measures have been initiated by the government for this activity. Section 4(2) of the Right to reformation Act, 2005 reads it shall be a constant endeavor for every public authority to take steps in accordance with the requirements of clause (b) of sub-section (1) to provide as much information suo motu to the public at regular intervals through various means of that the public have minimum resort to the use of this Act to obtain information. Organizations like Department of Publications, National Archives of India have started projects to digitize and provide access to Gazette of India Publications and Government records that have research and reference value.

References

[1] India Department of Science and Technology. National Data Sharing and Accessibility Policy, 2012. *Gazette of India,* Part 1, Section 1. 17 March 2012.

[2] Smith, Mackenzie. Exploring variety in digital collections and the implications for digital preservation. *Library Trends,* 2005, 54(1), 6 15.

[3] United Nation Educational Scientific and Cultural organization. Memory of the world: Safeguarding the documentary heritage of humanity, 2010.

Electronic Resources Management in Libraries, pp. 259–273

Use of E-Resources in Indian Institute of Technology Library Guwahati: A Survey

R.N. Mishra and Rosa Laltlanmawii

ABSTRACT

E-resources have a pragmatic value in teaching, learning and research. The present trend insist upon all the libraries to provide services in electronic form due to changing information needs of the users who principally depend upon the e-resources due to its easy accessibility, wide range of materials etc. This is more practical due to open access, Internet, subject portals, subject gateways etc. The paper primarily discusses on types of e-resources, use of e-resources, and its evaluation including some major initiatives taken by IITG library, a national repute organization to its users.

1. Introduction

Rapid technological developments and its application in different spheres including service sectors have altered the magnitudes of information gathering, and needs of the user communities in the present day of digital environment. Multidisciplinary researches have precipitated various ways and means for libraries and information centers to acquire multifarious information sources to provide authentic, reliable and constructive resources to the user communities. The emphasis in the digital environment has been primarily focused to develop core knowledge in multidimensional disciplines which requires sound skills to deliver of the same with legitimate and trustworthy at the door step of the user communities including on their desktops. Internet has become the uniquely identified component to provide the wide array of e-resources to the users in the relevant disciplines with quickest access. It is been recognized as the most powerful and indispensable tool for global communication and exchange of information. E-resources, the only option left out for proliferating research encompasses both documentary and non-documentary forms in electronic formats that provide a pointer including exhaustive information relating to the area of research that can be seamlessly accessed through computers. E-resources comprise databases, e-journals, e-magazines, e-books/Wiki books, e-news, e-images, data/GIS, digital library projects, electronic exhibitions, e-subject guides, portals, e-newsletter, e-white papers, e-conference proceedings, e-reports, e-studies, e-interesting development, e-directories, web searching tools etc. on a wide range of topics.

1.2 *IITG Central Library*

Consequently upon the requirements of multi-directional and multi-dimensional fabrics of information of the users due to advanced courses, multi-disciplinary research, it is hardly possible to confine to traditional documents, rather expanded its horizon to e-resources. Expanding horizon of knowledge compelled the library to keep pace with the changes. The IITG Central Library under study is reckoned as source of knowledge center and sharing of knowledge in multidimensional ways to its clienteles. Apart from more than one lakh volumes collection covering textbooks, reference books, conference proceedings, back volumes, standards, and non-book material such as CD-ROMs, audio tapes, video tapes, slides, the library also is subscribing 414 current periodicals published in both India and Foreign countries.

1.3 *E-Resources*

E-resources are the electronic products that delivers a collection of data through various means such as full-text, e-journals, image collections including other multimedia products, numerical, graphical and the products are being marketed by the vendors, publishers etc. on Internet platform. Further, e-resources available through various modes include, CD-ROM, tape etc. E-resources have become imperative in libraries due to the spiraling cost of publications, shrinking budget allocations, constraints in acquiring international publications, expansion of staffs, space problems, and above all information explosion. Availability of plethora of e-resources has dramatically altered the nature of collection developments, management and dissemination of services in libraries. Acquisition, organization, dissemination and use of e-resources have altered the magnitude of traditional library system and giving birth to the digital library.

Application of technologies has a considerable impact on libraries and information centers. Virtually most of the academic and special libraries, at least in the most developed countries, are now members of networks and different consortia that greatly facilitate the location of sources of information in electronic form and gaining access to them. Card catalogues and other form of services in the libraries have largely been replaced by online catalogue and online services respectively. Access to databases of various kinds including e-resources has become a routine job for many libraries. Further, most of the libraries both academic and public have also started adding electronic resources to their collection development through CD-ROM or other forms.

2. Classification of E-Resources

Electronic Journals: E-journals are available in electronic format. E-journals are also referred to as 'electronic publishing', 'electronic serials', 'online journals' and 'electronic periodicals'. An electronic journal is defined as the grouping of information that is sent out in electronic format, which is produced, published and distributed electronically. E-journals are electronic version of printed journals accompanied by extensive hyper linking. They can be read both online and offline. It is the principle source of information and fastest growing segment of the digital collection in most libraries. E-journals can be obtained freely, through subscription, pay-per-use through license to access. A physical, printed version is also available in e-format.

Electronic Books: An e-book is the electronic text and is represented to the reader visually. The electronic text is saved to a floppy, transferred onto a CD-ROM, downloaded from the Internet or provided on a palm-sized digital reader. In general e-books are two types: one type refers to a piece of hardware device created specifically for reading purpose, and another is an e-book in the form of electronic texts which are read on a PC or any other reading device either in the form of CD-ROM/DVD (offline) or over Internet (online) such as Amazon.com, SomonSays.com, O'Reilly.com are the best known e-book publishers, suppliers and sellers.

Electronic Reports: The reports are available both ongoing and completed projects electronically which allowed the researcher to generate new concepts concerning to his area of research. E-reports of any type are profusely available which can be accessed through Internet. These act as a substantial tool to promote research activity. It refers to activities of research, experimentation of analysis with regard to the development of innovative methods and contents in the field.

Electronic Theses and Dissertations: Electronic theses and dissertations (ETDs) are defined as those theses and dissertations submitted, archived, or accessed primarily in electronic formats, which include born digital and converted by scanning the documents made available in Portable Document Format (PDF), as well as hypertext and multimedia formats published electronically on CD-ROM or on the World Wide Web (WWW). Many libraries are now in the process of digitizing information in an effort to preserve it and to make it more widely available over network or Internet. The Networked Digital Library of Theses and Dissertations (NDLTD), funded by a grant from the U.S Department of Education, is a collection focused specifically on digitized versions of theses, dissertations and technical papers that began in 1996 at Virginia Tech. The NDLTD reports that more than twenty universities around the world are official contributing members.

Electronic-Reference Tools: Today vendors and publishers are providing users with various reference sources through their website and databases such as viz online dictionaries (www.dictionay.com, www.m-w.com, www.dict.leo.org, www.batleby.com), online handbooks (www.uia.au), yearbooks, encyclopedias etc. In reality electronic reference tools such as encyclopedias, dictionaries, atlases, almanacs at the same time and less then their print counterparts. It also offers words games, transcripts from a radio programme about language, and a brief history of English language.

Electronic Encyclopedias: E-encyclopedias and almanacs also offer search capabilities and hyperlinks leading the reader to a related article, but such tools do not always anticipate users' needs or habits. While updating it can be as often as desired, economics rather than a desire to be up to date is more often the driving force. An almanac's print version, may be more up to date and easier to use than some online versions of the same title depending on the company offering access to the title. Online atlases including those provided by the National Geographical Society, offer up-to-date maps accompanied by related flags and demographic information. The reader must wait for the graphic to load-a substantial period as compared with the time taken to turn the pages of print atlases, a weakness mitigated by the free content offered online. In the present scenario, e-encyclopedia is supplemented with webopedia, wikipedia etc. which add substantial value to promote research work.

Electronic Magazines: E-zines are periodicals application that are stored on a file server and that may be distributed or accessed via a computer terminal. They are also called web-zines. Some sources of e-zines are www.indiatoday.com, www.musicindia.com, www.bestindiansites.com, www.news.sify.com, etc.

Databases: It is a collection of records or a file or a collection of files brought together as a single file commonly accessible by a given set of programs. It is an organized, integrated and often inter-related collection of data, records, files or information. Databases can be divided into three types, *i.e.* bibliographic database, numeric database and full text database. Bibliographic databases contain bibliographic citation to a document which may include an abstract. Numeric database contain numeric or statistical data and full text databases contains the full text of the publication. The power and value of searchable databases have been developing by the introduction of DIALOG, MEDLINE/MEDLARS etc. Unlike CD-ROM, online indexes and abstracting services can be updated on a daily basis and are often linked to the complete text of the article that has been indexed.

Electronic Newsletters/Electronic Bulletin Boards: E-newsletters are offered by companies and organizations around the world. These newsletters are actually e-mail sent from e-servers, generally as text that the individual's mail reader may convert to another format. The obvious advantage of an electronic newsletter is that it can be sent to thousands of readers at once without postage. Electronic newsletters will likely grow in number and popularity as ease of access to the internet increases and the related cost decrease. They may be house organs, or they may contain individual contributions brought together by an editor or moderator. There are also electronic newsletters that are not subscription-based but that are available only on the web. These publications are usually less elaborate in design that online newspapers and magazines but recognizable as distinct publications. These online newsletters differ from web pages in that they are serial in nature and generally have archives of past issues. Electronic Bulletin Board (EBB) displays through Liquid Crystal Display

(LCD) the current information in a very short form which is mean for general awareness of the public at a large.

Electronic Newspapers: E-newspapers, may copy the typography of their printed counterparts, even though they are not laid out as the print versions are, and they used frames or sidebars to the list contents, on which readers may click in order to go straight to that section. There are photographs and other graphics in online newspapers, and often there are photo archives available online as well. Political and other cartoons are available in the online versions of some newspapers and there are often links to other sites where more of the same cartoons can be viewed or the cartoonist's home page may be visited. Crossword and other puzzles are also available for solving online or for printing and solving the old fashioned way with a pencil. Online newspapers offer web advertising that is link to the site so that advertising can see the site visitors' location and make some real connection between the advertising and responses to it. Demographic information about the user may also be available.

3. Use of E-Resources

Libraries now rely increasing on e-resources as many of them are not supported with sufficient print versions due to the above mentioned factors. Since the inception and induction of electronic materials through the technologies libraries have practically become flooded with digital resources which are a continuous process. Digital preservation in this juncture has become imperative to maintain and organize for sustainability for a good time. It is a process by which data is preserved in electronic form in order to ensure the usability durability and intellectual integrity of the information contained therein.

The emergence of electronic resources has drastically revamped the status of all the libraries and information centers across the world during the last decade. There has been a rapid urge of the user community to get more and more information from electronic resources. With the advancement of the information and communication technology applications, Internet and WWW, Library and Information Centers (LICs) have also shifted their collection from print to electronic resources. Electronic resources offer tremendous possibilities and advantages over print media which includes the ease of use, shareable nature, and availability of internet and universal acceptance of web technology. The enhanced features of online access provide value-addition to these sources:

- ***Multi-access:*** A networked product can in theory provide multiple points of access (offices, homes, classrooms, etc.) at multiple points in time (often called '24/7', referring to the fact that the resource is available 24 hours a day, 7 days a week) and to multiple simultaneous users.

- ***Speed:*** An e-resource often as being a lot quicker to browse or search, to extract information from, and to integrate that information into other material and to cross-search or cross-reference between different publications.
- ***Functionality:*** An electronic version will allow the user to approach the publication and to analyze its content in new ways (for e.g. with a dictionary one would no longer be restricted to searching under headword).
- ***Content:*** e-content acts as a solution for developing, managing and publishing content on the web which can be accessible on the Internet platform. Designed for enterprise, government and educational institutions, e-content provides ultimate flexibility through open source. E-content integrates content management, resource management, workflow, collaboration and personalization. With comprehensive support for managing content stored in databases, Extensible Markup Language (XML) repositories, and static files. E-content provides team-based enterprise-wide collaboration, reducing IT burden.
- ***Management:*** The management of e-resources otherwise known as Electronic Resource Management (ERM) refers to practices and software systems used by libraries to keep track of important information about electronic information resources, especially internet-based resources such as electronic journals, databases and electronic books. The development of ERM became necessary in the early 2000s as it became clear that traditional library catalogs and integrated library systems were not designed to handle metadata for resources as mutable as many online products are.
- ***Interoperability:*** It is a property which refers to the ability of systems and organizations to work together (inter-operate). The term is often used in a technical systems engineering sense, or alternatively in a broad sense, taking into account social, political and organization factors that impact system to system performance. Interoperability becomes a quality of increasing importance for information technology products as the concept that "The network is the computer" becomes a reality. Hence, it is a combination of software and hardware on different machines from different vendors to share data. With the advent of such standards as open Uniform Resource Locator (URL), it is possible to link to another elsewhere.
- ***Storage:*** e-storage provides a safe keeping for library data making sure that it can be retrieved properly at the time of need. It is also a remote site backup solution for the storage service subscribers, freeing the user from the worry of critical data loss due to the hardware crashes or unfortunate incidents from natural causes, theft, and break-ins, e-storage service allows to access personal and business data anytime anywhere with the Internet. E-storage is a remote storage at which the user can store and retrieve data via web browser or Storage Sync, a software client on the user's desktop. E-storage includes two principle functionalities such

as; Online Storage Service and, Internet Back Services. The feature comprises the following:

- Accessing of data anywhere at anytime with the Internet via the web browser.
- File Management features such as back-up, upload, download, delete, move, copy, access control etc.
- Upload and download specific files up to a maximum of 5 each time.
- Sharing of files.
- Encrypt and Decrypt features.
- Manage users (only for enterprise package), and
- Help and guidance to the users.

E-resources add lively substance to the modern library's collection and satisfy the varied needs of students, faculty and research scholars with minimum risk and time. Additionally, electronic resources carry the potential power to increase the learning opportunities offered to students in a particular, the interactive and multimedia elements provided by the electronic medium can offer a great variety of learning exercises and making courses much more lively and interactive. These e-resources enable instant feedback to students and facilitate students' ability to understand concept more clearly and easily by providing several supporting and supplementing resources for the courses so that students can visualize the material and its content without facing much difficulty in understanding.

4. Evaluation of E-Resources

Evaluation is defined in manifold directions. While, Wikipedia defines it as a means of systematic determination of merit, worth, and significance of something or someone using criteria against a set of standards, American Heritage Dictionary of the English Language (2003, 4th Ed) has defined evaluation as to:

- Ascertain or fix the value or worth of
- Examine and judge carefully; appraise
- Application of mathematical and statistical calculation etc.

Evaluation leads to

- Reveal the strength, weakness, opportunity and utility of the resources of the library
- Control and develop a realistic user-centric resource collection
- Justify for the increased of budget
- Increase the efficiency of the professionals to impart effective service in ICT environment
- Ascertain the relevance of the resources to fill up the information need gap of the users etc.

E-resources play a pragmatic role in providing the widest array of useful information as against the traditional documents and its evaluation has been mandatory to know the strength, usefulness, value etc. especially in a special library of national repute. A standard social research method is applied in evaluative process. It not only involves an assessment process by employing special techniques but also apply monitoring and other information to make judgments. Depending upon the type of data, the evaluation process is measured through its extent, efficiency, quality, performance and effectiveness.

5. Significance and Scope of the Study

Knowledge centre around the central Library as the library under discussion furnishes information/knowledge support for learning, teaching and research to its clienteles by countenancing access to e-resources maintained by the library along with various gateways. Growth and changes are the recognized predominant characteristics in the libraries which opened new vistas for collections of resources and their scientific organization including dissemination of services. In this perspective, the library under discussion is adapted to the latest technological innovations and its applications as well because it responds both to the changing need of the users' communities and collection developments including its organization in the ambit of information technology. Hence, collection of information must remain flexible enough to support to the causes of the information requirements of the users in the IITG Central Library in a changing technological scenario. In the present days, adoptions of information technology have compelled the library to be dependant upon digital materials which could be collected through Internet. The significance of the study is that it happens to the first and pioneer library in the field of science and technology with a national status in Assam to provide e-resources services to its clienteles. Moreover, the work aims at evaluating the flexibility of this library in this fluid environment as well as their capabilities in developing a process to integrate the changes in to a standard library practice to meet the current and update demands of the users' communities. IITG happens to be a special library where apart from technical teaching, research and development has been acknowledged as predominant. The research scholars and faculties of various departments of the institute under study require manifold information through e-form as traditional documents are not sufficient to meet their need. The work under study deals with extensively about the use and need of information resources in e-form including an evaluation of electronic resources used by the users in the library. However, the present study is limited only to Central Library, Indian Institute of Technology, Guwahati and no other IIT Central libraries or any other special libraries at Guwahati have been taken into account to make the study more authentic.

5.1 *Statement of the Problem*

To meet the varied demands of the clienteles, IITG central library facilitate services both traditional and electronic where, the library access of a versatile electronic resources including formats available through digital full-text, sound, graphics, images, multimedia and hypertext. This has necessitated the library to opt consequent upon the shriveling budgetary provision coupled with boosting price printed publications. Moreover the mounting publications in different streams also added substantially problems for the library to get the right choice of documents and also to the users to select appropriate materials for teaching and research. All these factors compelled both the library and the users to switch from traditional to electronic platform to get the appropriate resources available through consortia and subject gateways.

The problems associated with the study that in spite of the best efforts of the library supported with sound technical hands, the users find absence of information gap with regard to the use of e-resources due to varied reasons. Therefore, the present study aims at finding out the reasons including viable suggestions to overcome the tribulations.

5.2 *Objectives of the Study*

The objectives of the study are to ascertain the availability of different types of e-resources; to study the purpose, services provided by the library to the users; to determine the frequency of use of e-resources by the users of the library; and to evaluate the type of services provided by the library to its users.

5.3 *Research Methodology*

IITG Central Library comprises 11 Departments as on 2010, 2815 users comprising of 2300 students, 215 faculties and 300 supporting staffs. The present study is based on the published documents, records available including the URL of IITG Library. A stratified sampling technique was used to obtain a representative sample constitute a heterogeneous group. The population was grouped into several sub-population groups which are individually homogenous and items were selected from each stratum to constitute a sample and thus, the total sample size was confined to 300 comprising students, faculties and staffs. To obtain the data relating to the study, two structured questionnaires were prepared both for the users and the librarian.

Further the scholar applied both observation and interview methods with the users to ascertain the viability of use of e-resources, which facilitated the scholar to obtain primary data concerning to the research problem. The other sources of information such as unpublished dissertations, research articles, peer-reviewed journals, open access journals, etc. were explored to make the study more exhaustive and authentic.

6. Analysis and Findings

6.1 *Analysis by Designation*

Of the total 300 questionnaires circulated among 220 students, 50 faculties, 30 research scholars, 192 filled-in questionnaires were received back constituting 142 students, 32 faculties and 18 research scholars in Table 1.

Table 1: Types of Users

Sl. No.	*User Type*	*Questionnaires*	*Respondents*	*%*
1.	Faculty	50	32	64
2.	Research scholars	30	18	60
3.	Students	220	142	65
	Total	300	192	64

The table shows that students constitutes more in number, *i.e.*, 142 (65%), followed by 32 (64%) faculties out of 50 and 18 (60%) research scholars out of 30 respectively. Overall response was 192 (64%) out of 300. This reflects that the students are more conscious to reveal their mind followed by the faculties who are pre-engaged with their academic assignments and research scholars engaged in research.

6.2 *Analysis by Frequency of Visit to Library*

Frequency of visits to the library reveals the collection strength of the library as the users especially the students and the research scholars consider the resources for academic assignments and download the articles for learning and research purpose. Higher frequency of visit to the library also symbolizes accumulation of user-centric resources and its utilization in Table 2.

Table 2: Frequency of Visit

Sl. No.	*Frequency*	*Students*	*Faculty*	*Res. scholars*	*Total*
1.	Daily	74(71%)	21(20%)	9(9%)	104
2.	Weekly	63(78%)	11(14%)	7(9%)	81
3.	Occasional	5(71%)	0	2(29%)	7
	Total	142	32	18	192

Frequency of visit to the library depends upon the library resources where the users do their academic coursework. Frequency also signifies that the library is well equipped to provide adequate resources to the users both traditional and electronic. Analysis to the data shows that students are the high rated visitors followed by the faculties and research scholars respectively. Further, out of 142 students, 74 (71%) are daily visitors followed by 21(20%) faculties and Research Scholars 9(9%) respectively. This shows that the library is well equipped with resources.

6.3 *Analysis by Sources of Information*

Sources of information especially in a special library system play a significant role as the users require specific information and for that the library develop multidimensional collections to satisfy their information needs. Multifarious information being the need of the users due to technical subjects, the library could not restrict to the traditional documents and expanded to online resources, web-resources etc. The foregoing discussion on the component reveals the most preferred sources of information in Table 3.

Table 3: Preferred Source of Information

Sl. No.	*Source of Information*	*Students*	*Faculty*	*Res. Scholars*	*Total*
1.	Print material	30(68%)	8(18%	6(14%)	44(23%)
2.	Online resources	57(75%)	12(16%)	7(9%)	76(40%)
3.	Web resources	30(68%)	9(20%)	5(11%)	44(23%)
4.	CD-ROM	13(81%)	3(19%)	0	16(8%)
5.	Audio-visual tapes	11(100%)	0	0	11(6%)
	Total	142	32	18	192

It is one of the foremost activities of the library to provide the preferred source of information to the users. Analysis to the data reveals that, out of the five segments of the information sources, online resources followed by the print and web and CD-ROM are the most preferred source of information. This shows that the users are not confined to print rather, have switched over to e-resources available in different modes as 76 (40%) of the users out of the total respondents have given their preferences followed by 44 (23%) each for print and web resources. It is certain from the analysis that most of the users prefer to use the e-resources due to its flexible and convenient access. It could be further noticed that, the library maintains a healthy and user-centric collection.

6.4 *Purpose of E-resources Use*

Increasingly e-resources are gaining momentum almost all the libraries and IITG is no exception to it due to its flexibility, continuous access round the clock, global access etc. Building e-resources has become an integral part of the library as the users prefer mostly e-resources due to multiple reasons as stated above. Institution of consortia by the national body and its availability in IITG library, developing institutional database, individual subscription to e-journals, national and international databases, subject gateways are some of the important ventures taken by the library to promote teaching, research activity in the institute. It also added potential value in establishing knowledge in the respective subject areas for sustainable growth and development. Data relating to the purpose of the use of e-resources is given in Table 4.

Table 4: Purpose of Use of E-resources

Sl. No.	*Purpose*	*Students*	*Faculty*	*Res. scholars*	*Total*
1.	Update knowledge	63(85%)	07(9%)	04(5%)	74(39%)
2.	Research work	28(64%)	08(18%)	08(18%)	44(23%)
3.	Notes preparation	36(100%)	00	00	36(19%)
4.	Writing article	13(54%)	07(29%)	04(17%)	24(13%)
5.	Preparation for lecture/seminar	02(22%)	05(56%)	02(22%)	09(5%)
6.	Writing book	00	05(100%)	00	05(3%)
	Total	142	32	18	192

The respondents were asked to indicate the purpose of use of e-resources which differ from one user to another. The Table reflects the quantitative study that gives an indication of the core purpose of e-resources used by the users of IITG library. It is revealed from the table that, the major chunk of users *i.e.* 74 (39%) used e-resources of the library to update their knowledge out of which, the students constitute more followed by faculties and research scholars, while 44 (23%) of them used to support research work, 36 (19%) apply for notes preparation etc. The faculties and research scholars mostly employ the e-resources for research work, writing articles. Thus, e-resources are indispensable to all communities.

6.5 *Type of E-resources Used*

Multiple types of e-resources are available to suit to the users need. It is also essential to determine the most preferred type of e-resources as the library under discussion provides a wide array of e-resources to its users. Data relating to this facet grouped under six different types are as given below in Table 5.

Analysis of the Table shows that most of the faculty members and research scholars use e-resources. Out of that, 142 number of students, 32 number of faculty and 18 research scholars use multiple e-resources such as e-book, e-journals etc. It is further deduced from the analysis that, 84 (44%) users irrespective of the types prefer e-books followed by 83 (43%) prefer e-journals, and 9 (5%) choose DVDs. It is ascertained that the library is making progress in providing e-books and e-journals. It is noticed that the publishers are printing electronic forms due to high printing cost and this number is growing day-by-day.

Table 5: Type of e-Resources Used

Sl. No.	*Type of Resource*	*Students*	*Faculty*	*Res. Scholars*	*Total*
1.	E-journals	63(76%)	13(16%)	07(8%)	83(43%)
2.	E-books	65(77%)	11(13%)	08(10%)	84(44%)
3.	Bulletin board	04(57%)	03(43%)	00	07(4%)
4.	DVDs	05(56%)	02(22%)	02(22%)	09(5%)
5.	CD-ROM	04(57%)	02(29%)	01(14%)	07(4%)
6.	Floppy diskettes	01(50%)	01(50%)	00	02(1%)
	Total	142	32	18	192

6.6 *Frequency of E-resources Use*

This is one of the most important components of the questionnaire to determine the frequency of use of e-resources. Frequency of access to e-resources determines prior acquaintance of the skills, engagements in research work etc. Those who had operation skills such as use of computers, Internet, intranet etc. can take the best use of e-resources because of consortia based e-resources are being provided to the libraries through IP based access and the library provides e-resources through intranet to the users which is again IP based. However, users accessing e-resources from the library, computer centre etc. can directly access to the same. Data relating to the same are shown below in Table 6.

Table 6: Frequency of E-resources Use

Sl. No.	*Type of Resource*	*Students*	*Faculty*	*Res. Scholars*	*Total*
1.	Daily	44(66%)	18(27%)	05(7%)	67(35%)
2.	Weekly	63(85%)	09(12%)	02(3%)	74(39%)
3.	Monthly	32(70%)	05(11%)	09(20%)	46(24%)
4.	Never	03(60%)	00	02(40%)	05(3%)
	Total	142	32	18	192

Analysis of the data in the Table reveals that, users to access e-resources weekly are more compared to daily or monthly 74 (39%) users prefer to access e-resources weekly where the students population are more compared to other two segments and 67 (35%) users opt for daily and 46 (24%) users monthly. While making an analysis for the users who access daily, again the student populations are more followed by faculties and research scholars. It further reveals that the faculties are more who access e-resources daily compared to weekly. This is a healthy sign and it signifies the faculties involved in research activity.

6.7 *Access to Internet*

In recent years, Internet has emerged as the most powerful medium for storage and retrieval of information. With the unprecedented growth in the quantum of knowledge worldwide and easy accessibility, Internet has become an unavoidable necessity for every institution for higher learning and research. An Internet user has access to a wide variety of services such as electronic mail, file transfer, vast amount of e-resources, breaking news, shopping opportunities, and many more. The data indicates the average time spent on the use of Internet services of the library under study is shown in Table 7.

Table 7: Use of Internet

Sl. No.	*Internet use*	*Students*	*Faculty*	*Res. Scholars*	*Total*
1.	1–4 years	67	03	05	75
2.	5–7 years	50	05	08	63
3.	> 7 years	25	24	05	54
	Total	142	32	18	192

Analysis relating to the use of Internet shows that the highest number of students (67) used Internet with in the span of 1–4 years followed by 50 students during 5–7 years and 25 students have the experience to browse on Internet for more than 7 years. This shows that, during the recent time the students are more Internet literate. But among the faculties, the highest number, *i.e.*, 24 out of 32 are used to Internet during the last 7 years. This is again a healthy sign for the library where the users are used to Internet.

7. Findings

- From the above study, it could be ascertained that the library under study has adequate strength of resources including electronic resources. In the changing scenario, slowly it is dominating the traditional resources so as to overcome the weakness and to facilitate the users with adequate opportunities for sustainable development.
- The efficiency of the library has increased due to the skilled manpower as it is providing adequate electronic resources in multiple forms to the users.
- Efficiency of the library professionals by providing national and international databases and the quality of services also could be measured as the users are happy with the library services.

- Even if, the users are self sufficient to access the e-resources, the library professionals put much effort through various search techniques on the users for more effective use of the e-resources.

8. Conclusion

E-resources are becoming important information resource in today's electronic environment, as they are more up-to-date, and can be accessed anywhere, crossing all geographical boundaries. Through their various search techniques, electronic resources provide extensive links to explore additional resources or related content. Such resources added value to the R&D activities. There has been a rapid urge of the user community to get more and more information online. The development of ICT devices, the rapid rise of electronic databases, and modern e-book technologies have altogether changed the entire scenario of informatics. The user attitude to information is gradually shifting from printed documents to electronic resources and thus, it has become an important area of research for the information professionals in India.

Acknowledgements

The authors would like to convey their profound gratitude to Dr. Saibaba, Deputy Librarian and his staffs for providing the useful data and information for the Dissertation work based on which this paper is prepared.

Electronic Resources Management in Libraries, pp. 274–285

Promotion of E-Resources through Consortia in Science and Technology Libraries: Some Strategies and Future Outlook

K.V. Ratnakar, Aamir Jilani and K. Satyanarayana

ABSTRACT

The Library and Information Science scenario is currently undergoing a rapid and dynamic revolution leading to new generation of information centres with the emphasis on e-resources. At the same time, the cost of scientific journals is increasing at a rate of 8–10% per year. Due to continuing increase of user demands, diminished budgets, galloping subscription rates of periodicals, Libraries are unable to maintain the same number of journals and particularly unable to add any more subscriptions to new journals. A lot of efforts have been taken in past few years to overcome this problem of financial crunch by resource sharing through consortia approach. These revolutionary steps are providing scholarly resources including peer reviewed journals, databases, abstracts proceedings etc. Consortia based library subscriptions to e-journals and electronic full-text databases are picking up best momentum in Delhi. INDEST, CSIR, ICMR, ERMED, CeRA are some of the successful consortium examples in this regard. This paper discusses the promotion of e-resources through consortia in science and technology libraries with focus on Delhi library and information science centres.

1. Introduction

Scientific information is growing rapidly at a rate of about 5–6% every year. There are over 1.3 million papers published every year in scientific journals. To facilitate quick and ready access to such information from these journals to the users several methods have been devised like creation of subject-specific databases that will collect, compile and organize in a systematic way for rapid retrieval. With research becoming increasingly competitive, the demand for scientific information is growing rapidly. The budgets to libraries are also stagnating due to funds crunch. Therefore, libraries of various institutes/centres are under great pressure to provide reasonable access to readers of current information. The increasing cost of journals plays an impact on the libraries all over the world. Alternative innovative strategies are being considered that would ensure access to journals in a cost-effective manner. One of such options that is increasingly finding acceptance is consortia of scientific journals. Consortia is a system through which a common single subscription is obtained through a license from the journal publisher/aggregator readers at institutes/centres located at different sites (all over India) can simultaneously access the content of the database.

This strategy of using the consortia mode to promote access to journals has been widely used in India. A few decades back Lancaster talked about the "paperless society". That day has gone when it was only a dream, now that very idea sounded theoretical all over the world. However, we took a step towards a paperless society very rapidly and most of libraries have begun allocating separate funds for e-resources. Today, most of the librarians are faced with economic problems, especially in developing countries to collect all the new generated information and to satisfy the high degree of aspiration for knowledge of the user.

2. Library Consortia

Library cooperation is very old started long ago, through means as inter-library loan, document delivery, and library networks etc. which are internationally accepted. At present, the more accepted system of resource sharing is library consortia which have come into existence with a wide coverage. Consortia approach is one of the many ways of maintaining cooperation and coordination among the libraries and in fact, it has emerged as the "state of the art" in library cooperation in recent years. Typically the aim of the consortia is to achieve what the members of the group cannot achieve individually. A consortium is said to be a cooperative arrangement among group of institutions or an association or society (American Heritage Dictionary). Consortia are commonly formed to increase the purchasing power of the collaborating institutions to expand the resource availability and to offer automated services. With the advent of e-resources, the concept of consortia has been mooted mainly for the acquisition of e-journals. Today most of the resources procured through the consortium are mainly e-resources, it has become possible for the users to access and download the required materials without even going through the elaborate process of intra-library lending. Though library consortia have been created with narrow purpose, these can be turned into efficient instruments for sharing all types of library resources.

2.1 *Definition of Consortium*

A consortium could be described as a group of organizations who come together to fulfill a combined objective that usefully requires co-operation and the sharing of resources. The participant institutes/centres need to have a clear common goal in order to ensure their success. The aim therefore should be to deliver "more than the sum of the individual parts". A library consortium formation can be local, regional, state, inter institutional or at the national level.

2.2 *Need for Library Consortium*

The consortium is needed for libraries due to the following reasons:

- ***Information Explosion:*** The most challenging tasks for the Library and information centers all over the world are to collect and manage the huge information that is being acquired. It is impossible to monitor all the information published in various forms and provide the same to the users. To cope up with this situation, the phenomenon of consortia has become very important during the last few years
- ***Diversity of User Needs:*** The growing needs of users is increasingly diverse, interdisciplinary, ever expanding and the increase in research and the rapid Information and Communication Technology (ICT) developments have all changed the routines of traditional librarianship. As the information demand of the user to a greater extent is beyond the control of the capacity of librarians, Library consortia play an important role to overcome this problem.
- ***Financial Crunch:*** The explosion of information, in multidimensional form and voluminous development has urged the libraries to adopt new philosophies and technologies for collection development and reduce the costs of information. Today, most of the librarians are faced with economic problems, especially in developing countries to collect all the new generated information and to satisfy the high degree of aspiration for knowledge of the users.
- ***Difficulty to be Self Sufficient*:** The basic aim of an academic or research library is to meet the teaching, learning, scholarly-research and other information needs of its users and research scholars and that too effectively and efficiently. No library is self sufficient to purchase all the books, Journals and other library documents with in their library budget. So, users belonging to different institutions or libraries may use library resources through consortia.

3. Factors to be Considered before Formation of Consortia

Various factors have to be taken into consideration for starting and running an effective functioning of a successful consortium. Like resources identification on the basis of usage and usability, long term planning of the technology infrastructure, access to back runs of periodicals copyright and licensing, archival issue, price issue all of which make consortia economically favorable and attractive. Last but not the least, designing and launching a library consortium should be long term sustenance and robust models towards achieving the above goals.

3.1 *Types of Consortia*

Library consortia function in different ways. During the last three decades, libraries have developed a variety of organizational models. At one end of the spectrum are the loosely affiliated buying clubs where libraries come together primarily to share a discounted rate on electronic journals and databases, whereas on the other end are consortia that are tightly integrated organizations sharing a variety of resources which require a long term commitment and collaborative decision making at all levels. Theoretically, consortia may be of following types depending on their characteristics.

By Type of Libraries

Consortia of Multi-type Libraries: In this type of consortium participating libraries are of different types, such as public, academic and special.

Consortia of Same Type of Libraries: The members of such a consortium are of same type, such as consortium of public libraries, consortium of academic libraries, etc. DRDO or CSIR E-Journals Consortium is such a consortium.

By Geographical Region of Coverage

Local Level Consortia: This consists of libraries situated in a particular city, town of district, e.g. BOSLA (Bombay Science Librarians' Association), which was possibly the first library consortium in the country.

State Level Consortia: In such a consortium libraries of one particular state participate. There is perhaps no such consortium in the country at present.

National Level Consortia: Libraries belonging to a country are its members. INDEST is a national level consortium, but covering only libraries of scientific and technical institutions.

Regional Level Consortia: In such a consortium libraries of a particular region participate.

International Level Consortia: In this consortium libraries belonging to different countries participate. This may be formed either by individual libraries, such as OCLC, or by bringing different national consortia under one umbrella. Such federation of consortia is known as '*Meta Consortia*' such as 'International Coalition of Library Consortia' which comprises of nearly 150 library consortia from around the world.

By Subject or Area of Coverage

Single Discipline Consortia: In such a consortium organizations dealing with same or similar disciplines join hand, such as FORSA (Forum for Resource Sharing in Astronomy and Astrophysics).

Multi-discipline Consortia: Such a consortium deals with resources in multiple disciplines. UGC sponsored INFONET is such a consortium, which deals with multiple subjects.

From Organizational Point of View

Loosely Knit Federation: In such a consortium there is no central body of dedicated staff to look after the consortium activities. Some libraries join hand for some immediate gain for a particular purpose. It is often not of permanent nature.

Tightly Knit Organization: Such a consortium is of permanent type, having a central body with membership of participating libraries for guiding the activities of the consortium and also some dedicated staff for performing the consortium activities.

On the Basis of Formation

Non-sponsored Consortia: Such a consortium is formed voluntarily by participating libraries by sharing the expenses. FORSA again is such a consortium.

Sponsored Consortia: This type of consortium is sponsored by a central organization and the major expenses are borne by it. Here sometimes the sponsoring body itself carries out the major activities of the consortium. UGC-Infonet is such a consortium.

Obviously, the above categories are not mutually exclusive. Most of the existing consortia naturally fall in more than one category.

3.2 *Salient Features of Library Consortium*

- To eliminate the different problems faced by the libraries and to provide various services to the users.
- To meet the thrust of information of the vast people due to rapid growth of population all over the world.
- To cope up with the newly generated knowledge published in different forms, such as, printed and non-printed documents, electronic media on various disciplines, multi-disciplinary and new generated subject areas.
- To collect all the documents published at the national and international level because of financial crunch in the libraries; and
- To overcome to language barriers, *i.e.*, primary documents are being published by the developed countries like USA, UK, France, Japan *etc.* and among them the non-English speaking countries produce majority of scientific literatures in their mother languages.

4. Indian Scenario

The tremendous information revolution and proliferation have brought about drastic changes to the function and services in all types of libraries in India during the last two decades. Many libraries in India till today are not in a position to afford to procure all documents and subscribe to core journals in major disciplines or CD-ROM databases, due to their financial crunch. As a result, Indian library networks started with the initiatives of NISSAT in forming CALIBNET in 1986, DELNET in 1988 and other networks subsequently to promote resource sharing among libraries. The UGC (University Grant Commission, India) set up INFLIBNET in 1988. There are many libraries in India have set up consortia for resource sharing amongst the libraries, such as Indian Institute of Astrophysics (IIA) Library, Inter-University Centre for Astronomy and Astrophysics (IUCAA) Library, National Centre for Radio Astrophysics (NCRA) Library, Nizamiah Observatory (NO) Library, Physical Research Laboratory (PRL) Library, Raman Research Institute (RRI) Library, Tata Institute of Fundamental Research (TIFR) Library, Uttar Pradesh State Observatory (UPSO) Library. The main objectives of these consortia are for better resources sharing, to reduce information costs, for speedy delivery of documents, to keep abreast of new developments etc[6]. All the libraries in India are not able to come under any consortia system and most of the information generated by Indian scholar in different subject fields is not fully represented in the international scenario. That is why, there is a necessity to prepare Indian databases and link them up with consortium activities. Much emphasis should be given at the national level in India for the development of documentary information resources, because it is considered as vital resources to promote the development of economy, science, technology and culture etc.

4.1 *Consortia in Science and Technology Libraries in Delhi*

There are six major consortia viz. INDEST-AICTE, CeRA, CSIR (NKRC), DRDO, ERMED and ICMR based at Delhi. This paper covers all except DRDO E-journal Consortium.

INDES-AICTE Consortium

The INDEST (Indian National Digital Library of Engineering, Sciences and Technology) Consortium was set up by the Ministry of Human Resource Development (MHRD). The Ministry provides funds required for subscription to electronic resources for 57 institutions including IISc, IITs, NITs, IIMs and a few other centrally funded government institutions through the consortium headquarters set up at the IIT, Delhi. Besides, 60 government or government-aided engineering colleges and technical departments in universities have joined the consortium with financial support from the AICTE (All India Council of Technical Education). The consortium has an active mailing list and a website hosted at IIT, Delhi. The Consortium subscribes to over 12,000 electronic journals from a number of publishers and aggregators. The major publishers are ACM Digital Library, Emerald, EBSCO, IEEE/IEE Electronic Library, Springer etc. Nineteen Delhi based institutes are under INDEST.

CSIR Consortium

The Council of Scientific and Industrial Research (CSIR), a public-funded organization, is one of the India's largest R&D organization established in 1942 with a chain of 37 national laboratories and institutes. CSIR is carrying out the research work in various disciplines all over the country. It provides an access to 4500^{+} world-class e-journals, Patent databases, standards, bibliographic databases etc to all CSIR labs, as against the print base of 20–200 print journals. The major publishers are Elsevier, Oxford University Press, Sage, Springer, Emerald, and Blackwell. Six Delhi based institutes are under the CSIR consortia.

ICMR Consortium

The Indian Council of Medical Research (ICMR), the apex body in India for the formulation, coordination and promotion of biomedical research, having been founded in 1911, is one of the oldest medical research bodies in the world. ICMR has undertaken various activities to help address the challenges of digital technology to research scholars, scientists. A consortium is the best way to fulfill all the requirement of the Users. ICMR has undertaken various activities to help address the challenges of digital technology to research scholars, scientists. It covers 1940 journals received collectively at 29 institutions/centre of ICMR. Major publishers are Elsevier, Nature Publishing Group, Gist, etc. Four Delhi based institutes are under ICMR Consortium. ICMR has initiated two types of consortia:

- JCCC@ICMR covering all ICMR subscribed journals and full-text of over 200 free journals.
- ICMR e-consortia providing full-text of only subscribed e-journals.

ERMED Consortium

National Medical Library under Director General Health Services (DGHS), Ministry of Health and Family Welfare recently started ERMED (Electronic Resources in Medicine) electronic journal consortium for providing full-text electronic journal service to 39 medical colleges and institutions including 10 DGHS libraries and 28 ICMR libraries and the AIIMS library totaling Seventy-eight institutes and libraries. The Consortium offers over million articles in the open access mode from over 1600 medical journals. Major publishers covered are BMJ Publishing, Cambridge University Press, Cengage Learning, IOS Press, Lippincott William Wilkins, Oxford University Press, Proquest, and Royal Society of Medicine Press. Sixteen Delhi based institutes are under ERMED Consortium.

CeRA Consortium for e-Resources in Agriculture

CeRA is Consortium of e-journals being subscribed by NAIP, ICAR and provided access to 123 libraries of Agriculture (NARS) for the years 2008–10 (3 years). IASRI is also one of the Libraries among 123. To develop the existing R&D information resource base of ICAR institutes/universities, etc., comparable to that existing in world's leading institutions/organizations. The Consortium consists of Deemed Universities, ICAR Headquarters and *Krishi Anusandhan Bhawan*, National Bureau, Institutes, National Research Centres, Project Directorates, State Agricultural Universities. It covers total 123 libraries and institutes. It covers 2905 journals, Majors Publishers are Springer Link, Taylor and Francis, Elsevier, Informatics etc. Seventeen Delhi based institutes are under CeRA Consortium.

5. Analysis

To understand the success of ongoing consortia and to see whether the readers expectations are matching by the information provided, a survey was conducted through questionnaire. For collection of data, a questionnaire was prepared and circulated for relevant information from the member libraries and various consortia under study. These were circulated to the various consortia users, librarians and publishers in the Delhi region. Institutions were asked to furnish information about consortia management aspects and usages.

The following are the major findings:

- Delhi-based S&T libraries under consortia: It was found (table 1) that INDEST and ERMED have more institutions in Delhi than ICMR, CSIR, and CeRA.
- Population of users by discipline: It was found (table 2) that users of clinical discipline uses consortia more than library science, computer and engineering.
- Usage by gender: It was found (table 3) that usage of consortia by women is slightly higher than men.
- Population of users by type of institute they affiliated to: It was found (table 4) that majority of access and use of e-resources in S&T libraries based in Delhi are from research institutes (92.3%) followed by hospitals (7.7%).
- Awareness on subscription to Online Consortia. It was noted that majority of users (92.3%) are aware that their library has subscriptions to some online journals and consortia.
- Periodicity of Usage of Consortia. The majority of the users accessed e-journals through consortia either daily (38.5%) or weekly (38.5%). A considerable proportion of users (23%) accessed consortia seldom.
- Preference to online method of retrieving full-text journals: About 70% of users had preference for online method of retrieving full-text journal articles over print journals. None of the users working in hospitals preferred online retrieval whereas majority of users working in research institutes (75%) preferred online retrieval.
- Perception about e-journals and online searching.

- The perception about the usage of e-journals and online usage decreases the quality/vigour of research is agreed by considerable proportion of users. The majority of the female users (60%) are agreed with this statement while majority of male users (62.5%) disagreed and 37.5% are agreed. All users agreed that e-journals and online searching increases the scholarly productivity of the user.
- Advantage of e-journals.
- 77% users obtained information related to their study through e-journals.
- 85% of users exchanged more journal articles with colleagues because e-journals make distribution of articles easier and less costly.
- 92.3% of users agreed that user became more organized in archiving papers by using e-journals and creating own mini library.

Table 1: Consortia vs Number of Participant Libraries

Consortium	*Institutes in Delhi*
CeRA	7
ERMED	16
ICMR	4
CSIR	6
INDEST	19

Table 2: Subject Coverage vs Member Libraries

Discipline	*Number*	*%*
Clinical	18	69.2
Computer-related	2	7.7
Engineering	2	7.7
Library science	4	15.4
Total	26	100.0

Table 3: Participant Libraries vs Type of Libraries

Type of Institute	*Number*	*%*
Hospital	2	7.7
Research institute	24	92.3
Total	26	100.0

The following are the major findings of the perception about the e-resources by librarians.

- Librarians are willing to join the consortia to acquire e-journals
- The average list price of e-books increased by 25%
- Librarians acquire e-journals, books through e-consortia
- Librarians consider consortia to provide user-friendly front end, comprehensive database, support standard retrieval format, satisfactory usage. These features encourage librarian to go for consortia access
- Various marketing methods and tools follow for enhancement of user awareness and usage of e-journal consortia. Librarians adopted various methods for user's awareness which include library website, e-mail/news updates, orientation programmes/workshops, training users
- Usage of digital resources increases the growth of users
- Librarians save up to 75% of money by adopting of consortia.

The following findings were observed after the analysis of questionnaire on e-resources for publishers.

- Analysis shows publisher launches journals frequently. Commercial companies have a much higher journal growth rate than not-for-profit organizations.
- Linking from abstracting databases to article or from journal article citations to the full-text of the article cited.
- Publishers charge subscribers for access to back volumes.
- Publishers make back volumes available online—the majority from 1st volume, 1st issue.
- Publishers offer multi journal bundles by subject, or by journal type (*i.e.*, primary, review, abstract journal etc.).

6. Suggestions

6.1 *National Library Consortia*

The possibilities of ICTs, digital information, electronic document delivery, library consortia, web-based operations, etc. have helped to provide better services to the users. But wide disparity in the availability and use of academic and research information still prevails among different universities and research institutions in India. Moreover, establishment and maintenance of separate library consortium for each group of government and government supported institutions in a country has lead to the duplication of efforts and additional investment. Since the present pattern of higher education and research is inter-disciplinary, clear cut demarcation of areas of subject interest are cross-disciplinary and also at micro-level. This underlines the need for providing access of information in all subject areas to the students, teachers and researchers in all branches. Establishment of a National Library Consortium automatically will bring economy, efficiency and equality in information availability and use.

6.2 *International Library Consortia*

Library consortia have grown substantially over the past ten years globally. As this resurgent consortial movement has begun to mature, and as publishers and vendors have begun to adapt to consortial purchasing models, consortia have expanded their agendas for action. Library Consortia from India also join International Coalition of Library Consortia (ICOLC). FORSA and INDEST have already joined this International Coalition. More number of library consortia from India could join as a coalition with the International Coalition of Library Consortia (ICOLC) which has been in existence since 1996. The Coalition of these consortia facilitates discussion among consortia on issues of common interest and its members informed about electronic information resources, pricing practices of electronic publishers and vendors, and other issues of importance to consortium directors and governing boards. The Coalition helps the information provider community to discuss product offerings and issues of mutual concern.

6.3 *Virtual Library*

The present scenario requires a whole new approach to library cooperation. So far library cooperation has mainly been established in order to handle inter-library lending and document delivery on the individual document level. The new opportunities offered by the technological developments requires much more commitment and indeed much more ability from the management to give in an institutional autonomy in the sense that are library operations and services must be driven in cooperation with other libraries or even outsourced to other libraries. If the libraries really want to fight the current crisis they must interact in new ways. In reality what eventually must happen is that the concept of the single-primarily-self dependent library must fade away and the larger virtual library must be in place. We have for a number of years now talked about the virtual library. Now it must be in place very quickly.

7. Conclusions

It can be inferred that access to electronic information resources specially e-journals through consortia has numerous advantages and has to be taken more seriously to promote teaching, learning, scholarship, research and development activities. It is felt that the concept of consortia can work well among similar institutions. Although, it is debatable issue in developing country like India, as to whether electronic journals are a necessity or luxury. Even if they are considered to be a necessity, the few libraries in India that have managed to access electronic journals find it difficult to sustain them due to the exorbitant cost and the fluctuating license models offers by different publishers. Consortia in India are still in their infancy and there is a need to study their various models, guidelines and methodologies. The phenomenon of consortia formation among libraries in India is a recent development that started around last five years or so. However, library cooperation is a very old concept and a form of resource sharing. The new object of resource sharing has changed the old concept due to multidimensional growth of published documents through R&D activities in recent past, cost of the information, advancement of newly invented technologies for information processing and dissemination etc. Indian libraries should seriously rethink and reinitiate consortium movement like western countries for maximum utilization of resources at a reduced cost, time and space.

References

[1] Biswas, Ch, Bidhan and Dasgupta, K., Swapan (2003). Opportunities for libraries in managing and resource sharing through consortia: A New challenge for Indian librarians. In Salgar M., Mr S. and Kumbar S., Dr T. and Saraf, Dr Veena and Buvakutty, Dr M. and Chand, Mr Prem, Eds. Proceedings Convention for Accomodation of Libraries in Education and Research Institutions, Ahmedabad, India.

[2] Bedi, Shalu and Sharma, Kiran (2008). Library consortia : a step forward the Information Society. In Mahajan, Preeti and Vohra, Ranjana and Chakravarty, Rupak, Eds. Proceedings ICSSR Sponsored Seminar on "Trends and Strategic Issues for Libraries in Global Information Society." March 18–19, 2008, Organized by: Department of Library and Information Science, Punjab University, Chandigarh, Pages 185–189, Punjab University, Chandigarh.

[3] Rahman, Md Anisur, Nahar, Mahmudun and Akhter, Razina (2006). Resource Sharing, Networking and Library Consortia: problem and prospects in Bangladesh.4th Convention PLANNER-2006, Mizoram Univ., Aizawl, 9–10 Nov, 2006.

[4] Paul Pandian, M. and Karisiddappa, C.R. (2003). Technology issues for library consortia in India. CALIBER 2003, INFLIBNET.

[5] INDEST (http://paniitd.ac.in/indest).

[6] CSIR (http://www.csir.res.in).

[7] JCCC-ICMR (http://www.jccc-icmr.informindia.co.in).

[8] ICMR (http://icmr.nic.in).

[9] ERMED (http://www.nmlermed.in).

[10] CeRA (http://www.cera.jccc.in).

Section–VI

Digital Rights Management and IPRs

Electronic Resources Management in Libraries, pp. 289–298

Copyright in the Context of Open Access

Mangala Anil Hirwade and Anil W. Hirwade

ABSTRACT

Open Access (OA) movement is gaining throughout the globe. OA Journals and OA Archives are the two major vehicles of Open Access. The paper takes an overview of copyright issues in open access context. The paper discusses Creative Common License system to restrict the use and creation of new knowledge under open access. It also discusses golden road of open access and to have greater access and visibility to the scholarly publication. The authors follow Self Archiving which is done in three ways; by putting the published article on personal websites, by archiving it on Institutional repository or by archiving it in open archives. In this paper, a study has been carried out to trace the self archiving policies of Social Science journals. A total 3,062 journals in various subjects under Social Sciences indexed by Social Science Citation Index were selected and Sherpa Romeo database was used to trace the copyright policies of the publishers of these journals.

1. Introduction

Copyright is not a right to copy but protests the rights of owner by preventing others from exploiting the work without the Copyright owner's consensus. Copyright plays a vital role in the world of publishing scientific, medical and technical content. It provides authors with a set of rights to enable them to utilize their work and to recognize as the creator of the work. Publishers are empowered to act on behalf of the author through a copyright transfer or exclusive license to copy, publish, and adapt works, whilst protecting their integrity. In this way, publishers are empowered to do various things on behalf of the author, for example to ensure that the article is widely disseminated, that all requests for the rights to re-use content and provision of permissions are answered efficiently, and to ensure that the original is correctly attributed (Tempest, 2012).

Open Access (OA) is free, online access to the full text of research articles for anyone, web wide, without the severe restrictions on users commonly imposed by publisher copyright agreements. There are two roads to open access (Arunachalam and Muthu, 2012).

- ***Green Road:*** The "green road" of OA self-archiving, where authors provide OA to their own published articles, by making their own e-prints (the final accepted version) freely available to all by placing them on institutional or central repositories.

- ***Golden Road:*** The "golden road" of OA journal-publishing, where journals provide OA to their articles (either by charging the author/institution, a publication or processing fee instead of charging a subscription fee from the user/institution, or by simply making their online edition free for all and recouping the publication and production costs from other source).

The term was coined by the Budapest Open Access Initiative in 2002, and was given a quite explicit definition: "Open access to literature means free availability on the public Internet, permitting any users to read, download, copy, distribute, print, search or link to the full-text of these articles, crawl them for indexing, pass them as data to software, or use them for any other lawful purpose, without financial, legal or technical barriers other than those inseparable from gaining access to the Internet itself. The only constraint on reproduction and distribution, and the only role for copyright in this domain, should be to give authors control over the integrity of their work and the right to be properly acknowledged and cited" (Budapest OA Initiative, 2002).

2. Copyright and Open Access

Within OA publishing there seems to be a dilemma over copyright and the three choices facing an author: retain copyright, share it or transfer it (Hoorn and Graaf, 2006).

2.1 *Retain It—An Early OA Copyright Model*

The OA journals allow authors to retain their copyright and restrict reuse to educational purposes. This is an early OA Copyright Model in which:

- The author keeps the copyright.
- The copyright notice mentions that classroom use is free, but other uses depend on the permission of the authors.
- The journal asks only for a License to publish the article as the first publisher.
- The author is obliged to mention the journal reference as a source whenever the author later republishes the article on other platforms.

These early OA journals have frequently been published by the academics themselves without the involvement of a publisher or publishing organization. Leaving the copyright with the author spares the editors the trouble of answering permission requests.

2.2 *Share It—With a Creative Commons License*

Creative Commons (CC) was founded in 2001, being in part inspired by the open source software movement. Creative Commons has changed the copyright slogan "all rights reserved" into the slogan "some rights reserved," and has created various types of Licenses whereby the creators can protect their works while still encouraging certain defined uses.

2.3 *Transfer It (Partly)—Traditional Journals that go Open Access Way*

The journals that switched from the traditional model of publishing to an OA model use Licenses that keep the copyright with the author, but the author transfers all commercial exploitation rights to the publisher. The publisher here leaves the copyright with the author, only requiring an exclusive License to publish the article first and claiming all commercial exploitation rights. In addition, the publishing group gives the author a percentage of the royalties if they enter into a commercial republishing or redistribution deal on the basis of the author's article.

The advantage for authors is that they can do whatever they want with their own article without asking the publishing group's permission as long as commercial rights are not involved. The other advantage, of course, is that the model provides for potential revenue for the authors from royalties: so far, this seems a unique approach in the world of academic publishing.

2.4 *Creative Commons and Copyright*

The idea of universal access to research, education, and culture is made possible by the Internet, but our legal and social systems do not always allow that idea to be realized. Copyright was created long before the emergence of the Internet, and can make it hard to legally perform actions one take it for granted on the network: copy, paste, edit source, and post onto the Web. The default setting of copyright law requires all of these actions to have explicit permission, granted in advance. To achieve the vision of universal access, someone needed to provide a free, public, and standardized infrastructure that creates a balance between the reality of the Internet and the reality of copyright laws. That someone is Creative Commons.

The dual forces of copyright law restrictions and a new digital culture led to the launch of CC—a set of licensing tools that stands between the All Rights Reserved of traditional copyright and No Rights Reserved that is the public domain. In other words, Some Rights Reserved (Gordon-Murnane, n.d.).

Creative Commons is an alternative to traditional copyright, developed by a nonprofit organization of the same name. By default, most original works are protected by copyright, which confers specific rights regarding use and distribution. Creative Commons allows copyright owners to release some of those rights while retaining others, with the goal of increasing access to and sharing of intellectual property.

Creative Commons Licenses are becoming increasingly popular with both authors and publishers. Many OA publishers use Creative Commons Licenses to ensure that the content of the articles published in their journals are reusable in the widest sense: that is, they can be reproduced, abstracted, 'mashed up' with other material to produce new information, mined by text-mining and data-mining tools and so on.

Every CC license also ensures licensors get the credit for their work they deserve. Every CC license works around the world lasts as long as copyright lasts (because they are built on copyright). These common features serve as the baseline, on top of which licensors can choose to grant additional permissions when deciding how they want their work to be used.

3. Types of Licenses

According to Creative Commons, there are six types of licenses:

- ***Attribution CC BY:*** This license lets others distribute, remix, tweak, and build upon the work, even commercially, as long as they credit for the original creation. This is the most accommodating of licenses offered. It is recommended for maximum dissemination and use of licensed materials.
- ***Attribution-No Derivatives CC BY-ND:*** This license allows for redistribution, commercial and non-commercial, as long as it is passed along unchanged and in whole but credit goes to original author.
- ***Attribution-Non Commercial-Share Alike CC BY-NC-SA:*** This license lets others remix, tweak, and build upon the work non-commercially, as long as they credit original author and license their new creations under the identical terms.
- ***Attribution-ShareAlike CC BY-SA:*** This license lets others remix, tweak, and build upon the work even for commercial purposes, as long as they give credit to original author and license their new creations under the identical terms. This license is often compared to "copyleft" free and open source software licenses. All new works based on the original author's work will carry the same license, so any derivatives will also allow commercial use. This is the license used by Wikipedia, and is recommended for materials that would benefit from incorporating content from Wikipedia and similarly licensed projects.
- ***Attribution-Non Commercial CC BY-NC:*** This license lets others remix, tweak, and build upon the work non-commercially, and although their new works must also acknowledge the author and be non-commercial, they do not have to license their derivative works on the same terms.
- ***Attribution-Non Commercial-No Derivatives CC BY-NC-ND:*** This license is the most restrictive of six main licenses, only allowing others to download the works and share them with others as long as they credit the original author, but they cannot change them in any way or use them commercially.

4. Self Archiving and Copyright

When an author writes an article, he pursues three goals viz. to publish it in a refereed journal to get recognition, to get read by others and have more citations and greater impact. To be used and built upon, an article must first be accessed. A published article is accessible only to those researchers who happen to be at institutions that can afford to subscribe to a particular journal in which it was published. To have greater access and visibility, one solution is Self Archiving. It is achieved in three ways; by putting the article on personal websites, by archiving it on Institutional repository or by archiving it in open archives.

According to Wikipedia, self archiving involves depositing a free copy of a digital document on the World Wide Web in order to provide OA to it. Usually peer-reviewed research journals, conference articles and theses are deposited by the author himself/herself or any other with the consent of copyright holder in an institutional repository or any other open archive for the purpose of maximizing its accessibility, usage and citation impact. Self-archiving is a good method to promote open-access.

Self archiving is a matter of attitudes, awareness and scholarship. Authors who practice self archiving have to concentrate on copyright issues. Mostly authors deposit their pre-print articles before publishing in peer-reviewed conventional journals. That will be the authors final version of the article and in some cases authors should have to sign copyright agreements with the publisher or funding agency. Therefore, most of post-print articles require copyright holders consent prior to deposit them in an OA archive. Many digital archives tag the article as pre-print, post-print or peer-reviewed (Arachchige, 2009).

The publication process comprises (a) writing of a paper by an author, (b) submission of the written paper to a journal by the author, (c) reviewing of the submitted paper by referees and editors, (d) revision of the paper if needed, (e) submission of the revised paper by the author, (f) copyediting and formatting of the accepted paper by the publisher, and (h) publication of the paper by the journal. Self archiving in an e-print repository commonly takes place at two points in the publication process. Firstly, before the paper is refereed, the author may post it on the e-print repository as a "pre-print". Secondly, when the paper has been revised in response to referees' comments, the final version of the paper can be mounted on the repository as a "post-print". The post-print is normally formatted by the author and so may not incorporate changes made by the publisher at the pre-publication stage. At each of these stages the author creates metadata describing the paper which can be searched by users.

5. Sherpa-Romeo Database

There may be a confusion in the mind of the author while self archiving the published article, regarding copyright violation. Sherpa-Romeo database gives a solution to this problem. It has studied the copyright policies of the journal publishers worldwide and categorized the publishers into four categories viz. Green, Blue, Yellow and White. Green publishers allow archiving of pre-print, post-print and publisher's version/pdf; Blue publishers allow post-print and publisher's version/pdf; Yellow publishers allow archiving of pre-print only; and White publishers do not support self archiving at all (Sherpa website).

The present study has been carried out to trace the self archiving policies of social science journals. Total 3062 journals in various subjects under social sciences indexed by Social Science Citation Index (SSCI) were selected and Sherpa-Romeo database was used to trace the copyright policies of the publishers of these journals. SSCI is an interdisciplinary citation index product of Thomson Reuters. It is made available online through the Web of Science service for a fee. This database product provides information to identify the articles cited most frequently and by what publisher and author (SSCI). The Sherpa-Romeo database was studied in order to trace the archiving policies of Social Science Journals. The publisher's category was also observed and the details are given in Table 1.

Table 1: Archiving Policies of Social Science Journals

Sl. No.	*Subject*	*No. of Jls*	*% of Sherpa-Romeo Category*					
			Green	*Yellow*	*White*	*Blue*	*Ungraded*	*Not Found*
1.	Anthropology	65	32.31	33.85	7.69	1.54	23.08	1.54
2.	Area Studies	41	24.39	43.90	4.88	2.44	21.95	2.44
3.	Business Finance	62	38.71	40.32	4.84	0.00	11.29	4.84
4.	Business	78	43.59	39.74	3.85	5.13	7.69	0.00
5.	Communication	54	12.96	75.93	5.56	0.00	5.56	0.00
6.	Criminology And Penology	37	16.22	72.97	5.41	0.00	5.41	0.00
7.	Cultural Studies	8	25.00	75.00	0.00	0.00	0.00	0.00
8.	Demography	21	33.33	47.62	0.00	0.00	19.05	0.00
9.	Economics	223	43.05	44.84	3.59	1.35	6.73	0.45
10.	Educational and Educational Research	130	21.54	57.69	8.46	3.85	7.69	0.77
11.	Education Special	35	14.29	51.43	14.29	2.86	14.29	2.86
12.	Environmental Studies	69	46.38	39.13	1.45	4.35	8.70	0.00
13.	Ergonomics	13	46.15	38.46	7.69	7.69	0.00	0.00
14.	Ethics	35	51.43	31.43	2.86	8.57	5.71	0.00
15.	Ethnic Studies	13	7.69	84.62	0.00	0.00	7.69	0.00
16.	Family Studies	32	21.88	65.63	6.25	0.00	6.25	0.00
17.	Geography	52	26.92	55.77	5.77	0.00	9.62	1.92
18.	Gerontology	24	33.33	37.50	12.50	16.67	0.00	0.00

Sl. No.	*Subject*	*No. of Jls*	*% of Sherpa-Romeo Category*					
			Green	*Yellow*	*White*	*Blue*	*Ungraded*	*Not Found*
19.	Health Policy Service	47	40.43	42.55	10.64	0.00	6.38	0.00
20.	History and Philosophy	33	48.48	33.33	3.03	0.00	15.15	0.00
21.	History of Social Sciences	20	40.00	55.00	0.00	0.00	5.00	0.00
22.	History	23	21.74	65.22	4.35	0.00	8.70	0.00
23.	Hospitality, Leisure, Sport and Tourism	26	23.08	38.46	3.85	19.23	15.38	0.00
24.	Industrial Relations and Labor	18	27.78	50.00	0.00	0.00	22.22	0.00
25.	Information Science and Library Science	66	50.00	30.30	3.03	4.55	7.58	4.55
26.	International Relations	61	18.03	57.38	4.92	1.64	14.75	3.28
27.	Law	108	18.52	24.07	12.04	0.00	44.44	0.93
28.	Linguistics	106	44.34	37.74	4.72	2.83	7.55	2.83
29.	Management	111	45.95	38.74	2.70	4.50	7.21	0.90
30.	Nursing	70	21.43	52.86	5.71	0.00	20.00	0.00
31.	Planning and Development	45	28.89	64.44	4.44	0.00	2.22	0.00
32.	Political Science	107	19.63	58.88	3.74	0.00	14.95	2.80
33.	Psychiatry	95	38.95	35.79	12.63	1.05	11.58	0.00
34.	Psychology, Applied	60	35.00	46.67	13.33	5.00	0.00	0.00
35.	Psychology, Biological	14	85.71	14.29	0.00	0.00	0.00	0.00
36.	Psychology, Clinical	91	45.05	37.36	5.49	4.40	4.40	3.30
37.	Psychology, Developmental	61	42.62	42.62	9.84	0.00	3.28	1.64
38.	Psychology, Educational	47	17.02	21.28	6.38	0.00	55.32	0.00
39.	Psychology, Experimental	79	49.37	24.05	3.80	1.27	21.52	0.00
40.	Psychology, Mathematical	11	45.45	45.45	9.09	0.00	0.00	0.00
41.	Psychology, Multidisciplinary	109	26.61	46.79	6.42	1.83	15.60	2.75
42.	Psychology, Psychoanalysis	13	23.08	30.77	7.69	0.00	38.46	0.00

Sl. No.	*Subject*	*No. of Jls*	*% of Sherpa-Romeo Category*					
			Green	*Yellow*	*White*	*Blue*	*Ungraded*	*Not Found*
43.	Psychology, Social	52	40.38	44.23	9.62	1.92	3.85	0.00
44.	Public Administration	32	12.50	81.25	0.00	3.13	3.13	0.00
45.	Public, Environ. and Occupational Health	87	37.93	41.38	8.05	5.75	6.90	0.00
46.	Rehabilitation	56	23.21	35.71	17.86	3.57	17.86	1.79
47.	Social Issues	31	22.58	58.06	3.23	0.00	16.13	0.00
48.	Social Sciences, Biomedical	32	40.63	46.88	3.13	0.00	9.38	0.00
49.	Social Sciences, Interdisciplinary	65	36.92	49.23	6.15	0.00	6.15	1.54
50.	Social Sciences, Mathematical Methods	39	41.03	41.03	2.56	5.13	5.13	5.13
51.	Social Work	32	18.75	68.75	0.00	0.00	12.50	0.00
52.	Sociology	117	20.51	59.83	5.98	0.85	10.26	2.56
53.	Substance Abuse	24	33.33	50.00	4.17	0.00	12.50	0.00
54.	Transportation	18	72.22	22.22	5.56	0.00	0.00	0.00
55.	Urban Studies	35	22.86	57.14	8.57	2.86	8.57	0.00
56.	Women's Studies	29	13.79	65.52	6.90	3.45	6.90	3.45
Total Journals		3062	32.73*	47.34*	5.62*	2.27*	11.10*	0.93*
			* Average %					

From the Table it has been observed that:

- SSCI includes highest number of journals pertaining to Economics (223).
- Maximum numbers of Social Science journals are under Yellow category *i.e.* 47.34%, followed by Green category (32.73%). A small percentage (5.62%) of journals are under white category which do not allow self-archiving and 2.27% journals are under Blue category. 11.10% journals are ungraded and 0.93% journals do not provide details of self-archiving policies.

5.1 *Fair Dealing Button*

The articles published in the journals allowing self archiving can be immediately archived by authors. But the remaining journals either endorsed only the self-archiving of the un-refereed pre-print, or imposed an embargo of 6–12 months or more before their authors could make their refereed final drafts OA, or they did not endorse OA self-archiving at all. This was born and later called it as Request-a-Copy Button, the Email EPrint Request Button, the Fair Dealing Button, the Fair Use Button, etc. The button appears on an Institutional Repository's (IR) page describing the metadata for a refereed journal (or conference) article whose full-text is deposited in the IR as closed access rather than OA. The button then makes it possible for would-be readers to request that the author e-mail the EPrint to them for individual research purposes under the provisions of fair dealing in the world's Copyright Acts (Sale *et al.*).

6. Conclusions

Copyright in a work is always a collection of rights. In the case of scholarly written works, copyright covers what may be done with the work in terms of making copies, making derivative works, abstracting parts of it for citation or quotation elsewhere and so on. In order to increase the visibility and accessibility of the research output, the authors follow green road or golden road and make the creation available under open access. Creative Commons Licenses allow people to retain the copyright of their intellectual property while also specifying that those materials can be used under certain conditions. Self archiving is a concept which gives greater accessibility and visibility to the scholarly and peer reviewed works published in the works which are not covered under open access. Self archiving improves the citation index of the individual work. Sherpa-Romeo database helps the researcher tremendously before self archiving of the research publication and to know the copyright policies of the publishers worldwide.

References

[1] Arachchige, J.J.G. (2009). Promotion of open access through self-archiving in Sri Lanka: Getting experiences from E-LIS. Retrieved 15 February 2012 from http://eprints.rclis.org/ 16441/1/ NACLIS_full_paper_revised_2009.pdf

[2] Aunachalam, Subbiah and Muthu, Madhan (2012). Open access to scholarly literature in India—A status report (with emphasis on scientific literature). Retrieved 15 May 2012, from http://cis-india.org/openness/publications/open-access-scholarly-literature.pdf

[3] Budapest Open Access Initiative. (2002). Retrieved 10 May 2012, from http://www.soros.org/openaccess/read

[4] Creative Commons. Retrieved 14 May 2012, http://creativecommons.org/

[5] Gordon-Murnane. Creative Commons: Copyright Tools for the 21st Century. Retrieved 12 May 2012, from http://www.infotoday.com/online/jan10/Gordon-Murnane.shtml

[6] Hoorn, E. and Graff, M. (2006). Copyright issues in open access research journals: The authors' perspective. *D-Lib Magazine*, **12**(2).

[7] Sale, Arther and others. Open Access Mandates and the 'Fair Dealing' Button. Retrieved May 17, 2012 from http://eprints.soton.ac.uk/268511/1/saledraftv5.pdf

[8] Sherpa. Publisher copyright policies and self-archiving. Retrieved March 15, 2012 from http://www.sherpa.ac.uk/romeo.php

[9] Social Science Citation Index. Retrieved 20 March 2012 from http://thomsonreuters.com/products_services/science/science_products/a-z/social_sciences_citation_index

[10] Tempest, David (2012). Copyright in an Open Access World. Editor's Update (35). Retrieved 15 May 2012 http://editorsupdate.elsevier.com/2012/03/copyright-in-an-open-access-world

[11] Wikipedia. Self archiving. Retrieved 1 April 2012 from http://en.wikipedia.org/wiki/Self-archiving.

Electronic Resources Management in Libraries, pp. 299–305

Open Access Resources and Licensing Issues in University Libraries

Sujin Budisuwan and E. Rama Reddy

ABSTRACT

Scholarly publishing in the Open Access environment is revolutionizing and paving the way for transparency and quick access to the research findings. The evolution of libraries into the digital age has brought about a multitude of issues regarding rights and usage of electronic library materials. In the past, the traditional library model simply involved dealing with the physical book or journal. The rights regarding this material traditionally fell within the realm of the fair use clause of Copyright Act. Open Access resources use only a handful of licensing schemes as opposed to licenses for purchased materials, which can vary from publisher to publisher and title to title. The growth of purchased and free electronic resources available for immediate use by the library users has changed the traditional university library landscape through the use of resources by creators of Open Access (OA) content and publishers. The licensing workflows in the library can present opportunities for the university libraries to play an important role.

1. Introduction

Open Access (OA) to scientific research means universal availability of scholarly publications via the Internet without any barriers to access. They are licensed so as to allow redistribution and reuse as long as attribution is given. For example, a published article can be posted on a personal or institutional homepage, emailed to friends and colleagues, printed and sent to people, archived in a collection, distributed on CD-ROM, included in course-packs, quoted in the press, translated and further distributed as often and widely available. They can be permanently archived in an internationally recognized repository. The creation and continuous development of material within the OA has also created a dilemma for university libraries in the acquisition and handling of these freely available items on the Internet. Open Access material can be defined as the world-wide electronic distribution of the peer-reviewed journal literature and completely free and unrestricted access to it by all scientists, scholars, teachers, students, and other curious minds. The Budapest Open Access Initiative defines it as "free online availability of scholarly articles which users can "read, download, copy, distribute, print, search, or link to the full texts of these articles, crawl them for indexing, pass them as data to software, or use them for any other lawful purpose, without financial, legal, or technical barriers other than those inseparable from gaining access to the Internet itself" (Budapest Open Access Initiative, 2002).

University libraries have been struggling to get a clear grasp on how to handle paid licensed electronic resources while simultaneously addressing the increased patron demand for more online resources. The proliferation of electronic resources has led to multiple innovations to assist university libraries in dealing with copyright, fair use and to track patron usage. OA material is making slow, steady progress as a valuable resource in university libraries. As the amount of OA resources increase, university libraries are trying to develop additional workflows to accommodate the influx of OA material.

University libraries provide access to a variety of OA materials including journal titles, open courseware and faculty papers submitted to institutional repositories. All these freely available resources can be found under a variety of license agreements. All of these items are available to link to, print or in the case of items licensed under a Creative Commons (CC) license generally re-use. There are a limited number of licenses for OA material but there is no systematic tracking of these resources by university libraries. Lacking a standardized mechanism to convey OA usage terms to users means licensing information is not always consistent between institutions or within the same institutions.

2. Present Status

By virtue of purchasing electronic resources, the burden of determining access and license rights has now been placed on librarians and library staff. In the traditional model of purchasing the physical item, the book or journal was paid for and physically housed in the library. The rights regarding usage of the book copyright and usage are finite; they begin and end with the book. When librarians handle electronic resources, they are adding another complex layer to the work they do. Since there was no unifying standard for license information regarding electronic resources, electronic communication with vendors, users and other institutions became difficult and cumbersome. Not every institution or publisher uses the same language to describe the license restrictions of electronic resources. Libraries could no longer keep up with and enforce widely different license terms applied by the publisher and creator (Cave, Green and Martin, 2007).

University libraries need to find a way to manage the electronic resources, in addition to manage the workflow for traditional tangible resources. The process for handling tangible resources consists of "selecting, ordering, cataloguing and binding" and has now transformed into "selecting, evaluating, approving, licensing, billing and registering access" (Kasprowski, 2006). What happens if access is lost or there are technical difficulties? In the traditional workflow for university libraries, there was a beginning and end with a physical item(s). Now there would be an ongoing maintenance and technology component for libraries to provide continuous and uninterrupted access to all electronic resources.

3. Copyright

The traditional model of usage of materials involved a user going to the physical library location, taking the item off of the shelf either to check the book out and take it home or make photocopies. Users are allowed to use the copyrighted material purchased by the library through the "fair use" clause of the copyright act. The following guidelines determine fair use:

- The purpose and character of the use, including whether such use is of commercial nature or is for nonprofit educational purposes;
- The nature of the copyrighted work;
- Amount and substantiality of the portion used in relation to the copyrighted work as a whole; and
- The effect of the use upon the potential market for or value of the copyrighted work.

The distinction between "fair use" and "infringement" may be unclear and not easily defined (Copyright Act, 2006). This assumption of libraries and publishers of copyright compliance on the part of patrons is good for the physical item, but is questionable for electronic resources. In the case of the explosion of availability of digital resources, the speed in which copyrighted material can be copied in its' entirety is now almost instantaneous. In the era of electronic resources, the likelihood of obeying copyright restrictions is extremely thin due to "the ease with which digital files can be copied and transmitted" (Iannella, 2001). University Libraries are observing copyright rules and trying to prevent users from unauthorized use and access of digital materials. There are no longer the limitations of users need to go to the library and retrieving the item themselves. Articles, books and other items can be delivered instantly to the users' desktop/at home.

4. OA Resources and Creative Commons

A license is a contract which libraries or institutions can "modify default rights and obligations under law, add additional expectations as legally enforceable obligations. A license can address many issues including: price, permissions, number of users, whether files can be copied or transferred, who is the licensee, licensor, archival issues, obligations of both parties" (Robertson, 2006). For instance, university libraries could buy access to an electronic resource package 'A' that has three individual titles within the package. University libraries need to track a license for Package 'A' and individual licenses for the three titles. The library could end up with four different licenses for one journal package.

Open access resources use only a handful of licensing schemes as opposed to licenses for purchased materials, which can vary from publisher to publisher and title to title. Since 2002, Creative Commons (CC) has become a dominant entity in licensing OA material. The CC website states "share, reuse, and remix—legally." According to the CC website, over 65 million licenses linked worldwide as of 2011. The web site provides a very simple license option to ask the licensee if the work can be used commercially or can modifications of the work be made with limitations. In comparison to paid electronic resources, this type of license agreement is simple and relatively easy to understand.

"All CC licenses have many important features in common. Every license helps creators—we call them licensors if they use our tools—retain copyright while allowing others to copy, distribute, and make some uses of their work—at least non-commercially. Every CC license also ensures licensors get the credit for their work they deserve. Every CC license works around the world and lasts as long as applicable copyright lasts (because they are built on copyright). These common features serve as the baseline, on top of which licensors can choose to grant additional permissions when deciding how they want their work to be used" (http://creativecommons.org/licenses).

5. Digital Rights Management

University Libraries are required to convey any usage restrictions in the license agreement in order to ensure users adhere to the publisher requirements. Coyle (2004) says that "any rights or permissions beyond those included in copyright law are covered by contract or license". There is no prescribed way for a library to enforce these restrictions.

Usage restrictions for purchased electronic resources are commonly handled through the technology of Digital Rights Management (DRM). If the number of concurrent users must be restricted then libraries rely on DRM to enforce the specific restrictions of the license. Essentially, DRM can give access to a digital resource to the computer and not to an individual. If the individual patron attempts to send a digital resource that was allowed on his computer to another person's computer, the electronic resource would not work.

Typically the DRM is enforced through an institution approved IP address, an authentication process or user passwords. Not only restrictions are in place to comply with a publisher license agreement, but also to comply with copyright law.

5.1 *Electronic Resource Management*

In order to keep up with the license requirements of paid electronic resources, university libraries have turned to Electronic Resource Management (ERM) systems to keep track of license requirements and restrictions. The purpose for any ERM software is to store and make accessible information that relates to license terms—that is, the rights and responsibilities that a library has with relation to the resource being used.

Electronic resource management is defined as "a system that supports management of the information and workflows necessary to efficiently select, evaluate, acquire, maintain, renew/cancel and provide informed access to e-resources in accordance with their business and license terms" (Digital Library Federation, 2004).

5.2 *Workflows for OA Resources*

As university libraries began to adjust to licensing related issues, the emergence of OA and any accompanying license has highlighted the need to examine current workflows. Providing OA resources, free of any DRM restrictions, does not negate the responsibility of university libraries to enforce the license terms of the item. They should work to ensure compliance with license terms of items stored within the institution, whether in the online catalogue or through an institutional repository.

A search of current library literature on the role of libraries tracking licenses for OA materials provides few substantive results. There would be nothing to preclude the library from adding OA or CC licenses in which the ERM system alongside the purchases aside from the staffing issues and time needed to devote to the resources. Certainly, tracking licenses for OA material represents a new paradigm for libraries. The library should not necessarily become a CC license police force to ensure compatibility. But, university libraries should develop a centralized location for all electronic resources, paid and OA. Users could police themselves with librarians acting as moderators. If a user is re-using content and not following through on maintaining a CC license, the OA item can be flagged by users for further review by librarians.

6. OA and Libraries/Librarians

University libraries play a vital role in disseminating free and purchased information. If all license information can be put into a machine-readable form then all interested stakeholders can have a shared understanding of what the resource means and how the resources can be shared with others. Faculty members as authors are the first step in the OA process when they choose to deposit their articles either to an OA journal or an institutional repository. The OA movement, while increasing in numbers does still appears to be plagued by the lack of time, awareness and understanding by authors of the OA options available to them. The library catalogue can serve as the centralized location for the depositing of the self-archive record or other OA paper to be deposited by a faculty author.

If university libraries moved away from the model of separating the library catalogue from the institutional repository, the library catalogue could develop a more centralized role in creating and maintaining OA institutional repositories. One way to facilitate a central role would be to simplify the process for a faculty member to submit a paper directly into the library catalogue. If members of the faculty have time to search for articles and books, they would be able to easily deposit an article in the OA repository/catalogue.

Making the catalogue the central place for all OA transaction will help and strengthen the OA movement and ensure continual access to information without barriers. Library catalogues could also automatically give an option for search results to include institutional OA material. If discovering OA material was easy to find and always a part of the library catalogue, then faculty may be more willing to deposit materials to OA archives.

Librarians play a major role in ensuring compliance with copyright law for physical items in the library and compliance with license agreement(s) for paid electronic resources. University librarians can also take a role in educating and informing users of the OA licenses. Librarians and library staff should make a "sincere" effort to make users and staff aware of terms and live within them. The use of any license whether paid or open "is only as good as staff awareness about copyright issues, rights management procedures and robust policies underpinning the operation of education institutions" (Korn and Oppenheim, 2006). Failure of libraries and librarians to track license issues for OA material could result in a loss of trust between librarians and depositors of OA content if there is a perceived notion that librarians are not guarding the dissemination of OA knowledge.

7. Conclusions

During the last decade, university libraries have witnessed the evolution of tracking licenses for electronic resources from an endeavor requiring a heavy amount of staff time to a process, which can now be done in an almost completely automated environment. Licenses have grown exponentially through bundled journal title services and the plethora of available electronic resources. OA resources are not handled at all through any licensed tracking. ERM systems may have an occasional free resource, but a vast majority of staff resources focus has been on purchased licenses. If libraries must track and comply with license agreements and copyright law, compliance with licenses for OA material follows a natural progression of libraries being caretakers of knowledge within a reasonable means of enforcement for patrons to comply. Libraries do not have the resources to track every OA, those OA resources that the university provides access to should be tracked to ensure compliance with the license requirement and determine what types of information patrons are using.

Changing the workflow of university libraries to track OA licenses is just one step towards increasing awareness of OA resources and creating different workflow models for libraries in order to seamlessly integrate OA materials into a regular library workflow. Peter Suber pointed out that it is faculty members who must first to decide whether to pursue an OA avenue for their published works or not. If awareness is raised among the faculty members by librarians through outreach programmes such as blogs and other online tools and partnerships formed with faculty, the continual growth of OA material can be assured not only by the participation of the authors, but also by the central role played by libraries and librarians.

References

[1] Budapest Open Archive Initiative. Retrieved on 24 April 2012 from http://www.soros.org/openaccess/read.shtml

[2] Copyright and open licenses. (2007). *In* Giving knowledge for free: The emergence of open educational resources, Centre for Educational Research and Knowledge (Ed.). OECD. pp.71–86. Retrieved on 23 April 2012 from http://213.253.134.43/oecd/pdfs/browseit/9607041E.PDF

[3] Coyle, K. (2004). Rights expression languages: A report for the Library of Congress. Retrieved 20 April 2012 from http://www.loc.gov/standards/Coylereport_final1single.pdf

[4] Coyle, K. (2003).The Technology of rights: Digital rights management. Retrieved on 20 April 2012 from http://www.kcoyle.net/drm_basics1.html

[5] Creative Commons. Retrieved on 15 April 2012 from http://creativecommons.org/

[6] Digital Library Federation (2004). Report of the DLF electronic resource management initiative: Appendix A: Functional requirement for electronic resource management. Retrieved on 22 April 2012 from http://www.diglib.org/pubs/dlf102/

[7] Iannella, R. (2001). Digital rights management architectures. *D-lib Magazine,* 7(6).

[8] Kasprowski, R. (2006). Recent developments in electronic resource management in libraries. Retrieved on 20 April 2012 from www.asis.org/Bulletin/Aug-06/kasprowski.html

[9] Koppel, T. (2006). Introduction to the rapidly changing world of ERM standards, Retrieved on April 30, 2012 from http://www.exlibrisgroup.com/ files/Publications/Rapidlychanging worldofERMstandards.pdf

[10] Korn, N., Oppenheim, C. (2006). Creative Commons licenses in higher and further education: Do we care? *Ariadne*, 49. Retrieved on 26 April 2012 from www.ariadne. ac.uk/issue49/korn-oppenheim/

[11] Robertson, N.D.M. (2006). Managing our e-resource licenses: License expression standards. Retrieved on 30 April 2012 from http://smartech.gatech.edu/dspace/handle/1853/10407

[12] Suber, P. (Interviewee). (2008). Interview with Ellyssa Kroski. Retrieved on 20 April 2012 from http://www.archive.org/details/PeterSuberInterview

[13] US Copyright Office. (2006). Fair use. Retrieved on 29 April 2012 from www.copyright.gov/fls/fl102.html

[14] University of California Digital Library. Retrieved on 6 April 2012 http://www.cdlib.org/inside/collect/openaccess.html

[15] The Creative Commons copyright licenses. Retrieved on 26 April 2012 http://creativecommons.org/licenses

Electronic Resources Management in Libraries, pp. 306–320

Intellectual Property Rights, Role of LIS Professionals in Preservation and Communication of Traditional Biomedical Knowledge: Problems and Prospects

Surya Nath Singh

ABSTRACT

Traditional Biomedical Knowledge (TBK) is being used over the centuries however, claims have not been maintained due to various reasons. This paper provides an overview of protection of TBK and concept of Intellectual Property Rights (IPR) at national and international level. It describes various facets of TBK, viz. nature, contribution to progress and development of society, various components and different related terminologies used from time to time. The paper intends to study the detailed issues relating to the emergence and importance of IPR and challenges of managing it. It also provides a review of literature on IPR and TBK. It is proposed that countries invest in the establishment of sui generis regimes covering TBK and rights. It is necessary that Government of India should allocate resources and have proper IPR to protect TBK. This article concludes with changing roles of libraries, Library and Information Science (LIS) professionals in organization and management ICT based preservation and communication of TBK as well as IPR related problems, where LIS profession can take a lead of the above issues and initiate appropriate action to achieve the objective.

1. Introduction

The value of Traditional Biomedical Knowledge (TBK) has been realized globally because of its intrinsic value and knowledge management. In India, TBK began as art, later gradually evolved into a science over the ages. A large section of population in under developed and developing countries especially rural and tribal have been using TBK from generations. In the changing scenario, the new IP regimes will have wide range of socio-economic, technological and political impact. The protection of TK is one of the major issues addressed in the World Trade Organization (WTO) negotiations to implement in all National Systems of Intellectual Property Rights (IPRs), by following an agreed set of minimum standards (Mashelkar, 2001, 2002, 2003). This agreement was significant because TK consists of information in the public domain as well as trade secrets; novelty thresholds of patent laws of countries differ greatly. The pharmaceutical industry is strongest and has patentability nature under Trade Related Aspects of IP Systems (TRIPS), which does not require prior informed consent of countries or communities from, where organic and informational resources are procured. The notion of TK, how indigenous people had acquired TK and that went to the level of international debates on sustainable development as well as those on IPR protection (Posey, 1991) however, their usage is often leads to confusion. There have been various efforts to define the concepts of TK, indigenous knowledge (IK) and indigenous peoples, but failed to have a universally accepted adopted definitions. Different persons defined differently, depending on their intellectual persuasion and professional interest, while many often used the concept of TK interchangeably with IK (Mugabe, 1994). TBK is a heritage as well as part and parcel of our lives for much longer than modern medicine. It is a socio-cultural and historical aspect of our lives, hence it is difficult to internationalize, where a substantial component of knowledge passed on from generation to generation by the mainly oral communication.

1.1 *Intellectual Property Rights*

The IPR is an integral part as well as indispensable element of progress and development of human society. However, IPR refers to creation of human intellect, related to knowledge/information is a legal expression of privilege granted by the state for the use of one's creation and also inherently intangible. The IP law has recently received attention as a vehicle for technological innovations and industrial change. The various forms of IP are: (a) Patents, (b) Supplementary Protection, Certification, (c) Trademarks, (d) Designs, (e) Un-registered Design Rights, (f) Semiconductor Topography Rights, (g) Copyrights, (h) Confidentiality, and Trade Secrets, and (i) Plant Variety Rights. All these are also applicable to TBK and IPR. It has also been seen as a tool for promoting the conservation of biological diversity, sustainable use of its components. Several experts have argued that IP protection increases the costs of products, promotes genetic monoculture by concentrating industrial and agricultural activities on a few cultivated varieties or species, and, when extended to plants and animals, is in conflict with the morals of many societies (Acharya and Anshu, 2008; Anuradha, 1997; Chander and Sunder, 2004; Gopalakrishnan, 1998, 2002). IP laws also vary in their nature, disclosure conditions, duration and scope from one country to another as it is protected in one country may not be recognized in another country. Despite of the existence of various international agreements that attempt to harmonize its protection, these differences in national IP law are at the center of much of the debate on the IPR of indigenous and local peoples (Gopalakrishnan, 1998, 2002; Greaves, 1996; Gupta, 2001). The case of TBK of indigenous and local people has opened debate on the adequacy and ethics of IP protection on whether and how to extend IP. These issues are complex and controversial due to differences in conceptual treatment and often lack of clarity on the two concepts of TBK and IPR. Even the WTO has not confronted the implications of its Agreement on Trade-Related Aspects of Intellectual Property Rights for the protection and use of TK. On the whole, international debate on issues of IP protection in general and TBK in particular, is led to tension and inconsistency (Gupta, 2001).

Traditional Biomedical Knowledge vs. Intellectual Property Rights

In some Asian and African countries, up to 80 percent of the population relies on traditional medicine for their primary healthcare needs. Traditional/indigenous cultural knowledge has always been an open treasure box for the unfettered appropriation of items of value to Western civilization. While, we attentively protect rights to valuable knowledge among ourselves, but indigenous people have never been accorded similar rights over their cultural knowledge. Existing Western IP laws support, promote, and excuse the wholesale, uninvited appropriation of whatever indigenous item strikes our fancy or promises profit, with no obligation or expectation to allow the originators of the knowledge a say or a share in the proceeds (Greaves, 1996; WHO, 2008).

TBK resources include plants, animals, other material objects like tangible and intangible rights. These rights also include public law rights and customary law defined or accommodated in national and international laws. It also seeks to go beyond the concept of IPR and try to describe various rights existing and that can be developed with a view to afford protection to TBK and compensation for use of such knowledge. Furthermore, the panacea to these unresolved questions runs parallel to the concept of IPR, protects a base of knowledge and embraces the cultural fabric of people embodying religion, custom and tradition (Posey, 1991; WHO, 2008). Consequently, TBK has to be sought to be protected as IPR and as a cultural/intellectual right. The various IP law regimes to establish their adequacy in protecting TK are: The Paris Convention for the Protection of Industrial Property; Plant Breeders' Rights; Protection of Traditional Knowledge under TRIPS, etc. The several sources of TBK have been summarized in Figure 1.

International Scenario

Although laws and concepts behind copyright and patents are not new, the term intellectual property is relatively recent, dating from the 19th century, property as a common descriptor of the field probably traces to the foundation of the World Intellectual Property Organization (WIPO) by the United Nations (Mark, 2005). However, there are some organizations, which protect the IP. For example, Shaman Pharmaceuticals and the Body Shop are pharmaceutical companies' products development activities are largely based on TBK and to provide a certain measure of compensation to local people for the knowledge by returning some of the benefits from the commercialization of medicinal plants and traditional knowledge to the traditional people. The body shop sponsors projects to assist local people to establish enterprises for processing crude products. Traditional people (particularly the indigenous ones) and their knowledge are however, threatened with destruction. Modest estimates show that 85 Brazilian Indian groups became extinct in the first half of this century (Mark, 2005; Mugabe, 1994).

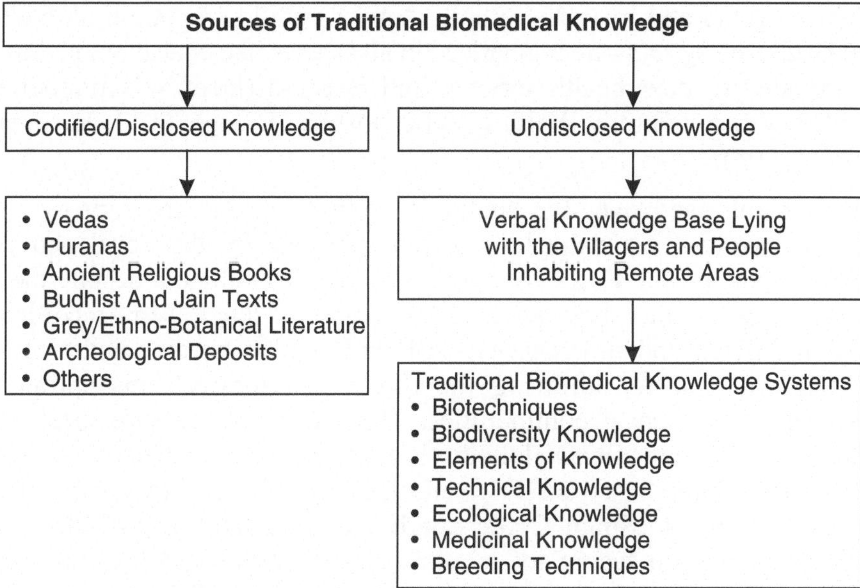

Fig. 1: Sources of Traditional Biomedical Knowledge

Indian Scenario

Indian civilization is one of the oldest heritages of mankind possessing comprehensive multi-faceted cultural aspects and co-existed since the emergence of humanity about three to five thousand years BC. The journey of TBK in developing and under developed countries is very much lengthy in view of time, cultures, languages, and geographical locations of countries as it was propagated in many cultures and countries. The present status of traditional health system in India is of poly-path practices but still predominantly, TBK practice is prevalent almost in all parts of India, especially rural and tribal areas, its education and research is mother of all traditional healthcare sciences as inseparable part and parcel of Indian culture. India has been using TBK systems, popularly known as AYUSH (Ayurveda, Yoga, Unani, Siddha, and Homeopathy) to overcome illness and sufferings to enhance the quality of life as oral tradition, passed generation to generation over many centuries. The TBK may include formalized aspects of folk medicine, *i.e.* longstanding remedies passed on and practiced by lay people. Consequently, it has a separate identity as well as status and is also the most pragmatic as well as progressive healthcare science. In a span of time, it is enriched with many new practices, procedures and materials assuming the present status *i.e.* existing recorded, semi-recorded and oral form of communication of knowledge. During ancient time, TBK was only method of healthcare as mentioned in the ancient Indian literature viz. Vedas, religious books, manuscripts, etc. The existing TBK is vast and comprehensive presented/documented in literature (*Punarbasu, Atreya*, the first Ayurvedic Medical School, *Charaka Samhita, Susruta Samhita* for surgery) and in verbal ethnic, family tradition in public domain. These traditional healthcare systems are regularized in all aspects like education, pharmaceutical industry, private practices health services and research (Dept. of Commerce, 2003; Ministry of Health and Family Welfare, 2002; Joshi and Singh, 2011; Krishnaswamy, 2005; WHO (2008)).

The TBK is being used over the centuries in India due to its very rich heritage. However, we have not maintained the claims as done by the developed countries. Consequently, some of our TBKs are being patented from abroad, despite the fact that above knowledge is ours but were orally communicated, semi-recorded and/or unrecorded in different Indian languages. TBK in India has become under considerable pressure and criticism for allowing the direct and indirect misappropriation of indigenous people and local communities. The piracy of turmeric, neem, Basmati Rice, more than 150 others items globally through patents stretched and demonstrated their limits and failures based on TBK and lack of IPR laws to protect the IPR of indigenous communities (Singh, 2003; Singh and Garg, 2003). As India enters into the 21st century, we are facing lot of problems about how to institutionalize new modes of access, control and production of information, knowledge and cultural resources. The rapid legislative activity on the Patent (Amendment) Act, 2005, has so radically shifted the goalposts of the debate that we are still to catch our breath. The traditional people have been defined as "those who hold an unwritten corpus of long-standing customs, beliefs, rituals and practices that have been handed down from previous generations. They do not necessarily have claim of prior territorial occupancy to the current habitat; that is, they could be recent immigrants. Consequently, traditional peoples are not necessarily indigenous but indigenous peoples are traditional (UNEP). The details of plants used for Indian Systems of Medicine as TBK have been summarized in Table 1.

The debate on protecting TBK in India best depicts the multi-dimensional character on the regulation of information, knowledge and cultural resources on the basis of the policy frameworks they offer to resolve of the problem. First, those who entrap the policy debate in colonialism, where wealthy Western nations and multi-national companies are seen to be expropriating our indigenous knowledge to immense profit. The moral panic centred around neem, Basmati and turmeric (Singh, 2003; Singh and Garg, 2003). The nationalist lens characteristic of this view prompts a regulatory response transferring control over TK resources to a selected cabal of state bureaucrats in a move that would rival to the nineteenth- and twentieth-century transfers of natural resources such as forests in the hands of the colonial forest department have, in fact, explored the scale and perversion of the expropriation, whereby state bureaucrats developed into a breed of rent-seekers over forest lands to the exclusion of tribal communities. There is little evidence to suggest that the state bureaucracies constituted and enacted Biological Diversity Act of 2002. Indian history in this regard teaches us that 'nationalizing' resources in the name of 'our' common heritage has a troubled legacy and, notwithstanding the emotive appeal of the biopiracy debate, we must resist such an option with TK (GOI, Department of Commerce, 2003; Ministry of Health Family Welfare, 2002; Gupta, 2001).

Table 1: Indian Systems of Medicine as TBK and Plants

Sl. No.	*Description*	*Nos.*
1.	Agro-climate zone	16
2.	Plant species	45,000
3.	Medicinal plants	15,000
4.	Plants used in Ayurveda: 7000 Unani: 700 Siddha: 600 Modern medicine: 30 Drug preparation:150	15,000
5.	Plants Endangered	150
6.	TKDL(CSIR)-Formulations)- 3,50,000 original text	16,000
7.	Registered practitioners of traditional medicine in India (Hospitals: 464 Dispensaries: 13,565	2,17,000

Source: Ministry of Health and Family Welfare, Department of ISMH, 2002, p. 241.

Components of TBK in India

There are five components of TBK in India popularly known as AYUSH. The first is Ayurveda, the main practicing family medicine throughout India; it is practiced by almost all medical systems practitioners in one or other form as supplementary measure or advices. The pure practitioners of Ayurveda are more in number than the integrated. The system of Ayurveda has a great history and started in about 400 BC. The Atharvaveda (science of life) gives enough details of various diseases and treatments. Due to many strong therapeutic measures like *Panchakarma* (bio-cleansing), and *Anushastra karmas* (minimal invasive para surgical measures and adoption of new technologies). This medical system is popular not only among Indians but also with other developed and developing countries. In India, Kerala state is flourishing because of Ayurveda in the form of health tourism.

Second is Yoga. The practices of yoga are not only considered as only physical exercises but also more body-mind measures. The yoga is widely practiced in urban educated population, rural and also in institutions. This is considered as a preventive measure to maintain positive health with yoga practices. There are several yoga gurus propagating the yoga art from time to time to cure several even dreaded disease and presently claims of Baba Ramdev is a living example along with other programmes on the TV channels and other public gatherings. However, the majority of them failed to provide scientific data evidences, causes lack of popularity in masses, despite the reality that it cures the diseases. Apart from these, there are ethno-botanical or traditional herbal family practices prevalent in remote tribal and rural areas. The knowledge or information here is not documented but based on family practices and many years of observations. This is considered a part and parcel of Ayurveda existing in the public domain. The Naturopathy is another healthcare system practiced in India mainly in urban population as a supplementary to main treatment. The Acupuncture is also practiced in India mainly in metro cities. The origin of Acupuncture is in Ayurveda, mentioned as *SiraVedha*.

The third is Unani traditional medicine, is mostly popular among the Muslim community but the propagation is not that wide like Ayurveda. The basic philosophy and practices are not much different from tose of Ayurveda. The dosage forms like *khamir* (jam type), *ark* distillate are specific to Unani medical system. The Sowa-regpa or Amchi medical systems are practiced mainly in Leh-Laddakh and Himachal Pradesh states of India. During the period of Lord Buddha, the monks propagated Ayurveda along with Budha teachings in the neighboring countries like Tibet, China, Sri Lanka, Thialand, etc. The main Ayurveda literature was translated in Tibetan language and the practices of Ayurveda influenced on the indigenous Tibetan health practices. The Sowa-regpa philosophy and practices are mostly similar to Ayurveda and some traces influence of Chinese medicine is also observed. Ayurveda along with this art was propagated long back in many neighboring countries but it is scientifically well developed in China. The other traditional health practices are of animal healthcare called *pashu* or *mriga* Ayurveda dealing with the common ailments mainly of tame animals utilized in agricultural works, horses, dogs, etc. Some practices called *vriksha* Ayurveda (plant/tree healthcare) exist in rural agricultural and horticultural working. This tradition is again on the verge of vanishing.

The fourth is Siddha system is one of the ancient traditional medical systems prevalent in Tamilnadu and some adjacent parts of Kerala and Puducherry states. The philosophy and practices are more or less like that of Ayurveda, all the original literature is in Tamil language. The therapeutic uses of minerals and metals are more in Siddha than

Ayurveda; it is the strength of that system. The other significant feature is that of *varma chikitsa,* treatment through vital spots.

The fifth is Homeopathy, originated in Germany but is also used and practiced widely in India, without much scientific evidences, despite the fact that people are being treated and cured as it has no much side effects (Acharya and Anshu, 2008, Anuradha, 1997; Chander and Sunder, 2004; Gopalakrishnan, 1998, 2002; Guha and Gadgil, 1993; Gupta, 2001; Ministry of Health and Family Welfare, 2002; Joshi and Singh, 2011; Mashelkar, 2001; WHO, 2008).

Traditional vs. Indigenous Knowledge (TBK)

Indigenous Knowledge (IK) is knowledge held and used by a people, who identify themselves as indigenous of place based on a "combination of cultural distinctiveness and prior territorial occupancy related to a more recently-arrived population with its own distinct and subsequently dominant culture. Traditional Knowledge (TK) on the other hand, is held by members of a distinct culture and/or sometimes acquired "by means of inquiry peculiar to that culture, and concerning the culture itself or the local environment in which it exists. TK plays a significant role in industries and R&D programs. But TK has been and continues to be an element in the commercialization of natural products; it has commercial interests and provided through databases, academic publications or other sources and it should be paid for in some form. This form is to some extent dictated by the market, but should also be established in light of the fact that the market will not reflect the true commercial value of TK. The IK fits neatly in the TK category but TK is not necessarily indigenous. In other words IK is TK but TK is not necessarily indigenous. Traditional knowledge comprises of the vast expanse of knowledge, innovations and practices of indigenous and local communities embodying their traditional life-styles while TK refers to tradition-based literary, artistic or scientific works; performances; inventions; scientific discoveries; designs; marks, names and symbols; undisclosed information; and all other tradition-based innovations and creations resulting from intellectual activity in the industrial, scientific, literary or artistic fields. 'Tradition-based' refers to knowledge systems, creations, innovations and cultural expressions which: have generally been transmitted from generation to generation; are generally regarded as pertaining to particular people or territory; and, are constantly evolving in response to a changing environment. Categories of TK could include: agricultural knowledge; scientific knowledge; technical knowledge; ecological knowledge; medicinal knowledge, including related medicines and remedies; biodiversity-related knowledge; expressions of folklore (Gopalakrishnan, 1998, 2002).

Healthcare, TBK and Library and Information Science (LIS) Professionals

Health has been declared as fundamental human right so as to health information for public, academicians, administrators/decision makers, researchers, clinicians and experts and other medical and paramedical services particularly in India. The LIS professionals of ancient India stored the TBK in scrolls, palm leaves, parchment papers, skins, clay tablets, stone writings, metal sheets, manuscripts, papers in a scattered manner. The dramatic change in library resources and Information Technology (IT) based services often blurs the lines between traditional job roles in Information Centres and Libraries (ICLs). Consequently, LIS professionals can play a vital role in preservation, organization and management of ICT based TBK. It also includes how some of the ways *of digital technology* can be used in managing TBK for dissemination and providing services to various professionals of health, academic, research, clinical practices. They can also focus on various innovative uses of IPR for strengthening health information and related to library services and also illustrates how it is more useful in health science areas, especially to manage digital TBK at global level. There are challenges to procure, store, preserve and communication TBK using modern technologies but are also more opportunities to LIS professional if one develops the expertise in this field.

1.2 *Research Questions*

A study was carried out to elicit information on the status of IPRs and protection of TBK. The basic questions to be answered in this study are:

- Is TBK on the verge of disappearance?
- Is the threat of bio-piracy merely one that comes from without due to lack of proper law for IPT?
- Would we be content if it were established that Indian pharmaceutical companies exploited this knowledge and have respect at par with industrial property based knowledge?

Objectives

- To find out the current situation of IPR to protect TBK at national and International level and also to discuss various issues related to generation, protection and exploitation of intellectual property (IP) due to high importance.
- To promote IPR by exchanging limited exclusive TBK rights for disclosure of inventions and creative works, society and the patentee/copyright owner mutually benefit and an incentive is created for inventors and authors to create and disclose their work.
- To study the issues and concerns related to TBK and emergence of digital technology, legal, challenges of managing IPR.

- To describe the roles and concerns of LIS professionals in preservation and management of TBK in the face of IPR viz. perpetual dependency, social rights, pricing access and ownership.
- To review situation in India and regional developments in TBK and identification of issues and suggest possible solutions.
- To identifying priority areas for collaboration between countries, formulate and agree on common IPR Program to protect TBK.

Hypothesis

- TBK is on the verge of disappearance which has got valuable knowledge in public domain needs a protection mechanism.
- There is no systematic law to protect TBK therefore no provision for novelty in IPR in India.

Scope

Study is descriptive and literature based hence it is difficult to derive meaningful conclusions. The study is restricted to TBK in India. This study also lacks to give a proper attention to scientific value of TBK, despite the facts efforts are being made at different levels.

2. Methodology

The study is based on descriptive methods based on the literature available especially case studies and primary and secondary sources. The possible models for material transfer and benefit sharing when products are created based on community knowledge are also included as supporting evidences. However, it is proposed to collect TBK (audio, visual, text, graphics, etc) in the local languages, store in digital form and translate it in various Indian and international languages. This will be followed by provision of Internet access by LIS professionals to global community.

3. Results and Discussions

There is big gap between TBK and modern science. The preservation of TBK is essential which is local in nature but global in use and importance. It is our TK, modern science and awareness towards IPR, India will emerge as super power. We have already started thinking preservation and digitization of our TK heritage. The TKDL project by NISCAIR, India is an example to this. It is for the LIS professionals to position themselves to suit their institutional missions. The study included the need for a fair play in technology transfer, creation of favourable economics' of essential medicines from the point of view of the third world, protection of TBK, etc. Based on several studies, the present study supports the hypotheses as a major part of TBK has lost forever and there in no full proof IPR law in India to protect it. The general observations are:

- It shows that conventional IP law does not adequately cover or protect TBK, innovations of indigenous as well as local peoples. However, non-patent forms of IP protection could be exploited to protect the TBK and innovations.
- TBK and IPR have been debated at different platforms and forums including patenting of that knowledge, where such knowledge is treated as a public good, however no concrete solution has been provided till date. Those who subscribe to or promote the first position often advance the following arguments.
  - ***First,*** they argue that extending IP protection to TBK will in fact promote technological innovation as it would facilitate the dissemination and development in the modern economic competition.
  - ***Second,*** recognition of IPR in TBK could generate incentives for local and indigenous peoples to conserve the environment and manage biodiversity.
  - ***Third,*** the industrialized countries have a moral obligation to ensure that indigenous and local peoples receive a fair and equitable share of benefits arising from the use of their TK and commercialization of genetic resources (Juma, 1989; Juma and Ojwang. 1996; Krishnaswamy, 2005; Laird. 1994; Mark, 2005).
- It has also been observed that TK has no scientific validations in majority of cases, hence should be validated. This will provide an authenticity to TBK however, even those who oppose the extension of IP to TK have also argued that such a move would in fact destroy the social basis for generating and managing the knowledge. It has also been observed that TBK is a communal property, passed on from one generation to the next. If it is protected under IP law it would be privatized, and this may deny future generations and industry to access such knowledge. It is crucial to remember that the underlying purpose of IPR is to turn knowledge into a marketable commodity, not to conserve such knowledge in its most fitting cultural context. This goal necessarily translates into a focus on segregating and isolating information into identifiable and manageable pieces that can be protected by law as intellectual property. In contrast, ethno-botanical knowledge by its very nature is integrative, holistic, and synergistic. It is most meaningful in situ where plants are understood in relation to the ecological and cultural environments in which they have been grown, managed, and used by local residents. IPR departs from such traditions by valuing the discrete properties of plants that can most easily be taken out of their natural and cultural context and replicated through artificial selection in a laboratory or greenhouse. Given the legal premises upon which IPR are based, it is unlikely that IPR will ever be a useful model for protecting ethnobotanical knowledge.

4. Suggestions

- Firstly, it is essential protect TBK and rights (compensation, novelty) of originators/ keepers. It is essential to document TBK, create databases properly, continuously and value added. Consequently, it is necessary to have a proper mechanism at different level. Hence, suggested that Government of India should allocate resources and invest in the creation of s suitable legislation and also to have proper IPR to protect TBK. It is suggested to use IPR for TBK in better way to avoid unnecessary controversies by redefining and clarify to enable users without any prejudice. Secondly, provision should explore the development of systems that will first protect TBK as IPR of indigenous and local community. Such systems should also encourage (or even require) the flow of benefits from bio-prospecting to indigenous and local peoples. As a right holder, they would have exclusive rights to withhold from third parties their consent to make, use, an offer for sale, or import the plant variety that they developed.
- There are provisions to protect TK in general but not for TBK as specific in most of the countries. Since, there is no systematic study/or suitable law in India, effort should be made to protect TBK and have specific IPR law in India for the same. Since, there are specific provisions to protect TBK in the developing countries, hence it is crucial that new researches to be conducted on traditional forms of IP and how TK was/is protected by indigenous and local peoples in different parts of the world. The same may be applied with suitable modifications for especially developing countries like India. Various case studies illuminating how indigenous and local peoples perceive intellect and whether they treat it as property worth protecting would be useful. The suggestions of this work would form the basis for national and international processes to establish property protection regimes suitable for TBK and innovations.
- The studies have shown that conventional international IP does not, at least adequately, protect the TBK of indigenous and local peoples. The international community has also recognized that there is a need to devise new regimes or enlarge existing ones to accommodate the protection of TBK. However, so far no coherent and inclusive international efforts are being made to address this concern. There are a number of alternatives that countries could exploit to protect TBK of indigenous and local community. Hence, a depth study is required in this regard.
- Since, there is no provision of publicizing TBK and IPR, it is essential to publicize the value of TBK and urge Governments to ensure its collection, preservation and communication. LIS professional and media can play a big role in this regard.
- The challenge before us is huge and it is accepted fact that much in the realm of TBK is unknown, disappeared/lost but it is certainly accepted and being practiced. Modern medicine is based on scientific discovery however, TBK needs to be

tested according to methods appropriate for it, and not by the same methods used for testing modern medicine (WHO, 2004). It is recommended that international organizations like WHO, UNESCO should support IPR for the preservation and communication of TBK.

- The National Population Policy states that TBK experts, researchers, scientists and clinicians should try to implement IPR to protect TBK and the Department of AYUSH, can play a vital role to regulate TBK programmes, while LIS professional may work towards safeguarding its collection, preservation and communication.
- It has also been observed that TBK is also available in the form of verbal, SLOKAS, poetry, dialogues, etc in many languages hence LIS professionals have to find such information from various sources for compilation and creation as well as access of various subject related databases.

6. Conclusions

The World Health Organization (WHO) has also accepted the importance of TBK in developing countries (Vicker, 2000; WHO Regional Office for SEA, 2004; WHO, 2008). Accordingly, India has a long tradition of TBK and "The first National Health Policy of 1983" mentions that use should be made of India's rich tradition of healthcare in national programmes. There are separate directorates of Indian Systems of Medicine and Homeopathy in 21 State Governments. The Government of India has an explicit and separate policy for Indian (Traditional) Medicine since 2002. The effort has been made to describe various aspects of IPR and TBK, how traditional and local peoples do not have strong institutional arrangements to safeguard their TBK. LIS profession can take a lead of the above issues and initiate appropriate action to achieve the objectives. In the developing countries like India and their peoples have contributed considerably to the global drugs industry. In due course of time, as we experienced with TBK looking into the new century, we need to devise a regulatory policy for information, knowledge and cultural resources which revitalizes and sustains a vibrant public domain.

Several studies also indicated that a commons based approach does not automatically mean that all resources must be committed to an unregulated public domain. On the contrary, a carefully designed legal strategy, such as open-source movement, responding to the political economy of computer software, needs to be imagined and deployed in fields ranging from traditional knowledge protection to trademark and patent law. It is only the vitality of our understanding and imagination and clarity of purpose that can see us through the battles over the regulation of TBK and cultural resources that lie ahead. In can be concluded that a significant part of the global economy is based on the appropriation and use of TBK. Indeed, it is increasingly contributing to production in modern economies, where property rights are inimical to community intellectual property. Modern economic policies and laws (particularly modern property laws) undervalue TBK: at best they ignore it and at worst they contribute to its destruction. The challenge before us is huge because much TBK is unknown, but it is certainly accepted and practiced even at grass root level. However, there is need for scientific validations of TBK and testing according to methods appropriate for it, and not by the same methods used for testing modern medicine. Although protection of TBK is a major issue but it is important to aid value to our lives by bridging gaps between TBK and modern science. Let us pursue this issue further, as practice invariably comes first followed by science.

References

[1] Acharya, D. and Anshu, S. Indigenous herbal medicines: Tribal formulations and traditional herbal practices. Jaipur, Aavishkar Publishers, 2008.

[2] Anuradha, R.V., In search of knowledge and resources who sows? Who Reaps? *Rev. Europ Community and Inten. Env. Law*, 1997, **6**(3), 263–271.

[3] Chander, Anupam and Sunder, Madhavi. The romance of the public domain. *Calif. L. Rev.*, 2004, 1331, 1366–1372.

[4] Gopalakrishnan, N.S. Impact of patent system on traditional knowledge. *Cochin University Law Review*, 1998, 219, 220.

[5] Gopalakrishnan.N.S. Protection of traditional knowledge: The need for a sui generis law in India, *J. World Intell. Prop,* 2002, **5**, 725.

[6] Department of Commerce. Protecting traditional knowledge; international dimension. International Seminar on System of Protection of Traditional knowledge. Organized by Department of Commerce, Government of India in collaboration with UNCTAD, 3–5 April, 2003, New Delhi.

[7] Greaves, T. Tribal rights. *In* Brush and Stabinsky (Eds.). Valuing local knowledge: indigenous peoples and intellectual property rights. Covelo, Island Press, 1996.

[8] Guha, Ramachandra and Gadgil, Madhav. This fissured land: an ecological history of India, 1993, pp.140–145.

[9] Gupta, Anil K. How can Asian countries protect traditional knowledge, farmers rights and access to genetic resources through the implementation or review of the WTO TRIPS Agreement? Address at the Joint ICTSD/CEE/HBF Regional Dialogue for Governments and Civil Society, Chiang Mai, Thailand (March 29–30, 2001), available at http://www.ictsd.org/ dlogue/2001-03-29/Gupta.doc (accessed on Nov. 3, 2005).

[10] Ministry of Health Family Welfare, Department of ISMH, 2002. p. 241.

[11] Joshi, P.P. and Singh, S.N. Organization and dissemination of traditional knowledge with special reference to viral diseases in Maharashtra. National Conference on Agricultural Librarians and user Community, 17–19 November, 2011. *In*: Transformation of Agricultural Libraries in Collaborative Era. Ed by Dr. M.S. Pathania, *et al.* BS Publications, Hyderabad, 2012, pp. 444–454.

[12] Juma, C. The gene hunters: Biotechnology and the scramble for seeds. Princeton, Princeton University Press, 1989.

[13] Juma, C. and Ojwang, J.B. In land we trust: Environment, private property and constitutional change. Nairobi, ACTS Press, 1996, pp. 282–283.

[14] Krishnaswamy, Sudhir. Intellectual property and India's development policy. *The Indian Journal of Law and Technology*. 2005, 1, 169–176

[15] Laird. Natural Products and the commercialization of traditional knowledge. *In* Greaves, T. (Ed.). Intellectual property rights for indigenous peoples: A sourcebook. Oklahoma City, Society for Applied Anthropology, 1994. pp. 145–149.

[16] Mark, A. Lemley, Property, intellectual property, and free riding. *Texas Law Review*, 2005, 83(1031), 1033.

[17] Mashelkar, R.A. *Current Science*, 2001; 81, 413–419.

[18] Mashelkar, R.A. Intellectual property rights and the third world. *J of IPR,* 2002, 7, 308–323.

[19] Mashelkar, R.A. Bridging the traditional knowledge and modern science (lecture). *CSIR News*, 2003: 348–54.

[20] Mugabe, John. Intellectual property protection and traditional knowledge: An exploration in international policy discourse. http://www.wipo.int/tk/en/hr/paneldiscussion/papers/pdf/ mugabe.pdf

[21] Mugabe, John. Technological capability for environmental management: The case of biodiversity conservation in Kenya. Ph.D. dissertation submitted to the University of Amsterdam, The Netherlands, 1994.

[22] Posey. Intellectual property rights for native peoples: Challenges to science, business, and international law, Paper presented at the International Symposium on Property Rights, Biotechnology and Genetic Resources, Nairobi: Kenya, 1991.

[23] Reid *et al.* (Eds.), Biodiversity prospecting: Using genetic resources for sustainable development. World Resources Institute, Washington, D.C., 1993.

[24] Singh, S.N. Bridging traditional biomedical knowledge and modern science in India and role of information centres and libraries. Proceedings of the National Convention of Medical Library Association of India, 3–5 December, 2003. New Delhi, Medical Library Association of India, 2003.

[25] Singh, S.N. and Garg, B.S., Bridging traditional biomedical knowledge and modern science in India: An overview. Proceedings of the National Convention of Medical Library Association of India, 3–5 December 2003. New Delhi, Medical Library Association of India. pp. 1–24.

[26] Singh, S.N., Digitization: Preservation and conservation of indigenous biomedical heritage knowledge in developing countries with special reference to India. IFLA International Conference on Interlending and Document Supply, Canberra, 28–31 October 2003.

[27] Sreenivasan, Padma. National policy for traditional knowledge in India. *World Health Forum* 1995, 16(2), 190–93.

[28] UNEP: Rural Advancement Fund International. Conserving indigenous knowledge: Integrating two systems of innovation. A study prepared for the United Nations Development Program, New York, 1994.

[29] UNEP: Property as a common descriptor of the field probably traces to the foundation of the World Intellectual Property Organization by the United Nations. *Texas Law Review,* 2005, 83(1031), 1033.

[30] UNEP/CBD/COP/3/Inf. 33, Annex 2, p. 9.

[31] Vicker, Andrews. Recent Advances in Complementary Medicine. *BMJ*, 2000, 321(72670), 683–86.

[32] WHO. World Health Organization, Regional Office for SEA. Review of traditional medicine in the South-East Asia Region. Report of the Regional Working Group Meeting New Delhi, India, 16–17 August 2004 (WHO Project No.: IND EDM 050).

[33] WHO. World Health Organization, Regional Office for SEA. SEA-Trad.Med.-83. New Delhi, November 2004.

[34] World Health Organization. Fact sheet no. 134: Traditional medicine. 2008-12-01. http://www.who.int/mediacentre/factsheets/fs134/en/index.html. Retrieved on 2 May 2009.

Section–VII

Standards and Metrics for E-Resources

Electronic Resources Management in Libraries, pp. 323–332

Role of Metadata Standards in Digital Preservation in the Context of Institutional Repositories

Surinder Kumar and C.R. Karisiddappa

ABSTRACT

The growth of institutional repositories and their valuable digital content raises questions as to how to preserve the content for a long term. Digital preservation is a complex process and there are many unsolved organizational, managerial and technical issues that make digital preservation a challenging task for those managing repositories. Reference Model for an Open Archival Information System (OAIS) that defined the functions needing to be supported by an archive responsible for preserving content is becoming a part of number of IR software. Metadata standards which are prevalent for discovery of content are playing major role in preserving the digital content. Metadata Encoding and Transfer System (METS) is an information package which stores information about all kinds of metadata. OAIS model are providing framework to implement preservation strategy and institutional repositories software a mean to implement these preservation strategies. METS profile need may be developed by organizations for the purpose of preserving metadata of digital object and may also be used for the purpose of interoperability across digital repositories.

1. Introduction

Institutions are the logical stake holders to implement institutional repositories as they have acknowledged responsibility for preserving of their digital assets. The focus of many repositories, to large extent, has been on creating repositories, depositing content, discovery and encouraging the necessary cultural change. Digital preservation has not been embedded as an integral part of the repositories workflow and also there is neither much experience nor commonly agreed practice how content would be preserved on a long term basis. Digital preservation is a complex process which has many unsolved organizational, managerial and technical issues that makes digital preservation a challenging task for those managing repositories. Digital preservation is a process which ensures the usability, durability and intellectual integrity of the information contained in the institutional repositories, which in precise is the storage, maintenance, and accessibility of a digital object over the long term. It is viewed as "series of managed activities necessary to ensure continued access to digital materials" over the years (Jones and Neil, 2008).

2. Institutional Repositories

Institutional Repository (IR) as defined by SPARC is a digital archive of the intellectual assets created by the faculty, research staff, and students of an institution and accessible to end users both within and outside of the institution, with few if any barriers to access (Crow, 2002). Lynch (2003) has clearly defined the role of IRs in long-term preservation of digital content submitted. IRs have some core functions such as metadata submission, access control, discovery, distribution and preservation.

As such IRs are not offering any solution for preserving the documents in a short or long term. However, some emerging IRs software provides some mechanism by storing the data in a bit stream so that data can be migrated to a newer system in future. The incorporation of persistent document identification such as CNRI or DOI system is another piece of an IRs preservation function (Weenink, Waaijers and Godtsenhoven, 2008).

3. Issues Involved in Digital Preservation

There are various organizational issues involved in digital preservation in the context of institutional repositories involved (Saha, 2006) are given as follows:

- Digital contents are becoming part of IR, ensure its preservation and to provide access with the changing hardware and software/file formats etc. is a kind of commitment to provide long term preservation thus helps authors more confidence in the future accessibility and more incentives to deposit the content.
- The majority of Institutional repositories are relying on a short-term funding, thus makes it hard to make long-term commitments.
- It is difficult to determine the cost estimation involved in digital preservation.
- Institutional Repositories should build trust on the ability of a repository to secure the information for long term.
- There is general lack of practical implementation of preservation standards, technical knowledge in handling technical issues involved in digital preservation.

3.1 *Technical Issues in Digital Preservation*

The followings are technical issues prevalent in the digital preservation of digital content are given as follows:

- ***File Format:*** There are hundreds of file formats (either born digital or digitized object from printed source) and not all formats are suitable for long-term preservation. Software programs offer the user a range of options that might influence the preservation of the object. The creator or author might not be aware of these risks. The digital repository manager should seek a balance between easy depositing and costly preservation operations. The file format choice can be influenced to a certain level, by limiting the file formats allowed (to open standard-based file formats, whenever possible) or by performing normalization on the digital objects. Guidelines in this regard will provide better understanding and raising awareness of the authors in preserving contents for a long time (Hockx-Yu, 2006).

- ***File Format Registries:*** There is certain information relating to the digital object which should be stored together such as character sets, supplier of the software, maintenance of the software, environment needed to run the software, necessary tools to render the software, newer versions or perhaps even the successor. Several initiatives have started to store this information in the form of file format registries that can be accessed on the internet. One such example is PRONOM, an initiative of the National Archives of the UK, describing the file format information of over 130 file formats (Weenink, Waaijers and Godtsenhoven, 2008).
- ***Preservation Levels:*** It is a fact that every institution may not have necessary wherewithal to ensure long-term preservation of its digital objects. It may start with building digital repository to preserve digital content at a minimal level, and after a certain period it may hand over the content of the repository over to an organization that is well equipped to perform digital preservation. A *'preservation level'* enables the institution to show the user of the object to which level the repository was able to take its responsibility. In this way, an institution can await the moment technology offers new opportunities to treat the object correctly according to a higher preservation level. Although there is not a fixed list of preservation levels, there are some widely accepted levels. The basic preservation level is 'bit stream preservation'; raw data are being stored and kept exactly as they have been delivered (Bradley, 2006).
- ***Persistent Identifiers:*** While storing a digital document in the repository, it is important to identify this object uniquely, for now and for the long run. Even in case the repository moves to another archive, the objects should keep a unique identifier, the 'persistent identifier'. This identifier enables the researchers and repository managers to identify the object, and use it in the scholarly process. Several systems have been developed such as Uniform Resource Name (URN), the Handle system (http://www.handle.net), the Digital Object Identifier (DOI) and the Persistent Uniform Resource Locators (PURL) (http://purl.oclc.org) (Weenink, Waaijers and Godtsenhoven, 2008).
- ***Migration:*** Migration is the most common preservation strategy which helps to make the digital content accessible in a new environment. Although migration is a widely accepted preservation strategy worldwide, however, it is not always full proof method that all the digital content available in earlier system would also be available in the new environment. Further, it has to be performed on a regular interval of time over the years. Another point is that testing of the results is difficult, time consuming and not yet automated. Migration requires thinking about the characteristics of the objects and it is highly unlikely that after migration all

characteristics are still available in the new object (Trusted Digital Repositories: Attributes and Responsibilities, 2002).

The process of migration from one particular file format to a newer version of the same format needs to be repeated whenever a new version is brought out. Research on this type of migration however, showed that more errors appeared when migrating from one version to the next version of software, then if the migration procedure skipped some versions (Mellor, Paul and Derek, 2002).

- ***Emulation:*** Emulation is the process of bringing digital objects back to life in their original environment on top of a different computer environment. This process is carried out by an emulator, which is, as phrased by the Digital Preservation Test-bed as 'a program that runs on one computer and thereby virtually recreates a different computer'. In this definition the word 'virtual' denotes that the emulator functions like the original computer, but differs physically. The original computer is called the 'target platform', the computer that executes the emulator is called the 'host platform' (Digital Preservation Test bed, 2003).

  Emulation can be done at three different levels: the application software level, the system software (operating system) level and the hardware level. Emulating both application and system software requires knowledge of their design and implementation. These products are complex and very often proprietary, which makes it difficult to emulate. Another issue with application level emulation is that each application requires a specific emulator. Since emulation is proposed as preservation action in the field of digital preservation, however, there is a debate whether it is only solution for a large class of digital objects or it is too complex and costly affairs to follow (Digital preservation through emulation, 2006).

4. Current Scenario in Digital Preservation

Digital preservation has to deal with software/hardware migration, physical deterioration of digital media, metadata, user needs and preferences. The Consultative Committee for Space Data Systems published a *Reference Model for an Open Archival Information System* (OAIS) (13) that defined the functions needing to be supported by an archive responsible for preserving content on behalf of a designated community. OAIS introduced the concepts of a Submission Information Package (SIP) and a Dissemination Information Package (DIP) as ways of bringing content into or delivering it from an archive, and outlined the kind of information needing to be included: not just files or pointers to them, but also the reference, provenance, context and fixity information needed for preservation management purposes. The schematic diagram of OAIS Reference Model has shown in Figure 1.

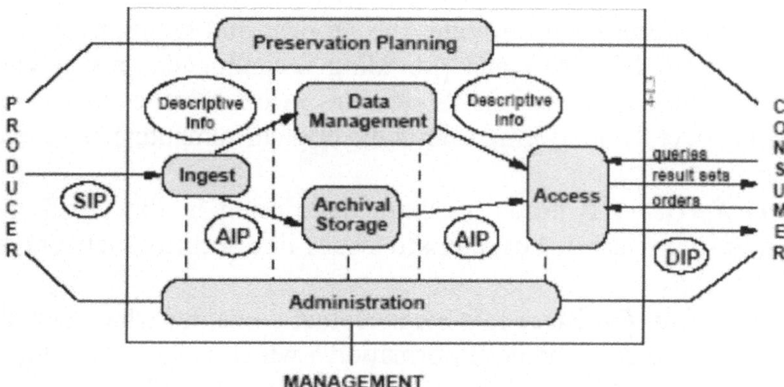

Fig. 1: OAIS Model (CCSDC, 2002)

Function of OAIS Model: OAIS model has the following six functions such as Ingest, Access, Data Management, Archival Storage, Administration and Preservation Planning. A seventh block, that is always present but not part of the figure, is Common Services.

Ingest: The Ingest function provides the services and functions to cover several activities around the Submission Information Package (the digital object), ultimately resulting in an Archival Information Package (AIP) that is fully prepared to be stored. This means, quality assurance checks have been performed and that the necessary descriptive information has been generated to make it possible for users to find the digital object in the archive.

Archival Storage: This entity provides the services and functions for the storage, maintenance and retrieval of AIPs. Functions like receiving Archival Information Packages from Ingest and adding them to permanent storage, managing the storage hierarchy, refreshing the media on which the holdings are stored, perform routine and special error checking provide disaster recovery capabilities and providing AIPs to Access to fulfill orders.

Management: It provides the services and functions for populating, maintaining and accessing both descriptive Information like descriptive metadata (which facilitates the access to the object) and administrative metadata used to manage the archive. This includes performing queries on the data, providing reports of these queries, performing database updates and administering the archive database functions.

4.1 *Administration*

It provides the services and functions for the overall operation of the archive system.

- ***Access:*** It provides the services and functions that support consumers in determining the existence, description, location and availability of information stored in the OAIS, and allowing consumers to request and receive information products.

- ***Preservation Planning:*** It provides the services and functions for monitoring the environment of the OAIS and providing recommendations to ensure that the information stored in the OAIS remains accessible to the Designated User Community over the long term, even if the original computing environment becomes obsolete.
- ***Common Services:*** It needs no extra description in the OAIS model, as this function is so pervasive, but refers to issues like security, network and operating system services.
- ***The Information Package:*** It is a conceptual container which contains two types of information, first, "Content Information", which is the actual digital object that the repository wants to preserve, and the second is "Preservation Description Information (PDI). The Content Information and PDI are viewed as being encapsulated and identifiable by the Packaging Information. The resulting package is viewed as being discoverable by virtue of the Descriptive Information.
- Information Package can be viewed differently keeping in view of its roles and functions from the perspective of OAIS Reference model as shown in Figure 1. The Information Package is called SIP (Submission Information Package) when the Information Package, coming from the producer, is sent to the OAIS archive. Once submitted and archived, it is called an Archival Information Package (AIP). When a member of the Designated Community via descriptive information retrieves one AIP or a set of related AIPs, it is called 'Dissemination Information package (DIP)'. In all cases the information package consists of the digital object but the information of the PDI is also connected.

5. OAIS Model for Institutional Repositories

An attempt has been made to present the scenario of digital preservation and role of metadata standards such as Metadata Encoding and Transfer System (METS) in the context of institutional repositories. DSpace is one such Institutional Repository software that has implemented METS Submission Information Package (SIP) and Dissemination Information Package (DIP) as a wrapper for containing descriptive, technical, structural metadata and its associated files.

A number of IRs software are using METS for exchanging metadata as well for preserving metadata to understand the changes happened in the life cycle of document. DSpace is open source IR software which is taking special care in preservation of bit stream of the digital object as well metadata in exporting in METS format.

6. METS Profile

METS, a Digital Library Federation initiative, attempts to build upon the work of MOA2 and provide an XML document format for encoding metadata necessary for both management of digital library objects within a repository and exchange of such objects between repositories (or between repositories and their users). Depending on its use, a METS document could be used in the role of Submission Information Package (SIP), Archival Information Package (AIP), or Dissemination Information Package (DIP) within the Open Archival Information System (OAIS) Reference Model (Metadata encoding and transmission standard, n.d., METS, n.d. and Bell and Lewis, 2006). A METS document consists of seven major sections:

- ***METS Header:*** The METS Header contains metadata describing the METS document itself, including such information as creator, editor, etc.
- ***Descriptive Metadata*****:** The descriptive metadata section may point to descriptive metadata external to the METS document (e.g., a MARC record in an OPAC or an EAD finding aid maintained on a WWW server), or contain internally embedded descriptive metadata, or both. Multiple instances of both external and internal descriptive metadata may be included in the descriptive metadata section.
- ***Administrative Metadata:*** The administrative metadata section provides information regarding how the files were created and stored, intellectual property rights, metadata regarding the original source object from which the digital library object derives, and information regarding the provenance of the files comprising the digital library object (*i.e.* master/derivative file relationships, and migration/transformation information). As with descriptive metadata, administrative metadata may be either external to the METS document or encoded internally.
- ***File Section:*** The file section lists all files containing content which comprise the electronic versions of the digital object. <file> elements may be grouped within <fileGrp> elements, to provide for subdividing the files by object version.
- ***Structural Map:*** The structural map is the heart of a METS document. It outlines a hierarchical structure for the digital library object, and links the elements of that structure to content files and metadata that pertain to each element.
- ***Structural Links:*** The Structural Links section of METS allows METS creators to record the existence of hyperlinks between nodes in the hierarchy outlined in the Structural Map. This is of particular value in using METS to archive Websites.
- ***Behavior:*** A behavior section can be used to associate executable behaviors with content in the METS object. Each behavior within a behavior section has an interface definition element that represents an abstract definition of the set of behaviors represented by a particular behavior section. Each behavior also has a mechanism element which identifies a module of executable code that implements and runs the behaviors defined abstractly by the interface definition.

7. Mets Profile in Dspace

DSpace (http://www.dspace.org) is an open source software platform that enables organizations to capture and describe digital material using a submission workflow module, or a variety of programmatic ingest options. It distributes an organization's digital assets over the web through a search and retrieval system and preserves digital assets over long term. METS document represent one DSpace item only. DSpace has defined a set of technical metadata elements for preservation and administration. This metadata includes a unique identifier, check sum, checksum type, mime type, file size, creation date and file path originally assigned to the file. In case, this data exist in the system, it should be included within the METS document. Inclusion of technical metadata should occur in the techMD element and should conform to PREMIS data dictionary.

DSpace includes a package disseminator and matching ingester for the DSpace METS SIP (Submission Information Package) format. Packagers are software modules that translate between DSpace Item objects and a self-contained external representation, or "package". A package ingester interprets, or ingests the package and creates an Item. A package disseminator writes out the contents of an Item in the package format. A package is typically an archive file such as a Zip or "tar" file, including a manifest document which contains metadata and a description of the package contents. The METS is a typical packaging standard. A package might also be a single document or media file that contains its own metadata, such as a PDF document with embedded descriptive metadata.

8. Discussion

Institution repositories must have policy in terms of content management, rights management, long term preservation policy etc. Peter Millington (2006) discovered that about two thirds of Open Access repositories did not have publicly stated policies for the permitted re-use of deposited items and OpenDoar has provided a tool (http://opendoar.org/tools/en/policies.php) to Institutional Repositories Manager to provide their IRS policy for such things as submission of items, long term preservation, etc. Various issues relating to digital preservation can be resolved by adopting metadata standard approach. METS, as it has been widely used in institutional repository software can be used as a means of transmitting a representation of an object (physical or digital or partially digital) from one system to another. It can:

- Fully describe the object and its components.
- Encode the metadata needed to aid its preservation and future access.
- Represent the physical and/or logical structure of highly complex objects.
- Represent collections of objects, even where these objects are not stored in the same repository.
- Support a range of submission and dissemination scenarios.

9. Conclusion

Digital preservation requires new workflow, new skills and close cooperation across different professions ranging from traditional preservation management to computing science. OAIS model are providing framework to implement preservation strategy and institutional repositories software a mean to implement these preservation strategy. As Australian National Library has developed Metadata Encoding and Transfer System (METS) profile as submission and dissemination package for integration of various services in Australia. Similar effort at National level in the country may be initiated so that single METS profile keeping in view of local need may be developed or adopting the existing profile as developed by international organizations for the purpose of preserving metadata of digital object and may also be used for the purpose of interoperability across digital repositories.

References

[1] Jones, M. and Neil B. (2008). The Preservation Management of Digital Material Handbook [online text], UK: Digital Preservation Coalition. Retrieved from the website: http://www.dpconline.org/graphics/handbook/. Accessed on 30 August 2012.

[2] Crow, R. (2002). The Case for Institutional Repositories: A SPARC Position Paper the Scholarly Publishing and Academic Resources Coalition, *ARL Bimonthly Report* 223. Retrieved from SPARC website: http://www.arl.org/bm~doc/instrepo.pdf. Accessed on 30 August 2012.

[3] Lynch, C.A. (2003). Institutional Repositories: Essential Infrastructure for Scholarship in the Digital Age, *ARL Bimonthly Report* 226. Retrieved from SPARC website: http://www.arl.org/newsltr/226/ir.html Accessed on 30 August 2012.

[4] Weenink, K., Waaijers, L. and Godtsenhoven, K.V. [Eds.] (2008). *A DRIVER's Guide to European Repositories*, Amsterdam: Amsterdam University Press. Retrieved from DRIVER website: http://www.driver-repository.eu/PublicDocs/D7.2_1.1.pdf Accessed on 30 August 2012.

[5] Saha, B. (2006). Digital archiving and preservation: present scenario. *In* 4th Convention PLANNER-2006, Mizoram Univ., Aizawl, 09–10 November, 2006. Retrieved from Shodhganga website: http://shodhganga.inflibnet.ac.in/dxml/bitstream/handle/1944/1258/265-274.pdf? Accessed on 30 August 2012.

[6] Hockx-Yu, H. (2006). Digital preservation in the context of institutional repositories. Retrieved from E-LIS website: http://eprints.rclis.org/archive/00007351/ Accessed on 30 August 2012.

[7] Bradley, K. (2006). Digital Sustainability and Digital Repositories. Retrieved from http://unpan1.un.org/intradoc/groups/public/documents/APCITY/UNPAN023378.pdf Accessed on 30 August 2012.

[8] *Trusted Digital Repositories: Attributes and Responsibilities* (2002), California: Research Library Group (RLG).

[9] Mellor, P., Paul, W. and Derek, S. (2002). Migration on Request: A practical technique for digital preservation. Retrieved from Camileon website: http://www.si.umich.edu/CAMILEON/reports/reports.html Accessed on 30 August 2012.

[10] Digital Preservation Test bed, "Emulation: context and current status" (The Hague,2003) http://www.digitaleduurzaamheid.nl/bibliotheek/docs/white_paper_emulatie_EN.pdf Accessed on 30 August 2012.

[11] *Digital preservation through emulation* (2006). Retrieved from Digitization 101 website: http://hurstassociates.blogspot.com/2006/11/digital-preservation-through-emulation.html Accessed on 30 August 2012.

[12] CCSDC (2002). *Reference model for an Open Archival Information System (OAIS): Recommendation for Space Data System, Blue Book*, Washington: CCSDC. Retrieved from CCSDC website: http://public.ccsds.org/publications/archive/650x0b1.pdf Accessed on 30 August 2012.

[13] Metadata encoding and transmission standard: primer and reference manual. Retrieved from Library of Congress website: http://www.loc.gov/standards/mets/METS%20 Documentation% 20final%20070930%20msw.pdf. Accessed on 30 August 2012.

[14] METS: an introduction and tutorial. Retrieved from Library of Congress website: http://www.loc.gov/standards/mets/METSoverview.v2.html Accessed on 30 August 2012.

[15] Bell, J. and Lewis S. (2006). Using OAI-PMH and METS for exporting metadata and digital objects between repositories. *Program*, 40(3), 268–276.

[16] Peter, M. (2006). *Moving forward with the OpenDOAR Directory* In 8th International Conference on Current Research Information Systems, Bergen, and 11th–13th May 2006. Retrieved from SHERPA website: http://opendoar.nottingham.ac.uk/documents/BergenPresentation20060512 Handouts.ppt Accessed on 30 August 2012.

[17] *Australian METS profile.* Retrieved from National Library of Australia website:_http://www.nla.gov.au/australianmetsprofile. Accessed on 30 August 2012.

Electronic Resources Management in Libraries, pp. 333–347

Heredity Blood Disorders: A Scientometric Analysis of Publications Output from India during 2002–2011

B.M. Gupta

ABSTRACT

This study analyses the heredity blood disorder research output carried out during 2002–11 on different parameters including the global publications share and citation quality of top 10 leading countries. India's growth, citation impact, share of international collaborative papers, contribution of major collaborative partner countries, contribution of various subject fields and by type of heredity blood disorder, pattern of research communication in most productive journals, productivity and citation profile of top Indian institutions and authors and characteristics of high cited papers. The SCOPUS Citation Database has been used to retrieve the data for 10 years (2002–11). It is found that there is a need to create comprehensive care services, including diagnosis and management of the heredity blood disorders in Indian context. For this purpose, there is need to undertake more R&D, develop trained manpower at different levels and create sufficient infrastructure to handle the problems associated with heredity blood disorders.

1. Introduction

The blood is living tissue made up of liquid and solids. The liquid part, called plasma, is made of water, salts and protein. Over half of your blood is plasma. The solid part of the blood contains red blood cells, white blood cells and platelets. Red blood cells deliver oxygen from lungs to our tissues and organs. White blood cells help fight infections and are part of body's defense system. Platelets help form clots to stop bleeding. Plasma, the liquid part of blood, contains many types of proteins. These include proteins that help the blood to clot and proteins that protect the body from viruses and infection. Plasma also contains substances such as dissolved salts, sugars, and hormones. Blood cells are produced by the soft tissue inside our bones, called bone marrow. Blood cells constantly die and your body makes new ones. Red blood cells live about 120 days, platelets 6 days and white cells less than a day. Blood is essential for life. It carries oxygen and nutrients to every part of the body. Blood also fights infections and heals injuries. Therefore, disorders of the blood can have a great effect on your health.[1] There are many different types of blood disorders. Some blood disorders are caused by excessive blood loss from injury, some are caused by other diseases and even still, some are caused by certain medications. Yet, there are some blood disorders that are hereditary. Heredity Blood Diseases or Disorders (HBD) are a group of diseases which are transmitted from parents to children and are caused by defects in the makeup of red blood cells resulting in blood cells that are unable to perform their natural functions. The most common hereditary blood disorders include hemophilia, von Willebrand disease, thrombophilia, thalassemia and sickle cell anemia.

Thalassaemia is a blood related genetic disorder which involves the absence of or errors in genes responsible for production of haemoglobin, a protein present in the red blood cells. Each red blood cell can contain between 240 and 300 million molecules of haemoglobin. The severity of the disease depends on the mutations involved in the genes, and their interplay. A haemoglobin molecule has sub-units commonly referred to as alpha and beta. Both sub-units are necessary to bind oxygen in the lungs properly and deliver it to tissues in other parts of the body. Genes on chromosome 16 are responsible for alpha subunits, while genes on chromosome 11 control the production of beta subunits. A lack of a particular subunit determines the type of thalassaemia (*e.g.* a lack of alpha subunits results in alpha-thalassemia). The lack of subunits thus corresponds to errors in the genes on the appropriate chromosomes. There can be various gradations of the disease depending on the gene and the type of mutations. The alpha and beta thalassaemias are the most common inherited single-gene disorders in the world with the highest prevalence in areas where malaria was or still is endemic.[3] Thalassemia in India the prevalence shows the estimated number of thalassemics in India is 1,00,000. On an average 8 to 10 thousand thalassaemia majors born in India every year.[4]

Sickle-cell anemia is a blood related disorder that affects the haemoglobin molecule and causes the entire blood cell to change shape under stressed conditions. In sickle cell anaemia, the haemoglobin molecule is defective. After haemoglobin molecules give up their oxygen, some may cluster together and form long, rod-like structures which become stiff and assume sickle shape. Unlike healthy red blood cells, which are usually smooth and donut-shaped, sickled red blood cells cannot squeeze through small blood vessels. Instead, they stack up and cause blockages that deprive organs and tissues of oxygen-carrying blood. This process produces periodic episodes of pain and ultimately can damage tissues and vital organs and lead to other serious medical problems. Normal red blood cells live about 120 days in the bloodstream, but sickled red cells die after about 10 to 20 days. Because they cannot be replaced fast enough, the blood is chronically short of red blood cells, leading to a condition commonly referred to as anemia.[5] According to ICMR survey, sickle cell gene is found amongst different tribal groups mainly in central and southern parts of India, which varies from 5 to 34% of their population.[6]

Haemophilia is a hereditary bleeding disorder, in which there is a partial or total lack of an essential blood clotting factor. It is a lifelong disorder, that results in excessive bleeding, and many times spontaneous bleeding, which, very often is internal. Haemophilia A is the most common form, referred to as classical haemophilia. It is the result of a deficiency in clotting factor 8, while Haemophilia B (Christmas disease) is a deficiency in clotting factor 9. This illness is a sex-linked recessive disorder. Due to the sex-linkage of the disorder, there is a greater prominence in males than in females.[7] With an estimated prevalence rate of 1:10,000, approximately 1,00,000 people are estimated to be haemophiliac in India, out of which 50,000 are likely to be severe. There are however, only about 13,000 registered patients.[8]

Von Willebrand's disease is a hereditary deficiency or abnormality of the blood protein von Willebrand factor, which affects platelet function. The von Willebrand factor is found in plasma, platelets, and the walls of blood vessels. When the factor is missing or defective, platelets cannot adhere to the vessel wall at the site of an injury. As a result, bleeding does not stop as quickly as it should.[9] Thrombophilia is a disorder in which the blood clots easily or excessively. Inherited and acquired disorders can increase blood clotting. Clots cause legs or arms to swell. Blood levels of proteins that control clotting are measured. People may need anticoagulants. Most disorders that cause thrombophilia increase the risk of blood clot formation in veins; a few increase the risk of clot formation in both arteries and veins.[10]

The Indian health ministry plan soon to roll out a national programme to prevent and manage hereditary blood disorders (HBDs) as per the report of the Planning Commission's Working Group on Health for the 12th Five Year Plan. A registry of hereditary blood disorders will be set up to collect actual data. For providing comprehensive care services, including diagnosis and management of HBDs, 120 medical colleges/hospitals across the country will be strengthened to have in it a haematologist/biochemist and a pathologist. Molecular genetics laboratory will also be set up at 20 Indian medical colleges that shall act as final referral centre for designated districts. These genetic laboratories will be developed in a phased manner with five new each year of the 12th Five Year Plan. In the first year of the plan, institutes like All India Institute of Medical Sciences (AIIMS), New Delhi; Christian Medical College (CMC), Vellore; King Edward Memorial Hospital (KEMH), Mumbai; Post Graduate Institute of Medical Education and Research (PGIMER), Chandigarh, along with the one in Kolkata will be strengthened. These institutes will also train gynaecologists/ sonologists to conduct prenatal diagnostic procedures for prenatal diagnosis for hereditary disorders. The Department of Haematology at AIIMS will coordinate the quality control for the diagnosis of haemoglobinopathies. Each molecular genetic lab will be supported with ₹ 25 lakh as a one-time grant and ₹ 20 lakh/year as recurring budget for human resource, drugs, reagents and other consumables. AIIMS and PGIMER, Chandigarh, and National Institute of Immunohaematology (NIIH), Mumbai, will serve as nodal training centres since these are already carrying out such comprehensive care. Counsellors may be trained in the psychiatric department of different medical colleges (tertiary care centres). A fully-fledged DM (Clinical Genetics) programme may be developed at one of the tertiary care centres. An amount of ₹ 25 lakh annual budget per year will be required for this scheme. According to the Commission, there are around 10,000–12,000 new thalassemia syndrome and 7,000–10,000 new sickle cell anaemia patients added annually in India. Besides, there are around 1, 20,000 haemophilia patients of which 14,000 are registered.[11]

There are no specific studies available in the literature dealing with scientometric analysis of publications in the area of heredity blood disorders. However, the author has carried out similar studies in Indian context on other diseases such as diabetes,[12] tuberculosis,[13] malaria,[14] asthma[15] and AIDS/HIV.[16]

2. Objectives

The main objectives of this paper is analyze Indian publications output in heredity blood disorders during the last ten years from 2002–11. In particular, the study focuses on the following objectives: (i) to analyse the contribution and citation impact of top 10 most productive countries and identify the place of India among them, (ii) to analyse the growth, citation impact and international collaborative share of Indian research; (iii) to study the contribution, citation impact and international collaborative share of different types of heredity blood disorders in India and in global context, (iv) to study research output in context of different subjects, (v) to study the research profile of most productive Indian institutions and authors; and (vi) to study the media of communication of research output and identification of characteristics of highly cited papers.

3. Methodology and Database Used

This study is based on the Indian publication data in heredity blood disorder retrieved from the Scopus Citation database [http://www.scopus.com/search/] for the 10 years (2002–2011). The string used to retrieve the data in heredity blood disorder was developed using the following keywords: heredity blood disorders, thalassemia, sickle cell anaemia, haemophilia, thrombophilia and von Willebrand disease along with India. The search using the above keywords becomes finally our main string. For citations data, three years, two year, one year and zero years citations window has been used for computing average citations per paper in heredity blood disorder research during 2002–08, 2009, 2010 and 2011. For searching and calculating the total international collaborative papers, a separate search strategy, which combines India's collaboration with 140 major countries, was prepared and this string was combined with the main string to generate India's total international collaborative output. For analyzing institutional, author and journals output, the separate search strategies for generating institutional, author and journal outputs were developed, which later combined with the main string to generate the desired output.

4. Contribution and Citation Impact of Leading Countries

The world has published 29773 papers in heredity blood disorders during the last ten years from 2002–11, which has increased from 13107 papers during 2002–06 to 16666 papers during 2007–11, witnessing a growth rate of 27.15%. Among the twenty leading countries contributing to heredity blood disorders research, the largest output of 7544 papers (with 25.79% share) comes from United States during 2002–11, followed by United Kingdom (2762 papers, 9.48%), Italy (2455 papers, 8.84%), France (1693 papers, 5.77%), Germany (1577 papers, 5.14%), Netherlands (1176 papers, 3.97%), Canada (1022 papers, 3.49%), India (921 papers, 3.09%), Spain (763 papers, 2.63%), Turkey (699 papers, 2.39%), Australia (682 papers, 2.29%), Greece (675 papers, 2.27%), Japan (617 papers, 2.07%), Brazil (600 papers, 2.02% share), China (595 papers, 2.00% share), Iran (535 papers, 1.80%), Israel (490 papers, 1.65%), Thailand (482 papers, 1.62%), Sweden (434 papers, 1.46%) and Switzerland (433 papers, 1.45%). Among the top 10 publishing countries in heredity blood disorders, the publishing share has increased in United States (from 25.63% to 25.92%), Italy (from 7.85% to 8.84%), Netherlands (from 3.96% to 3.98%), Canada (from 3.27% to 3.66%), India (from 2.91% to 3.23%), Spain (from 2.43% to 2.78%) and Turkey (from 2.33% to 2.44%), as against decrease in United Kingdom (from 10.43% to 8.73%), France (from 5.90% to 5.68%) and Germany (from 5.69% to 5.14%) from 2002–06 to 2007–11. In terms

Table 1: Contribution and Citation Impact of Top 10 Countries in HBD, 2002–11

Country	*Number of Papers*			*Share of Papers*			*Citations*	*ACPP*
	2002–2006	*2007–2011*	*2002–2011*	*2002–2006*	*2007–2011*	*2002–2011*	*2002–2011*	*2002–2011*
USA	3359	4319	7678	25.63	25.92	25.79	67713	8.82
UK	1367	1455	2822	10.43	8.73	9.48	27179	9.63
Italy	1029	1473	2592	7.85	8.84	8.71	19910	7.96
France	773	946	1719	5.90	5.68	5.77	11289	6.57
Germany	746	857	1603	5.69	5.14	5.38	11878	7.40
Netherlands	519	664	1183	3.96	3.98	3.97	11924	10.08
Canada	429	610	1039	3.27	3.66	3.49	9614	9.25
India	382	539	921	2.91	3.23	3.09	2235	2.43
Spain	318	464	782	2.43	2.78	2.63	4607	5.89
Turkey	305	406	711	2.33	2.44	2.39	2014	2.82
World	13,107	16,666	29,773	100.00	100.00	100.00		

of citation impact per paper during 2002–11, the highest among the top 10 countries was achieved by Netherlands (10.08), followed by UK (9.63), Canada (9.25), USA (8.82), Italy (7.96), Germany (7.40), France (6.57), Spain (5.89), Turkey (2.82) and India (2.43) (Table 1).

5. Indian Contribution, Citation Impact and International Collaboration

Indian contribution in heredity blood disorder has increased from 56 papers in 2002 to 111 papers during 2011, witnessing an annual average growth rate of 9.09%. Its cumulative contribution has increased from 382 papers during 2002–06 to 539 papers during 2007–11, witnessing a growth rate of 41.09%. The average citation per paper registered by India's research in heredity blood disorders during 2002–11 was 2.43, which has decreased from 3.35 during 2002–06 to 1.77 during 2007–11. India has contributed 10.31% international collaborative papers share in heredity blood disorder during 2002–11, which has decreased from 11.52% during 2002–06 to 9.46% during 2007–11 (Table 2).

In all 34 countries participated in international collaboration with India in heredity blood disorders during 2002–11, of which contribution of top 15 countries are listed in Table 3. The largest contribution to international collaborative papers of India in heredity blood disorder comes from United States (with 43 papers, 45.26% share), followed by UK (25 papers, 26.32%), Italy, Japan, Canada, Australia, France, Germany, Iran, Netherlands, Pakistan, Sweden, Thailand, Saudi Arabia and Taiwan (Table 3).

Table 2: India's Research Output, Citation Impact and International Collaborative Papers Share during 2002–11

Period	*TP*	*TC*	*ACPP*	*ICP*	*%ICP*
2002	56	98	1.75	5	8.93
2003	77	178	2.31	7	9.09
2004	76	209	2.75	9	11.84
2005	91	379	4.16	11	12.09
2006	82	416	5.07	12	14.63
2007	104	365	3.51	7	6.73
2008	98	233	2.38	10	10.20
2009	103	200	1.94	4	3.88
2010	123	121	0.98	14	11.38
2011	111	36	0.32	16	14.41
2002–06	382	1280	3.35	44	11.52
2007–11	539	955	1.77	51	9.46
2002–11	921	2235	2.43	95	10.31

Table 3: Share of Top 15 Countries in International Collaborative Papers of India during 2002–11

Country	*ICP*	*% Share*	*Country*	*ICP*	*% Share*
USA	43	45.26	Iran	6	6.32
UK	25	26.32	Netherlands	6	6.32
Italy	12	12.63	Pakistan	5	5.26
Japan	11	11.58	Sweden	5	5.26
Canada	11	11.58	Thailand	4	4.21
Australia	8	8.42	Saudi Arabia	3	3.16
France	7	7.37	Taiwan	3	3.16
Germany	6	6.32	Total	95	

6. Types of Heredity Blood Disorders

Under different type of heredity blood disorders, the maximum publication output (524) of India during 2002–11 was on thalassemia (with 56.89%), followed by sickle cell anaemia (193 papers, 20.96%), haemophilia (105 papers, 11.40%), von Willebrand disease (99 papers, 10.75%) and thrombophilia (85 papers, 9.23%). In terms of citation impact per paper, the maximum citation impact (4.58) during 2002–11 was in von Willebrand disease, followed by haemophilia (2.81), thrombophilia (2.25), thalassemia (2.13) and sickle cell anaemia (1.60). Compared to the world output, India's citation impact per paper was less in all types of HBDs. In terms of global share, the maximum was in thalassemia (6.52%), followed by haemophilia (3.92%), sickle cell anaemia (2.58%), von Willebrand disease (1.50%) and thrombophilia (1.33%) (Table 4–5).

Table 4: India and World Publication Output and Citations in Different Types of HBD, 2002–11

Types of HBD	*India*			*World*			*India's Share in World*
	TP	*TC*	*ACPP*	*TP*	*TC*	*ACPP*	
Thalassemia	524	1116	2.13	8035	36846	4.59	6.52
Sickle Cell Anaemia	193	309	1.60	7487	38142	5.09	2.58
Haemophilia	105	295	2.81	2680	11675	4.36	3.92
Von Willebrand Disease	99	453	4.58	6620	48455	7.32	1.50
Thrombophilia	85	191	2.25	6370	34150	5.36	1.33

Note: TP = Total papers; TC = Total citations; ACPP = Average citations per paper

Table 5: Indian Publication Output and International Collaborative Publications Share in Different Types of HBD, 2002–11

Types of HBD	*TP*	*IC P*	*%ICP*	*H-Index*	*Share in India's Output*
Thalassemia	524	47	8.97	16	56.89
Sickle Cell Anemia	193	13	6.74	12	20.96
Haemophilia	105	15	14.29	9	11.40
Von Willebrand Disease	99	19	19.19	13	10.75
Thrombophilia	85	6	7.06	9	9.23

Note. There is also some overlapping in the coverage of literature under different type of heredity blood disorder. TP = Total papers; TC = Total citations; ACPP = Average citations per paper.

7. Indian Heredity Blood Disorders Research Output in Context of Different Subjects

On analyzing the publication data, it was found that the Indian research output in heredity blood disorders during 2002–11 has been published in context of 6 subjects, with highest publications output coming from medicine (810 papers, 87.95% publications share), followed by biochemistry, genetics and molecular biology (175 papers, 19.00%), pharmacology, toxicology and pharmaceutics (37 papers, 4.02%), immunology and microbiology (20 papers, 2.17%), agricultural and biological sciences (11 papers, 1.19%) and neurosciences (9 papers, 0.98%). On analyzing the quality and impact of Indian heredity blood disorders research under different subjects, it was found that agricultural and biological sciences had scored the highest impact (4.00 citations per paper), followed by neurosciences (3.89), pharmacology, toxicology and pharmaceutics (3.62), medicine (2.36), biochemistry, genetics and molecular biology (2.30) and immunology and microbiology (2.20) during 2002–11 (Table 6).

Table 6: Subject-Wise Break-up of Indian HBD Publications during 2002–11

Subject	*Papers*	*Citations*	*ACPP*	*% Share*
Medicine	810	1914	2.36	87.95
Biochemistry, Genetics and Molecular Biology	175	403	2.30	19.00
Pharmacology, Toxicology and Pharmaceutics	37	134	3.62	4.02
Immunology and Microbiology	20	44	2.20	2.17
Agri. and Biol Sciences	11	44	4.00	1.19
Neurosciences	9	35	3.89	0.98
Total Indian Papers	921			

8. Research Profile of Most Productive Indian Institutions in Heredity Blood Disorders

The top 10 most productive Indian institutions involved in heredity blood disorders research have published 14 and more papers each during 2002–11. The publications profile of these 10 Indian institutions along with their research output, citations received and h-index values are presented in Table 7. These 10 Indian institutions involved in heredity blood disorders research together have contributed 60.69% share (with 559 papers) in the cumulative publications output of India in heredity blood disorders, with an average of 55.9 papers per institution. Only 4 Indian institutions have registered higher publications share than the group average. These are NIIH, Mumbai with 145 papers, followed by AIIMS, New Delhi (107 papers), KEMH, Mumbai (86 papers) and CMC, Vellore (65 papers). The average citation per paper registered by the total papers of these 10 Indian institutions is 2.88 during 2002–11. Only 2 Indian institutions have registered higher impact than the group average. The highest impact of 6.97 citations per paper was scored by the CMC, Vellore, followed by Sir Ganga Ram Hospital (SGRH), New Delhi (3.29 citations per paper). The average h-index value of these 10 Indian most productive institutions was 8.2 during 2002–11. The five Indian institutions have scored higher h-index value than group's average of 8.2. The highest h-index value (14) was achieved by CMC, Vellore, followed by NIIH, Mumbai and AIIMS, New Delhi (12 each), KEMH, Mumbai (11) and Sanjay Gandhi Postgraduate Institute of Medical Sciences (SGPIMS), Lucknow (9) (Table 7).

Table 7: Productivity and Citation Impact of Top 10 Indian Institutions in HBD, 2002–11

Sl. No.	*Name*	*TP*	*TC*	*ACPP*	*h-index*
1.	NIIH, Mumbai	145	335	2.31	12
2.	AIIMS, New Delhi	107	271	2.53	12
3.	KEMH, Mumbai	86	224	2.60	11
4.	CMC, Vellore	65	453	6.97	14
5.	PGIMER, Chandigarh	54	81	1.50	7
6.	SGPIMS, Lucknow	41	96	2.34	9
7.	Regional Medical Research Center (RMRC), Bhubaneshwar	19	51	2.68	6
8.	Armed Forces Medical College of India, Pune	14	34	2.43	4
9.	SGRH, New Delhi	14	46	3.29	4
10.	Institute of Medical Sciences, BHU, Varanasi	14	17	1.21	3
		559	1608	2.88	8.2

Note: TP =Total papers; TC = Total citations; ACPP = Average citations per paper.

8.1 *Contributions and Citation Impact of Most Productive Authors in Indian Heredity Blood Disorders*

Based on the publication output, 10 most productive authors having been identified who have published 18 and above papers in heredity blood disorder. Of these four authors are affiliated to NIIH, Mumbai, three to AIIMS, New Delhi, two to CMC, Vellore and one to RMRC, Bhubaneshwar. These 10 authors together contributed 459 papers with an average of 45.9 papers per author and account for 49.84% share in the cumulative publications output of India during 2002–11. Five authors have published higher number of papers than the group average (45.9). These are: K. Ghosh with 90 papers, followed by S. Shetty (63 papers), D. Mohanty (62 papers), R. Saxena (62 papers) and R.B. Colah (50 papers). Considering the quality/impact of papers, these most productive authors have received a total of 1447 citations for 459 papers with an average of 3.15 citations per paper. Two authors have registered higher impact than the average impact of papers of all authors (3.15). These are: A. Srivastava with 6.03 citations per paper and M. Chandy (5.14 citations per paper). Measuring the performance of these authors on the basis of h-index, five authors have achieved the higher h-index value than the group average of 9.5. These authors are A. Srivatava with h-index of 13, followed by K. Ghosh (12), S. Shetty (11), D. Mohanty (11) and R. Saxena (10) (Table 8).

Table 8: Productivity and Citation Impact of 10 Most Productive Indian Authors in HBD, 2002–11

Sl. No.	*Name*	*Institution*	*TP*	*TC*	*ACPP*	*h-Index*
1.	K. Ghosh	NIIH, Mumbai	90	248	2.76	12
2.	S. Shetty	NIIH, Mumbai	63	165	2.62	11
3.	D. Mohanty	NIIH, Mumbai	62	163	2.63	11
4.	R. Saxena	AIIMS, New Delhi	62	175	2.82	10
5.	R. B.Colah	NIIH, Mumbai	50	122	2.44	9
6.	A. Srivastava	CMC, Vellore	38	229	6.03	13
7.	V.P. Choudhry	AIIMS, New Delhi	29	91	3.14	9
8.	M. Chandy	CMC, Vellore	28	144	5.14	9
9.	M. Kannan	AIIMS, New Delhi	19	55	2.89	6
10.	R.S. Balgir	RMRC, Bhubaneshwar	18	55	3.06	5
	Total		459	1447	3.15	9.5

Note: TP =Total papers; TC = Total citations; ACPP = Average citations per paper.

8.2 *Research Communication in High Productive Journals*

The 20 most productive Indian and foreign journals publishing Indian research papers together contributed 415 papers in heredity blood disorder, which accounts for

45.06% share of the total output of India during 2002–11. The cumulative publications output share of these 20 most productive journals showed a decrease in India's publications output from 50.00% during 2002–06 to 41.56% during 2007–11 (Table 9).

Table 9: List of Most Productive Journals Publishing Indian Papers in HBD, 2002–11

Sl. No.	*Name of the Journal*	*Number of Papers*		
		2002–06	*2007–11*	*2002–11*
1.	Haemophilia	25	28	53
2.	Indian Journal of Paediatrics	19	28	47
3.	Indian Paediatrics	22	11	33
4.	Indian Journal of Pathology and Microbiology	13	19	32
5.	Journal of Association of Physicians of India	16	10	26
6.	Haemoglobin	15	9	24
7.	Haematology	10	14	24
8.	Annals of Haematology	9	10	19
9.	Indian Journal of Medical Research	5	14	19
10.	Indian Journal of Haematology and Blood Transfusion	6	12	18
11.	European Journal of Haematology	6	10	16
12.	British Journal of Haematology	6	8	14
13.	American Journal of Haematology	8	5	13
14.	Clinica Chimica Acta	2	11	13
15.	Indian Journal of Human Genetics	5	8	13
16.	Indian Journal of Clinical Biochemistry	5	6	11
17.	Clinical and Applied Thrombosis and Haemostasis	2	10	12
18.	Journal of the Indian Medical Association	7	3	10
19.	Blood Cells Molecules and Diseases	5	4	9
20.	National Medical Journal of India	5	4	9
	Total	191	224	415
	Total of India	382	539	921
	Share of top 20 journals in Indian output	50.00	41.56	45.06

8.3 *Highly Cited Papers*

The characteristics of top 13 most highly cited papers of India in heredity blood disorder are evaluated in this section. These 13 highly cited papers have received citations (since their publications till April 2012) from 30 to 266 during 2002–11. These 13 highly cited papers have received 926 citations, with an average of 71.23 citations per paper. Of these 13 highly cited papers, seven appeared as reviews, five as articles and one as conference paper. Of these 13 papers, eight involve international collaboration (three bilateral and five multilateral), one involve national collaboration and five papers zero collaboration. Of the 13 highly cited papers, three papers are in citation range of 100–266, three papers in citations range of 50–99 and seven papers in citations range of 30–49. The authors of these high cited papers are affiliated to 13 Indian institutions, including five papers from CMC, Vellore; two papers from AIIMS, New Delhi, and one paper each from Bombay Hospital, Mumbai; Central Drug Research Institute, Lucknow; CMC, Ludhiana; GB Pant Hospital, Delhi; Industrial Toxicology Research Centre, Lucknow; Lalitha Super Specialty Hospital, Guntur; Mahatma Gandhi Institute of Medical Sciences, Wardha; Ranbaxy Research Laboratories, Gurgaon; SGRH, New Delhi; Sree Chitra Tirunal Institute for Medical Sciences and Technology, Thiruvananthapuram and the Institute of Neurological Sciences, Care Hospital, Hyderabad. The 13 highly cited papers in HBD have appeared in 11 journals, including two papers each in *Blood Cells, Molecules and Diseases* and *Journal of Thrombosis and Haemostasis* and one paper each in *Annals of Haematology, Blood, Environmental Toxicology and Pharmacology, Expert Opinion on Drug Safety, Haemophilia, International Journal of Stroke, Journal of Gastroenterology* and *Haematology, National Medical Journal of India* and *Toxicology Letters.* A list of top 13 highly cited papers are given in Table 10.

9. Summary

India has published 921 papers in heredity blood disorder during 2002–11, accounting for 3.09% share in global publications output. India's global publication share in heredity blood disorder has increased from 2.91% during 2002–06 to 3.23% during 2007–11. India's publications output in heredity blood disorder has increased from 56 papers in 2002 to 111 papers in 2011, witnessing an annual average growth rate of 9.09%. The average citation impact per paper registered by Indian papers in heredity blood disorder was 2.43 during 2002–11, which has decreased from 3.35 during 2002–06 to 1.77 during 2007–11. Among the 10 most productive countries in heredity blood disorder, India registered the lowest citation impact per paper during 2002–11. The share of international collaborative papers in India's total publication output in heredity blood disorder was 10.31% during 2002–11, which has decreased from 11.51% during 2002–06 to 9.46% during 2007–11. Thirty four countries participated in international collaboration with India in heredity blood disorder during 2002–11, with largest publication share (45.26%) from USA, followed by UK (26.32%), Italy (12.63%), Japan and Canada (11.58% each), Australia (8.42%), *et al.* In terms of different types of heredity blood disorders, the largest contribution (56.89% share) in India was in

Table 10: List of Top 13 Highly Cited Papers in HBD during 2002–11

Authors	*Title*	*Source*	*Citations*
Sadler, J.E., Budde, U., Srivastava A. *et al.*	Update on the pathophysiology and classification of von Willebrand disease: A report of the Subcommittee on von Willebrand factor	*Journal of Thrombosis and Haemostasis,* 2006, **4**(10), 2103–2114	266
Kumar, S. and Bandyopadhyay, U.	Free heme toxicity and its detoxification systems in human	*Toxicology Letters,* 2005, **157**(3), 175–188	136
Rodeghiero, F., Castaman, G., Srivastava, A. *et al.*	The discriminant power of bleeding history for the diagnosis of type 1 von Willebrand disease: An international, multicenter study	*Journal of Thrombosis and Haemostasis,* 2005, **3**(12), 2619–2626	100
McCaughan, G.W., Amarapurkar, D., Chutaputti, A. *et al.*	Asian Pacific Association for the Study of the Liver consensus statements on the diagnosis, management and treatment of hepatitis C virus infection	*Journal of Gastroenterology and Hepatology,* 2007, **22**(5), 615–633	58
Premawardhena, A., Verma, I.C. *et al.*	The global distribution of length polymorphisms of the promoters of the glucuronosyltransferase 1 gene (UGT1A1): Hematologic and evolutionary implications	*Blood Cells, Molecules, and Diseases,* 2003, **31**(1), 98–101	57
Srivastava, A., Poonkuzhali, B., Shaji, R.V. *et al.*	Glutathione S-transferase M1 polymorphism: A risk factor for hepatic venoocclusive disease in bone marrow transplantation	*Blood,* 2004, **104**(5), 1574–77	53
Baronciani, L., Cozzi, G., Srivastava, A. *et al.*	Molecular defects in type 3 von Willebrand disease: Updated results from 40 multiethnic patients	*Blood Cells, Molecules, and Diseases,* 2003, **30**(3), 264–270	48
Peyvandi, F., Jayandharan, G., Chandy, M., Srivastava, A. *et al.*	Genetic diagnosis of haemophilia and other inherited bleeding disorders	*Haemophilia,* 2006, **12** (Suppl 3), 82–89	37
Dixit, A., Chatterjee, T.C., Mishra, P. *et al.*	Hydroxyurea in thalassemia intermedia—A promising therapy	*Annals of Haematology,* 2005, **84**(7), 441–46	37
Tiwari, A., Bansal, V., Chugh, A. *et al.*	Statins and myotoxicity: A therapeutic limitation	*Expert Opinion on Drug Safety,* 2006, **5**(5), 651–66	36
Kakkar, P. and Jaffery, F.N.	Biological markers for metal toxicity	*Environmental Toxicology and Pharmacology,* 2005, **19**(2), 335–39	36
Pandian, J.D., Padma, V. *et al.*	Stroke and thrombolysis in developing countries	*International Journal of Stroke,* 2007, **2**(1), 17–26	32
Kalantri S.P., Joshi R., Riley L.W.	Chikungunya epidemic: An Indian perspective	*National Medical Journal of India,* 2006, **19**(6), 315–22	30

thalassemia, followed by sickle cell anemia (20.96% share), haemophilia (11.40% share), von Willebrand disease (10.75% share) and thrombophilia (9.23% share) during 2002–11. In terms of sub-fields, the largest contribution of Indian heredity blood disorder research came from medicine (with 87.95% share), followed by biochemistry, genetics and molecular biology (19.00%), pharmacology, toxicology and pharmaceutics (4.02%), immunology and microbiology (2.17%), agricultural and biological sciences (1.19%) and neurosciences (0.98%) during 2002–11. The 10 most productive Indian institutions involved in heredity blood disorder research together contributed 60.69% share in India's total output with an average of 55.9 papers per institution during 2002–11.The average citation impact per paper and h-index of these 10 top Indian institutions was 2.88 and 8.2 during 2002–11. The 10 most productive Indian authors involved in heredity blood disorder research together contributed 49.84% share in India's total output with an average of 45.9 papers per author during 2002–11.The average citation impact per paper and h-index of these 10 top Indian authors was 3.15 and 9.5 during 2002–11 The top 20 most productive journals together contributed 415 papers, accounting for 45.06% share in Indian output during 2002–11, which has decreased from 50.00% during 2002–06 to 41.56% during 2007–11.

To conclude, there is a need to create comprehensive care services, including diagnosis and management of the heredity blood disorders in Indian context. For this purpose, there is need to undertake more R&D, develop trained manpower at different levels and create sufficient infrastructure to handle the problems associated with heredity blood disorders. Although, the Indian government has already taken some steps in this direction, but they are not totally sufficient to take care of all patients associated with heredity blood disorders in India.

References

[1] Blood and blood disorders. http://www.nlm.nih.gov/medlineplus/bloodandblooddisorders.html (accessed on 5 May 2012).

[2] Hereditary blood disorders explored. http://www.itpblooddisorder.com/blood-disorder/hereditary-blood-disorders-explored (accessed on 5 May 2012).

[3] Thalassaemia. http://www.who.int/genomics/public/geneticdiseases/en/index2.html (accessed on 5 May 2012).

[4] Thalassaemia. http://onlinelibrary.wiley.com/doi/10.1111/j.1751-2824.2011.01529.x/pdf (accessed on 5 May 2012).

[5] Sickle cell anemia. http://www.who.int/genomics/public/geneticdiseases/en/index2.html# SCA (accessed on 7 May 2012).

[6] Sickle Cell Anemia Control Programme. http://www.gujhealth.gov.in/Portal/Tender/20/ 1_sickle-cell-anemia-control-programme-add.pdf (accessed on 7 May 2012).

[7] Haemophilia. http://www.who.int/genomics/public/geneticdiseases/en/index2.html #Haemophilia (accessed on 5 May 2012).

[8] Gupta, Naresh. Plight of the haemophiliacs in India. *Times of India*. 17 April, 2011. http://www.timeswellness.com/index.aspx?page=article§id=1&contentid=2011041720110415115242531ecbf4d68.

[9] Von Willebrand's Disease. http://www.merckmanuals.com/home/blood_disorders/bleeding_and_clotting_disorders/von_willebrands_disease.html (accessed on 5 May 2012).

[10] Thrombophilia. http://www.merckmanuals.com/home/blood_disorders/bleeding_and_clotting_disorders/thrombophilia.html (accessed on 5 May 2012).

[11] Sinha, Kounteya. Drive to curb hereditary blood disorders in the offing. Times of India April 13, 2012. http://timesofindia.indiatimes.com/india/Drive-to-curb-hereditary-blood-disorders-in-the-offing/articleshow/12645607.cms (accessed on 5 May 2012).

[12] Gupta, B.M., Kaur, Har and Bala, Adarsh. Mapping of Indian diabetes research during 1999–2008. *DESIDOC Journal of Library and Information Technology*, 2011, 31(2), 71–80.

[13] Gupta, B.M. and Bala, Adarsh. Mapping of tuberculosis research in India: A scientometric analysis of publications output during 1998–2009. *COLLNET Journal of Scientometrics and Information Management,* 2011, 5(1), 33–51.

[14] Gupta, B.M. and Bala, Adarsh. A bibliometric analysis of malaria research in India during 1999–2008. *Journal of Vector Borne Diseases* September 2011, 48, 163–170.

[15] Gupta, B.M. and Bala, Adarsh. Mapping of asthma research in India: A scientometric analysis of publications output during 1999–2008. *Lung India* October–December 2011, 28(4), 239–46.

[16] Gupta, B.M., Bala, Adarsh and Kaur, Har. Mapping of AIDS/HIV research in India: A scientometric analysis publications output during 1999–2008. *COLLNET Journal of Scientometrics and Information Management,* 2011, 5(2), 185–203.

Electronic Resources Management in Libraries, pp. 348–357

Changing Research Impact Assessment Metrics in the Web 2.0

Sudhanshu Bhushan and Priya Bhushan

ABSTRACT

Increasing scholarly use of Web 2.0 tools like Facebook, Twitter, Mendeley, and blog-style article commenting presents an opportunity to track scholarly impact in novel ways. Metrics based on this diverse set of web sources could yield broader, richer, and more timely assessments of current and potential scholarly impact. Author has reviewed features of selected social media and alternative bibliometric tools, which are going to influence authors and researchers in the 21st century.

1. Introduction

Since the creation of the *Journal des Sçavans* and the *Philosophical Transactions of the Royal Society*, in 1665, papers have been physically bound to the journal in which they were published. Papers published in high profile journals with high circulation had a greater chance of being read and cited over the papers published in less widely available journals. For the past few centuries journals were a convenient way to organize papers by subject, but search engines now allow us to find individual papers on specific topics from across the entire spectrum of journals, so highly subject-specific journals might become obsolete or begin to amalgamate. Now scientific information is disseminated electronically, researchers are less likely to read entire journals; instead they conduct electronic literature searches on particular topics and find specific articles from a wide variety of journals.

Hence, papers now can be read and cited based on their own merits, independently of the journal's physical availability, reputation, or Impact Factor (IF). With the speed of communication today, researchers, and authors are impatient to get an indicator of its value. Waiting 1 to 3 years for publication and citation seems interminable. Conflating an article's impact with its journals' impact creates uncertainty, as well. Online, open-access journals, such as in the Public Library of Science (PLoS) family of journals, and online databases, such as the ArXiv system and its cognates, continue in gaining prominence. Using these open-access repositories, experts could find publications in their respective fields and decide which ones are worth reading and citing, regardless of the journal.

The IF was originally devised in the 1960s to guide academic libraries in their journal purchases (Archambault and Larivière, 2009). Although several other types of citation-based measures of journal impact have been recently devised, such as the SCImago Journal Rank (González-Pereira, Guerrero-Bote and Moya-Anegón, 2009), the Eigenfactor (West and Bergstrom, 2010) and the source normalized impact per paper (Moed, 2010), the 2-year IF compiled by Thomson Reuters is still the most widely used. The H-Index (Hirsch, 2005), G-Index (Egghe, 2006), Google Scholar Metrics (2012) and the JIF are all rather good indicators of scientific quality. However, in measuring real-world impact they are seriously flawed. Thinks for a moment of how impact is felt for whatever random topic you can think of. Every one of us will consider the publication itself, but probably also downloads, page views, blogs, comments, Twitter, different kinds of media and social network activity (Google+, Facebook), among other things. In other words, all activities that can be measured by 'talking' through social media and other online activities can be used to give a more realistic impression of the real impact of a given research article. Since talking about articles depends on actually being able to read the articles, this is where open access came into picture. The use of the proposed kind of article-level metrics only makes sense when many people are being able to discuss the actual content of published articles, which in turn is only possible when articles are open access. Alternative metrics refers to tools based on bookmarks, links, blog posts, tweets, and other online measures that presumably indicate ways that readers have been influenced by an article—in short, how much 'buzz' the paper is generating online.

2. Impact Measurement

Bibliometrics is a statistical tool used to understand the state of research using publication metrics. It is no different from the work economists do to understand the state of the economy (Judyluther, n.d.). Peer-review has served scholarship well, but is beginning to show its age. It is slow, encourages conventionality, and fails to hold reviewers accountable. Moreover, given that most papers are eventually published somewhere, peer-review fails to limit the volume of research. Citation counting measures are useful, but not sufficient. Metrics like the h-index are even slower than peer-review: a work's first citation. Citation measures are narrow; influential work may remain uncited. These metrics are narrow; they neglect impact outside the academy, and also ignore the context and reasons for citation.

The Journal Impact Factor (JIF), which measures journals' average citations per article, is often incorrectly used to assess the impact of individual articles. In the digital world, eagerness to know the impact of an article is high on priority for a scientist to see which paper's peers are talking about and where; an author to identify and respond to comments about the work, and an editor to track the trends and hot topics in the field of interest. New applications are designed, developed, and made available which are able to measure (Priem, Piwowar and Hemminger, n.d.):

- Citation in Web of Science, CrossRef, PubMed Central, Scopus, Wikipedia, etc.

- Scholarly bookmarking/reference-management services Mendeley, CiteULike, Zotero, etc.
- Blogs as tracked by Postgenomic, Trackbacks, Nature Blogs, Research Blogging, etc.
- Popular Web 2.0 services: Facebook, Twitter, Delicious, etc.
- Ratings by Faculty of 1000
- Comments from within the PLoS platform, as well as monthly PDF and html view counts.

3. Data Source for Metrics

Data mining techniques are brought to bear on massive social media databases and other online storehouses to search for fresh indicators of scholarly impact. Data sources for generating these matrics are based on:

- ***Facebook***: A social networking service. Facebook is a social utility that connects people with friends and others who work, study and live around them. People use Facebook to keep up with friends, upload an unlimited number of photos, post links and videos, and learn more about the people they meet (www.facebook.com). Data collected by knowing the number of users who
  - Shared a post about the item
  - Clicked on a post about the item
  - Commented on a post about the item, and
  - Liked a post about the item.
- ***Twitter:*** An information network. Find out what's happening, right now, with the people and organizations you care about. Instantly connect to what is most important to you. Follow your friends, experts, favorite celebrities, and breaking news. Twitter is a real-time information network that connects you to the latest stories, ideas, opinions and news about what you find interesting. Simply find the accounts you find most compelling and follow the conversations. At the heart of Twitter are small bursts of information called '*Tweets*'. Each Tweet is 140 characters long, but don't let the small size fool you—you can discover a lot in a little space. You can see photos, videos and conversations directly in Tweets to get the whole story at a glance, and all in one place (*twitter.com)*. Data collected by knowing the number of users who twitted and follows.
- ***CrossRef:*** It registers Digital Object Identifier (DOI) names and URLs in a central DOI directory on behalf of publisher members. Is has more than 50 million registered CrossRef links. CrossRef enables linking in scholarly content on a cross-publisher basis (article-level-metrics.plos.org). The metadata associated with a DOI can include: basic bibliographic values including all authors, volume, issue, page number or article number, article title. The references being cited within the item. A list of figures, tables, images or other parts of the item (we call these components) which may benefit

from having their own DOI for linking. The citation data reported for an article from CrossRef.

- ***PLOS Article-Level Metrics:*** It measures the impact of research. Provide a suite of established metrics that measure the overall performance and reach of published research articles (www.crossref.org). Data collected by knowing the number of times
  - Abstracts have been viewed on PubMed Central
  - Figures have been viewed on PubMed Central
  - Supplementary data has been viewed on PubMed Central
  - PDF has been viewed on PubMed Central
  - HTML has been viewed on PubMed Central
  - Full-text has been viewed on PubMed Central
  - The citation data reported for an article from PubMed Central
  - The citation data reported for an article from Scopus.
- ***Slideshare:*** it provides best way to share presentations, documents and professional videos (github.com). Data collected by knowing the number of times
  - The presentation has been downloaded
  - Presentation has been favorited
  - Presentation has been viewed, and
  - The number of comments received by the presentation.
- ***Github:*** A social, online repository for open-source software (www.slideshare. net). Data collected by knowing the number of people
  - Who have forked the github repository
  - Who are watching the GitHub repository.
- ***Topsy*:** Real-time search for the social web (topsy.com). Data collected by knowing the number of times the item has been initially tweeted and again tweeted by influential tweeters.
- ***Wikipedia*:** It is a free online encyclopedia that anyone can edit (www.wikipedia. org).
  - The number of Wikipedia articles that mentioned this object.
- ***Scopus*:** Scopus is world's largest abstracting and citation database of peer-reviewed literature covering nearly 18,000 titles from more than 5,000 publishers (www.scopus.com).
  - Citations number of times the item has been cited.
- ***CiteULike*:** It is a free service to help you to store, organise and share the scholarly papers you are reading (www.citeulike.org).
  - It provides number of users who have bookmarked this item.

- ***Delicious:*** Online social book marking service that keeps, shares, and discovers the best of the Web using Delicious, the world's leading social book marking service (delicious.com).
  - The number of bookmarks to this artefact (maximum=100).
- ***Mendeley:*** A research management tool for desktop and Web. Easily organize your papers, read and annotate your PDFs, collaborate in private or open groups, and securely access your research from everywhere (www.mendeley.com). Data collected by knowing the percent of readers by
  - Discipline, for top three disciplines (csv, api only)
  - Country, for top three countries (csv, api only)
  - Career stage, for top three career stages (csv, api only)
  - The number of groups and readers who have added the article to their libraries.
- ***Dryad:*** An international repository of data underlying peer-reviewed articles in the basic and applied Biology. Dryad contains 2060 data packages and 5475 data files, associated with articles in 157 journals (datadryad.org).
  - Dryad package views: number of views of the main package page
  - Dryad total downloads: combined number of downloads of the data package and data files.
- ***ScienceSeeker:*** Science news from science newsmakers. ScienceSeeker collects science articles from sources around the world, so you can find the latest science news and discussion on any topic (scienceseeker.org).
  - The number of blog posts that cited this item.
- ***PubMed:*** PubMed comprises over 22 million citations for biomedical literature from MEDLINE, Life Science journals, and online books. PubMed citations and abstracts include the fields of biomedicine and health, covering portions of the Life Sciences, Behavioural Sciences, Chemical Sciences, and Bioengineering. PubMed also provides access to additional relevant web sites and links to the other National Center for Biotechnology Information Molecular Biology resources (www.ncbi.nlm.nih.gov/pubmed). Data collected by knowing the number of citations by,
  - Editorials in PubMed Central
  - Review papers in PubMed Central
  - Research papers in PubMed Central, and
  - The article has been reviewed by F1000.

4. Tracking Tools for New Matrics

A number of article-level metrics services are currently in the start-up phase. They do by watching social media sites, newspapers and magazines for any mentions of scholarly articles. The result is an 'Altmetric' score which is a quantitative measure of the quality and quantity of attention that a scholarly article has received. The altmetric score is also implemented in UtopiaDocs, a PDF reader which links an article to a wealth of other online resources like CrossRef, Mendeley, Dryad, Scibite, Sherpa, and many more. PLoS also uses article level metrics to qualify articles by giving comprehensive information about the usage and reach of published articles onto the articles themselves, so that the entire academic community can assess their value. PLoS provides a complete score build on a combination of altmetrics, citation analysis, post-publication peer-reviews, pageviews, downloads and other criteria. ImpactStory also makes extensive use of the analysis of social media and other online statistics, to provide a tool to measure total impact of a given collection of scientific articles, datasets and other collections. Their focus on collections represents still another approach to the problem of evaluating scientific output. Researchers who want to know how many times their work has been downloaded, bookmarked, and blogged. Research groups who want to look at the broad impact of their work and see what has demonstrated interest. Funders who want to see what sort of impact they may be missing when only considering citations to papers:

- ***Altmetric Explorer:*** The Altmetric Explorer is a powerful, intuitive tool for measuring the attention that scholarly articles receive online. Altmetric collects the relevant discussions around each article from Twitter, Facebook, science blogs, mainstream news outlets and many more sources—then makes it all available to you in one place. Use it to deliver insights, track conversations and measure levels of attention over time or compared to your competitors. The optimal conditions for using altmetrics would be when articles would all be published as open access, but even with the current growth of open access published papers the method is already starting to make sense (Priem, n.d.).
- ***Scores for Quick Analysis and Comparison:*** Each article is given a score that measures the quantity and quality it has received. Demographics: the demographics for the social network users mentioning each paper e.g. Was an article unusually popular in Spain? Amongst doctors? Science communicators? The Explorer can tell everything to you. Powerful search and filtering is available to browse all articles in the database, or filter by journal, publisher or time last mentioned. Interested in specific papers? Enter DOIs, PubMed or arXiv IDs to track them. Search for articles with keywords in the title or author lists. Altmetric tracks three types of data sources:
  - Social media like Twitter, Facebook, Google+, Pinterest, and blogs
  - Traditional media—both mainstream (The Guardian, New York Times) and science specific (*New Scientist, Scientific American*)
  - Online reference managers like Mendeley and CiteULike.
- ***ImpactStory:*** ImpactStory is a website that makes it quick and easy to view the impact of a wide range of research output. It goes beyond traditional measurements of research output—citations to papers—to embrace a much broader evidence of

use across a wide range of scholarly output types (impactstory.it). The system aggregates impact data from many sources and displays it in a single report, which is given a permaurl for dissemination and can be updated any time. ImpactStory data can be:

- Highlighted as indications of the minimum impact a research artefact has made on the community
- Explored more deeply to see who is citing, book marking, and otherwise using your work
- Run to collect usage information for mention in bio-sketches
- Analyzed by downloading detailed metric information.

- ***ReaderMeter:*** ReaderMeter is a mash-up visualizing author-level and article-level statistics based on the consumption of scientific content by a large population of readers. Using readership-based metrics we can estimate impact on the basis of the consumption of scientific content by a population of readers. ReaderMeter adapts two popular impact metrics for authors (the H-Index and the G-Index) and redefines those using bookmarks instead of citations as an HR-Index and a GR-Index respectively: however the index values for an explanation of their meaning. Analysing readership data can help, discover areas of real-time impact that may not be visible to traditional citation-based measurements. Readership data is made available via the Mendeley API (ReaderMeter.org).
- ***ScienceCard:*** ScienceCard is a web service that collects Article-Level Metrics for scientific articles. Everyone can register via his/her Twitter account and can then add articles from PubMed via the DOI or PubMed ID. This is particularly useful for articles you have authored, as they will be listed in your ScienceCard profile. ScienceCard uses freely available sources for the Article-Level Metrics. ScienceCard retrieve contents from Twitter, Mendeley, PubMed Central, CiteULike, Wikipedia, and CrossRef (sciencecard.org).
- ***PLoS Impact Explorer:*** While it may be easy to dismiss the idea that social media metrics can be meaningful for scholars, PLoS has been developing a suite of measures over the last three years referred to as article-level metrics (ALM) that provide a view of the performance and reach of an article (www.altmetric.com/demos/plos.html). Their approach is to present totals of multiple data points including:
  - Usage data (HTML views and PDF downloads)
  - Citations (PubMed Central, Scopus, Crossref, and Web of Science)
  - Social networks (CiteULike, Connotea, Facebook, and Mendeley)
  - Blogs and media coverage (Nature, Research blogging, and Trackbacks)
  - Discussion activity on PLoS (reader's comments, notes, and ratings).

5. Discussion

There are numerous article-level metrics and each has its own advantages and problems. Citation counts are an excellent measure of influence and impact but are very slow to collect. Download statistics are rapid to collect but may be misleading. Comments can provide valuable and immediate feedback, but are currently sparse and require a change in the research reward culture to become more widespread and to improve quality. Book marking statistics can be both rapid to collect and contain high quality information but are largely untested and require the widespread adoption of unfamiliar tools. Alongside these we have 'expert ratings' by services such as Faculty of 1000 and simple rating schemes (Neylon and Wu, 2009).

The metrics are also useful in different contexts. Indeed, the fundamental problem of which paper to read can also have different contexts. Which new papers are relevant to you? Which papers should you read if you are going to pursue research question X? Which papers do you need to read before submitting your paper? Are you a funder interested in media coverage of work you have paid for or a textbook writer aiming to assess the most important contributions in a field? All these questions require different information at different times and may be better determined using different measures of article impact.

Altmetrics attempts to close that gap by providing more timely measures that are also more pertinent to the researcher and their article. Use metrics from downloads and blogs, and attention metrics such as tweets and bookmarks, can provide immediate indicators of interest. Although metrics associated with these activities are in the developmental stage, there is growing investment in the broader landscape to produce more current metrics that serve the researcher, their communities and funding agencies.

Scientific impact is not a simple concept that can be described by a single number (Bollen, Van de Sompel, Hagberg, Bettencourt and Chute, 2009). The key point is that journal impact factor is a very poor measure of article impact. And, obviously, the fact that an article is highly influential by any measure does not necessarily mean it should be. Many researchers will continue to rely on journals as filters, but the more you can incorporate effective filtering tools into your research process, the more you will stay up-to-date with advancing knowledge. The question is not whether you should take article-level metrics seriously but how you can use them most effectively to assist your own research endeavours. We need sophisticated metrics to ask sophisticated questions about different aspects of scientific impact and we need further research into both the most effective measurement techniques and the most effective uses of these in policy and decision making. For this reason we strongly support efforts to collect and present diverse types of article level metrics without any initial presumptions as to which metric is most valuable. Different users will need different information and it will take time before 'any metric proves useful. As Clay Shirky (n.d.) said, you can complain about information overload but the only way to deal with it is to build and use better filters. It is no longer sufficient to depend on journals as your only filter; instead, it is time to start evaluating papers on their own merits.

ImpactStory is in early development and has many limitations. BibTex import sometimes cannot parse or locate all objects, and does not display metrics with a zero value. Sometimes the artifacts were received without sufficient information to use all metrics. For example, the system sometimes cannot figure out all URLs from a DOI. Some sources have multiple records for a given artifact. ImpactStory only identifies one copy and so only reports the impact metrics for that record. It makes no current attempt to aggregate across duplications within a source how should not it be used?

6. Conclusions

Field of bibliometrics is moving fast and that Open Access will provide the key to the development and implementation of better ways to evaluate scientific output. Compounded with the fact that, in general, citations have become more widely spread among journals (Larivière, Gingras and Archambault, 2009), the electronic age and its new modes of disseminating and accessing scientific literature might bring forth the end of the IF as a useful measure of the quality of journals, papers, and researchers and have interesting implications for the future of scientific literature.

Our only options are to publish less or to filter more effectively, and any response that favours publishing less doesn't make sense, either logistically, financially, or ethically. The issue is not how to stop people from publishing; it is how to build better filters, both systematically and individually. At the same time, we can use available tools, networks, and tools built on networks to help with this task. So in the spirit of science, let's keep learning and experimenting, and keep the practice and dissemination of science evolving for the times. Future research must examine scholars' use of social media tools to gain a better picture of what a Twitter citation or a CiteULike bookmark, for instance, really means.

References

[1] Archambault, É. and Larivière, V., History of the journal impact factor: contingencies and consequences. *Scientometrics*, 2009, **79**(3), 635–649.

[2] González-Pereira, B., Guerrero-Bote, V.P. and Moya-Anegón, F., The SJR indicator: A new indicator of journals' scientific prestige. 2009. Available at: http://arxiv.org/ftp/ arxiv/ papers/0912/0912.4141.pdf Accessed on 15 September 2012.

[3] West, J.D. and Bergstrom, C.T., The EigenfactorTM Metrics: a network approach to assessing scholarly journals. *College and Research Libraries Journal*, 2010, 71, 236–244.

[4] Moed, H.F., Measuring contextual citation impact of scientific journals. *Journal of Informetrics*, 2010, 4, 265–277.

[5] Hirsch, J.E., An index to quantify an individual's scientific research output. *PNAS*, 2005, 102(46), 16569–16572.

[6] Egghe, L., Theory and practise of the g-index, *Scientometrics*, 2006, **69**(1), 131–52.

[7] Google Scholar Metrics. http://scholar.google.com/intl/en/scholar/metrics.html Accessed on 11 September 2012.

[8] Judyluther. Altmetrics—Trying to Fill the Gap. http://scholarlykitchen.sspnet.org/2012/07/25/altmetrics-trying-to-fill-the-gap/Accessed on 13 August 2012.

[9] Priem, Jason; Piwowar, Heather A. and Hemminger, Bradley H. Altmetrics in the wild: An exploratory study of impact metrics based on social media. http://jasonpriem.org/self-archived/PLoS-altmetrics-sigmetrics11-abstract.pdf Accessed on 13 August 2012.

[10] Priem, Jason. Altmetrics: A manifesto. http://altmetrics.org/manifesto/Accessed on 15 September 2012.

[11] Neylon, Cameron and Wu, Shirley. Article-level metrics and the evolution of scientific impact. *PLoS Biology*, 2009, **7**(11). e1000242 www.plosbiology.org

[12] Bollen, J.; Van de Sompel, H.; Hagberg, A.; Bettencourt, L. and Chute, R. Clickstream data yields high-resolution maps of science. *PLoS One*, 2009, 4: e4803. doi:10.1371/journal.pone.0004803. Accessed on 26 September 2012.

[13] Shirky, C. It's not information overload. It's filter failure. 2008 Available at http://www.web2expo.com/webexny2008/public/schedule/detail/4817. Accessed on 17 September 2012.

[14] Larivière, V., Gingras, Y. and Archambault, É., The decline in the concentration of citations, 1900–2007. *Journal of the American Society for Information Science and Technology,* 2009, 60(4), 858–62.

Electronic Resources Management in Libraries, pp. 358–374

Methodological Study of Recommendation Process in Recommender Systems

K. Nageswara Rao

ABSTRACT

Users are becoming overwhelmed by abundant information available online about items and products such as web pages, news items, movies, music, jokes, books, etc., In addition to increasing amount of information, advances in information technology have dramatically reduced the barriers in electronic publishing and distribution of information over networks virtually anywhere in the world. As a result, people find it difficult to locate and retrieve relevant information from phenomenally increasing terabytes of information base. To address the problems with the information overload and to sift through available information resources for useful information, recommender/filtering systems were emerged in the recent past. The researcher has collected literature on more than hundred recommender systems in various application domains, procedurally studied, identified and reported various steps involved in the recommendation process. Every recommender system needs some sort of input collected explicitly or implicitly to generate recommendations. Using this input, the recommender system builds user profile which represents any of the information retrieval/profile representation models viz., vector space model, semantic networks, weighted n-grams, associative networks etc. The recommender system matches the user profile with the descriptions of items or users with similar taste to recommend items of interest to the user. There are three matching techniques generally used by the recommender systems such as: content-based filtering, collaborative filtering, demographic filtering, knowledge-based filtering or hybrid techniques. Finally, these systems provide Top-N recommendations after fine tuning the user profile with the help of relevance feedback mechanism to retrieve more relevant items.

1. Introduction

The amount of published information about products and items in the world is growing phenomenally. Users are becoming overwhelmed by information about ever increasing items and products such as web pages, news items, movies, music, jokes, books, etc., books, etc., In addition to increasing amount of information, advances in information technology have dramatically reduced the barriers in electronic publishing and distribution of information over networks virtually anywhere in the world. As a result, people find it difficult to locate and retrieve relevant information from hundreds and thousands of terabytes of information base.

To address the problems with the information overload and to sift through all available information resources for useful information, recommender systems or filtering systems were emerged in the recent past. Commonly, these recommender systems were used online to suggest items that customers find interesting, thereby, benefiting both the customer and merchant. Recommender systems benefit the customer by making him suggestions on items that he is likely to purchase and the business for the merchants by increase of sales.

When people need to choose varieties of options with which they do not have any experience, they often rely on the opinions of others who do have such experience. However, when there are thousands or millions of options, like in the Web, it becomes practically impossible for an individual to locate reliable experts that can give advice about each of the options. By shifting from an individual to a collective method of recommendation, the problem could be managed more effectively. For example, people look for recommendations or suggestions when they have more alternatives or choices before them such as purchasing a book on a particular topic, to watch a good movie, to go to a restaurant for tasty food, to listen to music, to visit a website of interest, etc. In such circumstances, they often relay word-of-mouth recommendations made by relatives and friends, recommendations letters, books reviews or travel guides.

Generation of recommendations by the recommender systems follow similar steps that of information retrieval systems by incorporating advanced profile building techniques, item/user representation techniques, filtering and recommendation techniques and profile adaptation techniques. In this paper, the author has collected technical literature pertaining to 107 filtering/recommender systems, studied their functionality with respect to recommendation process and reported various techniques, methods and algorithms used to collect and maintain user interests implicitly or explicitly, match with existing collection of items and retrieve relevant information, fine tune the user profile using relevance feedback mechanisms to provide better recommendations.

2. Role of Profile in Information Filtering

The earliest mechanism of electronic information filtering originated from the concept of *Selective Dissemination of Information (SDI*). SDI was designed as an automatic way of keeping scientists informed of new documents published in their areas of specialization. The scientist was able to create and modify user profile of keywords that described his or her interests. SDI system used the profile to match the keywords against new documents in order to predict which new documents would be of most relevant to the scientist's interests. Recently, more or less the similar concept was incorporated in personalization, information filtering and recommender systems by building user profiles interactively and intelligently.

Conventional information retrieval is closely related to information filtering in that they have the goal of retrieving information relevant to what the user wants while minimizing the retrieval of irrelevant information (Salton and McGill, 1983, van Rijsbergen, 1979). The crux of the matter in information filtering is construction of user profile describing user's preferences to compare with incoming documents to determine documents of interest to a particular user.

In information filtering task, the important aspect is not only ranking relevant documents but also the construction of a user profile, which truly reflect the user's preferences. A simplistic approach for constructing a user profile is to describe the profile through a set of keywords, which requires provision of important and relevant keywords by the user. If the user is not familiar with the type of incoming documents, he might find it difficult to provide relevant keywords, which exactly represent his preferences. In addition, an attempt by the user to familiarize himself with the vocabulary of incoming documents might turn into a tedious and time-consuming task. In such an environment, the user may not precisely describe his profile. So, an alternative approach is to collect user information from his preferences implicitly and use such information to build user profiles.

In the very beginning stages of information filtering, user provides a set of keywords, which describe an initial profile of his preferences. As new documents arrive into the system, the system uses the initial profile to select documents, which are potentially of interest and shows them to the user. The user goes through relevance feedback cycle in which he indicates not only relevant but also non-relevant documents. The system then uses ratings information to adjust or tune the user profile description such that it reflects new preferences. The process of adjusting the user profile continues until the system stabilizes and filters documents actually required by the user. Once the user profile is stabilized and there are no more changes to the profile, unless the user's interest shifts suddenly from one subject to another, the information filtering task can be viewed as a traditional information retrieval task in which the documents keeps arriving the system.

Recommender systems are systems that build a representation of the user's likes and dislikes and suggest items to the user based on the profile representation. Different approaches have been employed for computing recommendations in different environments. Collaborative filtering systems and content-based filtering systems are the most common approaches/systems for generating recommendations. The other approaches/systems are demographic filtering systems, knowledge-based recommender systems and hybrid recommender systems.

3. Recommendation Process in Recommender Systems

Recommender systems are the systems meant for augmenting recommendation process in case people need help. The basic elements of any recommender systems are the users/customers, items/products and filtering techniques. A user/customer is a person who utilizes the recommender systems by providing his opinions or tastes about various items and receives recommendations about new or un-rated items from the system. The items/products includes details of books, products catalogs, movie programmes, music programmes, restaurants, travel information, curriculum details, TV programmes, online jokes, software features, trade fair events, email messages, news articles, RSS feeds, Usenet news and Web pages. Filtering techniques include content-based filtering, collaborative filtering, demographic filtering, knowledge-based filtering and hybrid filtering.

Based on the open literature collected on more than hundred filtering/recommender systems in various application domains and procedural study revealed that the recommendation process typically includes: (a) source of information—gathering information about thousands of items/products and users/customers and their likes/dislikes on vast collection of items (b) profile learning and representation—generation of user profiles using appropriate algorithms and representation of profiles (c) filtering or matching techniques—matching user profiles with items or profiles or other users of the system with similar tastes (d) recommendations—generation of list of recommendations or suggestions for the active user with relevance ranking and (e) relevance feedback—collecting users ratings and satisfaction level on recommended items and refining or fine tuning the user profile for generating more relevant and useful recommendations. Detailed study of various steps involved in the recommendation process is presented in the succeeding sections.

3.1 *Source of Information (Input Data Collection)*

Data Collection Using Registration

The user of recommender system needs to provide some form of input or feedback to the system, which plays an important role in the recommendation process. The simplest form of collecting user information requirements is through the user registration and provision of keywords. In many of the recommender systems, the process of registration is a time-consuming and tedious task because the user does not fully cooperate in filling up of registration form or may not be able to represent exact information requirements with suitable keywords.

Another type of information that could be used as input for filtering/recommendation is bookmarks. Bookmarks are not only the unit of sharing current information but also used to provide evidence that users are similar and so are good candidates for sharing recommendations. Therefore, bookmarks are considered as reliable and high-value evidence of peoples' tastes. Unlike rating-based approaches, bookmarks do not require users to perform additional explicit and perhaps fine-grained judgments, which is a difficult task (Hill *et al.,* 1995). For example, WebSIFT system (Cooley *et al.,*

1997) uses registration data in addition to server logs, HTML files and remote agent logs as input data.

Explicit Data Collection

Another source of information that could be collected from the user is through 'ratings', which represents the opinion of user on items. Such process of gathering input by the recommender systems is referred to as 'explicit data collection'. These ratings follow a specified numeric scale from most favorite to least favorite, for example, '1' for 'bad', '5' for 'excellent'. A common ratings scheme adopted in many filtering systems is the binary rating scheme, which allows only ratings of either '1' for 'interesting' or '0' for 'not interesting'.

Another simplest ratings scale is unary—where liked items are marked, all others are unknown to the user. Unary scheme is common in eCommerce applications, where all that is known is whether the user has purchased an item or not. However, binary scheme allows a separate designation for disliked items. Recommender systems often support 5-point, 7-point or 100-point scales for ratings as input.

For example, Amalthaea (Moukas and Maes, 1998), (Moukas, 1997), Bellcore Video Recommender (Hill *et al.*, 1995), Eigentaste (Goldberg *et al.*, 2001), Fab (Balabanovic and Shoham, 1997), (Balabanovic, 1997), Foxtrot Recommender System (Middleton *et al.*, 2002), ifWeb (Asnicar and Tasso, 1997), LIBRA (Mooney and Roy, 2000), PipeCF (Xie *et al.*, 2004), PORSCHE (Kawashima *et al.*, 2006), REFEREE (Cosley *et al.*, 2002), Ringo (Shardanand and Maes, 1995), (Shardanand, 1994), SmartRadio (Hayes and Cunningham, 2000, 2001), etc. use "numerical scale" for rating reference documents/items as input data collection method.

DEMOIR (Yimam-Seid and Kobsa, 2003) and Entrée (Burke *et al.,* 1996), (Burke *et al.,* 1997) uses "positive"/"negative" method; InfoFinder (Krulwich and Burkey, 1997), News Dude (Billsus and Pazzani, 1999), and NewsWeeder (Lang, 1995) uses "interesting"/"not interesting" methods for data collection, Movies2Go (Mukherjee *et al.,* 2001), SIFT Netnews (Yan and Garcia-Molina, 1995), Tapestry (Goldberg *et al.,* 1992) and WebSail (Chen *et al.,* 2000), (Chen *et al.,* 2002) uses "like"/"dislike" methods to build user profiles.

Syskill and Webert (Pazzani and Billsus, 1996) uses "hot"/"cold" method; GroupLens (Konstan *et al.*, 1997), (Resnick *et al.,* 1994) uses "text comments" method for collection of input data and representation of profiles.

Implicit Data Collection

Ratings can also be gathered from the user's purchase history, web logs, hyperlinks visited, browsing behavior, item/user viewing times, time spend on reading a particular item, etc. This type of input gathering is referred to as "implicit data collection".

For example, NCR News (Mobasher *et al.*, 2000), AVATAR (Blanco-Fernandez *et al.*, 2006), Foxtrot Recommender System (Middleton *et al.*, 2002), NAUTILUS (Gori *et al.*, 1999), Personal WebWatcher (Mladenic, 1996), PILGRIM (Brunato and Battiti, 2003), PORSCHE (Kawashima *et al.*, 2006), REFEREE (Cosley *et al.*, 2002), SELECT (Alton-Scheidl *et al.*, 1999), SurfLen (Fu *et al.*, 2000), The Wasabi Personal Shopper (Burke, 1999), WebInEssence (Radev *et al.*, 2001) and WebSIFT (Cooley *et al.*, 1997) uses "navigation behavior"/"browsing behavior" for collection of data for building user profiles.

Amazon.com (Linden *et al.*, 2003), Beehive (Huberman and Kaminsky, 1996), GroupMark (Pemberton *et al.*, 2000), LifestyleFinder (Krulwich, 1997) and VISCORS (Kim *et al.*, 2004) uses historical data of the user to construct user profiles.

Amalthaea (Moukas and Maes, 1998), (Moukas, 1997), Anatagonomy (Sakagami and Kamba, 1997), FAIRWIS (Buono *et al.*, 2001), GroupLens (Konstan *et al.*, 1997), (Resnick *et al.*, 1994), Krakatoa Chronicle (Kamba *et al.*, 1995), Recommendation Explorer (Efron and Geisler, 2001), REFEREE (Cosley *et al.*, 2002) and SmartRadio (Hayes and Cunningham, 2000, 2001) uses a form of "time spent"/"idle time"/"focus time"/"saving"/"scrolling"/"enlarging"/"printing"/"downloading"/"bookmarking", etc. for collection of data to build user profiles.

Demographic Data Collection

The other form of input data is demographic data, which refers to the information such as age, gender, marital status and educational qualification of the users. Such data is usually difficult to collect due to involvement of privacy issues. Demographic data is normally collected explicitly from the user and the recommendations are truly dependent on factual values.

For example, Grundy system introduced by Rich (1979) allows users to fill out a registration form and uses the entered demographic data for classification of users and recommendation of items to users.

Data Collection through Text Analysis

The other form of input/feedback is the content data, which is based on textual analysis of documents related to items rated by the user. The features of text are extracted by textual analysis and used as input to the filtering algorithm to generate user profiles.

For example, ARAS (Kilfoil *et al.*, 2005) uses "selection of course content"; COFIND (Dron *et al.*, 2003) uses "qualities of resources"; PEFNA (Kilander *et al.*, 1997) uses "creation of categories" and WebSell (Cunningham *et al.*, 2001a, 2001b) uses "creation of pathways" as input for the creation of user profiles and fine-tuning for good recommendation of items.

3.2 *Profile Building and Representation*

In recommender systems, one or more of the inputs are combined together to form the representation of user's likes and dislikes. The simplest representation found in several recommender systems is the user-item ratings matrix. For example, the ratings of user $U_i(i = 1, 2, 3 \ldots m)$ for item $I_j(j = 1, 2, 3 \ldots n)$ is denoted by R_{mn}, where each item's rating is a real number within the agreed numerical scale that has been incorporated in the given application. Such ratings are collected in mxn user-item matrix as shown below.

$$\begin{bmatrix} R_{11}U_1I_1 & R_{12}U_1I_2 & \ldots & \ldots & R_{1j}U_1I_j \\ R_{21}U_2I_1 & R_{22}U_2I_2 & \ldots & \ldots & R_{2j}U_2I_j \\ \ldots & \ldots & \ldots & \ldots & \ldots \\ \ldots & \ldots & \ldots & \ldots & \ldots \\ R_{m1}U_mI_1 & R_{m2}U_mI_2 & \ldots & \ldots & R_{mn}U_mI_n \end{bmatrix}$$

The filtering or recommender algorithm designed for a particular application employs suitable techniquè either on the rows, which correspond to ratings of a single user about different items or on the columns, which correspond to different user's ratings about a single item of user-item matrix. As per the study conducted on various filtering/recommender systems, it has been observed that vector space model, semantic networks, weighted n-grams, associative networks, neural networks, decision trees, Bayesian networks, etc. are used for learning and representing user profiles.

Associative Networks

Quillian (1968) introduced the principle of a semantic network and it played an important role in knowledge representation. An associative network defines a generic network, which consists of nodes representing information items (semantic entities) and associations between nodes, that express, not necessarily defined or labeled, relations among nodes. Links between particular nodes might be weighted to determine the strength of connectivity. For example, INFOrmer (Sorensen *et al.,* 1997) uses weighted associative network for representation of user profiles.

Semantic Networks

The concept of a semantic network is a fairly old in the literature of cognitive science and artificial intelligence. These networks were first appeared in modern linguistics modeling and adopted by computer science and machine translation (Quillian, 1968; Sowa, 1984). Semantic networks were developed in so many ways and for so many purposes for the past 20 years. For example, semantic networks have been used by linguists to represent the meaning of words, by data modelers to capture the static relationships among concepts and by artificial intelligence researchers as a mechanism for knowledge representation (Sanders, 1995). Quillian (1968) has described the semantic network as a "representational format that would permit the meanings of words to be stored, so that humanlike use of these meanings is possible" and most of the mainline research in semantic networks is continued with Quillian's original proposal. So, a semantic network is a directed graph consisting of vertices, which represent concepts and directed edges, which represent semantic relation between concepts. For example, Entrée (Burke *et al.,* 1996, 1997), ifWeb (Asnicar and Tasso, 1997), InterestMap (Liu and Maes, 2005) and SiteIF (Stefani and Strapparava, 1998) uses semantic networks for representation of user profiles.

Neural Networks

In the early 1940s, McCulloch and Pitts (1943) published a seminal paper titled "A Logical Calculus of the Ideas Immanent in Nervous Activity". In it, they proposed a mathematical model of a neuron, which could perform computations. This work described how networks of binary threshold neurons might be described in terms of sentences of first-order logic. One of the first neural networks developed was the "Perceptron". Created by a psychologist named Frank Rosenblatt in 1958, the "Perceptron" was a very simple system, which used interconnected neurodes to analyze data (Rosenblatt, 1958). In 1969, Minsky and Papert (1969) published "Perceptrons", a critique of this sort of neural network model. This work showed that two-layer networks were limited in the functions they could compute, thereby providing a major cause for a decline in neural network research during the 1970's. For example, NAUTILUS (Gori *et al.,* 1999) and Re: Agent (Boone, 1998) uses neural networks for representation of user profiles.

Decision Trees

The statistical and machine learning communities have pursued developing prediction and classification rules for various problem domains for several years. In this process, decision trees were developed and have become powerful and popular tools for classification and prediction. The attractiveness of decision trees is due to the fact that, in contrast to neural networks, they represent rules. Rules can readily be expressed so that humans can understand them or even directly used in retrieving records from databases with the help of query languages. Decision tree is a classifier in the form of a tree structure, where each node is either a leaf node—indicates the value of the target attribute (class) of examples, or a decision node—specifies some test to be carried out on a single attribute-value, with one branch and sub-tree for each possible outcome of the test. A decision tree can be used to classify an example by starting at the root of the tree and moving through it until a leaf node, which provides the classification of the instance. For example, InfoFinder (Krulwich and Burkey, 1997) and WebSell (Cunningham *et al*, 2001a, 2001b) uses decision tree technique for representation of user profiles.

Bayesian Networks

A Bayesian network is a graphical model for probabilistic relationships among a set of variables. Over the last decade, the Bayesian network has become a popular representation for encoding uncertain expert knowledge in expert systems (Heckerman, Geiger, and Chickering, 1995). A Bayesian network is a directed acyclic graph (DAG), which consists of nodes representing variables and arcs representing dependence relations among the variables. For example, LaboUr (Schwab *et al.,* 2000), News Dude (Billsus and Pazzani, 1999), Personal WebWatcher (Mladenic, 1996) and Syskill and Webert (Pazzani and Billsus, 1996) use Bayesian classifier for classification of items/documents.

N-grams

N-gram is a sub-sequence of N characters from a given word. It is called an N-gram model because the probability of occurrence of words is conditioned upon the prior occurrence of N-1 other words. The words in natural language tend to occur one after another significantly a high number of times. Weighted N-grams model is one in which the words are organized as weighted links representing the co-occurrence of different words based on the N-grams. N-grams have applications in correcting spelling errors (Angell, Freund, and Willett, 1983), (Zamora, Pollock, and Zamora, 1981). Applications of N-grams were also found in text retrieval and filtering (Cavnar, 1993), (Cavnar and Trenkle, 1994), (Kimbrell, 1988) and in other natural language processing applications (Suen, 1979), (Ullmann, 1977). For example, weighted N-grams technique is used in PSUN (Sorensen and McElligott, 1995) for representing user profiles.

Vector Space Model

Vector space model is an algebraic model used for information filtering, information retrieval, indexing and relevance rankings. It represents natural language documents in a similar manner that of vectors in a multidimensional space. In the vector space model, items or documents are represented as a vector of features commonly known as keywords or concepts with associated weights. The weights may be Boolean or a real value. The Boolean value represents the presence or absence of the keyword and the real value represents the frequency, relevance or probability of the keyword. For example, Amalthaea (Moukas and Maes, 1998), (Moukas, 1997), Anatagonomy (Sakagami and Kamba, 1997), ARAS (Kilfoil *et al.,* 2005), Beehive (Huberman and Kaminsky, 1996), CoFIND (Dron *et al.,* 2003), etc. uses vector space model for profile representation.

3.3 *Matching/Filtering Techniques*

Once the user profile is generated, which represents the information requirements of the user, the user profile needs to be matched with the descriptions of items or with other users of the recommender system for similar tastes to generate list of recommendations. In general, available techniques for matching or filtering are: content-based filtering, collaborative filtering, demographic filtering, knowledge/utility-based filtering or hybrid methods such as combination of any two or more filtering methods.

In content-based filtering, the content of user profile is matched against the descriptions of items for producing recommendations. Collaborative recommender systems aggregate ratings or recommendations of items, identifies commonalities between users on the basis of their ratings, and generate new recommendations based on similarity of ratings between users. In demographic filtering systems, users are categorized based on personal attributes and make recommendations based on demographic classes of users. Recommender systems, which make suggestions based on the computation of the utility of each item for a given user, are called as utility-based recommender system. Knowledge-based systems attempts to recommend items based on inferences about a user's needs and his preferences.

Apart from the above-mentioned three filtering approaches, some recommender systems use combination of two or more approaches for improving the efficiency of recommender system.

3.4 *Recommendations/Predictions*

The primary objective of the recommender system is to predict whether a user will like a particular item or document that the user has not encountered before. So, the output of a recommender system can be either a prediction or a recommendation. A prediction algorithm receives input data from the user and the items and produces specific ratings of items. These ratings are generally expressed as a numerical value, which represents the predicted opinion of the user for a particular item.

In general, the predicted value should necessarily fall within the same numerical scale as the input/feedback initially provided by the user seeking recommendations. This form of recommender system output is also referred to as 'Individual Scoring'.

When the output is a recommendation, then it is expressed as a list of items, which the user is expected to like the most. Usually the list includes only items that the user has not already rated, viewed or purchased. This form of recommender system output is also known as 'Top-N Recommendations' or 'Ranked Scoring' (Vozalis and Margaritis, 2003).

3.5 *Relevance Feedback*

In order to improve the efficiency of a recommender system, it is necessary to evaluate the relevance of recommendations provided by the system. The process of evaluating results for making the system more effective is called "*relevance feedback*". Relevance feedback is required for the recommender system because the interests of users may change over a period of time or the user might not have exactly represented his information requirements. So, in order to update the user profile continuously and provide better recommendations, the user need to provide feedback to the system by specifying a particular item is relevant (items liked) or non-relevant (items not liked). Generally, recommender systems collect relevance feedback from the information explicitly provided by the user or implicitly from the user's navigation behavior. Some systems utilize both implicit and explicit feedback for improving the quality of service.

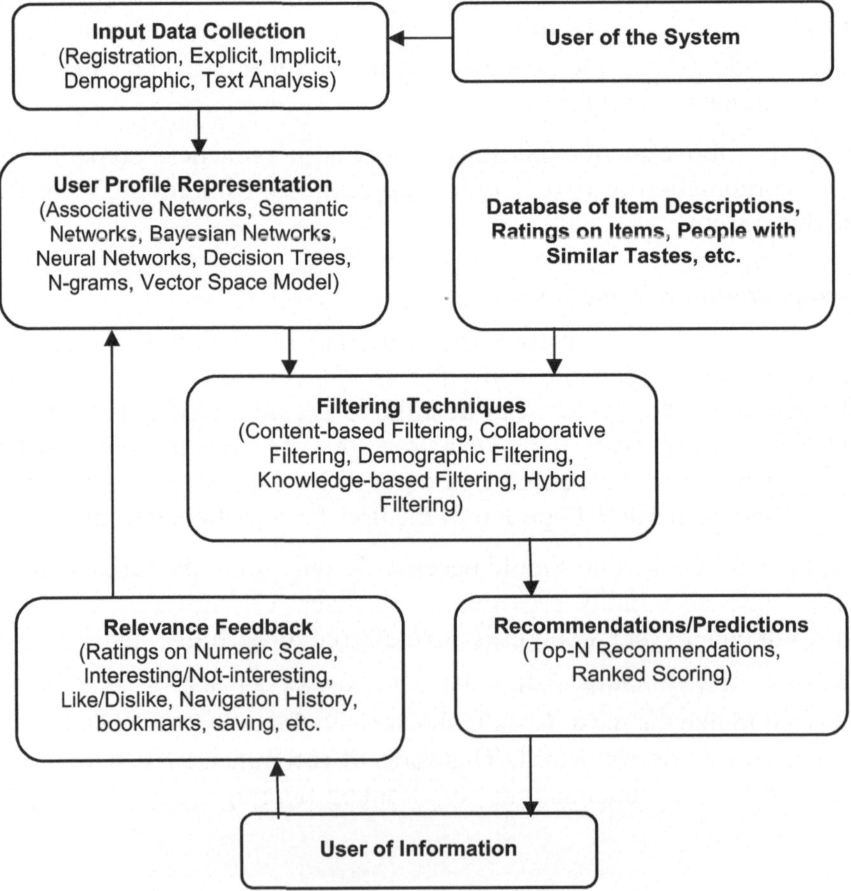

Fig. 1: Pictorial Representation of Recommendation Process in Recommender Systems

For example, some recommender systems expect ratings from users on "numeric scale"; some expect ratings as "interesting"/"not interesting"; some expect "negative"/ "positive"; some expect "like"/"dislike"; and some expect "text comments" for providing better recommendations as an explicit feedback. Examples of another type of feedback is implicit feedback, which includes "navigation history"/"browsing behavior"/ "bookmarks"/"access time"/"saving"/"downloading"/"viewing"/"printing"/"scrolling"/ "maximizing"/"resizing"/"visited hyperlinks", etc. Figure 1 shows the pictorial representation of recommendation process in recommender systems.

4. Conclusions

Queries in information retrieval play an important role in searching and retrieving relevant information from static collection of documents. But in the case of information filtering/recommender systems, profiles play an important role to filter relevant information from dynamic stream of incoming data. The researcher has studied various recommender systems and identified steps followed in recommendation process. Every recommender system needs some sort of input collected explicitly or implicitly to generate recommendations. Using this input, the recommender system builds user profile which represents any of the IR/profile representation models viz., vector space model, semantic networks, weighted n-grams, associative networks etc. The recommender system matches the user profile with the descriptions of items or users with similar taste to recommend items of interest to the user. There are three matching techniques generally used by the recommender systems such as: content-based filtering, collaborative filtering, demographic filtering or hybrid technique. Finally, these systems provide Top-N recommendations followed by fine tuning the user profile with the help of relevance feedback mechanism to retrieve more relevant items. All these 106 systems under study have their advantages and disadvantages in the process of recommending items to the targeted users. Hybrid recommender systems are more important and they are going to play vital role in the next-generation of recommender systems, because they minimize the disadvantages and maximize the utility of content-based filtering systems and collaborative filtering systems.

Acknowledgement

I thank Mr A.K. Chakrabarti, Director, Defence Research and Development Laboratory, Hyderabad for his encouragement and support to carry out this research work.

References

[1] Alton-Scheidl, R., Ekhall, J., van Geloven, O., Kovacs, L., Micsik, A., Lueg, C., *et al.* (1999). SELECT: Social and collaborative filtering of Web documents and news. A. Kobsa and C. Stephanidis (Eds.). *In* Proceedings of the Fifth ERCIM Workshop on User Interfaces for All, Dagstuhl, Germany. pp. 23–37.

[2] Angell, R.C., Freund, G.E., and Willett, P. (1983). Automatic spelling correction using trigram similarity measure. *Information Processing and Management,* 19(4), pp.255–261.

[3] Asnicar, F. and Tasso, C. (1997). ifWeb: A prototype of user model-based intelligent agent for documentation filtering and navigation in the World Wide Web. *In* Proceedings of the 6th International Conference on User Modeling. Chia Laguna, Sardinia. pp. 3–12.

[4] Balabanovic, M. (1997). An adaptive Web page recommendation service. *In* Proceedings of 1st International Conference on Autonomous Agents. California, United States. New York: ACM Press. pp.378–385.

[5] Balabanovic, M., and Shoham, Y. (1997). Fab: Content-based, collaborative recommendation. *Communications of the ACM,* 40(3), 66–72.

[6] Billsus, D., and Pazzani, M.J. (1999). A hybrid user model for news story classification. J. Kay (Ed.). *In* Proceedings of the Seventh International Conference on User Modeling, Banff, Canada. New York: Springer-Verlag. pp. 99–108.

[7] Blanco-Fernandez, Y., Pazos-Arias, J.J., Lopez-Nores, M., Gil-Solla, A., and Ramos-Cabrer, M. (2006). AVATAR: An improved solution for personalized TV based on semantic interface. *IEEE Transactions on Consumer Electronics,* 52(1), 223–231.

[8] Boone, G. (1998). Concept features in Re: Agent, an intelligent Email agent. K.P. Sycara and M. Wooldridge (Eds.). *In* Proceedings of the Second International Conference on Autonomous Agents, Minneapolis, Minnesota, USA. New York: ACM. pp. 141–148.

[9] Brunato, M., and Battiti, R. (2003). PILGRIM: A location broker and mobility-aware recommendation system. *In* Proceedings of the First IEEE International Conference on Pervasive Computing and Communications, Fort Worth (TX), USA. Washington, DC: IEEE Computer Society. pp. 265–272.

[10] Buono, P., Costabile, M. F., D'Atri, A., Hemmje, M., Jaeschke, G., Muscogiuri, *et al.* (2001). FAIRWIS: A system for improving online trade fair services. Stanford-Smith, B. (Ed.). *In* E-work and E-commerce Novel Solutions and practices for a Global Networked Economy, Venice. Amsterdam: IOS Press. pp. 519–525.

[11] Burke, R. (1999). The Wasabi Personal Shopper: A case-based recommender system. *In* Proceedings of the Sixteenth National Conference on Artificial Intelligence and the Eleventh Innovative Applications of Artificial Intelligence Conference, Orlando, Florida, USA. Menlo Park, CA: AAAI. pp. 844–849.

[12] Burke, R., Hammond, K., and Cooper, E. (1996). Knowledge-based navigation of complex information spaces. *In* Proceedings of the Thirteenth National Conference on Artificial Intelligence and Eighth Innovative Applications of Artificial Intelligence Conference, Portland, Oregon. AAAI Press/The MIT Press. pp. 462–468.

[13] Burke, R., Hammond, K., and Young, B. (1997). The FindMe approach to assisted browsing. *IEEE Expert,* 12(4), 32–40.

[14] Cavnar, W.B. (1993). N-gram-based text filtering for TREC-2. D.K. Harman (Ed.). *In* Proceedings of TREC-2: Text Retrieval Conference, Gaithersburg, Maryland, USA. Washington, DC: National Bureau of Standards. pp. 171–179.

[15] Cavnar, W.B., and Trenkle, J.M. (1994). N-gram based text categorization. *In* Proceedings of the Third Annual Symposium on Document Analysis and Information Retrieval, Las Vegas, Nevada, USA. pp. 161–175.

[16] Chen, Z., Meng, X., Fowler, R.H., and Zhu, B. (2000). WebSail: From on-line learning to Web search. Q. Li, Z.M. Ozsoyoglu, R. Wagner, Y. Kambayashi, and Y. Zhang (Eds.). *In* Proceedings

of the First International Conference on Web Information Systems Engineering, Hong Kong, China. Washington, DC: IEEE Computer Society. pp. 206–213.

[17] Chen, Z., Meng, X., Zhu, B., and Fowler, R.H. (2002). WebSail: From on-line learning to Web search. *Knowledge and Information Systems,* 4(2), 219–227.

[18] Cooley, R., Mobasher, B., and Srivastava, J. (1997). Web Mining: Information and pattern discovery on the World Wide Web. *In* Proceedings of 9th International Conference on Tools with Artificial Intelligence, Newport Beach, CA, USA. Washington, DC: IEEE Computer Society, pp. 558–567.

[19] Cosley, D., Lawrence, S., and Pennock, D.M. (2002). REFEREE: An open framework for practical testing of recommender systems using ResearchIndex. *In* Proceedings of 28th International Conference on Very Large Data Bases, Hong Kong, China. pp. 35–46.

[20] Cunningham, P., Bergmann, R., Schmitt, S., Traphoner, R., Breen, S., and Smyth, B. (2001a). WEBSELL: Intelligent sales assistants for the World Wide Web. *Kunstliche Intelligenz (KI),* 1, 28–32.

[21] Cunningham, P., Bergmann, R., Schmitt, S., Traphoner, R., Breen, S., and Smyth, B. (2001b). Intelligent support for online sales: The WEBSELL experience. R. Weber, and C. G von Wangenheim (Eds.). *In* Proceedings of the Workshop Programme at the Fourth International Conference on Case-Based Reasoning, Vancouver, British Columbia, Canada. pp. 104–109.

[22] Dron, J., Mitchell, R., Siviter, P., and Boyne, C. (2003). CoFIND—An experiment in N-dimensional collaborative filtering. *Journal of Network and Computer Applications,* 23(2), 131–142.

[23] Efron, M., and Geisler, G. (2001). Is it all about connections? Factors affecting the performance of a link-based recommender system. *In* Proceedings of ACM SIGIR Workshop on Recommender Systems, New Orleans, USA.

[24] Fu, X., Budzik, J., and Hammond, K.J. (2000). Mining navigation history for recommendation. *In* Proceedings of the 5th International Conference on Intelligent User Interfaces, New Orleans, Louisiana, United States. New York: ACM Press. pp. 106–112.

[25] Goldberg, D., Nichols, D., Oki, B.M. and Terry, D. (1992). Using collaborative filtering to weave an information tapestry. *Communications of the ACM,* 35(12), 61–70.

[26] Goldberg, K., Roeder, T., Gupta, D., and Perkins, C. (2001). Eigentaste: A constant time collaborative filtering algorithm. *Information Retrieval,* 4(2), 133–151.

[27] Gori, M., Maggini. M., and Martinelli, E. (1999). NAUTILUS: Navigate Autonomously and Target Interesting Links for Users. (Technical Report No. RT-DII-20/99). Dipartimento di Ingegneria dell'Informazione, Università di Siena, Italy.

[28] Hayes, C., and Cunningham, P. (2000). Smart radio—Building music radio on the fly. A. Macintosh, M. Moulton and F. Coenen (Eds.). *In* Proceedings of Expert Systems 2000, 20th SGES Conference on KBS and Applied AI. London: Springer Verlag. pp. 129–140.

[29] Hayes, C., and Cunningham, P. (2001). Smart Radio—Community-based music radio. *Knowledge Based Systems*, 14(3–4), 197–201.

[30] Heckerman, D., Geiger, D., and Chickering, D. (1995). Learning Bayesian networks: The combination of knowledge and statistical data. *Machine Learning,* 20(3), 197–243.

[31] Hill, W., Stead, L., Rosenstein, M., and Furnas, G. (1995). Recommending and evaluating choices in a virtual community of use. I.R. Katz, R. Mack, L. Marks, M.B. Rosson, and J. Nielsen

(Eds.). *In* Proceedings of the SIGCHI Conference on Human Factors in Computing Systems, Denver, Colorado, United States. New York: ACM Press. pp. 194–201.

[32] Huberman, B.A. and Kaminsky, M. (1996). Beehive: A system for cooperative filtering and sharing of information. (Technical Report). Dynamics of Computation Group, Xerox Palo Alto Research Center.

[33] Kamba, T., Bharat, K. and Albers, M.C. (1995). The Krakatoa Chronicle: An interactive personalized newspaper on the Web. In Proceedings of Fourth International World Wide Web Conference, Boston, USA. pp. 159–170

[34] Kawashima, H., Matsushita, T., and Satake, S. (2006). PORSCHE: A physical objects recommender system for cell phone users. *In* Proceedings of the Second International Workshop on Personalized Context Modeling and Management for UbiComp Applications, Orange County, California.

[35] Kilander, F., Fahraeus, E., and Palme, J. (1997). PEFNA: The Private Filtering News Agent. (Technical Report No. 97–004), Department of Computer and Systems Sciences, Stockholm University.

[36] Kilfoil, M., Xing, W., and Ghorbani, A. (2005). ARAS: Adaptive recommender for academic scheduling. In Proceedings of the 3rd Annual Communication Networks and Services Research Conference, Volume 00. Washington: IEEE Computer Society. pp. 307–312.

[37] Kim, C.Y., Lee, J.K., Cho, Y.H., and Kim, D.H. (2004). VISCORS: A visual-content recommender for the mobile Web. *IEEE Intelligent Systems,* 19(6), 32–39.

[38] Kimbrell, R.E. (1988). Searching for Text? Send and N-gram! *Byte*, May 1988, 297–312.

[39] Konstan, J.A., Miller, B.N., Maltz, D., Herlocker, J.L., Gordon, L.R., and Riedl, J. (1997). GroupLens: Applying collaborative filtering to Usenet news. *Communications of ACM,* 40(3), 77–87.

[40] Krulwich, B. (1997). Lifestyle Finder: Intelligent user profiling using large-scale demographic data. *Artificial Intelligence Magazine,* 18(2), 37–46.

[41] Krulwich, B., and Burkey, C. (1997). The InfoFinder agent: Learning user interests through heuristic phrase extraction. *IEEE Expert: Intelligent Systems and Their Applications,* 12(5), 22–27.

[42] Lang, K. (1995). NewsWeeder: Learning to filter netnews. Armand Prieditis and Stuart J. Russell (Eds.). *In* Proceedings of the Twelfth International Conference on Machine Learning, Tahoe City, California, USA, pp. 331–339.

[43] Linden, G., Smith, B., and York, J. (2003). Amazon.com recommendations: Item-to-item collaborative filtering. *IEEE Internet Computing,* 7(1), 76–80.

[44] Liu, H., and Maes, P. (2005). InterestMap: Harvesting social network profiles for recommendations. *In* Proceedings of IUI Beyond Personalization 2005: A Workshop on the Next Stage of Recommender Systems Research, San Diego, CA, USA, pp. 54–59.

[45] McCulloch, W.S., and Pitts, W.H. (1943). A logical calculus of the ideas immanent in nervous activity. *Bulletin of Mathematical Biophysics,* 5, 115–133.

[46] Middleton, S.E., De Roure, D.C., and Shadbolt, N.R. (2002). Foxtrot Recommender System: User profiling, ontologies and the World Wide Web. *In* Proceedings of the Eleventh International World Wide Web Conference, Honolulu, Hawaii.

[47] Minsky, M.L., and Papert, S.A. (1969). Perceptrons: An introduction to Computational Geometry. MIT Press.

[48] Mladenic, D. (1996). Personal WebWatcher: Design and implementation. (Technical Report No. IJS-DP-7472), School of Computer Science, Carnegie-Mellon University, Pittsburgh, USA.

[49] Mobasher, B., Cooley, R., and Srivastava, J. (2000). Automatic personalization based on Web usage mining. *Communications of the ACM,* 43(8), 142–151.

[50] Mooney, R.J., and Roy, L. (2000). Content-based book recommending using learning for text categorization. *In* Proceedings of the Fifth ACM Conference on Digital Libraries, San Antonio, Texas. New York: ACM Press, pp. 95–204.

[51] Moukas, A. (1997). Amalthaea: Information discovery and filtering using a multiagent evolving ecosystem. *Applied Artificial Intelligence: An International Journal,* 11(5), 437–457.

[52] Moukas, A., and Maes, P. (1998). Amalthaea: An evolving multi-agent information filtering and discovery system for the WWW. *Autonomous Agents and Multi-Agent Systems,* 1(1), 59–88.

[53] Mukherjee, R., Jonsdottir, G., Sen, S., and Sarathi, P. (2001). MOVIES2GO: An online voting based movie recommender system. *In* Proceedings of the Fifth international Conference on Autonomous Agents, Montreal, Quebec, Canada. New York: ACM Press, pp. 114–115.

[54] Pazzani, J.M., and Billsus, D. (1996). Syskill and Webert: Identifying interesting Websites. *In* Proceedings of the Thirteenth National Conference on Artificial Intelligence and Eighth Innovative Applications of Artificial Intelligence Conference, Portland, Oregon. AAAI Press/The MIT Press, pp. 54–61.

[55] Pemberton, D., Rodden, T., and Procter, R. (2000). GroupMark: A WWW recommender system combining collaborative and information filtering. Emiliani, P.L., and Stephanidis, C. (Eds.). *In* Proceedings of 6th ERCIM Workshop on 'User Interfaces for All', Florence, Italy.

[56] Quillian, M. R. (1968). Semantic memory. M. Minsky (Ed.): *In* Semantic Information Processing. Cambridge, MA: MIT Press, pp. 227–270.

[57] Radev, D.R., Fan, W., and Zhang, Z. (2001). WebInEssence: A personalized, web-based multi-document summarization and recommendation system. *In* Proceedings of NAACL Workshop on Automatic Summarization, Pittsburgh. pp. 79–88.

[58] Resnick, P., Iacovou, N., Suchak, M., Bergstrom, P., and Riedl, J. (1994). GroupLens: An open architecture for collaborative filtering of netnews. *In* Proceedings of the 1994 ACM Conference on Computer Supported Cooperative Work, Chapel Hill, North Carolina, United States. New York: ACM Press, pp. 175–186.

[59] Rich, E. (1979). User modeling via stereotypes. *Cognitive Science,* 3, 329–354.

[60] Rosenblatt, F. (1958). The Perceptron: A probabilistic model for information storage and organization in the brain. *Psychological Review,* 65(6), 386–408.

[61] Sakagami, H., and Kamba, T. (1997). Learning personal preferences on online newspaper articles from user behaviors. P.H. Enslow, M. Genesereth, and A. Patterson (Eds.). *In* Selected Papers from the Sixth International Conference on World Wide Web, Santa Clara, California. Essex: Elsevier Science. pp. 1447–1455.

[62] Salton, G., and McGill, M.J. (1983). Introduction to modern information retrieval. New York: McGraw Hill Publishing Company.

[63] Sanders, G.L. (1995). Data modeling. Danvers, MA: Boyd and Fraser Publishing Company.

[64] Schwab, I., Pohl, W. and Koychev, I. (2000). Learning to recommend from positive evidence. *In* Proceedings of the 5th International Conference on Intelligent User Interfaces, New Orleans, Louisiana, United States. New York: ACM Press. pp. 241–247.

[65] Shardanand, U. (1994). Social information filtering for music recommendation. M.S Thesis, Program in Media Arts and Sciences, Massachusetts Institute of Technology.

[66] Shardanand, U., and Maes, P. (1995). Social information filtering: Algorithms for automating "word of mouth". I.R. Katz, R. Mack, L. Marks, M.B. Rosson, and J. Nielsen (Eds.). *In* Proceedings of the SIGCHI Conference on Human Factors in Computing Systems, Denver, Colorado, United States. ACM Press/Addison-Wesley, pp. 210–217.

[67] Sorensen, H., and McElligott, M. (1995). PSUN: A profiling system for Usenet news. *In* CIKM '95 Workshop on Intelligent Information Agents, Baltimore.

[68] Sorensen, H., O'Riordan, A., and O'Riordan, C. (1997). Profiling with the INFOrmer text filtering agent. *Journal of Universal Computer Science,* 3(8), 988–1006.

[69] Sowa, J. (1984). Conceptual structures: Information processing in mind and machine. Reading, MA: Addison-Wesley Publishing Company.

[70] Stefani, A., and Strapparava, C. (1998). Personalizing access to Web sites: The SiteIF project. *In* Proceedings of the Second Workshop on Adaptive Hypertext and Hypermedia, Pittsburgh, USA.

[71] Suen, C.Y. (1979). N-gram statistics for natural language understanding and text processing. *IEEE Transaction on Pattern Analysis and Machine Intelligence,* 1(2), 164–172.

[72] Ullmann, J. R. (1977). Binary n-gram technique for automatic correction of substitution, deletion, insertion, and reversal errors in words. *The Computer Journal,* 20(2), 141–147.

[73] van Rijsbergen, C.J. (1979). Information retrieval (2nd ed.). London: Butterworths.

[74] Vozalis, E., and Margaritis, K.G. (2003). Analysis of recommender systems algorithms. *In* Proceedings of the 6th Hellenic European Conference on Computer Mathematics and its Applications, Athens, Greece.

[75] Xie, B., Han, P., and Shen, R. (2004). PipeCF: A scalable DHT-based collaborative filtering rccommcndation systcm. S.I. Fcldman, M. Urctsky, M. Najork, and C.E. Wills (Eds.). *In* Proceedings of the 13th International Conference on World Wide Web-Alternate Track Papers and Posters, New York, USA, pp. 224–225.

[76] Yan, T.W. and Garcia-Molina, H. (1995). SIFT—A tool for wide-area information dissemination. *In* Proceedings of USENIX 1995 Technical Conference on UNIX and Advanced Computing Systems, New Orleans, Louisiana. Berkeley, CA: USENIX Association, pp. 177–186.

[77] Yimam-Seid, D., and Kobsa, A. (2003). Expert finding systems for organizations: Problem and domain analysis and the DEMOIR approach. *Journal of Organizational Computing and Electronic Commerce,* 13(1), 1–24.

[78] Zamora, E.M., Pollock, J. J., and Zamora, A. (1981). The use of trigram analysis for spelling error detection. *Information Processing and Management,* 17(6), 305–316.

Section–VIII

Electronic Resources and Pedagogical Issues

Electronic Resources Management in Libraries, pp. 377–388

Future of Special Libraries: Vision 2020

Ramesh C. Gaur, Yogita Ahuja and Manorama Tripathi

ABSTRACT

The advent of new technologies has led to a very bright and exciting vision for future libraries. To reach out the users is the new slogan for future libraries. Vision 2020 for special libraries is dominated by mobile computing and its convergence with mobile communication technologies. This paper presents a vision 2020 for special libraries worldwide in general and Indian special libraries in particular.

1. Introduction

A special library is defined as a library that is neither academic library nor a public library and is not usually open to public use. It is meant for special category of clientele. We are in electronic age and a number of changes have been seen in special libraries during last two decades. Change is integral part of human life and it is inevitable. What more is to be seen in year 2020? Seamless 24 × 7 access to the library resources anytime, anywhere through multi-channel and in multi formats to anyone by 2020, or even earlier may be a vision in the minds of both users and librarians.

A futuristic vision of any kind of library is envisaged keeping people, technology, finance, physical, legal, social, and institutional and various other issues in mind. Last two decades, we have seen E-revolution which may continue for another few decades. Convergence of IT and telecommunications along with popularity of social networking tools has put new challenges for special libraries. Technology is not only the primary catalyst for changes in the library, but also the major impetus for changing the underlying culture of the library environment.

A library consists of trinity of users, staff and resources. Resources may have in its fold both technological tools and collections. Let's first begin with users as libraries exist for them only. Now users wants pinpointed information not only on computers but also on their mobiles, palmtops, tabulates etc. So, 2020 will be era of Web 2.0 *i.e.* Library 2.0. RSS Feeds, Blogs, Wikis, Podcasting, Photosharing, Facebook, Linked in, You-Tube, Twitter, Flickr, e-resources, instant messaging, chat service, virtual learning and virtual referencing will be seen as opportunities as well as challenges for both libraries and users.

By the year 2020, questions may be asked about the future of physical libraries. Ongoing debates on print versus electronic may have more reasons to look forward towards paperless society. Better networking connectivity, 24 × 7 seamless accesses to library resources, availability of information in multiple formats through multiple media and channels, towards creation of community based contents, flexible space and infrastructure for future innovations and creation of virtual libraries may be more significant issues in 2020. Better and more efficient storage solutions, improvements in Internet bandwidth, miniaturization of technological tools, advancements in mobile communication and computing may be seen as new opportunities. Availability of above technologies on affordable prices may help special libraries in the days of shrinking budget and increasing cost of publications.

In term of library techniques and methods instead of OPAC and digital library, you may see more and more library portals which may provide single window based access to all services and resources anytime, anywhere and to anyone. Mobile computing may be the focus of information dissemination in years to come. Taxonomy supported by global metadata standards, semantic web are new methods to optimize browsing and may improve access to information.

E-journals and other electronic databases have already become integral part of special libraries. E-books and digital repository are also trying to make some impact on libraries. Digital audio/video, and other images based resources need more suitable ways for reaching out to the users over intranet/Internet. Mixing and repackaging of the various forms of contents in the form of a single e-resource may find place in users selves in years to come. A number of e-security concerns, cyber crime, authenticity of information, web standards and plagiarism may be seen as challenges to both libraries and technocrats. The most critical challenge is the preservation of digital information. Physical media has some fixed life span such as stone tablets have survived for thousands of years, paper/palm leaf manuscripts are there since last 300–500 years but same is not true in case of digital information storage media such as CD/DVD, Hard disks etc. So, researcher working in the area of digital preservation may have some concrete solutions to offer in 2020.

Special libraries are changing and will continue to see more changes in year 2020. Same is true for changing role for librarians. A librarian has to be more technology savvy. To cope up with new user demands, he/she has to fine-tune library techniques and methods. Whatever may be the changes but the basic philosophy of the librarianship will remain same, *i.e.*, to provide right information, to right user, at right time in pinpointed or most suitable formats as per user's needs. Year 2020 may provide more opportunities and better solutions to many of the existing problems faced by the special libraries.

2. Review of Literature

Singh (2006) has pointed out that in most Indian special libraries, features such as Internet resources and other electronic/digital resources, subject gateways and networks and consortia, are fast gaining acceptance. New trends include the development of libraries' own websites, the sophisticated application of digital technology, more professional marketing of information products and services, outsourcing, flexible workforce, knowledge management and participative management are becoming the order of the day.

Special libraries are changing dramatically by adopting new means of technology in all activities from print to e-environments like printed library card catalogues have been replaced by computerized OPAC system with a variety of web-based Graphical User Interface (GUI) functions, online accessibility for 24 × 7, availability of numerous e-databases, e-journals, information resources, information literacy, online services for users. To face the new information explosion, special libraries will have to meet even more challenges and opportunities to serve users, all with much expectation and many more demands triggered by the growth of emerging and cutting edge technologies in electronic learning environments. Joshi (2003) has reported that special library acts as a disseminator of information, while doing the same manually, the special library has to face various short comes. In short, the day has come for changing the traditional library into a modern one. The opportunities are more for the special library, because of computer technology, networking, communication and information processing, advanced and can provide efficiency, accuracy and speed for delivering library and information services. He has also identified some of the main problems such as: effective management, lack of suitable manpower etc.

The Philippine Association of Academic/Research Librarians has defined that special libraries offer resources and collections in a specialized environment of interest, such as corporations, hospitals, the military, museums, private businesses, and the government. Special libraries can serve particular populations, such as the blind and physically handicapped, while others are dedicated to special collections (Paarl blog, 2011).

Kumar *et al.* (2005) have highlighted the use of IT in special libraries that special libraries have been in existence from the beginning of twentieth century, whereas information centres formed during the fifties and have now developed into major group of information institutions. Although special libraries and information centers have over lapping functional characteristics to some extent, the special libraries disseminate information and matter acquired by them to answers the research questions, and direct users on research information to appropriate one and use periodicals to keep them user informed about current developments in this field. Parent organization's special library serves a wide distributed group of users who may be linked with the common subject interest. Now, the concepts of special libraries have been changed in all aspects and librarians are known as cybrarians.

3. Special Library Vision 2020

The future of libraries is being shaped today by emerging new technologies that are transforming the way information is created and disseminated. One indicator of the future of libraries is the push to provide increasing amounts of information in electronic format. By the year 2020, many more opportunities and better solutions to the existing problems faced by the special libraries emerge; some new methods and technologies are given in the following paragraphs.

3.1 *Interactive Information Dissemination: Web 2.0 and Beyond*

With the emergence of Web 2.0 technologies, it has become easy to seek information interactively and making appointments effectively. It is associated with Web applications that facilitate interactive information sharing, interoperability, user-centered design, and collaboration on the World Wide Web. A Web 2.0 site gives free choice to its users to interact or collaborate with each other in a social media dialogue as creator of user-generated content in a virtual community, in contrast to website where users are limited to the passive viewing of content that was created for them. Examples are Social Networking sites, Blogs, Wikis, video-sharing sites, hosted services, Web applications, Mashups and Folksonomies (Wikipedia, 2011).

Web 3.0 is a term that is loosely used as a reference to the future of the Web. It is a term used to describe the evolution of Web usage and interaction that includes transforming the Web into a database. In Web 3.0 era we will upgrade the back-end of the Web, after a decade of focus on the front-end (Web 2.0 has mainly been about AJAX, tagging, and other front-end user-experience innovations). Web 3.0 technology is a move towards making content accessible by multiple non-browser applications, the leveraging of artificial intelligence technologies etc. The bandwidth will continue to improve to the point that is loading web pages, even high definition video file instantaneous. The virtual elimination of bandwidth restraints opens web developers to entirely new opportunities. Elements and experiences such as high definition graphics, 3-D animations and modeling, multi-player games and social networks, can all rise to new levels on an unlimited bandwidth of Internet. Web 3.0 is something called the Semantic Web, a term coined by Tim Berners-Lee. The idea behind the Semantic Web is to provide data on the web in a universal format that can be interpreted by software agents. This makes all data easily searchable and ubiquitous. A universal format also allows the data to be presented in different formats and modalities (Berners-Lee, 2001).

Web 3.0 will lead to the blurring of that artificial wall between the web browser and the desktop, providing a full but secure integration with devices and services exposed by the operating system. The first stage of Web 1.0 was about connecting information and getting over the Internet. Web 2.0 is about connecting people putting the "I" in user interface, and the "we" into a web of social participation. The next stage of Web 3.0 represents the meanings, connecting knowledge, and putting them to work in ways that make our experience of Internet more relevant, useful, and enjoyable.

Library 2.0: The term Library 2.0, first coined by Michael Casey in 2006 on his blog 'Library Crunch' and refers to a number of social and technological changes that are having impact upon libraries, its staff and their clientele, and how they could interact. It is a model for modernized form of library service that reflects a transition within the library world in the way services are delivered to users. The focus is on user-centered change and participation in the creation of content and community (Wikipedia, 2011).

The application of concepts and technologies of Web 2.0 as applied to the library services and collections is named as "Library 2.0". It is a concept that personified new generation of library services to meet the present day user's needs and expectations. Some of the core concepts of Library 2.0 are given below:

- Services would be made available at the point of need rather than making the users come to the services. Reach out the users and provide library services in a wide variety of services beyond the library, such as portals, virtual learning environments, and e-commerce systems etc.
- Allow data to be exposed, discovered and manipulated in a variety of ways in distinct fom form access to users.
- Develop the applications that can be easy to use, flexible, intelligent, and responsive to user's needs.
- Facilitate communication, community and user participation that are focused on the users and their needs (Pandey and Pandey, 2009).

Library 3.0: It is just around the corner and with foresight and planning we are confident that libraries will overcome the barriers. Current experience suggests that librarians will spend an increasing amount of their time in the electronic frontier. Many dimensions and properties of this electronic frontier is unfamiliar and uncharted territory and our survival depends on well we adapt our values and skills. With digital collections "remote access", and virtual reference; access is one point of need so the issue is function and service not people and service. Services will be in a variety of forms and places. So what does that mean for Librarian 3.0? Ability to collect and provide information and to offer instruction in research techniques and information use rather than by physical presence as somewhere people go. Librarian 3.0 will also have to offer alternative services such as help at the 'point of failure' and other value added services.

Librarians or library staff of the future will have to be prepared for lifelong learning. Some library staff may not be library trained so continual professional development will be part of their every day's work. No one person can be expert in the entire cyberspace and librarians will seek new alliances and develop new talents. Those libraries or librarians that do not or will not be around to work with Library 4.0; those that will be would have taken heed of the following words from the naturalist Charles Darwin 'It is not the strongest of the species that survive, or the most intelligent, but the one most responsive to change' (Saw and Todd, 2007).

3.2 *Library Management*

Digital Library: A digital library is an assemblage of digital computing, storage, and communication machinery together with the content and software needed to reproduce, emulate and extend the services provided by conventional libraries based on paper and other means of collecting, cataloguing, finding and disseminating information. A fully functional digital library must accomplish all essential services of traditional libraries and also exploits the well-known advantage of digital storage, searching and communication (Chowdhury and Chowdhury, 2003). It provides access to part of or all its collections, such as plain texts, images, graphics, audio/video materials and other library materials those have been converted into electronic form and made them accessible via the Internet and World Wide Web.

Virtual Reality: Virtual reality is a computer simulation of a real or imaginary system that enables a user to perform operations on the simulated system and shows the effects in real-time. It is used in libraries for many purposes.

Impact of Virtual Reality on Libraries

- Virtual Library (VL) a place where one can access to universal knowledge from the workplace, no matter wherever your workplace is.
- Sometimes VL referred as Library without walls.
- VL creates its own tools such as e-text databases, OPAC, e-mail, connection with libraries all around the world, queries to local and external databases, and access to the Internet.
- Virtual Library services like DDS and ILL to the user's home, Virtual Reference Desk, User training, Virtual Library Tours are latest techniques which many libraries are adopting by for their users benefits.

WebOPAC: Web OPAC (Online Public Access Catalogue) is used for accessing, retrieving and using the learning resources of the library with the help of their bibliographic details. Through Web-OPAC the documents can be searched by author(s) and editor(s), any keyword(s) from the title or subject heading(s). User friendly (and menu driven) help screens of the OPAC retrieval software help the users make searches with ease and promptness.

E-reference Services: In distance education and learning, Electronic reference (e-reference) services are playing an important role. Increasingly distance education is utilizing e-mail and web-based facilities to deliver teaching materials and providing interactive tutorial support across the Internet in both the industrialized and developing world. Library services now include databases, and online access to the full-text of electronic journals or specially digitized book chapters. Now libraries are engaged with in order to best serve the needs of distance learners. *e*-reference services are Internet-based question and answer services that connect users with experts in the information sources in a variety of subject areas through web forms and/or e-mail. E-reference can be interpreted to cover support via direct contact with reference librarians through e-mail, telephone, video-conferencing, and dedicated pages on the World Wide Web. E-reference provides an extra choice for users, and may take some of the load off a busy reference desk, although it does not lessen the overall workload for the library. Using e-reference could be a time saver for users, and using the Internet is generally cheaper than a telephone. E-reference may also provide the user with a degree of anonymity, or at least minimizes any embarrassment that they might feel in a face to face reference interview. The growing use of the Internet for information storage, retrieval and communication is perhaps the most significant development shaping into library and information services today. The advantages of developing e-reference services using the facilities of the Internet include 24 hours access for users, and the potential for easier referral of questions to services with more substantial collections or higher levels of expertise (Johnson, Reid and Newton, 2011).

RFID Library Management System: Radio Frequency Identification Device (RFID) is one of today's most exciting and fastest growing technologies for increasing efficiency, improving profitability and an important area of study in information environment.

Use of RFID in Libraries Services

- It has the capability for multiple applications and provides effective and efficient library detection system
- It has provided full autonomy to users in library transactions. The library can issue and return the books in a flexible manner irrespective of non-availability of staff.
- It has improved users satisfaction substantially
- It has enhanced the level of security to collections
- It has eliminated various repetitive work carried out by the staff
- It has enabled us to update the database in a real-time environment
- It has enabled self check-in/Check-out System
- Faster circulation transactions
- Perfect tracker and high-speed inventorying
- Simplified self-charging/discharging and highly reliable
- Automated identification of materials
- It is better than barcode.

Digitization of Library Collections: Library digitization is the process of using computers, databases, multimedia equipment, networks, video equipment and web technologies to electronically collect, classify, copy, compress, scan, store and transform the existing conventional library information resources into digital forms. Library digitization is different from a digital library as it focuses on the process of making diverse library information resources electronically available, while a digital library is a platform for accessing, collecting, managing, searching and storing distributed digitized information resources over the Internet and WWW (Khan and Waris, 2009). Thus, to provide access to these digitalized library collections, libraries need to set up and implement digital library projects which provide digitalized resources, network access and distribution management via network technology.

Institutional Repository: An Institutional Repository is an online locus for collecting, preserving, and disseminating—in digital form—the intellectual output of an institution, particularly a research institution.

The four main objectives for having an institutional repository are:

- To provide open access to institutional research output by self-archiving;
- To create global visibility for an institution's scholarly research;
- To collect content in a single location;
- To store and preserve other institutional digital assets, including unpublished or otherwise easily lost ("grey") literature e.g. theses or technical reports (Wikipedia, 2011).

Non-print Material: In the digital environment, every library wants to enrich not only in printed materials and services but also in non-print materials/products and services like:

- CDs, DVDs, Microfilms etc.
- Online Books, Online Journals.
- Online Databases.
- E-Reference sources.

Consortia: Membership with e-consortia: Technology is a driving force in the contemporary education systems. Successful implementation of high-tech programmes like INDEST and UGC-INFONET consortia resources will really get further strength and campus wide reach with the adoption of cabled network and wireless technologies.

3.3 *Library Services*

Tagging: It is another Web 2.0 application which is extensively used in library community and is described as the process by which the resources in a collection are assigned tags in the form of words, phrases, codes or other strings of characters. This allows users to add and change the data and metadata and at times give a local flavour to the data and metadata. The advantage of user tag is that it helps the data to be more easily searchable. The examples are Flicker, Delicious (Arora, 2009).

Instant Messaging Reference Service: It is one of the real-time electronic consulting and reference offered by academic libraries via specific software running on the

Internet platform. It is virtually instantaneous communication between two or more people using textual format, providing "real time reference" services, where patrons can synchronously communicate with librarians much as they would in a face to face reference context. The software often allow co-browsing, file sharing, screen capturing and data sharing and mining of previous transcripts. Libraries are already offering live reference service using 24 × 7 × 365 basis in a collaborative fashion.

Wiki's: Wiki is a website that uses wiki software, allowing the easy creation and editing of any number of interlinked web pages, using a simplified markup language. Wikis are often used to create collaborative websites, to power community websites and for note making (Wikipedia, 2011).

Blogs: A blog is a website, usually maintained by an individual, with regular entries of commentary, descriptions of events, or other material such as graphics or video (Wikipedia, 2011).

Social Networking: A social networking service is an online service, platform, or site that focuses on building and reflecting of social networks or social relations among people, e.g., who share interests and/or activities. Social networking sites allow users to share ideas, activities, events, and interests within their individual networks. Popular methods now combine many of these, with Facebook and Twitter, Hi5, widely used worldwide. Flicker, Twitter, Facebook, LinkedIn and Orkut are very popular in India (Wikipedia, 2011).

YouTube: YouTube is a website to upload and shared videos. On which users can discover, watch, upload, and share videos. There is a wide variety of user-generated video content, including movie clips, TV clips, and music videos, as well as amateur content such as video blogging and short original videos. Librarians, students of library and information science well as users can understand the library and library techniques by watching these videos (Wikipedia, 2011).

ListServe: It is an email based technology used a library to send simultaneously their users all the new arrivals list, newspaper clipping, TOC of Journals by a single click.

RSS: This is nothing but a coding of text in the XML form at which allows users to fix the preferences and with the help of subscription to collect or gather the content from the web feed on regular intervals like hourly, daily, weekly etc. Application of RSS feeds in the library services are:

- *RSS Book Lists:* Amazon is already involved in the production of a number of RSS feeds which aggregate book news under popular headlines (<http://www.amazon.com/exec/obidos/subst/xs/syndicate.html>).
- RSS table of contents for journals
- RSS feeds to improve the existing reference service
- It is new addition to the online catalog

- Creating an RSS feed tied to a library account for get notifications and/or information about overdue materials
- New programs and events posted on the library website
- Sending library's electronic newsletter
- Press releases and other media advisories are sent
- Library closings, including emergency closings
- Library job openings are posted
- Subscribe to a few RSS feeds, such as local news websites, and share the content on the library's website
- Interest to library customers and share the content on the customer's personalized library web page
- Professional RSS feeds and share with library staff on the library intranet.

SMS Alert Services: These provide current awareness and selective dissemination services by e-mail or SMS alerts. In the present environment every library should adopt these techniques for users, to provide current awareness services like contents of journals, newspaper clippings, and new arrival list etc. as per their requirement or regular intervals by using email or SMS alert service. Through this kind of services users can aware or up-to-date their knowledge in the field.

Mobile Computing: Librarians have always been enthusiastic in applying and adopting new technologies to serve their clientele. Many libraries in foreign countries have successfully exploited novel web-based technologies, including social networking, chat technologies, instant messaging, SMS etc. All these technologies are increasingly being used on mobile devices (Library and Information Association' Blog, 2011).

Libraries today are covering most of the technologies given by mobile industry like PDA's, Blackberry, iPod, Cellphones, UM PC's (Ultra Mobile PC) and mobilising library contents in a portable form suitable for small screen and delivering short services in the form of contents/information with device's multiple searching features. Mobile Optimized Catalogs and Ready References, ILS vendors are starting to make Mobile Optimized Catalogs—so that patrons can access library catalogues through their mobile device. More and more library users are using their cell phones or other mobile devices (e.g., PDAs, smartphones, etc.) for much more than talking and texting. Many patrons are searching and browsing the web, reading magazines and books, and generally doing things that recently used to do by computers (Khare, N., 2009).

Future Potentials of Mobile Application in the Libraries: More and more changes are expected within four to five years in the field of mobile technology and its application to the libraries, the day is not too far when we will use phone to read barcodes or RFIDs in the library and OPACs will develop GIS sensitivity and be able to communicate with users through their mobiles for holds, fines, late notices, alerts, etc.

4. Conclusions

The Road Map of new generation of libraries can bring revolutionary changes in contemporary information infrastructure. Technology has enabled diverse distributed collection of contents to become integrated at the metadata and/or content levels, for widespread use through powerful interfaces that will become increasingly personalized. Due to advancement of information technology, many of the library users satisfy their information needs at home/cyber cafe through Internet. Library services based on the conventional service model due to lack the new information services and there exist a large gap between user needs and the actual offered before the library services. This communication provides true intellectual information access in the form of indexing, cataloguing and classification. Standards, advanced technology, and powerful systems can support a wide variety of types of users, providing a broad range of tailored services. The new generation of libraries glorifies the information access services and optimizes the infrastructure with user's requirement.

Privacy and copyright should be matter of concern in future due to the availability of web contents 24 × 7 basis and possibilities of its damage and loss in the computer and also mobile searches by all the individuals without any authentication or identification, as it is going to be the fastest growing application in the next five years even today It is already a major feature of Apple iphones user. The librarian has to understand fully the capabilities and potentials of the Information Communication Technology and its use in libraries in near future by providing the quality services matching with the needs of the user.

References

[1] Arora, J. (2009). Library 2.0: Innovative technologies for building libraries of tomorrow. *In* Kataria S. *et al.* (Ed.). *Conference Proceeding of Emerging Trends and Technologies in Libraries and Information Services ETTLIS-2009*. New Delhi, KBD Publications. pp.19–30.

[2] Berners-Lee, J., Hendler, T. and Lassila, O. (2001). The semantic web. *Scientific American*, 284(5), 35–43.

[3] Blog. Wikipedia, the free encyclopedia. Accessed on 13 May 2011 from http://en.wikipedia.org/wiki/Blog.

[4] Chowdhury, G. and Chowdhury, S. (2003). Introduction to digital libraries. London: Facet Publishing.

[5] Institutional Repository. Wikipedia, the free encyclopedia. Retrieved on 13 June 2012 from http://en.wikipedia.org/wiki/Institutional_repository.

[6] Joshi, H.N. (2003). Computer application in special libraries: a study report. *CALIBER 2003*. Ahmedabad, Inflibnet Centre.

[7] Khan, M.H. and Rao, A.K.W. (2009). Digital libraries: Problems, issues and challenges *In* Kataria S. *et al.* (Ed.), *Conference Proceeding of Emerging Trends and Technologies in Libraries and Information Services ETTLIS-2009*. New Delhi, KBD Publications, pp. 592–599.

[8] Khare, N. (2009). Libraries on move: Library mobile applications. *In 7th International CALIBER-2009,* Pondicherry University, Puducherry, Ahmedabad, INFLIBNET Centre. Vol. 1, pp. 272–278.

[9] Kumar, H., Nageswaran, S.N. and Singh, S.N. (2005). Plan and management for library automation and use of new information technology in special libraries. *3rd Convention PLANNER -2005.* Assam Univ., Silchar. pp. 207–216.

[10] Library 2.0. Wikipedia, the free encyclopedia. Retrieved on 12 May 2011 from http://en.wikipedia.org/wiki/Library.

[11] Microsoft Press (2002). Microsoft computer dictionary. Ed 5. New Delhi, Microsoft Corporation.

[12] Mobile Computing and Libraries. LIA–Library and Information Association Blog. Retrieved on 30 May 2011 from http://liamofmauritius.wordpress.com/2010/01/21/mobile-computing-libraries

[13] Pandey, P. and Pandey, M. (2010). Library 2.0 technology: an advance approach to information handling. In Kataria S. *et al.* (Ed.), *Conference Proceeding of* Emerging *Trends and Technologies in Libraries and Information Services, ETTLIS-2010.* New Delhi, KBD Publications, pp. 61–63.

[14] Saw, G. and Todd, H. (2007). Library 3.0: Where art our skills? *In World Library and Information Congress, 73rd IFLA General Conference and Council, Durban, South Africa,* pp. 1–15.

[15] Singh, S.P. (2006). Special libraries in India: Some current trends. *Library Review*, 55(8), 520–530. Retrieved on 3 February 2011 from http://www.emeraldinsight.com/journals.htm?issn=00242535&volume=55&issue=8&articleid=1571431&show=abstract; DOI: 10.1108/00242530610689365

[16] Social Network. Wikipedia, the free encyclopedia. Retrieved on 12 June 2011 from http://en.wikipedia.org/wiki/Social

[17] Web 2.0. Wikipedia, the free encyclopedia. Retrieved on 12 May 2011 from http://en.wikipedia.org/wiki/Web.

[18] Wiki.ikipedia, the free encyclopedia. Retrieved on 13 May 2011 from http://en.wikipedia.org/wiki/Wiki

[19] YouTube. Wikipedia, the free encyclopedia. Retrieved on 14 May 2011 from http://en.wikipedia.org/wiki/YouTube.

Electronic Resources Management in Libraries, pp. 389–395

Placing Media and Information Literacy at the Core of Instruction to Promote Critical Thinking and Independent Learning among Students

Jagtar Singh

ABSTRACT

Information has become fourth need for surviving and thriving in the Internet era. With emergence of the Internet and the ascent of multimedia, it has become very difficult to manage quality information for decision-making and convert pertinent information into tacit knowledge for problem-solving. For the emerging knowledge societies, competency building is necessary to make sense of the chaos on the Internet particularly in the public domain. Similarly, various TV channels are also adding to the problems of the viewers. Instead of informing the masses, these channels in India are competing with each other and sometimes make issues of the non-issues. What is breaking news in the morning becomes barking news in the evening. Media is virtually setting the agenda and many-a-times misguiding the masses. In such a situation, it is required to equip the stakeholders with media and information literacy skills to promote critical thinking among them and also to convert the typical information consumers into informed citizens. Only vigilant viewers and critical thinkers can contribute to the sustainable socio-economic development of nations. This paper is based on the assumption that majority of the students are moving away from the libraries and consider 'Google' as their Godfather to solve their education and learning related problems. This is a very dangerous trend. It is high time to take these students out of the clutches of the 'Google' by making their respective libraries their as second home. For this, media and information literacy courses must be offered across frontiers at all levels of education. Since today's students will be tomorrow's leaders, it is better to catch them young. This paper builds a strong case to place media and information literacy at the core of instruction to promote critical thinking and independent learning among the students.

1. International Initiatives

Article 19 of the Universal Declaration of Human Rights stipulates that everyone has the right to freedom of opinion and expression. This means that everyone is free to hold opinions without interference, and to seek, receive and impart information and ideas through any media across frontiers. Media and Information Literacy (MIL) empowers people with competencies needed to survive and thrive in this world full of fierce competition. UNESCO and IFLA have taken MIL as one of their top priorities. UNESCO has the 'Information for All Programme (IFAP)' and IFLA has the 'Freedom of Access to Information and Freedom of Expression (FAIFE)' core programme. Hence, before dealing with the central theme of this paper, it would be appropriate to give a brief overview of the international initiatives that have taken place in the field of media and information literacy. MIL initiatives have gained ground at the international level. Gunwald Declaration of 1982 emphasized on the need for political and educational systems to promote citizens' critical understanding of the phenomenon of communication and their participation in both old and new media. Similarly the Alexianderia Declaration of 2005 underlines to place MIL at the core of lifelong learning. This paper is based on the spirit of the Alexandria Declaration because the author strongly believes that MIL empowers information seekers to seek, evaluate, use and create information effectively to obtain their personal, educational, professional and social goals. It is the basic human right that promotes equity to bridge digital divide and info-divide. Fez Declaration in 2011 endorses a far-reaching vision that today's digital age and convergence of communication technologies necessitate the combination of media literacy and information literacy in order to achieve sustainable human development, build participatory civic societies, and contribute to the consolidation of sustainable world peace, freedom, good governance, and the fostering of constructive intercultural knowledge, dialogue and mutual understanding. Similarly in 2011, UNESCO has also designed MIL Curriculum for Teachers. This curriculum focuses on the required core competencies and skills which can be seamlessly integrated into the existing teacher education without putting too much strain on already overloaded teacher trainees. The curriculum suggests nine core modules pertaining to citizenship, freedom of expression and information, access to information, democratic discourse, lifelong learning, understanding the news, media and information ethics, representation in media and information, languages in media and information, advertising, new and traditional media, Internet opportunities and challenges, information literacy and library skills, communication, MIL and learning—a capstone module. The non-core modules cover audience, media, technology and global village; digital editing and computer; camera shots and angles-conveying meanings; transnational advertising and super brands.

Prior to this, a UNESCO Expert Group Meeting on the Development of Media and Information Literacy Indicators was held at Bangkok (Thailand) from 04–06 November 2010. This meeting ascertained the MIL indicators in two tiers. Tier-1 indicators were input related to measure enabling factors that impact individuals acquiring MIL skills. Tier-2 indicators were meant to measure individual competencies among teacher-trainers, teachers in training and in service, as well as among students. Keeping in view that the MIL skills must enable people to achieve their personal, educational, occupational, and social goals and also develop critical thinking and public opinion to survive and thrive in the world which is highly competitive, insecure, and uncertain, the author conducted an IFLA sponsored International Workshop on Health Information Literacy (IWHIL) at East West University, Dhaka (Bangladesh) from 27–30 July 2011. This workshop was based on the premise that people are most important source of a nation and only healthy people can contribute to the progress of society. After this, one more workshop on Health Information Literacy (HIL) was conducted at the same university in January 2012 for the students and faculty in universities in Bangladesh. The Governing Board of IFLA has also endorsed the IFLA Media and Information Literacy Recommendations at its meeting held at Den Haag, The Netherlands on 07 December 2011. IFLA recommends that governments and organizations to commission research on MIL, support professional development, embed MIL education in all lifelong curricula, recognize MIL and lifelong learning as key elements for accreditation of all education and training programmes, include MIL in continuing education programmes, implement MIL programmes to increase employability and entrepreneurial capacities, and support thematic meetings which facilitate the MIL skills and lifelong strategies across frontiers.

2. Empowering-8 and the IMIL Survey

Earlier the 'Empowering-8 Model of Information Literacy' was developed by the participants of the IFLA Sponsored Workshop on Information Skills for Learning, hosted at Colombo in 2004 by the National Institute of Library and Information Sciences (NILIS), University of Colombo, Sri Lanka. This model is specially developed for the information seekers and teachers in the Asia-Pacific region. It contains eight steps to effectively access and use reliable information. Follow-up workshops were held at Patiala (India) and Kuala Lumpur (Malaysia) respectively in the years 2005 and 2006. After this, to create a ripple effect at grass root level, eleven UNESCO sponsored Training-the-Trainers in Information Literacy Workshops were held in different countries of the world. Comprehensive report of these workshop is published in a special issue of 'International Information and Library Review' by Prof. F. Woody Horton, Jr. Now a UNESCO sponsored International Media and Information Literacy Survey (IMILS) is being undertaken by twenty countries of the Asia-Pacific to generate baseline data for UNESCO about the information seeking behavior, attitudes, problems and media preferences of graduate information seekers. Later on this project will be extended to the other regions of the world. As all these documents are easily available from the Internet by making a Google search, no references are given to them in this paper to save space. The author has been an active role player in all these events and is hopeful that the International Conference on Media and Information Literacy for Knowledge Societies being held at Moscow from 24–28 June 2013 would certainly set new standards for the promotion of MIL skills at the grass root level.

3. The Google and Libraries

The future of libraries is uncertain as the end-users have fallen in the hands of commercial database providers and search engines like Google. Preservation of and access to our documentary heritage has been the historical mandate of libraries but now-a-days instead of buying documents, libraries are buying access from the commercial database providers. The commercial providers are always interested in their profit and not in the public good. On the other hand, the Net Generation thinks that Google has answer to all their problems. That is not true, and at stake is the quality of information and future of libraries. Hence, there is an immediate need to develop media and information literacy skills of the stakeholders, and turn the rote learners into independent lifelong learners and critical thinkers. This is necessary as information from incredible sources is not always reliable. Information is now in over abundance and finding reliable information from the Internet is just like drinking from the fire hoses. Moreover, there is a lot of information deluge and the researchers are required to carefully find the way to the pertinent information they need. It is difficult than ever to be a good researcher because there is such a huge mix of reliable and unreliable information available on the Internet and in the libraries. Searching, browsing, and retrieving reliable information are critical challenges these days. In fact, accessing relevant information on the Internet is just like hitting the moving object. The Net Generation is mesmerized with the speed with which Google presents links to them. But many a time quality is at stake. Inaccurate information can mar the future of students in a fraction of a second as accurate information is instant power. Though libraries these days are not the only sources of information, yet they are reliable sources of information. It is very well said that if you have time to waste go to Google and if you don't have time to waste then go to a library. In libraries, everything is selection based and in control. But on the Internet, a lot of effort and skills are needed by the information seeker to manage access to quality information. Moreover, Google and the commercial publishers are another name for commoditization of information, whereas library is a social agency for the public good. Students need be equipped with the MIL skills and libraries need be made second home for them. Otherwise inaccurate information would lead to wrong decisions that would further mar the future of students, in other words the future of nations.

4. Promises and Perils of the New Media

TV channels and the new media have virtually overtaken the print-on-paper paradigm. Though the new media has the capacity to provide 24 × 7 real-time access to information, yet various TV channels are also adding to daily problems of the viewers. Instead of informing the masses, these channels in India are competing with each other and sometimes make issues of the non-issues. What is breaking news in the morning becomes barking news in the evening. Media is virtually setting the agenda and many-a-times misguiding the masses. In such a situation, it is required to equip the stakeholders with media and information literacy skills to promote critical thinking among them and also to convert the typical information consumers into informed citizens. Only vigilant viewers and critical thinkers can contribute to the sustainable socio-economic development of nations. People must be able to ascertain the role, functions, and motives of the media. They should also be aware of the conditions under which media operates. Gagging, censorship and misuse of media must not be allowed by the vigilant citizens. Similarly media must also not be allowed to twist arms of the stakeholders without any rationale. Content evaluation and then ethical and legal use of information and media are most important aspect of MIL skills. Similarly stakeholders must also be trained in content creation and communication. Simply speaking, the MIL skills are the *sine qua non* for creating and leading change in the emerging knowledge societies. The critical challenge for present day teachers and academic librarians is to effectively educate and train students in the art of strategically collecting information from the Internet and other sources in ways that give the best sources in a cost-effective manner in the smallest amount of time. To be effective information managers, students must equipped with media and information skills for effective searching. Students need to look beyond their academic assignments to be able to complete their research work. If educational institutions are to prepare graduates to be world-class professionals, then they must place media and information literacy skills at the core of instruction in across frontiers. This can best be accomplished when librarians in collaboration with classroom faculty instill media and information literacy instruction into the curriculum. "Librarians, librarianship and libraries have always a leading role in the advancement of knowledge and the pursuit of learning. It has been the extremely close symbiotic collaboration between school teachers and school librarians that led to the information literacy idea in the first place" (Horton Jr., 2009).

5. The Challenge before Librarians

The challenge before librarians is how to develop partnership with classroom faculty to share the responsibility of teaching students the value of the library. Another challenge is to free the information seekers from the clutches the Google and the Wikipedia. Google and Wikipedia can be good starting points, but these tools cannot be the final authority on reliable information. Librarians must collaborate with the faculties to understand the problems that students face when they use computers and networks for searching and browsing the web-based information. This can be done only by treating the MIL skills as the heart of education, and faculty-librarian partnership must be encouraged to develop critical thinking and independent learning in students. The Net Generation is not well versant with the print-on paper paradigm and the treasures of learning resources which libraries have for them. They most likely did not grow up with a stock of good books in their homes because for them the Internet has quickly replaced print sources as a primary and reliable platform for information.

The problem with replacing the print-on-paper encyclopedia with the Wikipedia is in "assuming" the reliability of information that comes from the Web. The implications using the information that is retrieved only from the Internet without the filter of media and information literacy skills are immediately visible to anyone who teaches research-based writing. The following example clearly shows innocence of the students with which they trust the reliability of information they find on the Internet. One of the students retrieved unreliable information from the Internet and also used information from a credible source without giving its reference. When the teacher warned him of the inaccuracies of the retrieved information and the plagiarism issue of the not cited source, the student innocently told the teacher that no one have ever taught him such things. This speaks volumes about a teacher's responsibility to equip students with MIL skills. The best way to do this is to introduce MIL courses at all levels of education across different streams.

6. Shift from Stacks to Computers

Majority of students enter a library to turn away from the books stacks and use networked computers to navigate beyond the boundaries of the library databases to the seamless horizons of information on the Web. Going to library as a place to access virtual resources and services is against the spirit of a library's mandate, as well as the 24 × 7 nature of the Internet. ICTs and the Internet have given a death blow to the traditional constraints of space and time but these dynamic developments have not been able to change the static mind-set of the majority of the information seekers. Techno-savvy students know how to blog, create websites, download, text and post to YouTube, but don't have the critical abilities to use the Internet as a research tool and resource. This means that teachers must revise the curriculum to include media and information literacy. But librarians also have a pivotal role to play. "If, as all available evidence indicates, students and faculty are increasingly relying on Internet sources, then it is vital that what they rely on be of good quality and readily accessible. This is of importance not only for library patrons but also for librarians themselves" (Proctor, 2009).

7. Conclusions

Recognizing the challenges that face novice researchers, librarians and teachers can help students to beat the info-glut that exists on the Internet. Rather than being overwhelmed by a flood of information, students can learn how to carefully search and browse the Internet. MIL skills are not innate, rather these need be taught in a systematic and cumulative way in the classroom and in the library and at any place where research is conducted. This is a task that is best accomplished by teachers who collaborate with librarians enabling students to see librarians as the information service professionals who can make students effective information managers. It means that libraries must redefine their role and library professionals must aggressively promote user education and MIL skills. ICTs cannot provide human touch but librarians can certainly do that by becoming pro-active professionals and effective MIL trainers. Having a collaborative approach to teaching media and information literacy skills reinforces the notion that library and research skills are integral to any education system that seeks to prepare students to be critical thinkers and independent lifelong learners. We need to change perception of the libraries as repositories and redefine them as pro-active service centers staffed by information professionals who are educated and trained in effectively using the entire information and communication system by which information is created, shared, stored, managed, and used. The challenge before librarians is how to collaborate with teachers to promote among students the use and value of the library. Another challenge is to free them from the grips of the Google and clutches the Wikipedia and the blogs. The librarians and the faculty must work together to understand the obstacles that students face when they use computers and networks for searching and browsing the web-based information. This can be done by treating the media and information literacy as the heart of educational programmes and placing the MIL skills at the core of instruction for developing critical thinking and independent learning skills in students. In fact, if information is fish then MIL is the art of fishing. It is incumbent upon the faculty and librarians to equip students with the MIL skills to enable them to be quality information managers, critical thinkers, independent learners, opinion makers, and vigilant citizens who understand the role and function of the media and the conditions under which the media operates and with which motives. MIL skills can enable students and other stakeholders to enjoy the bliss of truth and truthful living.

References

[1] Horton Jr., F. (2009). Woody. Information literacy and learning to learn. *In* Library and Information Science in Digital Age (Essays in honour of Prof. M.P. Satija), edited by Jagtar Singh, Malhan, Indervir, and Trishanjit Kaur. New Delhi, Ess Ess., pp. 117–119.

[2] Training-the-Trainers in Information Literacy. *International Information and Library Review*, 2009, 41(2), (Special Issue).

[3] Proctor, Edward (2009). Facilitating research on the Internet: The rationale behind design of an academic resources website. *In* Library and Information Science in Digital Age (Essays in honour of Prof. M.P. Satija), edited by Jagtar Singh, Malhan, Indervir, and Trishanjit Kaur. New Delhi, Ess Ess., pp. 19–442.

Electronic Resources Management in Libraries, pp. 396–401

Research Avenues in Library and Information Science

Pratibha Gokhale

ABSTRACT

Education in any profession is bound by the complex and reciprocal relationship of training and prevailing practices in the profession. The filed of Library and Information Science is not an exception to this. With the intensification of research activities during recent years, the need for organizing knowledge in developmental work and in research, is more pronounced. The goal of any such activity is to assimilate information from the natural world, then structure it into a comprehensible form, so that it is put to use. Any piece of information needs to be tested, experimented, scrutinized and verified on several parameters before it is to be utilized for meaningful purpose. Information is a self renewing resource; which if managed properly, can stimulate thinking, improve levels of productivity and can ensure consistent maintenance of quality. The present paper has taken a brief overview of the Library and Information Science education scenario and attempts to explore the different research avenues in the field.

1. Introduction

Formal Library education in India has a history of more than a century behind it. Chronological developments as reported in the literature reveal that:

- John Macfarlane who was the first Librarian of the Imperial Library (now the National Library) at Calcutta started the first in-service training programme for the staff in 1901.
- W.A. Borden—initiated training for Librarians at the invitation of Maharaja Syajirao Gaikwad II of Baroda state in 1911.
- Asa Don Dickinson stared a systematic training programme at the Punjab University in Lahore in 1915. This was first university course in (the undivided) India. He also prepared a manual namely, *The Punjab Library Primer.*
- Andhra Desa Library Association founded in 1914 started conducting training classes for Library personnel in 1920 at Vijaywada. This is described as the "*Peoples' Movement.*"
- M. Vishveshwaraiah, the then Dewan of Mysore state in 1920, started training course for librarians at Bengaluru as *Programme of Library Development.*

- University of Madras, in collaboration with the Madras Library Association, started offering a certificate course in Librarianship from 1929 which was fully taken over by the University in 1931.
- Andhra University, the Imperial Library and Bengal Library Association imparted training through certificate/diploma courses for shorter duration of varying period.
- University of Madras converted the Certificate Course in Librarianship to Post-graduate Diploma Course of one year duration in 1937. Subsequently, Benaras Hindu University (1941), University of Bombay (1944), Calcutta University (1946), Delhi University (1947) started diploma courses.
- Aligarh Muslim University is the first university to start the BLibSc course in India.
- At present, there are about 100 universities in the country which are imparting different levels of courses in Library and Information Science ranging from certificate course to Ph.D. DRTC and INSDOC (now *NISCAIR*) started offering two years Associateship programme. DRTC now conducts two-year MS (LIS) course.

The major objectives of university's academic work are teaching, research and publications, out of which research is the core function. Apart from Ph.D., the components of research at elementary level are also covered through following ways:

- M Phil. Course.
- MLISc projects/dissertations.
- Individual or team research projects sponsored by UGC, ICSSR, DST, MHR.
- Self supported research.

2. Research in Library and Information Science—International Scenario

Research in Library and Information Science (LIS) does not have a very long history—both at the international as well as at the national level. Melvil Dewey, the then Director of the New York State Library School at Albany in 1891, moved the idea of conferring an Honorary Ph.D. degree for outstanding professional achievement in the field. However there is no record available whether the degree was ever granted. The Graduate Library School at the University of Chicago in 1926, first time made provision for granting an earned Ph.D. degree in LIS. Eleanor S Upton, from University of Chicago is the first Ph.D. in Library Science in 1930 for his thesis, "*A Guide to Source of 17th Century English History in Selected Reports of the Royal Commission on Historical Manuscripts.*" In UK, the first School of Librarianship was established in 1919 at the University College in London. But, University of Sheffield is considered as the pioneer in formal doctoral research activity in LIS since 1963.

3. Research in Library and Information Science in India

University of Delhi has the credit of starting the MPhil programme for the first time in the country in 1976. There are about 21 universities in the country which offer both MPhil and Ph.D. programmes; where as about 37 universities are offering only Ph.D. Programme. Kota Open Universitie and Yaswantrao Chavan Marathwada Open University offer Ph.D. under Distance Education mode. So far only one DLitt has been awarded in LIS by Utkal University in 1992 to Dr B.B. Shukla for his thesis, *The Work and Impact of a Pioneer in LIS: A Critical Study of the Work of Prof. P.N. Kaula.*

University of Delhi instituted the doctoral programme leading to Ph.D. in Library Science in 1951. Dr. D.B. Krishna Rao is the first awardee in 1958 from University of Delhi, under the guidance of Dr. S. R. Ranganathan, for the topic, *Facet Analysis and Depth Classification.* However, the second Ph.D. degree in Library Science was awarded to Dr Pandey S.K. Sharma by Punjab University in 1977 only after 19 years of first Ph.D. degree. He received the degree under the guidance of Dr J.S. Sharma for his topic, *Expansion and Modification of DDC (Ed18) for Classifying Indological Books with Special Reference to Indian Philosophy and Indian Religion.*

4. Research Output in Indian Universities

As per the record available about award of Ph.D. degree in LIS, analysis is as under:

Table 1: Chronological Growth of Doctoral Work in LIS Research (Manjunath, 2010)

Year	*No. of PhDs*	*%*
1950–80	27	2.6
1981–85	47	4.5
1986–90	105	10.0
1991–95	259	24.8
1996–00	167	16.1
2001–05	245	23.5
2006–10	193	18.5
Total	1043	100.0

4.1 *Research Output in Indian Universities Subject-wise Analysis*

Broad subject analysis of Ph.D. research topics in LIS as reported in literature is as under:

Table 2: Subject-wise Analysis

Subject	*%*
Types of libraries	26.21
IT application, computer, communication technology, network, GIS related…	15.85
Library services…	11.65
LIS profession and education…	9.95
Users' surveys, information needs…	9.26
Bibliometric studies, biographical works, foreign topics	7.52

Subject	%
Technical processing…	7.03
Librarianship in general library history, universe of knowledge	6.55
Reading material, children's literature patents, periodicals, non-book material…	5.33
Grey literature	.728
Total	100

4.2 *Faculty Affiliation of Library Science School/Departments*

It is interesting to note that the subject of LIS is placed under as many as 15 Faculties by different universities in the country. After re-grouping them under broad subject categories, it reveals following faculty affiliation.

Table 3: Faculty Affiliation of LIS in Universities

Social sciences	30
Arts and humanities	29
Sciences	8
Education	4
Non-affiliated departments	4
Library science	3

5. Influence of Allied Disciplines

Though the field of LIS has developed its own professional techniques, subsequently it has adopted some of the application areas from other disciplines to suit the contemporary requirements. One of the earliest disciplines to have made a strong influence on Library Science is Management followed by Computer Science, IT-related Areas, Research Methods from Social Science, Statistical Techniques from Statistics, Behavioral Science from Psychology and Econometric study of Information from Economics also have a strong impact on study and research in Library and Information Science.

6. New Avenues of Research in Library and Information Science

Jesse Shera (1972) has mentioned that research is the Key to the future of the Profession and is an important means by which institutional programme is enriched. The Association for Library and Information Science Education (ALISE) held a conference in 1997 on the theme Reinventing the Information Profession. It highlighted the changing research avenues in the highly competitive environment. The ALISE leaders approached the Kellogg Foundation for funding a project known as the KALIPER research project

(Kellogg-ALISE Information Profession and Education Renewal Project). Broad research areas as identified by the KALIPER Committee are;

- Life cycle of information
- Physical and virtual collection in libraries
- Costing and pricing of information
- Bibliometrics and webometrics
- Organization of information
- Search retrieval techniques
- Computer–human interface
- Expert systems
- Information policy
- Information literacy.

Exploring Research in LIS in India: Research in LIS in India can be undertaken under

- Minor research project
- Major research project
- Ph.D. level research
- Post-doctoral research
- Individual/team research for the institution.

Traditional/Historical/Theoretical Subjects: Much work needs to be done at root level of LIS taking into consideration the local needs. For example, comprehensive study on reports of different committees/commissions, their findings, analysis, recommendations, circumstances under which they were made; their interpretation etc. needs to be done immediately. State-of-affairs of library legislation, in the country needs to be studied in detail.

Research in Semi-technical Subjects: Topics like classification, cataloguing, citation analysis, subject-based thesaurus construction, reference and information service, library management and planning should be re-invented in the changed circumstances for ontology, metadata, ergonomics and so on.

Technology/IT-based Topics: Large number of topics can be explored for further research such as webometrics, content management, digital data management, data mining, data warehousing, and expert systems in LIS. These are the upcoming areas for the future of library profession.

Form-based Topics: Clear understanding is needed for identifying the difference between ephemeral material, archival material, non-book and non-print material, audio-visual material, institutional repositories etc. Lot of potential research avenues exist in finding out innovative techniques for organizing different forms of records, standards, patents, maps, engineering drawings, non-confidential consultancy reports and so on. Creating their database, giving key words, formulating a classification scheme, preparing a model for clearing house... are some of the challenging areas of research.

Integrated Research-based Areas: Research can be explored in work flow management, work study analysis, time -event network analysis techniques, security systems in libraries, capacity determining factors, intelligent web searching, review of library portals and their evaluation. These studies can be undertaken with other disciplines. Whichever topic is undertaken for research, *global scenario* along with local needs must be taken into consideration.

7. Conclusion

In conclusion it can be stated the field of library and information science has undergone through significant transitions, which in fact is a most welcome change. However, great expectations are in store to establish its durability and survival in future. In order to withstand the challenges, the professionals have to set global standards in quality of research. The task involves progressive but definite changes in overall capacity building efforts with right type of a mind set.

References

1. Manjunath, K. *et al. Information Age*, 2010, **2**, p. 6.
2. Shera, J. Foundation for Education in Librarianship. New York, Becker and Hayes, 1972.

Electronic Resources Management in Libraries, pp. 402–408

Role of IASLIC in Capacity Building of LIS Professionals

J.N. Satpathi

ABSTRACT

Indian Association of Special Libraries and Information Centres (IASLIC) is a pioneer association in India that has been working for the development of library and information services since its inception in 1955. IASLIC has adopted various multifaceted activities for the healthy growth of library services and to safeguard the interest of library professionals as well as library users. IASLIC has been working to resolve various discrepancies particularly in selection of hardware and library software packages, interchange formats, training for digitization and to set a standard that ideally suits the most of the libraries in our country. After introduction of computer applications in LIS in the later part of 1980s, libraries urgently required adequate computer trained workforce to perform library services. Understanding the scenario and anticipating the future needs, IASLIC has been giving prime importance to manpower development programme. A brief overview of IASLIC activities like conferences, seminars, workshops, study circles, special interest groups, publications, lectures by experts, etc. related to computer training organized by IASLIC and its role as a advisory organization to Government for making policies related to LIS has also described in this article.

1. Introduction

Library is a significant characteristic of civilization and we find a large number of libraries in any civilized society irrespective of countries, race and communities. India is not an exception of it. We find a good number of modern libraries in both government and private sectors, with all modern facilities. But it is not a common picture of library service in India. It is found that libraries are operational in different part of the country with their own systems and resources. Librarians are trying to develop their own library with the guidelines of their governing authority. To ensure better library services to our society, it is very important to think of the betterment of library service, correct and timely policies and certainly the betterment of the professional skill for all the libraries in the country instead of developing of one particular library. Here lies the importance of library associations those can coordinate all the libraries nationwide and help the Library and Information Science (LIS) profession to uplift its skill and expertise. If the professionals of the country having their active participation and support accept a professional association, the association practically becomes the key force to influence the government as well as the society. It is natural because a professional organisation can understand the problems, prospects and the need of the hour better than any other governing authority of the library.

2. Objectives of the Association

The objectives of a Library Association may be divided into three basic categories:

- ***Societal Objective:*** Library movement is a social welfare activity that develops spontaneously as a product of collective initiative to development library awareness among all sections of the society with ultimate objective of hastening the process of social, cultural and economic growth of the society. Objectives of Library Association further include promotion of reading
- ***Professional Objective*:** Distinct from a general occupation, a learned profession has a philosophy to render a public service with theories of action underlying specialized knowledge and skills necessitating education, research, development and application.
- ***Political Objective:*** When libraries are set up and run by legislative or administrative laws, a Library Association has to keep vigil on such actions and act as a 'watch dog' to safeguard the interest of LIS professionals as well as the library user community.

The Indian Association of Special Libraries and Information (IASLIC) was established in 1955 as a non-profit making national professional body with the following objectives:

- To promote quality of library and Information services
- Coordinate the activities
- Improve the technical efficiency of the professionals
- To act as a center of research and studies in special libraries etc.

3. Scenario of Computer Applications in LIS Field

Application of computers in LIS profession started in 1980s still in preliminary level. Significantly, during the next two decades, library and information services promptly switched over to computerized system without having the scope and time for training adequate manpower to support it. It needs no explanation that there was a gap between the supply and demand of computer literate workforce in the LIS profession. Not only that, it is observed that newly passed out students from LIS schools also require some special hands-on-training to gain expertise and confidence. The present days challenges of LIS professionals are IT applications, web based library services, networking and server based services, e-consortia and legal issues related to cyber activities, creating digital repository, use of open source software and so on.

IASLIC could anticipate the future needs of LIS professionals and to bridge the 'gap' between the demand and supply of computer literate human resources, several programmes have been taken.

IASLIC has by and large fulfilled its role coordinating and harnessing the professional responsibilities in bringing out a harmonious development of the profession and library information services in India. The main activities of the IASLIC in this direction are:

- Holding annual seminars and conferences in different parts of the country
- Conducting study circle meetings at its headquarters and some state branches
- Organizing special short term training courses
- Bring out serial publications, monographs and pamphlets etc.

4. Conferences and Seminars

The IASLIC holds a biennial seminar and conference in alternate years (Tables 1 & 2). Through this forum the Association keeps with members in different parts country,

Table 1: National Conferences Organized by IASLIC

Sl. No.	*Year*	*Topic*	*Place*
1.	1977	Planning of national network	Dharwar
2.	1981	I. Organisation of data services in India II. Users education and training programmes	New Delhi
3.	1989	Manpower planning for library and information centers in India	Jaipur
4.	1993	Information management in library and information centers in India	Kurukshetra
5.	1995	Information technology products of 1990s and library and information centers	Lucknow
6.	1997	Information superhighway: its impact on library and information services in India	Coimbatore
7.	1999	Information management in the context of fast emerging information society	Agra
8.	2001	Content management in India in digital environment	Thiruvanan-thapuram
9.	2003	Knowledge management in special libraries in digital environment	Dehra Dun
10.	2005	LIS profession in India: vision for 2010	Chennai
11.	2007	Digital media and library information services	New Delhi
12.	2009	Library/Information users in Digital Era	Bhubaneswar
13.	2011	Library vision 2020	Srinagar

rotating the venue in various research and academic institutions. Special attention was given on computer training after introduction of computer in LIS in India. From the tables it is evident that special attention was given on computer training after introduction of computer in LIS.

During the conferences/seminars organized once a year, papers are invited in the two Special Interest Groups (SIGs) viz. Social Science Information, and Computer Applications. Emphasis is given to computer and information technology in the SIGs for the development of computer skill among LIS processionals.

A national conference on Planning of National Network that took place in Dharwar (Karnataka) in the year 1977 which recommended some important proposals and guidelines those in later years implemented by UGC and Govt. of India to promote library networking as well as to build national information policy.

Table 2: National Seminars Organized by IASLIC

Sl. No.	*Year*	*Topic*	*Place*
1.	1978	I. Standardization of techniques and procedures for information handling II. Library and Information system for rural development	Chennai
2.	1980	I. Role of information centers in technology transfer. II. Role of state-level and national library associations in library development of India	Nagpur
3.	1982	Information services in India	Kanpur
4.	1992	Information retrieval: models and techniques	Annamalai Nagar
5.	1994	Networking of libraries: Problems and prospects	Mumbai
6.	1996	Meeting the information challenge for development and self-sufficiency	Kolkata
7.	2000	Library and information profession at the cross-roads	Bhopal
8.	2002	Digital information systems and services	Patiala
9.	2004	Information Support for Rural Development	Kolkata
10.	2006	Open source Movement—Asian perspective	New Delhi
11.	2008	Library Profession in search of a new paradigm	Kolkata
12.	2010	Reading Habits in changing Scenario	Gorakpur

In addition to the national conferences and seminars, IASLIC organized two International Conferences viz. International Conference on Information Management in a Knowledge Society at Mumbai in 2005; and International Conference on Digital Libraries and Knowledge Organization at Gurgaon in 2010.

5. Workshops/Trainings

Trained manpower is the essential pre-requisite in the evolution of an effective information service. Accordingly, IASLIC conducts short-term courses on special subjects. Such short tern courses are the essential functions of a professional association, both to supplement the full time academic courses for students and to ensure continuing education for practicing library professionals. Understanding the demand from the professionals, IASLIC organized several workshops (Table 3) to develop computer skills among LIS professionals.

Table 2: Workshops/Training Courses Organized by IASLIC

Subject	*Training Programmes*	*Total No.*
Application of IT	Computer applications [2] Library software [10] WebPages designing [1] D-Space [3] Resource sharing [1] Information management technology [5] Open source [2]	24
Information Processing and Retrieval	Indexing [3] Thesaurus [4] Information acccss [2]	9
Information Service	Information consolidation [1] Access to social science information [2]	3
Management	Management [2] Marketing [1] Customer satisfaction [1] Reprography [1] Conservation and Preservation [3]	8
Information Communication	Audio-visual [3]	3
Library and Society	Special librarianship and documentation (1 year diploma) [1]	1

6. Study Circles

Apart from the above-mentioned conferences, seminars and workshops, IASLIC also conducts a series of Study Circles and invited eminent speakers expert in different fields on a specialized topic related to LIS. From the statistics of study circles, it needs no explanation that emphasis has been given on the issue of manpower development in LIS profession specially computer application in LIS environment. These meetings help to promote the ability of members to discuss problem and issues and also serve as a system of harnessing the intellectual growth in the profession.

Subject	*Total No. of Study Circles*
Application of IT in LIS	60
Information Processing and Retrieval	52
Information Services	70
Management	05
Information and Communication	05
Library and Society	94
Others	23
Total No. of Study Circles	309

The topics of IASLIC Study Circles reflect the trend of changes after introduction of computer in library. The changes were wisely anticipated by IASLIC and tried its best to train the LIS professionals on the new developments, which were the 'need of the hour'. The study circles are not limited to lectures by experts but also included the commercial enterprises to aware LIS professionals about new IT products and services. In this way, IASLIC opened a new platform to bridge the gap between conventionally trained LIS professionals and the state of art technology introduced in the market. Further, the study circles are not limited to the problems and prospects of LIS in India, but also extended to experts from other countries. Speakers from USA, UK, Japan, Russia, Bangladesh etc. delivered lectures in those study circles. This effort certainly leads to build a global LIS community with greater awareness.

7. Efforts to Improve LIS Professionals

Towards enhancement of professional skills IASLIC brings out publications like *IASLIC Bulletin* (quarterly), *Indian Library Science Abstracts* (yearly), and *IASLIC Newsletter* (monthly) for commutation of current professional thinking and dissemination of knowledge. The Association publishes books, pamphlets, journals and conference/ seminar papers. So far 25 Seminars and 27 Conferences had taken place different parts of the country along with a few monographs and technical papers.

To promote Library and Information service and to motivate the LIS professionals in the country, members of IASLIC have introduced 5 awards those are awarded annually. These efforts recognize the professional expertise in LIS field. Also IASLIC annually organizes two special lectures viz. Ranganathan Lecture delivered by a senior library and information professional and Dr R.C. Gupta. Annual Special Lecture delivered by eminent personalities in the society.

8. Status of LIS Professionals

In the last few decades the scenario of Special Libraries in India has changed dramatically and drastically. The librarians have been redefining their roles and responsibilities according to the need of the hour—from mere book keeper to librarian to document list to information scientist to knowledge manager. This may is because of importance of library and information services gained in recent times, not only in academic fields, but also in other areas, i.e. IT, industry, trade, research, etc. To justify the demands of LIS professionals, IASLIC has been negotiating with government with various issues related to the facilities of LIS professionals in the country. At the same time, it would not be irrelevant to say that there are a large number of LIS professionals working in private sectors, which are neither organized nor paid adequately for their services. IASLIC always try to do its best for their betterment in all respects but the main problem is LIS professionals working in private sector are not united.

9. Conclusions

IASLIC has rightly chosen to provide conscious support to the national effort in evolving an effective library and information services in the country. The collective thinking and the national debate on vital aspects of national information services in a digital environment provided by IASLIC through seminars, conferences, SIG meetings/training programs, study circle etc should provide sound guidelines to the national planners and policy-makers. The contributions made by the IASLIC and its future potential should be fully realized and should be represented on all policy-making bodies involved in the development of a national information system.

It should also be admitted that there are some issues associated to develop human resources like mental rejection of staff, trade unions, lack of interest from the higher authority etc. However, those issues can affect, but cannot stop the process to professional developments. The growth and increasing popularity of IASLIC during 1955 to the begging of 2012 is the proof of this truth.

Electronic Resources Management in Libraries, pp. 409–415

Enhancing the E-Resources for Educational Use and their Impact

M. Natarajan

ABSTRACT

This paper deals with the electronic resources (e-resources) and their different types. The use of different types of e-resources by students, researchers and faculties are discussed here. Explored the Open Educational Resources (OER) created by different organizations are emphasized for open access. Open CourseWare (OCW), which is available in audio-visual and textual OER are given examples in this paper. A case study has been conducted with AIS students about the usage of e-resources with the help of a questionnaire. The impact of e-resources is highlighted along with its evaluation. It has been concluded that e-resources helpful to everyone because they are available anytime and easy to access for the researchers to carry out the research on time.

1. Introduction

Higher education institutions are increasingly everywhere under pressure to produce graduates who can effectively function in today's information and knowledge economy. For this, libraries play an important role in making available pertinent information resources and services, inculcating information literacy skills and fostering a culture of lifelong learning among students. Using electronic information resources to support the students in higher education has been common practice for a number of years from now. Educators are increasingly aware of the need, and concomitant demand, for graduates to have skills to access the information to enable them to continue learning throughout their careers. Both during their studies and within the workplace, a demand for safe and effective use of e-resources is necessary with the skills in order to incorporate research findings into practice. Nowadays, publishers try to produce many publications in digital environment. Accordingly the libraries are able to make them available to their users the form of different types of electronic resources (e-resources). The way of searching for information by the users' has also changed and they require the current information at the earliest. There has been a rapid urge from the user community to get more and more information online. The development of the Information Communication Technologies (ICT), the rapid rise of electronic databases, and recent e-book technologies have altogether changed the entire scenario of today's informatics. It has become the need of the hour for library and information centers to make them available with network connectivity. This study deals with the types of e-resources available, in particularly for educational purpose, and their availability including the Open Access (OA) resources. Here, a case study by the students of Associateship in Information Science AIS) is discussed with the impact of e-resources on them.

2. Electronic Resources

Electronic resources are regarded as the mines of information that are explored through modern ICT devices, refined and redesigned and more often stored in the cyber space in the most concrete and compact form and can be accessed simultaneously from many points by a large number of people. As digital resources increased exponentially over the last decade, academic libraries have heavily invested in e-books, research databases, as well as e-journals, and made them accessible via their library web portals. The phrase "electronic resources", has broadly been defined as, information accessed by a computer, may be useful as bibliographic guides to potential sources but, as of yet, they infrequently appear as cited references in their own right (Graham, 2003). Moreover, e-resources refer to that kind of documents in digital formats which are made available to library users through an online information retrieval system. E-resources include online databases, sources from web pages, e-journal articles, electronic personal papers, e-mail messages, newsgroup postings, newsletters, government publications, e-theses and dissertations, e-newspapers, CDs/DVDs, e-books, e-databases, HTML links, digital library materials, institutional repositories, social networks, OA materials, e-theses, etc. The Internet is said to be the right and most extensively used channel to find out the majority of e-resources through different search engines and WebOPACs and, of course, some offline databases on CD/DVD formats that can even be accessed without the help of Internet.

3. Availbility of E-Resources

Electronic resources are usually referred as databases, e-books, e-journals, e-newspapers, e-zines, e-archives, e-theses, e-conference papers, examination papers, government papers, research reports, scripts and monographs available in an electronic form (Nicholas *et al.*, 2007). With the rapid development of ICTs, e-resources have been increasingly becoming readily available and easily accessible (Prabha, 2007). This is particularly in the case in higher education in which e-resources have become critical parts of an integrated learning environment. Besides organizations having their web pages wherein the html links provide e-information related to the organization and resources they possess; experts as resource persons as a databases, digital library resources, institutional repositories, OA resources (more than 500 journals are on education and training alone), search engines, subject directories, etc. Also the Indian library consortia like CSIR's National Knowledge Resource Consortium, Indian National Digital Library in Engineering Science and Technology (INDEST) consortium, DRDO E-Journals Consortium, Forum for Resource Sharing in Astronomy (FORSA), MCIT

Library Consortium, ICMR e-consortium, Consortium for e-Resources for Agriculture (CeRA), etc. are also providing full-text articles from Indian and foreign journals for the benefit of the users in different subject fields on subscription base. National Institute of Science Communication and Information Resources (NISCAIR) Online Periodicals Repository (NOPR), an OA collection of full-text articles for all its journals published available online in OA mode. Even though different types of resources are available, students, staff and others may not be able use in proper way, like searching the Internet, searching from databases and e-journals, etc. National Council of Educational Research and Training (NCERT) provides its textbooks in e-format for the students. There are many educational institutions that are running e-learning programs, by providing different modules in different subjects that are accessible by enrollment (may be with payment). There are free e-books available in different subjects, which are also made available in many of the IIT websites, by giving linkages to those sites. Some of the free e-book sites are as follows:

http://www.ebookdirectory.com
http://www.free-ebooks.net
http://www.gutenberg.org
http://www.ebooklobby.com
http://www.getfreeebooks.com

Taylor and Francis publisher has more than 200 journals with full text on different aspects of education. There are many more e-resources available for educational purpose. Directory of OA journals (www.doaj.org) also provides full text journal articles for approximately 8000 journals. Also, www.doabooks.org provides 755 peer reviewed e-books from 23 publishers are available OA mode.

Today's researchers are using a wide variety of sources for information. Students usually respond positively to recommendations of specific resources by their teachers, friends, or librarians, but convenience remains the most important factor for information use. Users in general prefer e-journals because they make their work easier and give them the information they need. Fast online access, and the ability to download, print, and send articles electronically are top advantages of e-resources for all. But the concerns remain over the quality of web resources, particularly among faculty and librarians who fear the students for using the web indiscriminately.

4. Open Educational Resources

The open educational resources (OER) and open courseware (OCW) are some of the recent innovations that are especially relevant for achieving equitable access to quality education. OER are open content that is freely accessible worldwide from a common portal or gateway. Indian institutions also have recognized the importance and impact of OER to bridge the learning divide in the country. Recently, India's National Knowledge Commission (NKC) has called for a National E-content and Curriculum

Initiative to stimulate the creation, adaptation and utilization of OER by Indian institutions. In addition to NKC, University Grants Commissions, National Association of Software and Services Companies and many others dealing with advocacy, advisory and policymaking bodies in India are supporting the cause and bridging knowledge and skill gaps (Ghosh, S.B. and Das, 2007; Das, 2011). India has been experiencing the incremental growth of OER, where a number of national institutions have established OER portals for providing nationwide access to their educational resources. Innovative technology, enabled learning environments create an atmosphere of effective learning and knowledge retention. If a popular technical teacher delivers a lecture from the classroom of an internationally reputed institute and makes the presentation materials freely available on the NET, remotely located students of professional colleges can access the same and gain in-depth subject knowledge. The OER developers are expecting an incremental increase of awareness level and self learning motivation so that OER will be reached to lifelong learners across the professions and occupations.

5. Indian Initiatives of OERS

Indian OER can be broadly categorized as audio-visual OER and textual OER. Few of the Indian OER initiatives are targeted at school students, whereas most others are targeted at students of technical and vocational education and training (TVET), tertiary education and lifelong learning. Some of the OERs are as follows:

- National Programme on Technology Enhanced Learning (NPTEL) (http://www. nptel. iitm.ac.in).
- Learning Object Repository of the Consortium for Educational Communication (CEC) (http://www.cec-lor.edu.in).
- Project Open Source Courseware Animations Repository (OSCAR) (http://oscar. iitb. ac.in/;http://ekalavya.iitb.ac.in/oscarHome.do).
- eGyanKosh of Indira Gandhi National Open University (IGNOU) (http://in. youtube.com/IGNOU)
- Online textbooks of the National Council of Educational Research and Training (NCERT) (http://www.ncert.nic.in/html/textbooks.htm).
- National Science Digital Library (NSDL) of the National Institute of Science Communication and Information Resources (http://nsdl.niscair.res.in)
- Vidyanidhi digital library and e-scholarship portal for theses and dissertations (http://www. vidyanidhi. org.in/)
- Rai OpenCourseware (http://www.rocw.raifoundation.org)

Other than the above OERs, there are many e-resources available in the form of digital libraries, institutional repositories, OA resources/journals, etc at various sites accessible freely on the Internet.

6. Case Study

Students, researchers and faculties use the resources of print and e-resources for their study and teaching. A survey was carried out with 20 students of AIS batch 2010–12 for their usage of e-resources using a detailed questionnaire. It was found that most of them use e-journals (90%) for preparation of their assignments and for their studies. Only 10% of them use print materials for their studies. In other studies also it was found that enthusiasm for using e-journals vary among the various fields of science. There are 15 male students and 5 girl students. The age group range of the students varied from 22 to 34. All of them are fully aware of the existence of e-resources, except few students from SARRC countries. The qualifications vary from B.Tech., M.A., M.Sc., and B.Pharm. From the questionnaire, it has been found that they use e-resources in the computer laboratory, library and in off-campus (hostel). The types of resources used by them are Library catalogue, online journals, website information, online newspapers, online magazines, archives, theses, examination papers, placement details—company information, etc. They use these e-resources almost daily, except on holidays.

The main purpose of using the e-resources being to get answers to specific questions/ topic, assignments, for seminar presentations, general information, for literature review, synopsis preparation for proposed dissertation topic, paper preparation, etc. They choose the e-resource because of ease to access, saves time, abundance of free literature on NET, availability of search tools and many full text articles from e-journals, etc. They have also been trained to do the search in more efficient and effective manner, by the use of advanced searching facility, use of truncation, etc. They use these types of tools for searching. They have also informed that the e-resources also added with printed sources, which they collect from the National Science Library (NSL) of NISCAIR. However, they informed that e-resources are extremely useful, which gave new insights/ideas and also to compare different views.

Despite this overall positive attitude, students have also experienced some frustrations while trying to use electronic resources. This frustration is usually experienced during searching, navigating and finding the relevant source, accessing it and downloading content (Tsakonas and Papatheodorou, 2007). The causes of frustration are due to the confusing search interfaces; the amount of time spent scanning and downloading, restricted access, such as availability of computers, the Internet connection, and the requirement for login password, and membership. These suggest that a more positive attitude towards e-resources could be expected with an improved application of ICT. For example, a revamp of the interface for access to e-resources could render it more user-friendly and to direct users to find the required information. A faster and more reliable Internet connection would increase the speed of download. The position and the educational background of the students were closely related to the nature of work and study and competence in using electronic resources.

7. Impact of E-Resources on Students

The use of e-resources by the students and faculties are increasing. The impact is:

- Students feel more at ease using online (Web-based) resources than CD-ROM databases. The library is responding to this by subscribing to more Internet/Web-based academic resources.
- Students prefer to use the Web for e-mail (the high percentage that uses Hotmail, Yahoo Mail, Gmail, etc.).
- Training—basic training on IT skills are provided during starting weeks of the course.
- Opening hours—weekend opening hours has to be increased.

Both browsing and searching remain important information-seeking behaviors, but there is some evidence that the amount of time for searching is going up when students have to access multi-title, full-text databases. Browsing through of print journal issues or e-journals is done for core journal titles. Articles from non-core journals are most often located through searching. Students are highly responsive to recommendations of specific resources by their teachers, friends, or a librarian. Educating the students in the best resources including how to evaluate Web resources, and search strategies are important. Desktop access, speed of access, and the ability to download, print, and send articles are top advantages of e-journals for all. Use of e-journals is increasing every year, among faculty members, students, and other professionals, higher the use of e-journals is accompanied by a decrease in visits to the physical library. Most readings will come from a relatively small percentage of the collection, but users will read from a greater variety of titles when they are made freely and easily accessible to them (Tenopir, 2003).

8. Conclusion

The e-resources available in different formats helps and supports the students and faculty to carryout the research and for teaching in an efficient manner and quickly, as the e-copies are available anytime and anywhere. The production and use of OER raises a number of issues including the open licensing. If materials are to be openly and freely shared, they must be licensed in a manner that promotes the desired objective. This article explored the different e-resources and mechanism of use and their impact on the library professionals particularly students and faculties. The interrelationship between the utilization of e-resources and outcome of the utilization may be further explored by the future researchers.

References

[1] Das, Anup (2011). Emergence of open educational resources (OER) in India and its impact on lifelong learning. *Library Hi Tech News*, 28(5), 10–15.

[2] Ghosh, S.B. and Das, A.K. (2007). Open access and institutional repositories: a developing country perspective—a case study of India. *IFLA Journal*, 33(3), 229–50.

[3] Graham, S.R. (2003). Historians and electronic resources: A citation analysis. *JAHC*, 3(3), 18–24.

[4] Nicholas, D., Huntington, P. and Jamali, H.R. (2007). The use, users, and role of abstracts in the digital scholarly environment. *The Journal of Academic Librarianship*, 33(4), 446–53.

[5] Prabha, P. (2007). Shifting from print to electronic journals in ARL university libraries. *Serials Review*, 33(1), 4–13.

[6] Tenopir, C., Hitchcock, B. and Pillow, S.A. (2003). Use and users of electronic library resources: An overview and analysis of recent research studies. Available at: http://www.clir.org/pubs/reports/pub120/sec4-5.html

[7] Tsakonas, G. and Papatheodorou, C. (2007). Exploring usefulness and usability in the evaluation of open access digital libraries. *Information Processing and Management*, 44(3), 1234–50.

List of Contributors

Ms Yogita Ahuja
Information Analyst
Library and Information Centre
TERI, India Habitat Centre
Lodhi Road, New Delhi–110003
E-mail: yogita_ahuja83@yahoo.com

Ms Priya Bhushan
Librarian
Govt. Girls Senior Secondary School
New Delhi–110054

Mr Sudhanshu Bhushan
Scientist
Defence Scientific Information &
Documentation Centre
Metcalfe House, Delhi–110054
E-mail: subhushan@gmail.com

Dr Sujin Budisuwan
Asst. Prof. & Vice President, MSU
School of Information & Communication
Management Technology
Faculty of Informatics, Mahasarakham
University (MSU), Thailand
E-mail: Sujin.b@msu.ac.th

Mr Sanjay Garg
Freelance Institutional Information
Disseminator & Website Designer
E-mail: sg1572@gmail.com

Dr Ramesh C. Gaur
University Librarian
Jawaharlal Nehru University
New Meharuli Road, New Delhi–110067
Tel: 011-26742605, 26704551
Fax: 011-26741603
E-mail: rcgaur@mail.jnu.ac.in,
rcgaur66@gmail.com

Dr Pratibha Gokhale
Associate Professor
Department of Library & Information
Science & Librarian, University of Mumbai
Vidyanagari Kalina, Santacruz (east)
Mumbai–400098
E-mail: pagokhale@mu.ac.in,
pratibha_gokhale@yahoo.com

Dr P.R. Goswami
Director, NASSDOC
Indian Council of Social Science Research
35 Firozshah Road, New Delhi–110001
Tel: 09818981644
E-mail: prgoswami@hotmail.com

Mr Sumit Goswami
Directorate of Management Information
System and Technologies
DRDO HQrs, New Delhi–110011
E-mail: sumit@hqr.drdo.in

Mr K. Sudhakar Goud
Consultant, UNICEF
Flat No. 403, SK Residency, Lane B-36
DD Colony, Hyderabad–500013
E-mail: k.sudhakargoud@gmail.com

Dr B.M. Gupta
National Institute of Science, Technology &
Development Studies (NISTADS), CSIR
New Delhi–110012
E-mail: bmgupta1@gmail.com

Dr Anil Hirwade
In-Charge Librarian
National Institute of Intellectual Property
Management
Nagpur–440001
E-mail: hirwade2004@indiatimes.com

Dr Mangala Anil Hirwade
Assistant Professor
Department of Library & Information Science, RTM Nagpur University
Nagpur–440010
E-mail: hmangala@rediffmail.com

Mr Aamir Jilani
Indian Council of Medical Research
P.O. Box No. 4911, Ansari Nagar
New Delhi–110029
E-mail: aamirjilani123@gmail.com

Dr Daulat Jotwani
Librarian
Indian Institute of Technology, Bombay
Powai, Mumbai–400076
E-mail: d.jotwani4@gmail.com

Dr Umeshareddy Kacherki
Deputy Librarian
Indian Institute of Science Education and Research, 900, NCL Innovation Park
Dr Homi Bhabha Road, Pune
Maharashtra–411008
E-mail: ureddy@iiserpune.ac.in

Prof C.R. Karisiddappa
UGC-Emeritus Fellow (2008–10)
Visiting Professor, Dept. of Library & Information Science, Karnatak University
Dharwad–580003
E-mail: karisiddappa@gmail.com
Tel: 0836- 2215260 (O)
0836-2776656 (R)
9880329880 (M)

Mr G. Karunakar
Information Management Area
Indian Institute of Chemical Technology
Uppal Road, Tarnaka
Hyderabad–500607
Ph: 040-27193203
Fax: 040-27160911

Mrs Sunita Koya
Chief Knowledge Manager
Ramoji Knowledge Centre
Ramoji Film City, Hyderabad–501512
E-mail: koyasunita@yahoo.com

Dr Surinder Kumar
Senior Technical Director
National Informatics Centre
A-Block, CGO Complex, Lodhi Road
New Delhi–110003
E-mail: suri@nic.in
Tel: 011-24305503

Ms Rosa Laltlanmawii
M.Phil. Student
Dept. of Library & Information Science
Mizoram University, Tanhril
Aizawl–796004

Dr Margam Madhusudhan
Assistant Professor
Department of Library and Information Science, University of Delhi
Delhi–110007
E-mail: mmadhu@libinfosci.du.ac.in

Prof A. Jack Meadows
Emeritus Professor of Library and Information Studies
Department of Information Science
Loughborough University
Loughborough, Leicestershire
LE11 3TU, UK
Tel: 44 (0)1509 223052
E-mail: a.j.meadows@lboro.ac.uk

Dr R.N. Mishra
Asst. Professor (SS)
Dept. of Library & Information Science
Mizoram University, Tanhril
Aizawl–796004
Tel.: 0389-2331608, 2331607
E-mail: rabinarayan_mishra@rediffmail.com

Ms Achala Munigal
Asst. Librarian
University College of Science, Saifabad
Osmania University
Hyderabad–500007

Dr Usha Mujoo Munshi
Librarian
Indian Institute of Public Administration
New Delhi–11002
E-mail: umunshi@gmail.com

Dr S.S. Murthy
Former Director
DESIDOC & Consultant, DELNET
Coordination Unit
3, Gruha Lakshmi Colony, Vikrampuri
Secunderabad, Hyderabad–500015
E-mail: murtyssn39@yahoo.co.in

Dr U. Nagalingam
Deputy Librarian, University Library
Pondicherry University
Puducherry–605014
E-mail: nagalingamu@gmail.com

Dr M. Natarajan
Head, Education & Training Division
Senior Principal Scientist, NISCAIR
14, Satsang Vihar Marg
New Delhi–110067
E-mail: m_natarajan@hotmail.com

Mr Manoj Pant
Editor, DESIDOC
DRDO, Metcalfe House
Delhi–110054
E-mail: pantmanoj28@gmail.com

Mrs Pushpa Raina
Technical Officer D (Retd)
DESIDOC, Metcalfe House
Delhi–110054
E-mail: pushpar49@rediffmail.com

Dr C.K. Ramaiah
Professor & Head
Dept. of Library and Information Science
Pondicherry University, R.V. Nagar
Puducherry–605014, Mobile: 9487605773
E-mail: ckramaiah.lis@pondiuni.edu.in,
ckramaiah@gmail.com

Dr D.B. Ramesh
Principal Technical Officer & Head Library
Institute of Minerals and Materials
Technology-CSIR, Bhubaneswar–751013
E-mail: dbramesh@immt.res.in,
db_ramesh@yahoo.com

Dr Ramesha
Associate Professor
Dept. of Library and Information Science
Bangalore University, Bangalore–560056
E-mail: bbramesha@gmail.com

Ms Kanchan Rani
Junior Information Assistant
Parliament Library, New Delhi–110001
E-mail: kanchangautam@ymail.com

Dr M. Koteswara Rao
Former University Librarian
University of Hyderabad
Hyderabad–500046
E-mail: mk-rao@hotmail.com

Dr K. Nageswara Rao
Defence Research & Development Laboratory
Kanchanbagh (PO), Hyderabad–500058
E-Mail: knrao_hyd@refiffmail.com

Dr Siriginidi Subba Rao
Chief Scientist & Head, Information Technology
Head, Knowledge Resource Centre
CSIR - Central Leather Research Institute
Adyar, Chennai–600020
E-mail: siriginidi@gmail.com

Dr K.V. Ratnakar
Indian Council of Medical Research
P.O. Box No. 4911, Ansari Nagar
New Delhi–110029
E-mail: venkat60a@gmail.com

Dr E. Rama Reddy
Visiting Professor
School of Information & Communication Management Technology
Faculty of Informatics
Mahasarakham University (MSU), Thailand
E-mail: enukondar@gmail.com

Dr M. Sankara Reddy
Professor (Retd) in Library and Information Science
Potti Sriramulu Telugu University
Hyderabad–500007
Senior Fellow, Ministry of Culture
Govt. of India. Mobile: 9291374462
E-mail: sankara_reddy@rediffmail.com

Prof C. Sasikala
Dept. of Library & Information Science
Andhra University
Visakhapatnam–530003
Tel: (O) 0891-2844388, (M) 09848278454
E-mail: prof.csasikala@gmail.com

Dr N.V. Sathyanarayana
Managing Director
Informatics (India) Ltd.
337, Karuna Complex, Sampige Road
Malleswaram,
Bangalore–560003
E-mail: sathya@informindia.co.in

Dr J.N. Satpathi
President
Indian Association of Special Libraries & Information Centres
P-291 CIT Scheme 6M
Kankurgachi, Kolkata–700054
E-mail: satpathijn@rediffmail.com

Dr K. Satyanarayana
Indian Council of Medical Research
P.O. Box No. 4911
Ansari Nagar
New Delhi–110029
E-mail: kanikaram_s@yahoo.com

Mr V. Senthil
Scientist
Defence Scientific Information & Documentation Centre
Metcalfe House
Delhi–110054
E-mail: senthildrdo@gmail.com

Dr Jagtar Singh
Professor
Dept. of Library and Information Science
Punjabi University
Patiala–147002
E-mail: jagtar.kindu@gmail.com

Dr K.P. Singh
Senior Assistant Professor
Dept. of Library and Information Science
University of Delhi
Delhi–110007
E-mail: singhkp_1972@yahoo.co.in

Dr Surya Nath Singh
Group Leader, Information and Library Services
Sr. Library, Information Officer
National Institute of Virology (ICMR)
Pune–411001
E-mail: singh.sn@niv. co.in, snsingh@niv.co.in

Ms U. Baby Soujanya
Technical Assistant
Indian Institute of Chemical Technology
Uppal Road, Tarnaka
Hyderabad–500007
Ph: 040-27193203
Fax: 040-27160911

Dr M.G. Sreekumar
UNESCO Coordinator
Greenstone Support for South Asia
Center for Development of Digital Libraries
Indian Institute of Management Kozhikode
Kozhikode–673570
E-mail: mgsree@iimk.ac.in

Mrs Sarminah Tamsir
Manager (Information Services)
National Trade Union Congress
No. 1, Marina Boulevard
#10-01, One Marina Boulevard
Singapore 018989
E-mail: sarminah@ntuc.org.sg

Ms Chaynika Taneja
Directorate of Management Information
System and Technologies, DRDO HQrs
New Delhi–110011
E-mail: chaynika@hqr.drdo.in

Dr Manorama Tripathi
Dy. Librarian
Jawaharlal Nehru University
New Meharuli Road
New Delhi–110067
E-mail: manoramatripathi@mail.jnu.ac.in

Dr S.J.D. Varaprasad
Scientist G & Head
Information Management
CSIR-Indian Institute of Chemical Technology
Uppal Road, Tarnaka, Hyderabad–500607
Ph: 040-27193203, Fax: 040-27160911
E-mail: varaprasad@iict.res.in

Dr K. Veeranjaneyulu
University Librarian & CCPI, e-Granth Project
ANGR Agricultural University
Hyderabad–500030
E-mail: veeru_1963@rediffmail.com.

Dr P. Visakhi
Deputy Librarian
Indian Institute of Science Education and Research Library, Sector-81, Knowledge City, P.O Manauli, S.A.S Nagar
Mohali–140306, Punjab. 09779981971 (M)
E-mail: visakhi@iisermohali.ac.in

Prof V. Vishwa Mohan
Professor, Head & Chairman, BoS
Dept. of Library & Information Science
Osmania University, Hyderabad–500007
Mobile: 09949701855
E-mail: profvmohan@gmail.com

Author Index